WORKSHOP INSTRUCTION MANUALS

ALL MODELS, 1957-1966

A COMPILATION OF THREE FACTORY WORKSHOP & INSTRUCTION MANUALS

1 - Lightweight & Heavyweight Singles and Twin cylinder models 1957-1964

2 - Lightweight Singles 250cc & 350cc 1958-1966

3 - Instruction Book for Competition Models

AMC MOTOR CYCLES LIMITED

Plumstead Road

London . S.E.18

England

INTRODUCTION

Welcome to the world of digital publishing ~ the book you now hold in your hand was printed using the latest state of the art digital technology. The advent of print-on-demand has forever changed the publishing process, never has information been so accessible and it is our hope that this book serves your informational needs for years to come. If this is your first exposure to digital publishing, we hope that you are pleased with the results. Many more titles of interest to the classic automobile and motorcycle enthusiast, collector and restorer are available via our website at www.VelocePress.com. We hope that you find this title as interesting as we do.

NOTE FROM THE PUBLISHER

The information presented is true and complete to the best of our knowledge. All recommendations are made without any guarantees on the part of the author or the publisher, who also disclaim all liability incurred with the use of this information.

TRADEMARKS

We recognize that some words, model names and designations, for example, mentioned herein are the property of the trademark holder. We use them for identification purposes only. This is not an official publication.

INFORMATION ON THE USE OF THIS PUBLICATION

This manual is an invaluable resource for those interested in performing their own maintenance. However, in today's information age we are constantly subject to changes in common practice, new technology, availability of improved materials and increased awareness of chemical toxicity. As such, it is advised that the user consult with an experienced professional prior to undertaking any procedure described herein. While every care has been taken to ensure correctness of information, it is obviously not possible to guarantee complete freedom from errors or omissions or to accept liability arising from such errors or omissions. Therefore, any individual that uses the information contained within, or elects to perform or participate in do-it-yourself repairs or modifications acknowledges that there is a risk factor involved and that the publisher or its associates cannot be held responsible for personal injury or property damage resulting from the use of the information or the outcome of such procedures.

WARNING!

One final word of advice, this publication is intended to be used as a reference guide, and when in doubt the reader should consult with a qualified technician.

PAGE NUMBERS

Please note that the page numbers relate to the individual manuals. The number to the bottom of the final page is the total number of pages in the manual.

FOREWORD

THIS MANUAL has been compiled as a practical guide to enable service staff and private owners alike to undertake overhauls and repairs, in the sequence as applied by the factory service department.

In contrast to the orthodox service manual, the possible faults, engine noises and also lubrication troubles are detailed, to enable the operator to readily diagnose the source and cause of the trouble, thus saving work hours and possibly unnecessary fitting of new parts.

Dismantling instructions are given step by step, in short paragraphs, obviating prolonged and confusing reading matter.

Whenever possible, figures shown in parenthesis, or part numbers are quoted in the text for reference to the subject depicted, and so enable the operator to determine the location and application of any part described. Where suitable instruments are available to measure engine and gear box parts, reference should be made to technical data for normal dimensions. Elementary details such as valve grinding are covered in the handbook issued with each new machine.

CONTENTS

		PAGE
Table of Models		3
Technical Data		4
Engine and Lubrication	Section A	10
Gears and Gear Box	" B	48
Forks	" C	57
Frame	" D	63
Wheels and Brakes	" E	65
Transmission	" F	74
Carburetter	" G	76
Electrical	" H	78
Supplement For 1963/1964 and Later Models		101
Supplementary Instruction Book For Competition Models		111

NOTE

Additional Manual For 'Lightweight' Models (Only) Begins After Page 124 Of This Manual

TABLE OF MODELS DESCRIBED

HEAVYWEIGHT MODELS

1957   Models
350 cc. ... ... G3 LS   16 MS
350 cc. Trials ... ... G3 C   16 MC
350 cc. Scrambler ... G3 LCS   16 MCS
500 cc. ... ... G80 S   18 S
500 cc. Scrambler ... G80 CS   18 CS
500 cc. Twin G9   20
600 cc. Twin G11   30

1958   Models
350 cc. ... ... G3 LS   16 MS
350 cc. Trials ... ... G3 C   16 C
350 cc. Scrambler ... G3 LCS   16 CS
500 cc. G80   18
500 cc. Scrambler ... G80 CS   18 CS
500 cc. Twin G9   20
600 cc. Twin G11   30
600 cc. Twin ... ... G11 CS   30 CS

1959   Models
350 cc. G3   16
350 cc. Trials ... ... G3 C   16 C
500 cc. G80   18
500 cc. Scrambler ... G80 CS   18 CS
600 cc. Scrambler ... TCS
500 cc. Twin G9   20
500 cc. Twin ... ... G9 CSR   20 CSR
500 cc. Twin ... ... G9 CS   20 CS
650 cc. Twin G12   31
650 cc. Twin ... ... G12 CSR   31 CSR
650 cc. Twin ... ... G12 CS   31 CS

1960-1961   Models
350 cc. G3   16
350 cc. Trials ... ... G3 C   16 C
500 cc. G80   18
500 cc. Scrambler ... G80 CS   18 CS
600 cc. Scrambler ... TCS
500 cc. Twin G9   20
650 cc. Twin G12   31
650 cc. Twin ... ... G12 CS   31 CS
650 cc. Twin ... ... G12 CSR   31 CSR

1962   Models
350 cc. (Short stroke) ... G3 G3S   16 & 16 S
350 cc. Trials ... ... G3 C   16 C
500 cc. G80   18
500 cc. Scrambler ... G80 CS   18 CS
600 cc. Scrambler ... TCS
650 cc. Twin G12   31
650 cc. Twin ... ... G12 CSR   31 CSR

1963-1964   Models
350 cc. 16
350 cc. G3
500 cc. 18
500 cc. G80
500 cc. ... ... G80 CS
650 cc. ... ... Twin

LIGHTWEIGHT MODELS

1958-1959   Models
250 cc. G2   14
250 cc. Scrambler ... G2 CS   14 CS

1960-1962   Models
250 cc. ... ... G2 & G2 S 14 & 14 S
250 cc. Scrambler ... G2 CS   14 CS
350 cc. G5   8

1962 ... ... G2 CSR   14 CSR

1963-1964   Models
250 cc. ... ... 14 & CSR
250 cc. ... ... G2 & CSR

3

TECHNICAL DATA

	250 cc. and Sports	250 cc. Scrambler	350 Lightweight	350 Heavyweight
Cylinder bore size	2.7513—2.7503	2.7513—2.7503	2.835—2.834	2.7197—2.7187
Compression ratio	7.8	10.5	6.9	7.4
Piston skirt diameter Top	2.7429—2.7421	2.7429—2.7421	2.8286—2.8276	2.718—2.7172
Piston ring gap	.008"—.012"	.008"—.012"	.008"—.013"	.008"—.013"
Gudgeon pin bush	.7505—.7508	as 250	as 250	$\frac{7}{8}"$—.00025" $\frac{7}{8}"$—.00075"
Con rod diameter	H 1.7037 L 1.7035	2.016—2.01575	2.016—2.01575	H 1.7037 L 1.7035
Crank pin diameter	H 1.20375 L 1.20350	1.516—1.5158	1.516—1.5158	H 1.20375 L 1.20350
Crank pin rollers	$\frac{1}{4} \times \frac{1}{4}$ (20)	$\frac{1}{4} \times \frac{1}{4}$ (28)	$\frac{1}{4} \times \frac{1}{4}$ (28)	$\frac{1}{4} \times \frac{1}{4}$ (30)
Valve spring free length	1.53/64"	1.43/64"	1.53/64"	2.5/64"
Valve spring wire diameter	.176"	$\frac{3}{16}"$	.176"	.168"
Drive side bearing	$\frac{7}{8} \times 2 \times \frac{9}{16}$	$\frac{7}{8} \times 2 \times \frac{9}{16}$	$\frac{7}{8} \times 2 \times \frac{9}{16}$	$1 \times 2\frac{1}{2} \times \frac{3}{4}$
Drive side bearing				$1 \times 2\frac{1}{4} \times \frac{5}{8}$
Timing side bush	H .8755 L .8750	H .8755 L .8750	H .8755 L .8750	H 1.1255 L 1.1250
Cam wheel bushes (all)				$\frac{1}{2}$+.0005 $\frac{1}{2}$—.0005
Rocker box bushes (all)				$\frac{5}{8}$+.00075 $\frac{5}{8}$—.00075

NOTE: Technical details given for the 250 cc. Scrambler apply also to the 250 cc. C.S.R. model with the exception of the compression ratio which is 8 to 1.

Finished cylinder bore size 1964   350 (2.835"—2.834")   500 (3.387"—3.386")   350 trials (2.835"—2.834")

	350 Short Stroke	500 Heavyweight	500 Scrambler	600 Scrambler
Cylinder bore size	2.915—2.914	3.2505—3.2495	3.386—3.385	3.5005—3.4995
Compression ratio	8.5	7.3	8.7	9.2
Piston skirt diameter Top	2.9063—2.9055	3.2475—3.2467	3.3795—3.7870	3.492—3.491
Piston ring gap	.008"—.013"	.010"—.015"	.010"—.015"	.012"—.016"
Gudgeon pin bush	$\frac{7}{8}"$—.00025" $\frac{7}{8}"$—.00075"	as 350	as 350	as 350
Con rod diameter	H 1.7037 L 1.7035	H 1.7037 L 1.7035	H 2.016 L 2.01575	H 2.016 L 2.01575
Crank pin diameter	H 1.20375 L 1.20350	H 1.20375 L 1.20350	H 1.5156 L 1.5154	H 1.5156 L 1.5154
Crank pin rollers	$\frac{1}{4} \times \frac{1}{4}$ (30)	$\frac{1}{4} \times \frac{1}{4}$ (30)	$\frac{1}{2} \times \frac{1}{4}$ (14)*	$\frac{1}{4} \times \frac{1}{4}$ (28)*
Valve spring free length	$1\frac{17}{32}"$	$2\frac{5}{64}"$	$1\frac{17}{32}"$	$1\frac{17}{32}"$
Valve spring wire diameter	$\frac{3}{16}"$	.168"	$\frac{3}{16}"$	$\frac{3}{16}"$
Drive side bearing	$1 \times 2\frac{1}{2} \times \frac{3}{4}$	$1 \times 2\frac{1}{2} \times \frac{3}{4}$	$1 \times 2\frac{1}{2} \times \frac{3}{4}$	$1 \times 2\frac{1}{2} \times \frac{3}{4}$
Drive side bearing	$1 \times 2\frac{1}{4} \times \frac{5}{8}$	$1 \times 2\frac{1}{4} \times \frac{5}{8}$	$1 \times 2\frac{1}{4} \times \frac{5}{8}$	$1 \times 2\frac{1}{4} \times \frac{5}{8}$
Timing side bush	H 1.1255 L 1.1250	H 1.1255 L 1.1250	H .8757 L .8752	H .8757 L .8752

* 1962 $\frac{1}{4} \times \frac{1}{4}$ (28)

Cam wheel bushes (all)	$\frac{1}{2}" \times .0005"$ $\frac{1}{2}" —.0005"$			
Rocker box bushes (all)	$\frac{5}{8}" \times .00075"$ $\frac{5}{8}" —.00075"$			

	500 cc. Twin	600 cc. Twin	650 cc. Twin
Cylinder bore size	2.598"+.0005" —.0015"	2.835"—2.834"	2.836"—2.835"
Compression ratio Std.	7 to 1	7 to 1	7.5
Compression ratio Sports	8 to 1	8 to 1	8.5
Piston skirt diameter Top	2.5933"—2.5925"	2.8341"—2.8334"	2.8295"—2.8287"
Piston ring gap	.006"	.006"	.006"
Gudgeon pin diameter	ALL	.7499—.7497	ALL
Gudgeon pin rod diameter	,,	.7505—.7500	,,
Crankshaft diameter (crankpin)	,,	1.62575—1.62525	,,
Crankshaft diameter (centre bearing)	,,	1.62675—1.62625	,,
Crankshaft bearings (2 off)	$3 \times 1\frac{3}{8} \times \frac{11}{16}$	$3 \times 1\frac{3}{8} \times \frac{11}{16}$	$3 \times 1\frac{3}{8} \times \frac{11}{16}$
Camshaft bushes	ALL	0.8125"—0.8135"	ALL
Rocker bushes	,,	0.500"—0.501"	,,
Intermediate shaft diameter	,,	0.7485"—0.7490"	,,
Intermediate bush diameter	,,	0.7495"—0.7502"	,,
Cam follower spindle diameter	,,	0.373"—0.374"	,,

CARBURETTER SPECIFICATIONS

1957 Models

Model:	350 cc. OHV	500 cc. OHV	500 cc. Twin	600 cc. Twin
Carburetter type	376/5	389/1	376/6	376/78
Bore size	1 1/16"	1 5/32"	1"	1 1/16"
Main jet	220	260	240	280
Main jet (air filter)	210	250	230	270
Slide	3½	3½	4	3½
Pilot jet	30	30	30	30
Needle jet	.106	.106	.106	.106
Needle location	central	central	central	central

1958 Models

Model:	350 cc. OHV	500 cc. OHV	500 cc. Twin	600 cc. Twin
Carburetter type	376/5	389/1	376/6	376/78
Bore size	1 1/16"	1 5/32"	1"	1 1/16"
Main jet	210	260	220	280
Main jet (air filter)	200	250	210	270
Slide	3½	3½	4	3½
Pilot jet	30	30	30	30
Needle jet	.106	.106	.106	.106
Needle location	central	central	central	central

1959 Models

Model:	350 cc. OHV	500 cc. OHV	500 cc. Twin	500 cc. C.S.	650 cc. Twin	650 cc. C.S.R.
Carburetter type	376/5	389/1	376/6	376/6	389/49	389/22
Bore size	1 1/16"	1 5/32"	1"	1"	1 1/8	1 1/8"
Main jet	210	260	220	220	400	430
Main jet (air filter)	200	250	210	210	380	400
Slide	3½	3½	4	4	3	3½
Pilot jet	30	30	30	30	30	30
Needle jet	.106	.106	.106	.106	.106	.106
Needle location	central	central	central	central	central	central

1960 Models

Model:	350 cc. OHV	500 cc. OHV	500 cc. Twin	650 cc. Twin	650 cc. C.S.R.
Carburetter type	376/5	389/1	376/6	389/18	389/22
Bore size	1 1/16"	1 5/32"	1"	1 1/8"	1 1/8"
Main jet	210	260	220	390	450
Main jet (air filter)	200	250	210	340	390
Slide	3½	3½	4	4	4
Pilot jet	30	30	30	20	20
Needle jet	.106	.106	.106	.106	.106
Needle notch location	central	central	central	4th	4th

1961–1962 Models

Model:	350 cc. OHV	500 cc. OHV	500 cc. Twin	650 cc. Twin	650 cc. C.S.R.
Carburetter type	376/5	389/52	376/209	389/50	389/49
Bore size	1 1/16"	1 5/32"	1"	1 1/8"	1 1/8"
Main jet	210	300	200	390	450
Main jet (air filter)	200	300	180	340	390
Slide	3½	3½	4	4	4
Pilot jet	30	25	25	20	20
Needle jet	.106	.106	.106	.106	.106
Needle notch location	central	central	central	4th	4th

Lightweight Models (1959–1962)

Model:	250 cc. OHV	350 cc. OHV	250 cc. C.S.R.
Carburetter type	376/99	389/42	389/82
Bore size	1 1/16"	1 1/8"	1 1/8"
Main jet	180	220	200
Main jet (air filter)	180	220	200
Slide	3½	3	3
Pilot jet	25	25	20
Needle jet	.106	.106	.106
Needle notch location	central	central	central

Trial and Scrambler Models (1959-1962)

Model:	*250 cc. Scrambler*	*350 cc. Trials*	*500 cc. Scrambler*	*500 cc. Scrambler*	*600 cc. Scrambler*
Carburetter type	376/276	376/59T	T5GP	Monobloc	T5GP
Bore size	$1\frac{1}{16}$″	$1\frac{1}{16}$″	$1\frac{3}{8}$″	$1\frac{3}{16}$″	$1\frac{3}{8}$″
Main jet	230	210	290	450	320
Main jet (air filter)	200	—	—	430	—
Slide	$3\frac{1}{2}$	3	7	3	7
Pilot jet	25	30	—	30	—
Needle jet	.106	.107T	—	.106	—
Needle notch location	central	central	central	central	—

350 cc. Short Stroke 1962

Carburetter type	389/68
Bore size	$1\frac{1}{8}$″
Main jet	230
Main jet (air filter)	230
Slide	3.5
Pilot jet	25
Needle jet	.106
Needle notch location	central

TABLE OF CHAINS

Chain sizes (Heavyweight Model)

Front chain	$\frac{1}{2}$″+.305″
Rear chain	$\frac{5}{8}$″+.380″
Magneto chain	$\frac{3}{8}$″+.225″
Dyno chain	$\frac{3}{8}$″+.225″

1957 Models

	350 cc.	350 cc. Trials	500 cc.	500 cc. Scrambler	500 cc. Twin	600 cc. Twin	650 cc. Twin	C.S.R.
Front	67 links	66 links	68 links	67 links	67 links	68 links		
Rear	98 „	97 „	98 „	97 „	97 „	97 „		
Magneto	46 „	46 „	46 „	46 „				
Dyno	50 „	50 „	50 „	50 „				

1958 Models

	350 cc.	350 cc. Trials	500 cc.	500 cc. Scrambler	500 cc. Twin	600 cc. Twin	650 cc. Twin	C.S.R.
Front	67 links	66 links	68 links	67 links	67 links	68 links		
Rear	98 „	97 „	98 „	97 „	97 „	97 „		
Magneto	46 „	46 „	46 „	46 „				
Dyno	50 „	50 „	50 „	50 „				

1959 Models

	350 cc.	350 cc. Trials	500 cc.	500 cc. Scrambler	500 cc. Twin	600 cc. Twin	650 cc. Twin	C.S.R.
Front	67 links	66 links	68 links	67 links	67 links		68 links	67 links
Rear	98 „	94 „	98 „	97 „	97 „		97 „	97 „
Magneto		46 „		46 „				

1960-1962 Models

	350 cc.	350 cc. Trials	500 cc.	500 cc. Scrambler	500 cc. Twin	600 cc. Twin	650 cc. Twin	C.S.R.
Front	67 links	66 links	69 links	67 links	67 links		68 links	67 links
Rear	98 „	94 „	98 „	98 „	97 „		97 „	97 „
Magneto		46 „						

Chain sizes (Lightweight Models)

Front chain	$\frac{3}{8}$″+.225″
Rear chain	$\frac{1}{2}$″+.305″
Front Scrambler	$\frac{1}{2}$″+.225″

1959-1962 Models

	250 cc. and Sports	250 cc. Scrambler	350 cc.
Front	72 links	55 links	72 links
Rear	123 „	131 „	123 „

Late 1962 Models

	250 cc. and Sports	250 c.c. Scrambler	350 cc.
Front	72 links ($\frac{3}{8}$″+.225″)	72 links	72 links
Rear	123 „	133 „	123 „

1962 C.S.R. Models

	250 cc. and Sports	250 cc. Scrambler	350 cc.
Front	72 links (.315″×.625″ Duplex)		
Rear	123 „ ($\frac{1}{2}$″×.305″)		

SCRAMBLES MODELS 1957 to 1959
Gear Ratios.

	First gear	Second gear	Third gear	Fourth gear (top)
Internal Ratios	2.67	1.77	1.35	1.1

Engine	Sprocket size	First gear	Second gear	Third gear	Fourth gear (top)
	16 teeth	18.39 to 1	12.19 to 1	9.30 to 1	6.89 to 1
(A)	17 ,,	17.30 to 1	11.47 to 1	8.74 to 1	6.48 to 1
	18 ,,	16.34 to 1	10.83 to 1	8.26 to 1	6.12 to 1
(B)	19 ,,	15.48 to 1	10.26 to 1	7.83 to 1	5.80 to 1
	20 ,,	14.71 to 1	9.75 to 1	7.43 to 1	5.51 to 1
	21 ,,	14.01 to 1	9.29 to 1	7.08 to 1	5.25 to 1
	22 ,,	13.37 to 1	8.86 to 1	6.76 to 1	5.01 to 1

(A) Standard for 350 cc. Scrambles Models.
(B) Standard for 500 cc. Scrambles Models.

TRIALS MODELS
Gear Ratios.

	First gear	Second gear	Third gear	Fourth gear (top)
Internal Ratios	3.28	2.39	1.47	1.1

Engine	Sprocket size	First gear	Second gear	Third gear	Fourth gear (top)
	16 teeth	22.59 to 1	16.46 to 1	10.12 to 1	6.89 to 1
(A)	17 standard	21.25 to 1	15.48 to 1	9.52 to 1	6.48 to 1
	18 ,,	20.07 to 1	14.62 to 1	8.99 to 1	6.12 to 1
(B)	19 ,,	19.02 to 1	13.86 to 1	8.52 to 1	5.80 to 1
	20 ,,	18.07 to 1	13.16 to 1	8.10 to 1	5.51 to 1
	21 ,,	17.22 to 1	12.54 to 1	7.71 to 1	5.25 to 1
	22 ,,	16.43 to 1	11.97 to 1	7.36 to 1	5.01 to 1

(A) Standard for 350 cc. Trials Models.
(B) Standard for 500 cc. Trials Models.

Sprocket sizes.
Clutch	42 teeth
Gear box	16 ,,
Rear wheel	42 ,,

250 cc. SCRAMBLES MODELS, 1959 to 1960
Gear Ratios.

	First gear	Second gear	Third gear	Fourth gear (top)
Internal Ratios	2.92 to 1	1.85 to 1	1.30 to 1	1 to 1

Gear Ratios with 17 teeth Engine Sprocket.
First gear	Second gear	Third gear	Top gear
23.4 to 1	14.8 to 1	10.4 to 1	8.0 to 1

Sprocket sizes
Clutch	46 teeth
Gear box	17 ,,
Rear wheel	73 ,,

250 cc. SCRAMBLES MODELS, 1961 to 1962.
Gear Ratios.

	First gear	Second gear	Third gear	Fourth gear (top)
Internal Ratios	2.42 to 1	1.85 to 1	1.30 to 1	1 to 1

Gear Ratios with 17 teeth Engine Sprocket.
First gear	Second gear	Third gear	Fourth gear (top)
21.62 to 1	16.6 to 1	11.63 to 1	8.95 to 1

350 cc. LIGHTWEIGHT MODELS, 1960 to 1962
ALSO 250 cc. C.S.R. MODEL
Gear Ratios.

	First gear	Second gear	Third gear	Fourth gear (top)
Internal Ratios	2.92 to 1	1.85 to 1	1.30 to 1	1 to 1

Gear Ratios with 22 teeth Engine Sprocket.
First gear	Second gear	Third gear	Fourth gear (top)
18.68 to 1	11.82 to 1	8.32 to 1	6.39 to 1

Sprocket sizes.
Clutch	46 teeth
Gear box	18 ,,
Rear wheel	55 ,,

GEAR BOX RATIOS, 1957 and 1958 TWINS

Engine	Sprocket size	First gear	Second gear	Third gear	Fourth gear (top)
	19 teeth	15.48	10.26	7.83	5.80
(A)	20 ,,	14.71	9.75	7.43	5.51
	21 ,,	14.01	9.29	7.08	5.25
(B)	22 ,,	13.37	8.86	6.76	5.01
	23 ,,	12.78	8.47	6.46	4.79

(A) Standard 500 cc. Engine sprocket.
(B) Standard 600 cc. Engine sprocket.

Gear box internal ratios.
First gear	Second gear	Third gear	Fourth gear (top)
2.67 to 1	1.77 to 1	1.35 to 1	1 to 1

Sprocket sizes.
Clutch	42 teeth
Gear box	16 ,,
Rear wheel	42 ,,

HEAVYWEIGHT GEAR RATIOS
Single cylinder Models (1957-1962)

Engine	Sprocket size	First gear	Second gear	Third gear	Fourth gear (top)
	17 teeth	16.6 to 1	11.05 to 1	7.91 to 1	6.48 to 1
	18 ,,	15.65 to 1	10.39 to 1	7.46 to 1	6.12 to 1
(A)	19 ,,	14.85 to 1	9.86 to 1	7.07 to 1	5.80 to 1
(C)	20 ,,	14.11 to 1	9.37 to 1	6.73 to 1	5.51 to 1
	21 ,,	13.42 to 1	8.93 to 1	6.41 to 1	5.25 to 1
(B)	22 ,,	12.81 to 1	8.52 to 1	6.11 to 1	5.01 to 1

(A) Standard for 350 cc. Touring Models.
(B) Standard to 500 cc. Touring Models.
(C) S/C Engine Sprocket.

TWIN CYLINDER MODELS 1959-1962
Gear Ratios.

Engine	Sprocket size	First gear	Second gear	Third gear	Fourth gear (top)
(C)	19 teeth	14.85	9.86	7.07	5.80
	20 ,,	14.11	9.37	6.73	5.51
(A)	21 ,,	13.42	8.93	6.41	5.25
	22 ,,	12.81	8.52	6.11	5.01
(B)	23 ,,	12.23	8.15	5.85	4.79

(A) Standard 500 cc. Engine Sprocket.
(B) Standard 650 cc. Engine Sprocket.
(C) S/C Engine Sprocket 500 cc.
(A) S/C Engine Sprocket 650 cc.

Gear ratios Models C.S. and C.S.R.
First gear	Second gear	Third gear	Fourth gear (top)
11.51 to 1	7.65 to 1	5.49 to 1	4.5 to 1

Sprockets.
Location	Number of teeth
Clutch	42
*Gear box	16 or 17
Rear wheel	42

* 17 teeth used on C.S.R. Models.

Gear box ratios (internal).
First gear	Second gear	Third gear	Fourth gear (top)
2.56 to 1	1.70 to 1	1.22 to 1	1 to 1

Chain sizes.
Front (all Models)	$\frac{1}{2}$" by .305"
Rear (all Models)	$\frac{5}{8}$" by $\frac{5}{8}$"

Chain length.
Front	350 Single	67 links	Rear	350 Single	98 links
,,	500 Single	69 ,,	,,	500 Single	98 ,,
,,	500 Twin	67 ,,	,,	All Twins	97 ,,
,,	650 Twin	68 ,,			

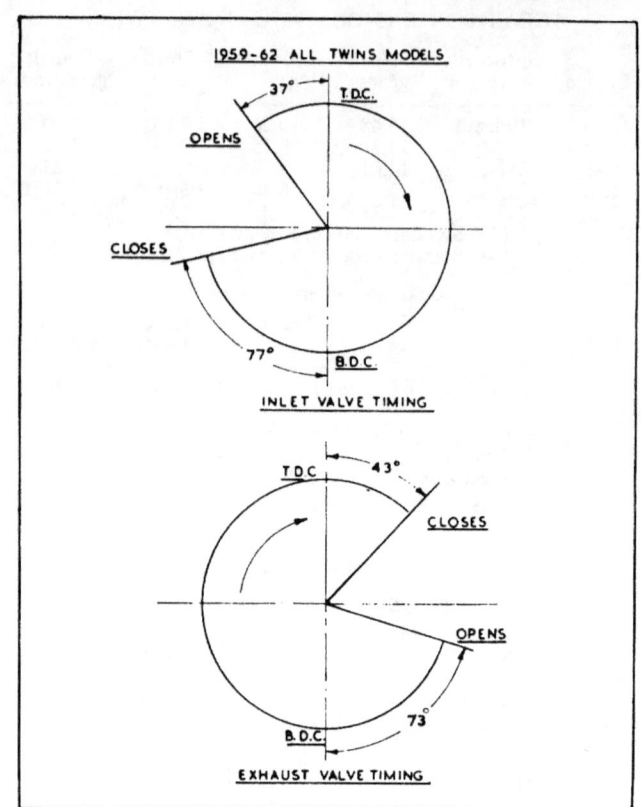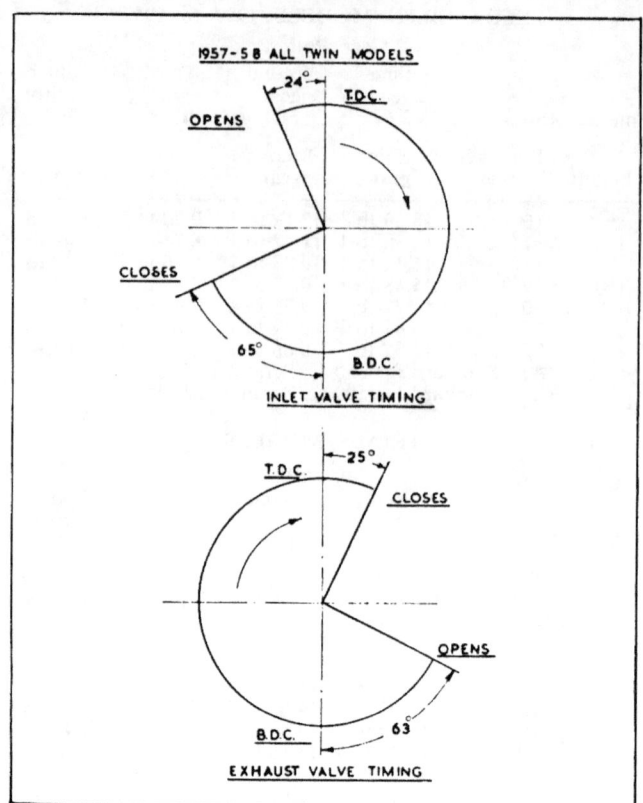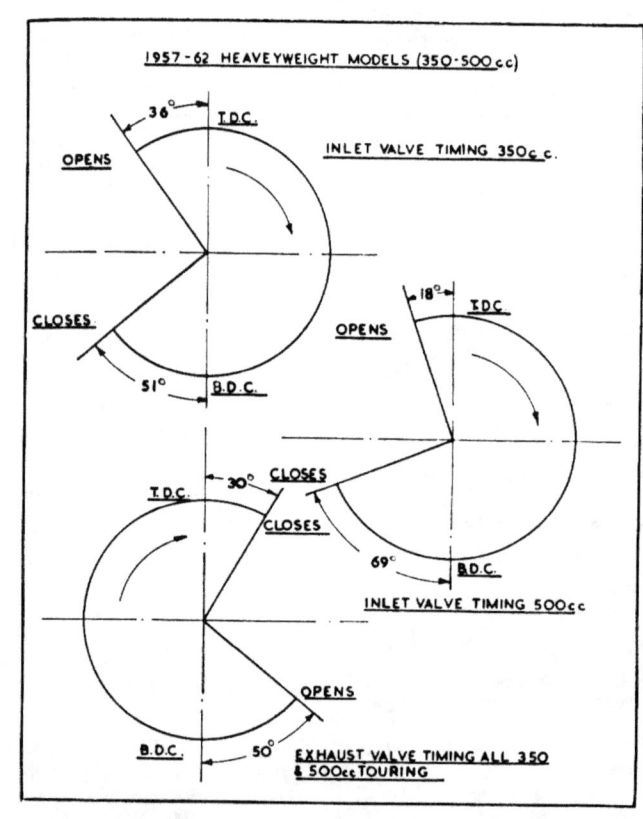

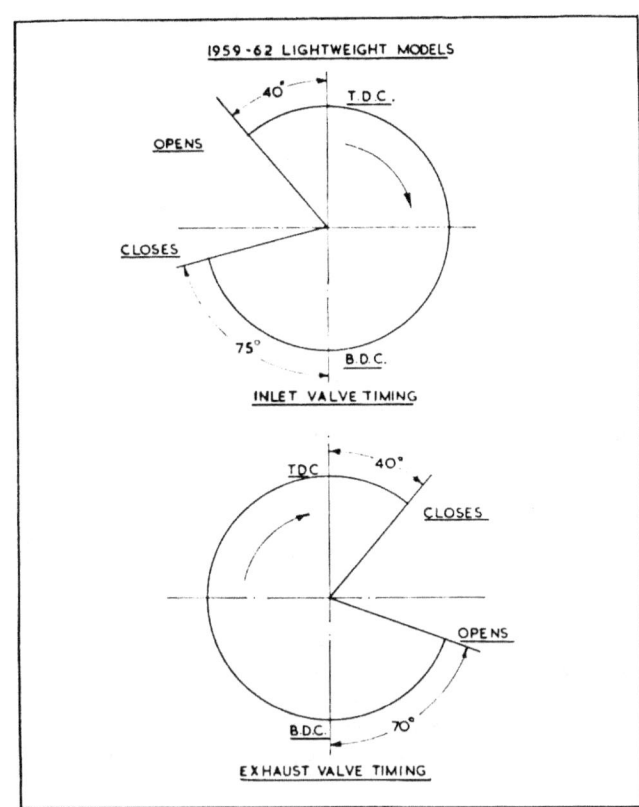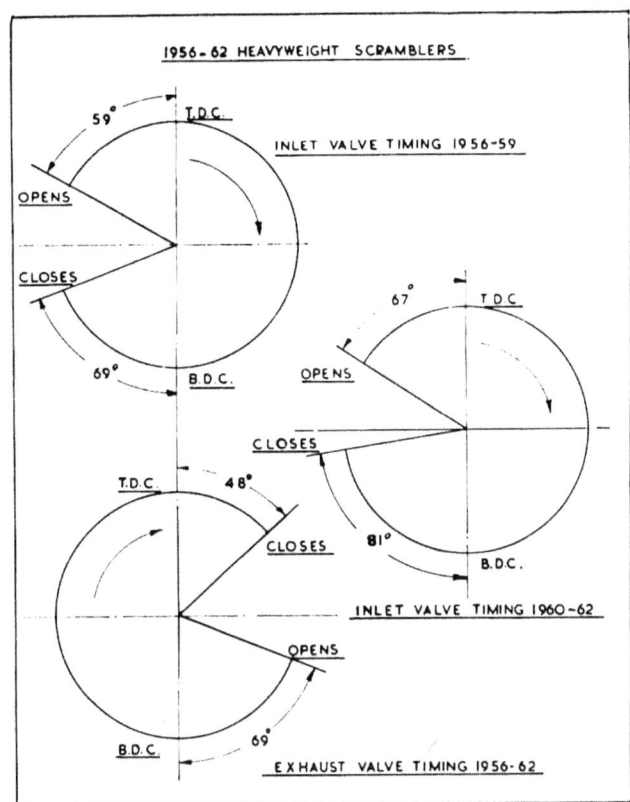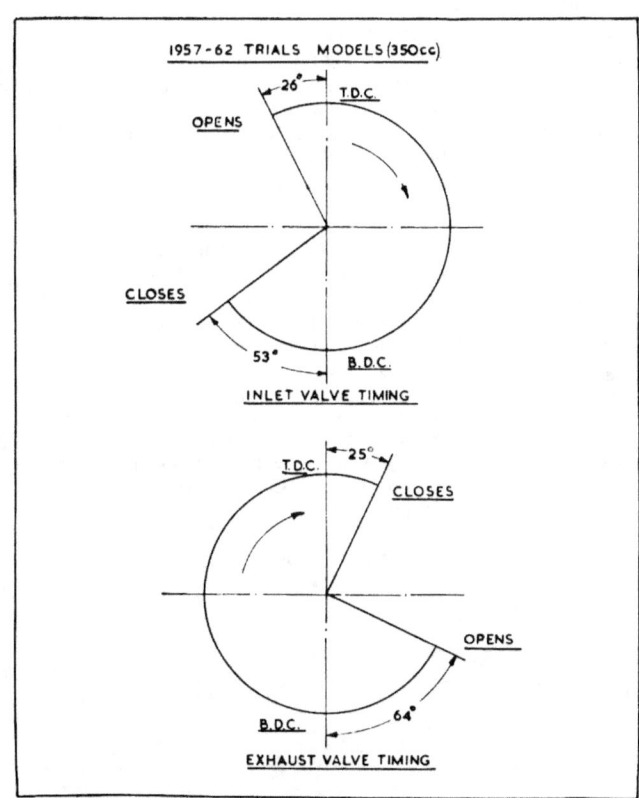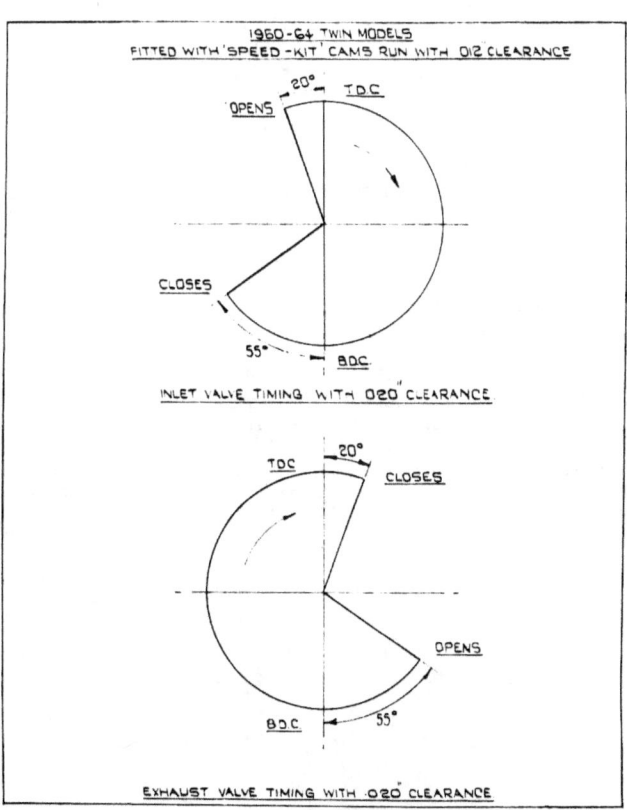

LUBRICANTS TO USE.

Efficient lubrication is of vital importance and it is false economy to use cheap oils and greases.

We recommend the following lubricants to use in machines of our make.

For Engine Lubrication

HOT above 50° F	COLD 32° F to 50° F	EXTREME COLD below freezing point (32° F)
SAE 50	SAE 30	SAE 20
Mobiloil **D** Castrol **Grand Prix** Energol **SAE 50** Essolube **50** Shell **X-100** Motor Oil **50** Regent **Havoline 50**	Mobiloil **A** Castrol **XL** Energol **SAE 30** Essolube **30** Shell **X-100** Motor Oil **30** Regent **Havoline 30**	Mobiloil **Arctic** **Castrolite** Energol **SAE 20** Essolube **30** Shell **X-100** Motor Oil **20/20W** Regent **Havoline 20**

Note: For the British Isles and much of Europe the **Cold** and **Hot** recommendations approximate to **Winter** and **Summer** conditions respectively. The **Extreme Cold** recommendations refer to wintry conditions in parts of Northern Europe, Canada, the Baltic and Scandinavian countries, and high mountainous districts where extreme cold is the average condition.

For Gear Box Lubrication

HOT above 50° F	COLD 32° F to 50° F	EXTREME COLD below freezing point (32° F)
SAE 50	SAE 50	SAE 30
Mobiloil **D** Castrol **Grand Prix** Energol **SAE 50** Essolube **50** Shell **X-100** Motor Oil **50** Regent **Havoline 50**	Mobiloil **D** Castrol **Grand Prix** Energol **SAE 50** Essolube **50** Shell **X-100** Motor Oil **50** Regent **Havoline 50**	Mobiloil **A** Castrol **XL** Energol **SAE 30** Essolube **30** Shell **X-100** Motor Oil **30** Regent **Havoline 30**

Note: For the British Isles and much of Europe the **Cold** and **Hot** recommendations approximate to **Winter** and **Summer** conditions respectively. The **Extreme Cold** recommendations refer to wintry conditions in parts of Northern Europe, Canada, the Baltic and Scandinavian countries, and high mountainous districts where extreme cold is the average condition.

For Hub Lubrication and all Frame Parts Using Grease.

MP Mobilgrease Castrolease **Heavy** Energrease **C3**
Regent **Marfak MP2** Shell **Retinax A.** or **C.D.**

For Teledraulic Front Forks

Mobiloil **Arctic** (SAE-20) Castrolite (SAE-20) Energol SAE 20
Essolube 20 (SAE-20) Havoline 20
Shell **X-100** Motor Oil 20/20W (SAE-20)

For Rear Chains

Mobilgrease No. 2 Esso Fluid Grease Energrease A.O.
Regentgrease 904 Castrolease Grease Graphited
Heated until just fluid.

When buying oils and greases it is advisable to specify the **Brand** as well as the grade and, as an additional precaution, to buy only in sealed containers or from branded cabinets.

PERIODICAL MAINTENANCE

Regular maintenance attention to lubrication and certain adjustments must be made to ensure unfailing reliability and satisfactory service.

Daily

Oil reservoir	Inspect oil level and top-up if necessary. Check oil circulation.
Petrol tank	Check level and refill if necessary.

Weekly

Oil reservoir	Check level and top-up if necessary.
Tyres	Check pressures and inflate if necessary.

Every 500 Miles (800 Kilometres)

Oil reservoir	Drain at first 500 miles and re-fill with new oil, and clean filters.
Ignition	Check contact breaker points. Regrease felt pad.
Gear box	Drain at first 500 miles and re-fill.
Chaincase	Check level of oil when machine is standing vertically on level ground.
Battery	Inspect each cell for level of electrolyte and top up with distilled water if necessary. Level of electrolyte should just be over top of plates. Beware of overfilling.

Every 1,000 Miles (1,600 Kilometres)

Oil reservoir	Drain at first 1,000 miles and re-fill with new oil.
Rear chain	In wet weather remove and soak in molten grease.
Gear box	Check oil level.
Small parts	Smear all moving parts with engine oil and wipe off surplus.
Chaincase	Drain, and re-fill, or monthly.

Every 2,000 to 5,000 Miles (3,200 to 8,000 Kilometres)
(according to road conditions).

Air filter	(If fitted) clean and re-oil filter element.

Every 3,000 Miles (4,800 Kilometres)

Rear chain	In dry weather remove and soak in molten grease.
Brake pedal	Inject small amount of grease.
Speedometer	Inject grease into gear box if nipple is fitted.
Ignition	Clean contact breaker points and re-set if necessary.
Plug	Clean sparking plug and re-set points as necessary.
Steering head	Test steering head for up and down movement and adjust if necessary.
Bolts and nuts	Check all nuts and bolts for tightness and tighten if necessary but beware of over-tightening.
Rockers	Check O.H.V. rocker adjustment and correct if necessary.

Every 5,000 Miles (8,000 Kilometres)

Oil reservoir	Drain and re-fill with new oil. If machine is only used for short runs renew oil every three months instead of mileage interval.
Filter	Clean filter in crankcase.
Ignition	Clean and adjust contact points. Check gap.
Front fork	Drain and re-fill with fresh oil. Insufficient oil content is indicated by abnormally lively action.
Carburetter	Remove carburetter float chamber side cover and clean interior. Also detach petrol pipe banjo and clean gauze strainer.

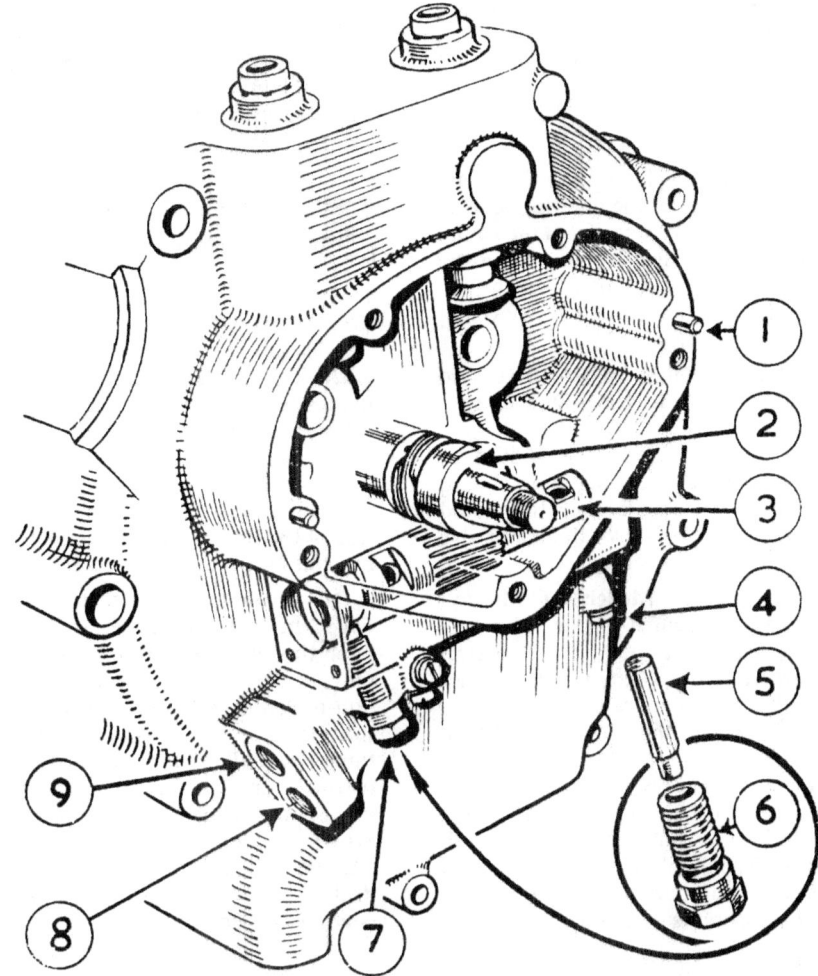

Fig. 1

The rotating oil pump plunger is here shown *in situ*, together with the guide screw which registers in the plunger profiled groove, thereby providing the reciprocating movement.

1. Dowel peg, locating timing gear cover.
2. Timing side flywheel axle with integral gear for driving oil pump plunger.
3. Oil pump plunger.
4. Screw (one or three) with fibre washer, plugging oil passages cast in crankcase.
5. Guide pin, for oil pump plunger. Inserted relieved tip downward as shown.
6. Screwed body to accommodate the oil pump plunger guide pin.
7. Body, with guide pin in position engaged in profiled cam groove of oil pump plunger.
8. Tapped hole, for pipe feeding oil to oil pump.
9. Tapped hole, for pipe returning oil to oil tank.

SINGLE CYLINDER ENGINE, 1957 to 1962 TYPES
LUBRICATION

The oil pump. The pump has only one moving part, this is the plunger (see Fig. 1), which revolves and reciprocates. Rotation is made by the worm gear on the timing side axle. Reciprocation is created by the two piece guide pin, engaged in the profiled groove machined in the pump plunger. Oil is fed by gravity to the lower of the two connections on the crankcase

Damaged or worn teeth on pump plunger. Slight amount of teeth marking, by engagement, is normal after considerable mileage. Where the teeth are worn or mutilated on the full diameter of the plunger, examine the plunger for evidence that the guide pin has been incorrectly located and has been in contact with the body of the plunger adjacent to the profiled groove. There will also be "witness" on the extreme end of the guide pin. Where the damage is confined to a small number of the teeth, this can be due to obstruction in the oil feed to either the big end, or to the rocker box. The obstruction should be removed before replacing the damaged parts. An incorrectly located timing side axle will have the same effect. When overhauling engines made before 1961 the correct type timing side axle should be used, which can be identified by the wider tooth gear for the latest type shaft.

Oil fails to return to the tank. This can only be due to:

(a) An air leak between the square cap at the rear end of the plunger housing and the crankcase.

(b) There is obstruction in the oil passage (cast in the crankcase) from the crankcase sump to the plunger housing, such as a piece of broken piston ring, etc.

(c) The housing in the crankcase where the large diameter of the plunger operates is either worn or scored. This is based on the assumption that the plunger revolves and is undamaged.

In the case of (b) it is sometimes possible to dislodge the obstruction without dismantling the engine (heavyweight models) by removing the oil pump plunger also the crankcase drain plug. A thin cycle spoke inserted through the drain plug aperture may dislodge the obstruction. The remedy for (c) is to replace the timing side half crankcase. Should oil seep into the engine when stationary, this can also be associated with (c).

Oil feed to rocker box cut off (all single cylinder engines). If the rocker box feed pipe is unobstructed examine the end of the pump guide pin for wear. A flat worn on this pin will cut off the oil supply to the rocker gear.

LIGHTWEIGHT MODELS (only)

Oil fails to return from the sump. Take out the crankcase filter and verify that the cap in the end of the filter tunnel is in position and not sealing the oil return passage from the sump. Examine also the right side of the plunger housing to ensure that the steel sleeve 042044 is correctly located also the 'O' ring is undamaged. Other details given for the heavyweight models apply also to this type engine.

Heavy oil consumption (250 cc. Models). Where there is no evidence of cylinder wear, or scored bore, use a Duaflex type piston ring 043097 as fitted to the 1962 engine.

Note: The oil supply to the inlet valve guide should be restricted as far as possible, in fact the regulating screw should be opened to the smallest amount possible from the closed position. There is considerable suction down the inlet valve guide, coupled with the down draught inlet port.

Crankcase release valve (Heavyweight Models). On heavyweight models this is a flap valve, located on the drive side crankcase adjacent to the drive side shaft, comprising a steel diaphragm located in a serrated seat. If the valve becomes inoperative causing oil leaks, the diaphragm is probably trapped between the serrated seat and the crankcase. When refitting this valve apply a grease to the serrated seat to retain the diaphragm in position during assembly. A slight oil discharge (condensed oil mist) is normal, a heavy oil discharge indicates oil is accumulating in the crankcase (see paragraph 'Oil fails to return to tank'). The crankcase release valve on the Lightweight engines is timed and ported in relation to the piston position. The ported portion is rotated by a woodruff key in the driving side shaft (see paragraph 'Engine noises'). A heavy oil discharge through the release valve tube (located behind the rear portion of the front chain case) indicates an oil accumulation in the crankcase, or abnormal positive crankcase pressure caused by gas leakage past the piston rings.

LUBRICATION
TWIN CYLINDER MODELS, 1957 to 1962

The design of the oil pumps for the Twin Cylinder Models, first introduced in 1949, has remained unaltered by reason of their reliability and longevity. Both pumps are of the gear driven type, the feed pump circulates 26 gallons per hour at 6,500 r.p.m. The widest of the two pumps is for the return to efficiently scavenge the crankcase. The two pumps can be inadvertently reversed (see paragraph 'Over oiling'). The general arrangement of the pump assemblies are shown in Fig. 2. To keep the return pump 'wet' thus ensuring an immediate oil return, when the engine is just started, a bleed valve (see Nos. 1, 2 and 3 in Fig. 2) is mounted in the left-hand side of the pump plate. Access to the ball and spring is made by removing the grub screw (No. 3, Fig. 2).

Oil circulation. (Refer to general arrangement drawing, Page 20). Oil is fed under pressure from the feed pump to the filter tunnel under the influence of the pressure relief valve plunger 026133. At the drive side end of the filter tunnel a non-return valve 026139 which is spring loaded, is also part of the filter assembly. When oil pressure is built up in the filter tunnel the ball 011645 is moved off its seating, oil passes to the two-way drilling for the main crankshaft bearings, with a by-pass to the oil distributor compartment. From here oil is distributed to the rocker gear by the oil distributor bush 022385, which is rotated by the exhaust camshaft. The oil drilling in the crankcase is via the aperture for the bolt 014292, which is sealed by the rubber backed washer 022580. Oil is

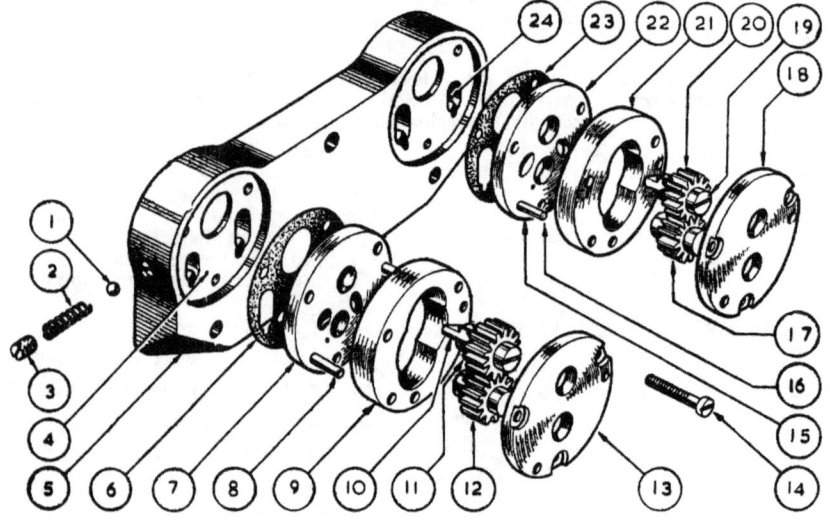

Fig. 2
Delivery Oil Pump (on the right). **Return Oil Pump** (on the left).

1 Ball, for non-return valve.
2 Spring, for non-return valve.
3 Plug, retaining non-return valve spring and ball.
4 Bleed hole.
5 Plate, carrying oil feed and return pumps.
6 Paper washer for oil return pump.
7 Back plate of oil return pump.
8 Dowel pin, locating pump plates and body.
9 Body of oil return pump.
10 Dog end of pump gear to engage in end of camshaft.
11 Driving gear, for oil return pump.
12 Driven gear, for oil return pump.
13 Front plate of oil return pump.
14 Screw (1 of 6) used to retain plates and bodies of oil pumps to the carrying plate.
15 Back plate of oil feed pump.
16 Dowel pin, locating pump plates and body.
17 Driven gear, for oil feed pump.
18 Front plate of oil feed pump.
19 Screwdriver slot, to enable driving gear to be correctly positioned during assembly.
20 Driving gear, for oil feed pump.
21 Body of oil feed pump.
22 Back plate of oil feed pump.
23 Paper washer for oil feed pump.
24 Bleed hole.

fed to a channel machined in both portions of the crankcase (see paragraph 'Oil leaks from the cylinder base'). Two metering plugs are used at this point to balance the oil feed to the camshaft tunnels and the O.H.V. rocker gear. Drillings in the face of the crankcase line up with holes machined in the cylinder barrels also cylinder heads through which oil is fed to the rocker spindles and bushes, which in turn falls by gravity down the push rod tunnels into the camshaft chambers. The main oil feed is taken to the centre web bearings, where it is diverted to the connecting rod bearings. Overspill from the camshaft tunnels causes oil to build up in the timing side crankcase, lubricating the train of gears. A pre-determined oil level hole in the crankcase wall keeps the oil level constant.

TWIN CYLINDER MODELS

OILING FAULTS

Oil builds up in crankcase (over oiling). This can be due to:

(a) The oil pumps have been reversed.
(b) There is an oil leak between the pump and the pump plate (faulty gasket) or between the pump plate and the crankcase.
(c) Obstruction in the form of a broken portion of a piston ring, sucked into the oil passage cast in the crankcase to the return pump drilling, or the pumps are loose on the pump plate.
(d) The gears are damaged, on the return pump, by the introduction of foreign matter (portion of piston ring).

In the case of (b) if the pump plate is bruised or deformed at the point where the oil pick up takes place, the oil return will be spasmodic. When there is evidence of air bubbles emerging from the spout in the oil tank, this indicates an air leak. If difficulty in dislodging the obstruction occurs, a good tip is to feed a line of $\frac{1}{4}$" diameter ball bearings down the passage cast in the crankcase and when nearly full apply pressure on the last ball, which should push out the obstruction. If a machine is left stationary for a lengthy period, oil can accumulate in the crankcase, due to a slight seepage past the oil feed pump, which is inevitable. Should this happen after standing for a short period, check the feed pump for loose fixing screws on the pump plate (No. 18, Fig. 2).

Oil discharge from crankcase into chaincase. This is usually due to the crankcase release valve being deranged. This valve also retains the engine sprocket to the crankshaft. Should the diaphragm be buckled or trapped oil will escape from the crankcase into the front chaincase. This oil discharge will also occur if oil builds up in the crankcase as previously described. Abnormal positive crankcase pressure caused by gas leakage past the piston rings can have a similar effect. A distance piece is used between the engine sprocket and the main crankcase bearing. The outside diameter of this distance piece is a close fit in the crankcase, being designed to prevent oil leakage. If the aperture is damaged or deformed, an efficient seal cannot be made, which would result in a build up of oil in the front chaincase.

Oil shortage to rocker gear. If the oil supply to the rocker gear is cut off, first check the metering plugs 018890 in the cylinder heads by removing both heads and take out, in turn, the rocker spindles which are held in position by the clamp bolt (No. 10, see Fig. 4) and note the location of the plain also spring washer. The oil feed hole drilled in the rocker post will now be exposed. Force petrol through this aperture which should emerge through the metering plugs, if they are unobstructed. Check also the oil hole in the cylinder, which may be masked by the base washer or head gasket. If it is found that the metering plugs are obstructed use a $\frac{1}{32}$" drill held in a pin vice to clear the drilling. The drill should be manipulated with care to avoid breakage. If it is desired to remove or replace these plugs, apply gentle heat to the cylinder head, then push the plug through the drilling, when it will come out of the hole in the rocker post. Insert the new plug, small end inwards, a light tap with a centre punch inserted in the larger hole will retain the plug in position.

Oil failure to big end journals. The big end shells used on the Two Cylinder Models are materially and dimensionally identical to those used on high-powered racing motor car engines. With smooth journals and a continuous supply of clean oil, these bearings will be trouble free for many thousands of miles. If the oil supply is cut off, even temporarily, the bearings will run and usually the drive side is the first to be affected. This is because the overspill from the timing gear falls on to the timing side crankshaft, which keeps the bearing 'alive' for a slightly longer period. When the bearing 'runs' the clearance between the con rod and the crankshaft increases considerably. The hammering effect produced will tend to loosen the con rod nuts, which gives rise to the opinion that loose nuts are responsible for the trouble. With further use, and the engine in this condition, can result in a broken con rod, with additional damage. It follows that should an unusual noise develop, the cause should be investigated without delay. It is imperative that the reason for the oil shortage is traced and rectified before the crankshaft is assembled also reinstalled into the crankcase.

Possible cause of oil failure. If the fault develops after an oil change or when the engine has been refitted to the frame, the oil pipes may be reversed at the oil tank end.

Crankcase filter. Early 1960 engines were issued with a close mesh gauze metal filter (see table of oiling modifications). If this type of filter has collapsed, this indicates that oil cannot pass through the filter. Lack of cleaning and the use of additives, which tend to varnish the outside diameter of the filter, prevents oil penetrating. This type of filter should be discarded and replaced with the modified, felt type.

Non-return valve. Make sure the ball can be lifted off its seat, the spring may be corroded.

Pressure relief valve. This is a vital part of the oiling system. On earlier type engines (see table of oiling modifications) this valve was located in the timing side crankcase, just below the dyno fixing stud. The valve consists of a spring loaded plunger, the spring will be exposed when the timing cover is removed. If the spring is buckled, or there is foreign matter in the plunger orifice, the plunger will be held off its seat, thus cutting off the oil supply to the engine.

Twin Cylinder Models, made in 1960 and onwards, the pressure relief valve was transferred to the base of the filter compartment (see 'general arrangement' Drawing Fig. 6), the plunger 026133 is retained by a spring, washer and circlip. The possibility of this valve becoming deranged is extremely remote. A case has been known where the valve washer 026134 has been trapped in the square bottom recess machined in the timing cover. Originally this recess was $\frac{1}{2}$" diameter, which in the interest of safety should be enlarged to $\frac{17}{32}$". With the engine in a dismantled state, test the plunger for free movement by pressure on the plunger with a suitable object.

Oil distributor bush (022385). As previously described, this rotating bush delivers oil to the rocker gear and needs no attention. It is of paramount importance to use a copper washer of the correct thickness, between the cap 014247 and the crankcase, the washer should be $\frac{1}{16}$" thick. The use of a thin washer will lock the bush solid with serious damage to the crankcase.

Checking the oil pressure. After engine overhaul, or when an oil feed shortage has taken place, when the engine is refitted to the frame, the oil pressure should be checked. An oil pressure gauge reading from zero to at least 150 lbs. per square inch is required. It must be mentioned that when a pressure relief valve is not incorporated in the oiling system (see table of oiling modifications) the engine must idle for several minutes until the oil has become warm and the viscosity lowered. Spinning the engine in a cold condition will generate a pressure of about 300 lbs., which can burst the gauge. The application of the gauge can be seen in Fig. 3. The shank of the gauge should be $\frac{1}{4}$" B.S.P. (.518) $\times$ 19 T.P.I. Use a filter compartment cap of an early type 016179 assembled with ball and spring to accommodate the gauge, for test purposes. When an oil pressure relief valve is fitted, the recorded pressure when cold is between 100 to 110 lbs. per square inch falling to 25 to 30 lbs. when hot. Without a relief valve the pressure is about 140 lbs. after warm up and 25 to 30 lbs. hot. In the event of damage to the thread in the crankcase for the cap 016179 use a tap $1\frac{1}{8}$" $\times$ 20 T.P.I. to clear the threads. This tap can also be used for the oil distributor cap orifice.

Oil leaks (Twin Cylinder Models). If the engine is carefully assembled, oil leaks are extremely rare, providing the gaskets are sound and not deformed during the process of assembly.

Oil leaks from cylinder head joint. If the oil leak is persistent and does not respond to the use of new gaskets, the cylinder head face may be distorted. To remedy, the head face should be 'rubbed down' on a face plate, alternatively, use a sheet of reasonably coarse emery cloth placed on a stout sheet of glass until the head face is perfectly flat. Use also heat treated cylinder head holding down nuts (Part No. 028082).

Oil leaks from cylinder base. An oil leak from this part of the engine may develop after the cylinders have been removed. When the leakage persists, and when the base joint is remade, without improvement, it is quite likely that the leak is from the crankcase joint and not from the cylinder base. As explained previously in paragraph 'oil circulation', oil is fed under pressure to a channel in the crankcase midway between the two cylinders. During the process of removing and refitting the cylinders, the crankcase joint has broken down, particularly if the bolts passing through the crankcase have been released, or if the cylinders have been 'racked' sideways to remove them. To prove if the leak does come from the crankcase joint, take off the right side cylinder head and barrel. Use a WESCO pressure oil gun, with the spout placed in one of the two oil holes drilled in the crankcase spigot aperture, seal off the other hole with one of the fingers of the free hand. Work the gun to build up pressure, if the crankcase joint is leaking, oil will emerge between the two halves of the crankcase midway between the two cylinders.

Engine noises (Twin Cylinder Models). No engine will remain mechanically quiet throughout the whole period of its life, so after considerable mileage some engine noise is inevitable. Under such conditions the possible engine noises are detailed together with the symptoms to assist in quick detection. Firstly, disregard the so-called experts' diagnosis of 'worn small end bearing' (wrist pin), as this does not happen on the twin engine.

Fig. 3

Overhead rocker noise. This can develop if the rocker clearance is excessive and is easy to locate. An oil shortage to the rocker gear will produce a similar noise, with the possibility of wear on the valve ends, also rockers. If the wear on the rocker end (which makes contact with the valve) is to any noticeable extent the use of a feeler gauge will give a false reading. If the wear is slight, the rocker gear can be hand stoned to remove the ridge formed by wear.

Cam follower wear. This noise is usually audible when running between 30 to 40 m.p.h. and is not affected by load on the engine. As a temporary measure close up the rocker clearance to .002 on all valves. If the noise is still there, the followers are worn. If after examination, the exhaust cam followers only are worn, this would suggest overload by the valves being tight, or prone to seize in the valve guides. After reassembly the valve motion should be checked to verify that the valve springs do not become coil bound when the valve is at full lift. This can happen when pattern valve springs are used, or the lower valve spring seat has been fitted upside down. The wide face of the spring seat should abut against the valve guide boss on the cylinder head.

Big end noise. Can be detected when engine is running at a small throttle without load, or when the machine rotates the engine on down gradient. This noise usually disappears when the engine is pulling.

Technical aspect of the Twin Cylinder Models. The twin cylinder engine for Touring Models was first produced in 1949. Since this time the design has undergone many changes, far too numerous to describe in this manual.

In the main the technical details given are to cover engines made from 1957 onwards, although a description of lubrication modifications are mentioned in preceding chapter for earlier models.

Engine design. Originally the cubic capacity of the 500 cc. Twin was 498 cc., bore size 66 mm., stroke 72.8 mm. Then the 600 cc. engine was introduced, capacity 592 cc., bore 72 mm., the stroke being the same as the 500 cc. version. From this it is apparent that the technical aspect of both engines are identical with the exception of carburetter settings and engine sprocket size, which are given in Technical Data.

The 650 cc. engine was first introduced in 1959, which has a cubic capacity of 646 cc., bore size 72 mm., stroke 79.35 mm. The standard engine uses a compression ratio of 7.5 to 1. The CS and CSR models have a ratio of 8.5 to 1, which necessitates a slightly retarded ignition timing (see paragraph 'setting ignition') and KLG FE220 sparking plugs.

Camshafts. An improved type of camshaft was introduced in 1959 for the CSR Models which can be used in all twin cylinder engines. Earlier types are no longer available. Replacements now issued will be of the improved type.

Fitting new camshafts. It is essential when new camshafts are fitted particularly to early type engines, that the valve motion is checked when the engine is assembled as far as adjusting the rocker clearance. Deal with each valve in turn by turning the engine until the valve is at full lift (fully open) when it should be possible to compress the valve spring further by applying pressure on the rocker to a minimum of .040" (1 mm.). This is to ensure the valve springs are not coil bound, or closing up solid at full lift. This can also happen if the valve spring seats have been reversed (the wide face should go against the cylinder head) or pattern type valve springs are used. An incorrectly located valve guide will also limit valve movement thus causing cam gear wear.

Cam followers. If premature wear occurs with this part of the engine, the cause can be due to overload (see paragraph 'Valve springs'). The use of unsuitable lubricating oil will affect cam gear wear. If the wear is confined to the exhaust cam followers only, the exhaust valves may be tight in the valve guides when the engine reaches its normal running temperature (see Technical Data for dimensions). Continual short distance running can have some bearing on this trouble. The use of delcrome cam followers used on late 1962 engines will offset premature wear.

Cylinder heads. Cylinder heads on the 500 cc. and 600 cc. engines were identical prior to 1957 when a slightly larger valve head diameter was introduced. The inlet port was also enlarged to 1 1/16" for the 600 cc. engine. A new design of cylinder head is used on all twin engines made for 1960 onwards. The head sphere is more shallow, with an alteration to the shape of the piston crown. The new parts do not interchange with earlier types.

To convert, new cylinders also cylinder heads and pistons together with new type head gaskets, are required.

Connecting rods. All connecting rods used on the twin engine since its conception are materially and dimensionally identical with one exception, namely, the detachable cap on the connecting rod which is chamfered to clear the crankcase for the 650 cc. engine. If an early type rod is used as a replacement, the cap must be filed to give the required clearance There is also a chamfer on one side of the connecting rod just above the big end 'eye'. The rod should be assembled with the chamfer pointing away from the centre of the crankshaft to clear the crankcase.

Raising the compression ratio. This is accomplished by exchanging the pistons. A table of pistons available for twin cylinder engines indicates the part number, also ratio for identification. The part number for the bare piston is quoted, which is stamped on the piston crown.

500 cc.	1957-59	1960-62
Standard ratio	022415 (7/1 C.R.)	026323 (8/1 C.R.)
H.C. ,,	022598 (8/1 C.R.)	---
600 cc.		
Standard ratio	022226 (7.4/1 C.R.)	---
H.C. ,,	023503 (8/1 C.R.)	---
650 cc.		
Standard ratio	025042 (7.5/1 C.R.)	026324 (7.5/1)
H.C. ,,	025045 (8.5/1 C.R.)	026325 (8.5/1)

Valve springs. Whilst the valve springs used on various Twin Cylinder Models are similar in appearance, they differ in free length, also on poundage when assembled.

It is important to use the correct type of springs to avoid overloading the cam gear, apart from the risk of the springs being coil bound, when the valve is at full lift.

TABLE OF VALVE SPRINGS

All 500 cc. and 600 cc. engines (1949-1959).

Part No.	Free length.	Number of coils.	Wire gauge.
011770 Inner spring	1 13/32"	7	12 S.W.G. (.104)
011769 Outer ,,	1 3/4"	6	9 S.W.G. (.144)

500 cc. and 650 cc. engines (1960—onwards).

018347 Inner spring	2.030"	8 3/4	.116"
018348 Outer ,,	2.523"	8	.140"

Note: This type of valve spring must NOT be used on engines made before 1960. These springs are rated, the end marked with yellow paint is assembled against the cylinder head. The inner spring is an interference fit with the outer spring to prevent valve spring surge.

TABLE OF SPRINGS (Twin Lubrication System)
1957 Models (only)

Spring for crankcase release valve 018282 9/16" + 3/8" 10 coil 26 gauge.

1957-1959

Spring for filter non-return valve 014241 1 1/2" + 5/16" 15 coil 17 gauge.

Spring for pump bleed valve 000701 19/32" + 1/4" 10 coil 26 gauge.

1960-1962

Spring for pressure relief valve 026132 .984" + .423" 9 coil 18.1 gauge.

Ball for pump bleed valve 1/4" diameter.
Ball for non-return valve 3/8" diameter.

Timing gear noise. This is due to backlash between the train of gear wheels in the timing cover, and is most pronounced when the engine is idling. Wear on the bush or shaft for the intermediate pinion can be responsible. A new pinion with closer mesh is also beneficial.

Piston slap. A little piston noise when the engine is cold is not unusual, particularly when high compression pistons are fitted. In the ordinary way this noise clears up when the normal running temperature is reached. Should the noise prevail, a seized piston is suspect.

Rattle in top part of engine. A noise that is difficult to locate can develop as a result of either one, or both, exhaust pipes becoming loose in the exhaust ports, when the engine is hot. Rocking the pipe sideways to get it out of the port tends to close in the pipe. Drive a steel or hard wood tool shaped like a carrot into the pipe end to 'bell out' the end to make it a close fit in the port.

TABLE OF OILING MODIFICATIONS

1956 Twin Cylinder Models

1. A balanced oil feed to cam tunnels and O.H.V. rocker gear introduced, by using two metering jets in the channel machined in the crankcase (see 'Lubrication').

2. Crankcase pressure relief valve discarded.

3. Oil hole in oil distributor bush $\frac{1}{32}$".

4. Magnetic filter incorporated in drain plug for crankcase.

5. Oil feed to O.H.V. rocker gear diverted to the top front crankcase bolt. Bolt is sealed with rubber-faced washer.

1957 Models

Non-return valve for filter compartment now a sealed unit 023331.

Oil hole in distributor bush enlarged to $\frac{3}{64}$".

Tufnol diaphragm for crankcase release valve discarded and replaced with steel type, use spring also for diaphragm.

1958 Models

Hole $\frac{3}{64}$" in oil distributor bush discarded. Bush now uses a flat machined on outside diameter of bush.

1959 Models

The four metering plugs in the cylinder heads discarded. New type crankcase release valve sealed unit type introduced.

1960 Models

A $\frac{3}{32}$" hole drilled in the cylinder spigot aperture (drive side only) the intention being to increase the oil supply to the drive side cylinder and piston. Engines with number X1994 to X2619 had a similar hole in the cylinder spigot. These cylinders must be used on the right (timing side) side of the engine.

An improved type of pressure relief valve introduced and now located in the base of the crankcase filter compartment. The fabric type crankcase filter discarded and replaced by fine metal gauze type with valve attached.

1961 Models

The $\frac{3}{32}$" hole in crankcase spigot (see 1960 Models) now transferred to the end of inlet camshaft tunnel.

Oil spills from the hole on the inside wall of the drive side crankcase so falling on to the crankshaft bob weight. From here oil is flung up and into the near side cylinder to augment oil supply. The four cylinder head metering plugs discarded in 1959 re-introduced.

1962 Models

Duaflex rings incorporated to improve oil consumption.

1962 Twin Cylinder Models

A new type crankcase filter 028496 using a felt fabric surrounding the gauze filter is used on the above Models. This filter can be used in 1960 and 1961 Models. Clean filter every three thousand miles.

TWIN CYLINDER

Overhead rocker adjustment. This adjustment is effected by turning the eccentric rocker spindle to increase, or decrease, the rocker clearance as desired. As quietening curves are used on the camshafts the engine must be correctly positioned to obtain correct clearance.

All twin engines made before 1960 use a clearance of .006" and .008" after 1960, engine cold.

Tools required are:—Allen Key 018055 for rocker cover; open end spanner 015264 for clamp nut; feeler gauges or strip foil .006" or .008".

Deal with one cylinder at a time by removing the rocker cover, also the sparking plug. Close the throttle, turn engine slowly until the inlet rocker goes down and returns. The piston is now approximately on T.D.C.

Insert a spoke, or stiff wire through plug hole to ensure the piston is exactly on T.D.C. by rocking the engine backwards and forwards. Slack off slightly the nut (8) (Fig. 4), turn the rocker spindle (12) to raise the rocker away from the valve (there is a slot in the spindle end).

Put the feeler gauge on the valve stem, turn the spindle in reverse direction until the rocker just 'nips' the gauge, re-tighten the clamp nut without undue force.

If the clearance appears to be in excess refer to paragraph 'overhead rocker noises'. Inspect gaskets for rocker covers and renew if they are damaged.

Note: Do not unscrew the clamp nut unduly, the thrust washer will come out of position.

TWIN CYLINDER ENGINE SERVICE

To remove cylinder heads. To ensure the various parts of each head are not intermixed, it is recommended that only one head is removed at a time.

Remove the petrol tank.

Remove the rocker box covers, as already described.

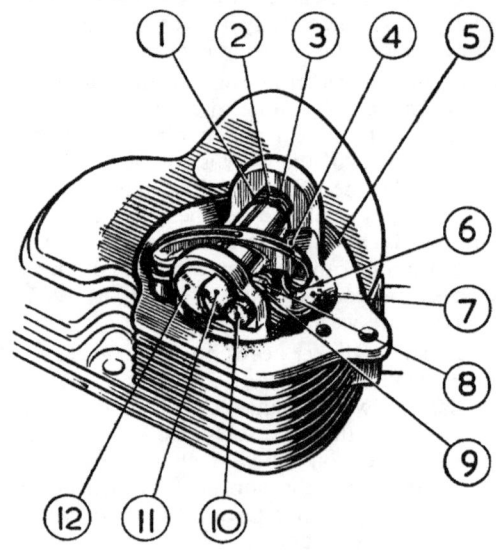

Fig 4
Rocker adjustment.

1 Plain washer—mentioned above.
2 Spring washer.
3 Plain washer.
4 Rocker.
5 Cylinder head.
6 Rocker Clearance .008".
7 Valve spring cap.
8 Clamping bolt nut.
9 Clamping bolt washer.
10 Clamping bolt.
11 Cutaway on rocker spindle.
12 Eccentric rocker spindle.

Remove the sparking plugs.

Remove the exhaust pipes and silencers (no need to separate pipes and silencers) by taking away nuts and washers holding pipes to stays and silencers to rear frame, pulling silencer end of each assembly outwards far enough to allow fixing studs to disengage and then pulling each assembly forwards till disengaged from the cylinder head.

Remove air filter (if fitted).

Remove carburetter by taking away the two fixing bolts and withdrawing to the rear.

Lay carburetter aside.

Remove inlet manifold by taking away the four fixing nuts and washers and withdrawing to the rear. Take care not to damage the gaskets between manifold and heads or rubber ring insert.

Remove cylinder head steady plate (secured by three bolts and nuts).

Remove heads by using box spanner 015213 to remove the four nuts that retain each head.

After removal invert each head to dislodge the spacers under the nuts and lay aside to await re-assembly.

The cylinder head gaskets will generally adhere to the tops of the barrels, but care must be taken not to damage them.

To remove the valves. First remove rockers from cylinder head (see Fig. 4). The importance of correctly locating the valve spring seats is stressed, the wide face of the seat abuts against the cylinder head. Reversal will make the springs coil bound and cause damage to the valve gear. Proceed by removing the rockers (see Fig. 4 for assembly sequence). If a valve spring compressor is not available, use a wood block 2″ in cube to support the valve with the head on a bench.

Compress the springs to extract the split collets, which are a taper fit. A sharp tap on the spring collar will release them.

If the valve springs are retained, identify their location for refitting. Check the four metering plugs in cylinder heads for obstruction, before refitting rockers.

To remove valve guides. Both guides are a force fit and located by circlips, the cylinder head must be uniformly heated, the guide can then be pressed out of the port sufficiently to remove the circlip.

Reheat the head, press down the guide from outside the port.

Removing cylinder barrels and pistons. Unless it is desired to inspect the pistons and rings during decarbonisation, they are, as already advised, best left undisturbed. Having removed the cylinder heads, withdraw the cylinder barrels by: Lift away the four push rods, identify them for refitting and lay aside. Dealing with one barrel at a time, exert upward pressure on a barrel, slightly rocking to and fro while doing so, and steady the piston with one hand as it emerges from the barrel. Cover the crankcase throat with clean rag to prevent entry of foreign matter.

To remove piston. Using 011188 circlip pliers, contract one of the gudgeon pin circlips and with a rotary motion, gently withdraw the circlip from its housing. The gudgeon pin may then be pushed out of the piston, which action frees the piston from the connecting rod.

(Being a parallel, floating fit in the piston and connecting rod, small end it is immaterial from which side the gudgeon pin is withdrawn.)

Note: It may be necessary to apply a little heat to the piston to permit free gudgeon pin removal and replacement.

Rings may be removed from a piston by peeling off or by introducing behind them three thin and narrow metal strips, equally spaced round the piston, and then sliding them off, taking care not to scratch the piston.

Carefully examine the contact edge of each piston ring and replace any which do not show a bright surface over the whole circumference.

Oversize or undersize parts: The following are the only 'oversize' variations provided for the vertical twin machines:

Big-end and crankshaft centre main bearings:

Undersize: .010 below normal (journals to be re-ground to suit).
.020 below normal (journals to be re-ground to suit).
.030 below normal (journals to be re-ground to suit).

Cylinder re-bore: .020″ and .040″ oversize. (See 'Technical Data' for normal size.)

Pistons and rings: .020″ and .040″ oversize. (See 'Technical Data' for normal size.)

Fitting pistons and cylinder barrels. Pistons to be free of carbon on their crowns and all piston ring grooves to be clean.

Piston rings to be clean and on pistons.

Fit a piston to its connecting rod by: Smear gudgeon pin with clean engine oil. Place piston over connecting rod, introduce gudgeon pin to piston and pass through connecting rod, press right home against the circlip still *in situ*. Then again using pliers 011188, contract the other circlip, introduce same into its groove in the piston, using a rotary movement. Make quite certain that the circlip lies snugly in its groove because failure to do so will inevitably lead to serious damage. (See *Note* above.)

Before fitting the cylinders, make sure they are clean and examine the base washers and renew same if not perfect.

To fit new cylinder base washer, first clean off the old washer and all traces of jointing compound. Then smear one side of the new washer with jointing compound and, when that is nearly dry ('tacky') apply to the cylinder.

Place rings on piston, scraper first, then the two compression rings.

On all models, the top compression ring is chromium plated. These chrome plated rings have a slightly tapered exterior and when new are clearly marked with the word 'TOP' on one side to indicate assembly position.

After use, this word tends to become indiscernible, but over a large mileage the assembly position can be determined by brightness of the edge contacting cylinder wall. This bright edge is the lower one. When as the result of wear, contact with the cylinder wall appears uniform over the whole width of the ring, it is immaterial which way round it is refitted. The 650 cc. two-piece ring, if used, is marked 'TOP'. Space the piston rings so that the gaps are 120° to each other, smear piston and rings and bore of barrel with clean engine oil and supporting the piston with one hand, gently pass over the barrel, compressing each piston ring with the fingers, as it enters the barrel. Press the cylinder barrel right down into the throat of the crankcase.

Fit the second piston, gudgeon pin, rings and barrel in a like manner.

Revolve the engine till the pistons are at the top of their strokes and then, with a clean rag, wipe off all surplus oil. All is now ready to re-fit the cylinder heads.

To re-fit the cylinder heads. *Note:* If the nuts retaining the cylinder heads are finally tightened before the manifold is fitted, a bias can develop between the manifold to cylinder head joint, causing a bad air leak.

Clean the valve stems and the bores of the valve guides with rag moistened with petrol, make sure all other parts are clean, then smear each valve stem with clean engine oil and proceed to re-fit the valve stems by reversing the procedure taken to dismantle them.

Insert the four valve push rods into their original positions and after making sure that the cylinder head gaskets are undamaged and in position, proceed to fit the two heads and *leave the two sets of four cylinder head retaining nuts finger tight.*

Now refit the inlet manifold, making sure the two paper gaskets are undamaged and leave the four retaining nuts only just tight enough to ensure correct alignment.

Next, fully tighten down the four retaining nuts on each head, treating each diagonally bit by bit, till all are fully down.

Then fully tighten the inlet manifold retaining nuts and refit the carburetter. Next, carefully check each rocker clearance, as previously described and reset if necessary.

The gasket under each rocker cover should be inspected and if not sound, should be replaced, after which the rocker covers can be refitted.

Next refit the cylinder head steady plate and securely tighten the three fixing bolts.

Note: Before refitting carburetter make sure the rubber ring in manifold joint face is in position and undamaged.

To re-time the ignition—Twins (Magneto Models). Before proceeding to time the ignition it is advisable first to check the contact breaker point gap, which should be from .012″ to .015″, and correct if necessary.

Having loosened the nut securing the magneto driving pinion, release same from the tapered end of the magneto shaft by means of a special extractor, as described on page 19.

Remove the inlet rocker cover from the off-side cylinder head.

Remove the sparking plug from the off-side cylinder.

Insert a small rod into the sparking plug hole, feeling the piston with the end of this rod, carefully turn the engine in its normal direction of rotation until the piston is exactly at the top of the stroke after the inlet valve has closed.

Hold the rod vertical in plug hole, mark the rod where the plug boss registers. Take out the rod, make another mark higher up $\frac{3}{8}″$ for the 500 cc. and 600 cc. twins or $\frac{11}{32}″$ for the 650 cc. models. Re-insert the rod, turn engine *backwards* until the higher mark registers with the plug boss. This applies also to the standard twins. Place the ignition control lever in the fully advanced position.

Next, taking care not to disturb the piston position, turn the magneto in a clockwise direction (looking at the contact breaker end of the magneto) until the contact breaker points are just about to separate by reason of the fibre block on the bell crank lever commencing to mount the lower cam hump.

The exact point of separation is best found by inserting between the contact points a strip of thin tissue paper when the separation point can be determined by the paper just being released with a light pull. Having obtained this position, press the magneto driving gear on to its taper with the fingers and lightly tighten the securing nut.

Re-check the timing by re-positioning the piston and when correct, securely tighten the nut fixing the ignition drive gear.

$$\tfrac{3}{8}″ = 39° \qquad \tfrac{11}{32}″ = 35°$$

Thoroughly clean off all traces of jointing compound from face edges of the timing cover and crankcase, then smear both faces with new jointing compound, which leave till tacky and then re-fit the cover to the crankcase. ('Wellseal' recommended.)

The whole operation of timing the ignition will be found quite simple if the foregoing instructions are carefully followed.

Note: The sparking plug high tension cable for the off-side cylinder is that connected to the rear pickup on the magneto.

To re-time the ignition (Alternator Twins). First refer to Electrical Section, paragraph 'Coil Ignition Standard Twins', to understand the principle of the distributor, then remove the distributor cover.

Check the contact gap which should be between .014″ and .016″, release clamp bolt, etc.

Position the engine as described for the Magneto Models. If the distributor has been removed, the distributor shaft with the rotor fitted when replaced should be in the approximate position as shown, which is the firing position for the left-hand cylinder. From the near side of the machine turn the rotor in a clockwise direction (fully advanced position). Whilst retaining this position turn the distributor body until the contact points are just about to break (see method described for Magneto Models).

Re-tighten the clamp bolt and re-check the timing.

VALVE TIMING. ALL TWIN MODELS

	1957-1958	1959-1962
Inlet valve opens	24° b.t.d.c.	37° b.t.d.c.
Inlet valve closes	65° a.b.d.c.	77° a.b.d.c.
Exhaust valve opens	63° b.b.d.c.	73° b.b.d.c.
Exhaust valve closes	25° a.t.d.c.	43° a.t.d.c.

(Check valve timing with .012″ rocker clearance.)

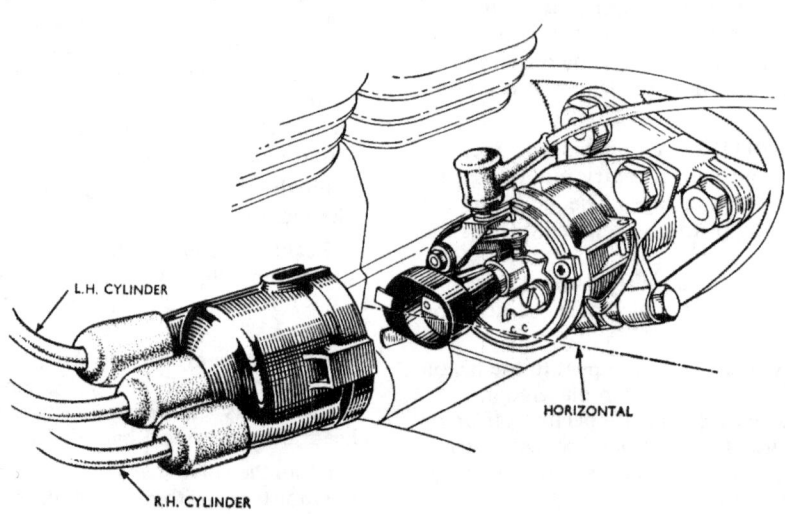

Fig. 5
Coil Ignition timing.

Upon removing the timing gear cover (secured by 10 screws) also the pump plate assembly, it will be observed the valve timing gears are marked to facilitate correct assembly.

One tooth gap of the mainshaft small pinion is marked with one centre punch dot and a tooth of the idler pinion into which it meshes, is similarly marked. With these two marks coinciding it will be seen that a tooth on each side of the intermediate pinion is marked with two centre punch dots which also coincide with a similarly marked tooth gap on each of the camshaft driving gear wheels.

During assembly it is only necessary to mesh the gears with these various marks coinciding to ensure correct valve timing. The dynamo and magneto drive pinions are not marked.

The dynamo does not need 'timing' and if, for any reason, the magneto timing has been disturbed, it is reset as described earlier.

Removal of gears. When completely dismantling the engine there is no necessity to remove the small timing pinion from the crankshaft before splitting the crankcase because the complete crankshaft can be taken away with the pinion still in position.

If, however, it is desired to remove the pinion without completely dismantling the engine a special extractor is required (part number 015273). This consists of a nut, threaded externally and internally. The external threads enable it to be screwed into the threaded centre of the pinion and the internal threads accommodate a specially designed and hardened bolt which, upon screwing down, pulls off the pinion. This same tool is used for the removal of the magneto gear.

The intermediate gear needs no extractor.

The gears on the two camshafts (secured by nuts having left-hand threads) have to be mechanically withdrawn and each has two holes drilled and threaded to accommodate the two bolts of a bridge type extractor (part number 015374), which has a central bolt threaded in the bridge. The two outside bolts are screwed into the holes in the gears whereupon application of the centre bolt being screwed into the bridge bears on the end of the shaft thereby causing the gear to be withdrawn.

The gear on the dynamo needs no extractor because the dynamo, complete with gear assembled, is easily and quickly removed from the engine and the subsequent removal of the gear from the dynamo shaft is a simple workshop operation.

Alternator Twins. To remove distributor pinion, spring outwards the circlip, take out the parallel pin passing through the pinion and distributor shaft—the pinion can then be removed.

TWIN CYLINDER MODELS

Removing engine from frame. Commence by removing the cylinder heads, cylinders and pistons as detailed earlier.

Removing the chain case (Alternator and Magneto Models). Take out the drain plug and catch oil in a tray.

Remove left side footrest.

Remove brake rod adjusting nut.

Remove inspection cap and alternator wires from connectors.

Remove 14 screws and central fixing nut.

Depress brake pedal and pull chaincase cover away.

Removing the engine sprocket and clutch. Straighten the tab washer, use a close fitting ring spanner for the engine sprocket nut, which is also the crankcase release valve.

Refit the brake rod adjuster, engage top gear.

Press on the brake pedal and give the ring spanner a series of sharp blows to release the nut.

Remove the three clutch spring adjusters and take out the springs and cups, then the pressure plate or pull off the plate with the springs and cups in it.

Use a stout box key for the gear box mainshaft nut $1\frac{3}{8}''$ across the flats, press again on the brake pedal and remove the nut. Take out the chain connecting link the clutch, rotor (if fitted) and engine sprocket, watch for the engine sprocket distance piece behind the sprocket.

Instead of using the rear brake whilst releasing the clutch and engine sprocket nut, the 'easy to make tool' shown in Fig. 51 will provide a more positive means to release these nuts. See Lightweight.

Removing rear portion chaincase. Remove three countersunk screws at front end. Remove central nut, if alternator is fitted. Remove chaincase portion. Drain the oil tank.

Disconnect both oil pipes at crankcase end first, then detach the pipes from the oil tank. A piece of wood or a stout screwdriver placed under the tank can be used as a lever to separate the pipes from the tank. If an engine overhaul is contemplated take off the oil tank for a thorough cleaning.

Removing the crankcase assembly. Remove distributor cover and l.t. wire or magneto control wire and h.t. cables, whichever fitted. Remove the dynamo if fitted.

Remove all bolts passing through the crankcase and frame and release only the two gear box fixing nuts. Grasping the cylinder studs, lift the crankcase clear of the frame.

Dismantling the engine. Cleanliness in working is of paramount importance in dealing with an engine of this kind. Clean down the crankcase and get rid of all road grit from the bottom portion, before the assembly is placed on the bench.

Have available magneto pinion extractor 015273, extractor for cam wheels 015374. If the work involved is confined to the cam gear, the magneto, or distributor can be left *in situ*. The pinion for ignition can be marked with a red paint line, with a similar marking on the inlet cam wheel in register, thus leaving the ignition timing undisturbed.

Remove the timing gear cover screws 011820.

Remove nut fixing dynamo.

Remove timing cover.

Remove three nuts 014903 securing pump plate to crankcase and take away pump plate.

At this stage a tool to hold the crankshaft from turning is desirable. A tool for this purpose is described in table of 'improvised tools'. Alternatively, put back the engine sprocket and use a chain bar as shown in Fig. 52.

Note: The two nuts securing the camshaft pinions have a *left-hand* thread 011653.

If the magneto has to come off, use the extractor which is also made to remove the small timing pinion 016209.

Remove the two cam wheel nuts 011653, fit the bridge type extractor by engaging the two outside bolts into the holes in the pinion, screw in the central bolt to pull off the pinions.

Remove intermediate gear pinion 021506, the small timing pinion 016209 can remain in position as it will pass through the crankcase, as will the dyno pinion.

Remove crankcase filter unit 026139, the oil distributor cap 014247 and take out the distributor, three 014292 crankcase bolts and bottom crankcase stud.

Note: A rubber-backed seal washer is used on the top front bolt 014292.

Set both con rods at bottom dead centre.

Remove timing side half crankcase from drive side crankcase.

Remove both camshafts, cam followers and spacers (note their location), also tunnels 016472.

Remove six centre web stud nuts 011843.

Remove crankshaft with centre web assembled, the inner members of the two main bearings will come away with the cranksahft.

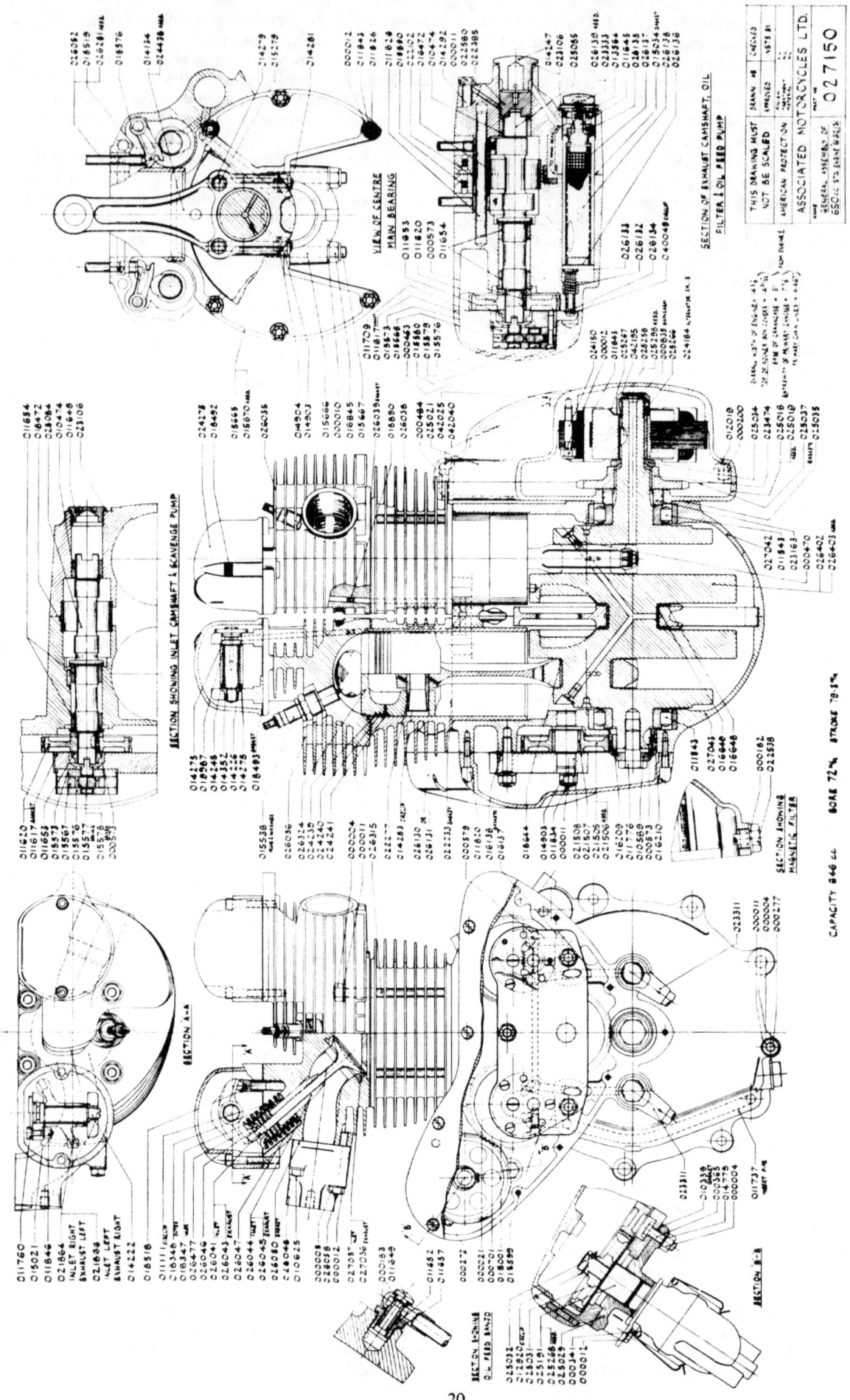

Fig. 6

To remove the magneto. The magneto is located by a spigot on the magneto body. A paper gasket is used between the magneto body and the crankcase. With magneto pinion removed, remove the three nuts fixing the magneto. The two top nuts are on studs, a detachable bolt is used for the lower fixing.

To remove the distributor (fixing as for magneto). Spring outwards the circlip, the parallel pin can then be pushed out through the pinion and distributor shaft. The pinion can then be removed.

EXTRACTOR TOOLS IN USE

Fig. 7

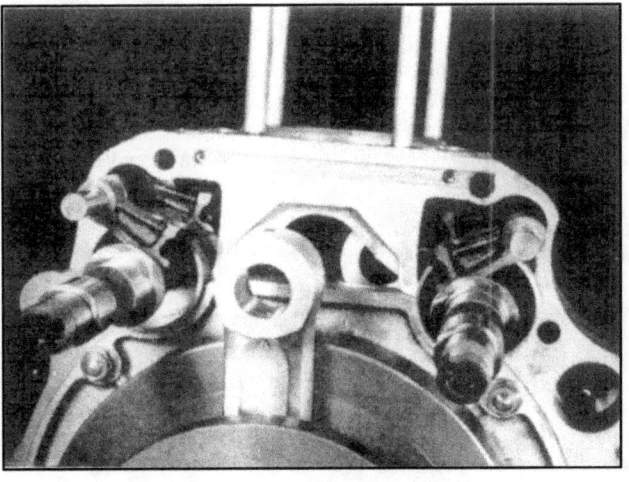

Fig. 8   Camshaft Removal

To remove the main bearings. The inner member for the main bearing will remain on the crankshaft when it is extracted. Use two screwdrivers, or levers, to prise off the bearing.

Dismantling the pressure relief valve. Press on the plunger via the crankcase filter tunnel and extract the circlip 040049. Take off the washer and spring and remove the plunger.

The centre web. The detachable cap is marked with a letter 'O', the centre web has a similar mark for location after machining. Hold the web in a vice, remove the two self-locking nuts and lift up the crankshaft which will dislodge the cap.

Removing the con rods. The caps on both connecting rods are marked after machining, with an oblique stroke (/), running across the cap and con rod.

Removing the main bearing sleeves. These are a close interference fit in each side of the crankcase, some patience is needed to remove them if damage to the crankcase is to be avoided.

First remove the metal extruded during the process of 'peening' on assembly. Use the sharp point of a scraper, or similar tool, to do this.

Apply heat to the crankcase, concentrated round the bearing housing. In this condition, dropping the crankcase face downwards on to a clean wooden bench, will start the movement of the sleeve sufficiently to get a drift on to the sleeve. Drift out the sleeve parallel with the bore to avoid scruffing the housing.

Removing the camshaft bearings. Two flanged bushes 011654 and one plain bush 010474 are fitted to each camshaft. The plain bush is located in the driving side crankcase. Support the case and drift out the plain bushes, towards the inside of the case.

There is a cavity in the camshaft tunnel between the two flanged bushes.

To extract the inner bush, use a short length of $\frac{5}{16}''$ rod, or bar, about the same width as the outside diameter of the bush. If a rod is used, file two flats on each end. Insert the rod or bar diagonally so that it rests on the bush forming a 'bridge'. Place a drift on the 'bridge' and drive out the bush. The second bush can be dealt with without difficulty.

Removing the intermediate pinion shaft. The shaft for the intermediate pinion 021508 is a force fit in the crankcase. To remove, it is preferable to heat the crankcase and drive it out, with the crankcase supported, from inside the case.

Checking the con rod and centre web shells. If attention to the crankshaft bearings is due to excessive movement between the con rods and the crankcase journals, and if the mileage covered is not excessive, a close examination of the bearings shells should indicate the reason for the excessive movement. As already explained, bearings of this kind do not wear prematurely providing the journal surface is smooth and there is a continuous supply of clean and uncontaminated oil passing under pressure through these bearings. If the shells are down and the copper backing is showing with deep score marks, and the *Indium* flash is piled up at one end, this indicates the bearing has 'run', which can only be due to an oil shortage—even temporarily.

Before doing anything further, the cause of the oil shortage should be carefully investigated and before an attempt is made to re-assemble the engine. Where the mileage is considerable, wear on the centre web bearings will cause a fall in oil pressure. Refer to possible cause of oil failure, page 13.

When the bearing shells have a grey matt finish and where the crankshaft journals are worn considerably, abrasive wear is responsible.

Where a groove is cut in the shells, in register with the oil feed hole in the crankshaft, this indicates the presence of foreign matter in the oil. A similar marking will result if the chamfer for the journal oil hole is not restored after a regrind.

If a con rod bearing has been deprived of oil, and the bearing has 'run', without prompt attention the hammering effect, due to the increase in clearance between the bearing and the crankshaft journal can cause ovality in the connecting rod eye.

Usually there is a witness in the con rod eye and in this condition the con rod is scrap. On no account should the faces between the detachable cap and the con rod be filed.

Checking the crankshaft journals. The normal diameter of the journals is shown in Technical Data. If the wear, ovality or taper exceeds .001″ a regrind is necessary. See Page 24 for dimensions.

During the process of regrinding, the radius between the journals and the crankshaft webs must not be removed as this would weaken the structure and possibly cause a fracture.

Whenever possible the crankshaft should be returned to the factory service department.

After regrinding the crankshaft, restore the chamfer for the oil holes in the crankshaft. The journals must have a mirror like finish. A rough surface will tear up the big end shells within short distance.

A simple tool to hold the crankshaft to polish the journals is shown in Fig. 9. A suitable tool for the polishing operation is also depicted. Strips of superfine emery cloth are used and the polishing should be made in the direction of engine rotation.

Force either petrol or paraffin through the oil ways to remove abrasive material.

Fig. 9

The small end bearing. The con rod is not bushed for the gudgeon pin. Wear at this point is unknown even after considerable mileage.

Fitting the bearing sleeves. Heat the crankcase in the vicinity of the bearing housing and fit the sleeves before contraction takes place.

Peen the crankcase in three equi-distant positions to prevent the sleeve from moving outwards.

Fitting the camshaft bushes. Introduce into the crankcase the inner flanged bush 011654. Use a draw bolt with two steel washers with an outside diameter of $1\frac{3}{32}''$ and pull the bush into position. Deal with the outer bush in a similar manner, but leave this bush protruding approximately $\frac{1}{32}''$ so that the end play can be adjusted.

Now fit the plain bush chamfered end first, from inside the case, which is a straightforward assembly.

Ream all bushes to $\frac{13}{16}''/+.001''/-.000''$.

Fig. 10

Adjusting the end play. When the nut securing the cam wheel pinion is tightened, the pinion will bear hard against the bush flange. A light tap on the pinion fixing nut will move the bush sufficiently to allow free movement. The minimum end play is .005″.

Fitting the intermediate gear shaft. Heat the crankcase in the vicinity of the shaft aperture and press the shaft firmly home.

Assembling the centre web. Hold the straight portion of the web in a vice with soft jaws, with the letter 'O' stamped on it facing the operator.

Fit the bearing shells to the web and cap, apply a little clean grease to each side of the shells (to retain the thrust washer in position). Paint the centre journal with either colloidal graphite or Molybdenum Disulphide. Fit the crankshaft with the drive side facing the operator.

Fit the centre web, cap and thrust washers with the oil slots facing outwards.

Use new self-locking nuts and tighten to 20 ft. lbs.

The crankshaft should be free to turn if the assembly is correct.

Fitting the con rods. Leave the centre web in the vice, paint the big end journals with anti-scruffing compound as prescribed for the centre web.

Fit in turn the con rods, locating the caps with the marking.

Use new self-locking nuts and tighten to 22 ft. lbs. With new parts and dry bearing the con rod to journal clearance is .00225″. The side play is between .025″ and .032″, and the rod should fall by its own weight.

Assembling the crankcase. The interior of both halves of the crankcase must be perfectly clean.

Carefully examine both crankcase face joints, which must be free from bruises or blemishes particularly at the point where oil is fed under pressure to the channel at the top of the crankcase.

To restore these face joints use a surface plate to remove blemish.

Verify the metering jets are unobstructed.

Oil and re-assemble the pressure relief valve (if fitted) and make sure the plunger works freely, when operated by hand. Needless to say, any moving parts in the engine should be treated with clean oil before fitting.

Fitting the crankshaft. Assemble the two inner members for the main bearings on to the crankshaft.

Insert the crankshaft and centre web assembly into the drive side crankcase, fit the six retaining nuts and washers and tighten to 6 ft. lbs.

Refit the small timing pinion.

Jointing Compound. The use of a shellac base compound should be avoided as this material becomes 'flaky' and particles dislodged can obstruct metered oil passages and cut off the oil supply. A non-flaky compound such as 'Wellseal' is the correct medium to use for an oil-tight joint.

Assembling the crankcase. With the crankshaft in position, apply jointing compound to the driving side crankcase face. Fit the *Paper Gasket* 015304 surrounding the filter tunnel. Paint the camshafts and cam followers with anti-scruffing compound and continue the assembly in the following sequence.

Fit two lower cam followers and two distance pieces.

Fit two camshaft tunnels 016472.

Fit two upper cam followers.

Fit exhaust camshaft 025085.

Fit inlet camshaft 025084, then position the con rods at B.D.C.

Fit timing side crankcase.

Fit three crankcase clamping bolts and bottom stud.

Fit the magneto or distributor and dyno if fitted.

Fit the cam gear pinions to marking (see paragraph 'Valve timing'), remembering the left-hand nuts for the camshaft pinion and firmly tighten these nuts.

Note: If new camshaft bushes have been fitted see paragraph 'Fitting the camshaft bushes'.

Fit two gaskets 016137 (see Fig. 2 for location).

Fit one gasket 016138 for feed pump. A little oil on the crankcase will hold these washers in position.

Fit the pump plate with three self-locking nuts.

Note: If the marking on the small timing pinion is not visible, it may be obscured by the washer. The mark is opposite the pinion keyway.

Fig. 11

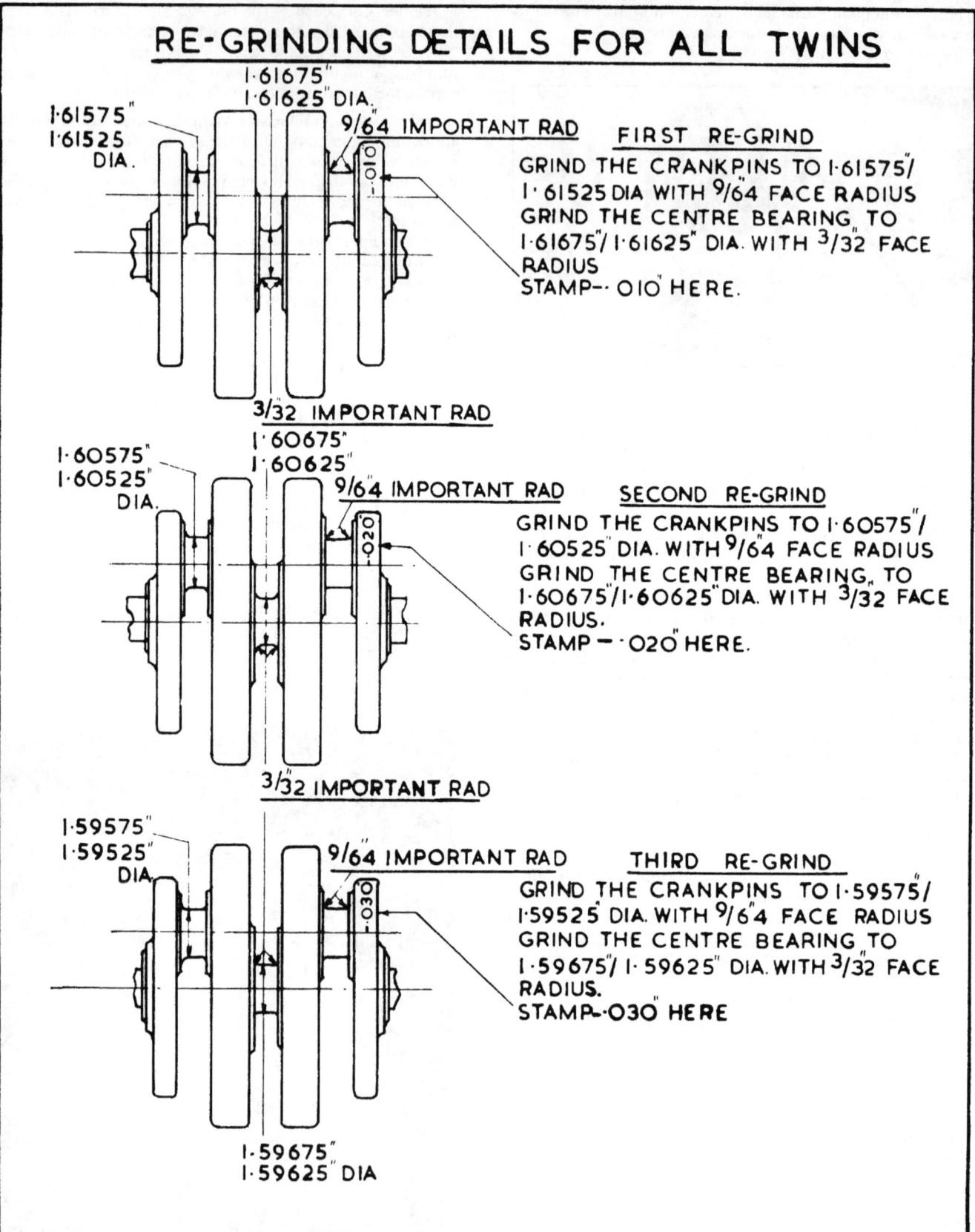

Clean the crankcase filter and see the ball for the non-return valve is free to move, then insert it into the crankcase. Oil and fit the oil distributor bush 022385. Make sure the correct type of washer 023106 for the cap covering the distributor bush hole is used, which is made from copper $\frac{1}{16}''$ thick.

Warning: If a thin washer is used between the cap and crankcase, the distributor bush will be end loaded and seize in the crankcase.

Re-tighten the caps on the drive side crankcase when hot.

Re-installing the engine. Pack some clean rag round both con rods to prevent the entry of foreign matter. For ease in handling, the crankcase assembly can be refitted to the frame.

Continue engine assembly as far as fitting both cylinders, then the ignition timing can be set or rechecked, as the piston travel can be measured more easily at this stage.

Before fitting the cylinder heads, flood the camshaft tunnels by pouring some clean oil down the push rod apertures in both cylinders.

Observe the following precautions:

(1) Leave the cylinder head nuts loose until the manifold has been fitted, then tighten to 22 ft. lbs.
(2) Make sure the oil pipes are correctly positioned at the oil tank end.
(3) Refill the oil tank, with the feed pipe connection loose, allow some oil to drain out and exclude air bubbles to prevent an air lock.
(4) Verify oil is returning to the tank after running engine for a short period.
(5) Do not fit the rocker covers until the oil feed has been checked and reset the rockers if necessary, after settling down.
(6) Retighten the cylinder head nuts.

Re-assembling the primary drive. Assemble in the reverse sequence described for dismantling.

Tightening the rotor (Alternator Models). A hammer tight spanner must *not* be used for this operation.

ENGINE NOISES

HEAVYWEIGHT SINGLE CYLINDER MODELS

Big end assembly. A high periodicity rattle audible when the engine is running without load, or when the machine is rotating the engine on down gradient, is due to slight movement in the big end assembly. This does not indicate that the assembly is beyond further use, as the movement is usually microscopical and is only audible by reason of the mechanically quiet valve gear. When the rattle is first manifest a further six to eight thousand miles can be covered before replacements are needed. Usually in the initial stages a new set of big end rollers will suffice, providing the roller track has not broken up by detonation or 'pinking' as a result of excess ignition advance, low octane fuel, with a high compression ratio. *Note:* The side movement in the con rod is .010".

Piston noise. Piston slap is audible when the engine is pulling or on changing up to a higher gear. A noise of this kind is inevitable in high efficiency engines or when ultra high compression ratio pistons are used. This noise is purely a matter of clearance between the piston and the cylinder barrel. On Touring Models, if the noise does not clear when the engine temperature rises, a rebore with oversize pistons is the only remedy.

Bearing noise. A high pitch whine which increases as the engine speed rises is caused by a pitted or worn driving side bearing in the crankcase. A tightly adjusted front chain will also create the same noise. On specially tuned engines, used for races of long duration, an improved type roller bearing Hoffman RMS10 ($2\frac{1}{2} \times 1 \times \frac{3}{4}$) is recommended.

Timing gear noise. Backlash between the small pinion and the cam gear will cause a rattle, usually audible when the engine is idling. As it is unusual for the cam gear bushes to wear, a new small timing gear pinion will give the desired effect.

Rocker box noise. A noise from this part of the engine is an uncommon occurrence. A clicking noise will develop if a valve spring is distorted causing contact between the rocker box and the spring. Should end movement develop in the rocker arm bearings, the movement can be taken up by removing the rocker axle and steel sleeve, and tapping outwards one of the rocker bushes until the movement is absorbed. A short exhaust valve lifter inner cable will hold the valve lifter arm on to the valve, affecting push rod adjustment, thus creating a rattle.

ENGINE NOISE

LIGHTWEIGHT MODELS

The details given for the Heavyweight Models apply also to its smaller counterpart. After considerable mileage and where high r.p.m. has been sustained for lengthy periods, wear can develop on the cam levers, which operate the push rods. If the wear is shown on the closing side of the lever ramps, this would indicate valve float. On engines with a number before 6850 a rattle can develop which can be mistaken for movement in the big end assembly. This rattle is due to movement of the crankcase release valve stator 042220. The noise can be overcome by removing the release valve tube 042221 (which locates the stator) and increasing the effective diameter on the end of the tube by an electrical deposit of either chrome or copper. The tube should be thus treated over a length of $\frac{3}{8}''$ from the tube end. Alternatively the engine can be dismantled to use a modified tube 044083 and stator 044084. The new stator is threaded internally with a threaded tube. If difficulty occurs in inserting the release valve tube, pass a spoke or similar object through the aperture in the crankcase, rotate the engine slowly until the hole in the stator is in register.

Note: The screwed release valve tube is tightened by torque spanner set to 10 ft. lbs.

Push rod adjustment (all Single Cylinder Models). Owing to the expansion of the alloy cylinder head when the engine has reached its normal running temperature, allowance for expansion must be made when the push rod adjustment is carried out. It is for this reason the engine should be warm when this adjustment is effected. As the term 'engine warm' is difficult to define, if the engine is allowed to idle for approximately four minutes and after an interval of two to three minutes with the engine stationary, the heat from the cylinder head will 'creep' into the rocker box.

It is at this stage the adjustment should be carried out.

Alternatively, take the machine on the road for two to three miles, then after an interval of a few minutes, heat transference to the rocker box will permit the correct adjustment to be made.

Without delay remove the rocker cover, position engine so that the piston is at the extreme top dead centre of the firing stroke (both valves closed). Use a piece of wire through the spark plug hole to ascertain piston position.

Release the lock nut (2) (Fig. 12) holding the sleeve (5) with a second spanner. Move the adjusting screw (3) until there is no appreciable up and down movement, the push rod being just free to rotate by finger application. Securely tighten the lock nut when the correct adjustment is found.

Note: After overhaul, this adjustment is best carried out after the engine has been run sufficiently long enough to enable all the parts to settle down.

Do not overtighten the rocker cover nuts.

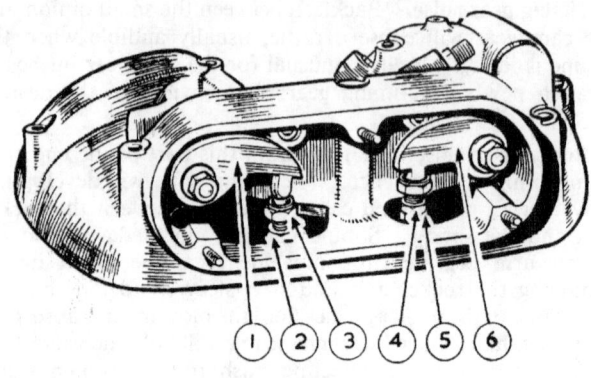

FIG. 12
Tappet Adjustment.
1 Inlet rocker arm (tappet end).
2 Nut, locking adjusting cupped screw.
3 Cupped adjusting screw.
4 Cupped adjusting screw and lock nut.
5 Sleeve, to accommodate adjusting screw, on top end of push rod.
6 Exhaust rocker arm (tappet end).

SINGLE CYLINDER HEAVYWEIGHT MODELS

To remove the rocker box. Remove the petrol tank.
Remove the three nuts and fibre washers retaining the rocker box side cover and take away the cover.
Disconnect the oil pipe feeding oil to the rocker box.
Turn over engine until both valves are completely closed.
Remove engine steady bracket by removing bolt from frame clip and nuts and washers from the rocker box bolt extensions.
Remove the nine bolts retaining rocker box to cylinder head.
Disconnect valve lifter cable.
Tilt upward the right-hand side of rocker box and extract the two long pushrods. Lay these aside so they may be identified and replaced in their original position.
The rocker box may then be lifted off.

To replace the rocker box. Carefully clean the top of cylinder head and lower face of rocker box.
Revolve engine until both tappets are down, i.e. the top dead centre of firing stroke.
Lay the composition jointing washer on cylinder head. This must be faultless. If necessary, renew.
Lay the rocker box in position then slightly raise the right hand side to allow the long push rods to be inserted into the original respective positions.
Insert all nine rocker box fixing bolts and note that the bolt with short head is in the centre right-hand position, and the bolts with threaded extensions are fitted one each side of the central short head bolt.
Tighten each bolt in turn bit by bit until all are fully home.
Replace the engine steady stay.
Turn engine over several times to ensure parts have bedded home.
Re-fix valve lifter cable.
Re-fix rocker box oil pipe union nut using two spanners to ensure that the union screwed into rocker box does not turn while the nut is being tightened.
Check tappet clearances and re-set if necessary.
Inspect rubber fillet on rocker box side cover and renew if not perfect.
Replace the side cover ensuring that a fibre washer is fitted under each of the three retaining nuts.
Beware of over tightening these nuts, the joint being made by the rubber fillet excessive pressure is not necessary.

To remove the cylinder head. Remove the petrol tank, the sparking plug, the rocker box.
Remove the exhaust system by removing nut and washers, retaining exhaust pipe to its stay; remove nut and washers, retaining silencer to its stay.

Remove complete exhaust system by pulling away from stays and then downwards from the exhaust port in cylinder head.
Remove carburetter by air filter connection and unscrew two carburetter retaining nuts. Take away carburetter and lay aside.
Remove the four bolts retaining cylinder head to barrel, and head is free to be taken away.
While doing this the push rod cover tubes will come away with the head.
Note: If the sparking plug resists removal, do not use force but brush penetrating oil round the body and leave for a time to soak before making further effort.

To remove and replace the valves and guides. Remove the cylinder head.
Remove the valve springs by inserting a finger in the spring coil and sharply pull upward.
The top spring collar and split collet can then be removed leaving the valve free to be withdrawn.
A sharp light tap on the valve collar may be necessary to free the taper split collet. It will be observed that the valve spring seat has a raised impression on its under side which registers with a hole drilled on the valve guide boss to ensure accurate positioning.
To remove the valve guides apply gentle heat, press the guide upwards sufficiently to permit removal of the external circlip. Then, clean the top of the guide, and press downwards to remove. Re-heat when replacing and see that correct projection is obtained, viz. $\frac{1}{2}''$. Also see that oil hole in guide is in correct alignment.
Note: The special valve spring compressor tool is not part of the standard tool kit, but can be obtained from any of our dealers (Part No. 018276).
It is essential that the collets are correctly located on the valve stems. It will be observed that the collet has two grooves machined in the bore and those two grooves must register with the two rings on the valve stem. If fitted so that only one of the grooves engages the ringed valve stem, damage will almost certainly result.
On 350 cc. the inlet valve head is larger in diameter than the exhaust. Therefore unintended interchange is not possible.

To replace a valve. After cleaning valve guide bores, smear each valve stem with clean oil, insert, and apply top collar and split collet.
Then apply the valve springs which although possible to fit by hand are more easily manipulated with a special compressor tool Part No. 018276 (Fig. 13). To operate this tool apply the top end of the valve spring to its groove in the top cap, then insert a short rod (one of the rocker box fixing bolts suits admirably) through the holes in this tool and the valve spring coils and pull outward and upward until the ends of the prong of the spring can be rested on the seat, then press down with the fingers. Withdraw the bolt or rod when the compressor lies against the cylinder head, retaining pressure with the fingers until the bolt has been withdrawn and the tool removed, when the spring can be readily pushed down to its proper location with the prongs laying flat upon the seat.

To replace the cylinder head (Singles). A gasket is fitted between cylinder head and barrel.
The top ends of the push rod cover tubes have rubber gaskets between tubes and head; they are a push fit and metal washers are located between the top edges of the gaskets and the cylinder head recesses.
If the cover tubes are pulled away from the head, the gaskets will probably remain in position in the head.
A rubber gland is fitted at the bottom of each cover tube.
Replace the cylinder head by carefully cleaning the top edge of the cylinder barrel and the under face of the cylinder head.

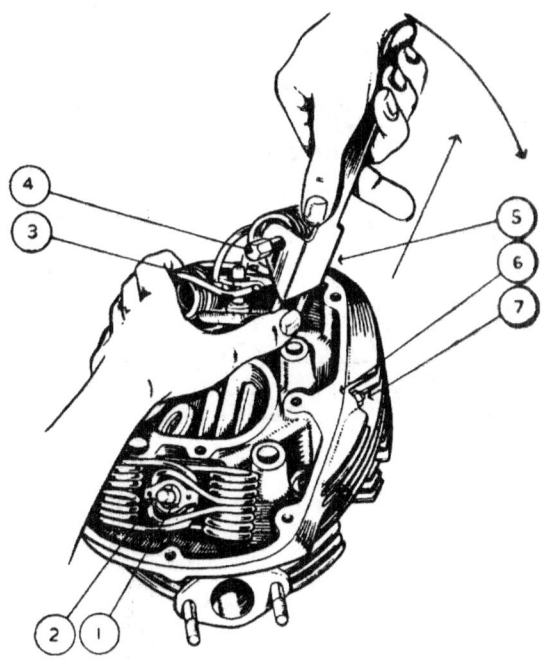

Fig. 13
Application of Valve Spring Compressor.
1 Collet, for valve.
2 Collar, for valve spring.
3 Collar, for valve spring.
4 Bolt through tools and coils of valve spring.
5 Valve spring compressor tool.
6 Oil passage from rocker box to inlet valve guide.
7 Screw with lock nut adjusting oil feed to inlet valve.

Fit the cover tubes with their rubber gaskets and metal washers into the cylinder head.

Place the cylinder head gasket in position on the top edge of the cylinder barrel.

Place a rubber gland round each tappet guide.

Place the cylinder head in position.

Ensure each cylinder head securing bolt has a plain steel washer on it and then replace the bolts and engage each a few turns.

Finally, screw down the cylinder head securing bolts, in turn, bit by bit, until all are fully home.

Replace the sparking plug, but before doing so it is desirable to coat the threads with 'Oil Dag' or graphite paste to prevent seizure upon next removal. The rocker box, carburetter, exhaust system and the petrol tank.

Note: If old gaskets are re-fitted they must be in an undamaged state, otherwise new must be used.

Whether new or re-used, the gasket should be annealed just prior to fitting. This is done by heating to 'blood-red heat' and plunging into clean cold water.

To remove the cylinder barrel and piston. Remove the cylinder head, the four nuts retaining cylinder barrel to crankcase.

Take away cylinder barrel. (Ensure piston is not damaged in doing this. Steady piston with hand as barrel is withdrawn.)

Fill throat of crankcase with clean rag to prevent entry of foreign matter.

Remove one gudgeon pin circlip. It is immaterial which circlip is removed. Use special pliers included in tool kit. Remove gudgeon pin by pushing it out of piston.

Take away piston.

Note: The gudgeon pin is an easy sliding fit in both piston and connecting rod small end bush.

Rings may be removed from a piston by introducing behind the rings three pieces of thin steel spaced at 120° from each other and then sliding off the rings. (Do not scratch the piston.)

To replace the piston and cylinder barrel. All parts must be clean.

Place rings on piston, scraper first, then the two compression rings. On all models the top compression ring is chromium plated. These chrome plated rings have a slightly tapered exterior and when new are clearly marked with the word 'TOP' on one side to indicate assembly position. After use, this word tends to become indiscernible, but over a large mileage the assembly position can be determined by brightness of the edge contacting cylinder wall. This bright edge is the lower one. When, as the result of wear, contact with the cylinder wall appears uniform over the whole width of the ring, it is then immaterial which way round it is re-fitted.

Smear gudgeon pin with clean engine oil.

Introduce piston over connecting rod and insert the gudgeon pin in position, then pass it through connecting rod small-end bush and centralise.

Re-fit circlips. (Use special pliers.) Use rotary action when bedding circlips in their grooves and make sure each circlip lies snugly in its groove. This is essential, otherwise considerable damage will result.

Note: The word 'FRONT' is stamped on the piston crown to indicate location.

Re-fit cylinder barrel by taking new cylinder base washer, coat one side with liquid jointing compound and apply it to cylinder base.

Smear cylinder bore and piston with clean engine oil.

Space piston rings so that the gaps are evenly spaced at 120° to each other.

Gently fit barrel over piston and carefully compress each ring in turn with the fingers, as it enters the chamfered mouth of the barrel.

Remove rag from crankcase throat.

Replace cylinder barrel holding down nuts, screwing each down, in turn, bit by bit, till all are fully home.

Cam Contour. On the flanks of the cams are quietening curves which are very slight inclines from the base circles to the feet of the humps. Therefore, it is necessary to ensure the tappet ends are on the base circles when checking valve clearances and valve timing. It is for this reason valve clearances must be checked when the piston is at the top of its compression stroke, at which position both tappets are well clear of the quietening curves.

Valve timing. Taken with valve .001" off its seat.

Inlet valve timing:

Inlet valve opens 36° before top dead centre—350 cc. Models.

Inlet valve opens 18° before top dead centre—500 cc. Models.

Inlet valve closes 51° after bottom dead centre—350 cc. Models.

Inlet valve closes 69° after bottom dead centre—500 cc. Models.

Exhaust valve timing:

Exhaust valve opens 50° before bottom dead centre—All Models.

Exhaust valve closes 30° after top dead centre—All Models.

Camshaft timing marks. Use mark 1 for exhaust cam—all Touring Models.

Use mark 2 for inlet cam—500 cc. Touring and Competition Models.

Use mark 2 for exhaust cam—all Competition Models.

Use mark 3 for inlet cam—350 cc. Touring Models.

When checking the valve timing the tappet clearances must be set .016", so that the tappets may be well clear of the quietening curves of the camshafts.

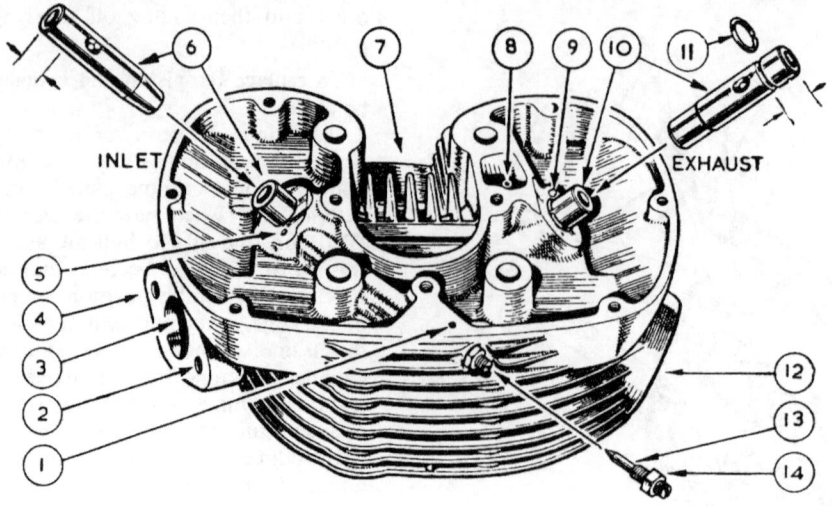

Fig. 14

The valve guides and the needle adjusting screw are also shown withdrawn.

1 Plain hole, for oil feed to inlet valve.
2 Tapped hole, to accommodate carburetter retaining stud.
3 Inlet port.
4 Tapped hole, to accommodate carburetter retaining stud.
5 Hole, to accommodate dowel locating valve spring seat.
6 Guide, for inlet valve.
7 Tapped hole, for sparking plug.
8 Plain hole, for oil feed to exhaust valve.
9 Hole, to accommodate dowel pin locating valve spring seat.
10 Guide, for exhaust valve.
11 Circlip.
12 Exhaust port.
13 Needle screw, adjusting oil feed to inlet valve.
14 Lock nut, for needle adjusting screw.

The timing gears are marked to facilitate their replacement.

To re-set the valve timing, by using the marks on the gears, proceed as follows:—

Turn over the engine till the mark on the small timing pinion is in line with the centre of the inlet (rear) camshaft bush. Insert the inlet camshaft so that the No. 2 or No. 3 mark on it is in mesh with the mark on the small timing pinion, according to model. Rotate the engine in a forward direction till the mark on the small timing pinion is in line with the centre of the exhaust (front) camshaft bush. Insert the exhaust camshaft so that the No. 1 mark on it is in mesh with the mark on the small timing pinion.

Small timing gear pinion (Singles). The pinion is a taper and keyed on to the timing side shaft, the retaining nut has a *left-hand thread*.

The timing mark on the pinion is central with the key way.

Ignition timing. To understand the principle, a study of Fig. 22 should be made. The automatic timing control is a taper fit on the shaft for the inlet cam, retained by a central bolt. The cam separating the contact points is rotated by two pegs engaged in the plates for the unit springs.

As the cam is detachable, the position of the cam should be noted, before it is removed.

Before setting the ignition timing it is essential to check the contact breaker gap.

Check contact breaker gap (see also 'Electrical Service'). Remove two screws securing the cover mounted on the timing case, also the cover.

Rotate engine to fully separate contact points.

Check the gap, which should be .014-.016".

To adjust the gap release slightly the two inner screws securing the fixed contact plate and adjust the gap as required by moving the pivot plate in the required direction.

Removing the automatic timing control. After taking off the cover remove the two screws passing through the slotted holes in the fixed contact breaker plate and remove the plate.

Remove the bolt securing the automatic timing control to the cam wheel shaft.

Fit a 024328 withdrawal bolt in place of the fixing bolt removed which should be lightly tightened. A sharp blow on the end of withdrawal bolt will dislodge the unit from the shaft.

Do not disturb the contact breaker cam.

Setting the ignition timing. The maximum advance is 34° (8.9 mm.) before top dead centre, with the automatic timing control wedged open to the fully advanced position.

Alternatively the firing point can be set with the piston 19° or ⅛" (3.175 mm.) before top dead centre with the automatic timing device in the fully retarded position.

To set the timing have available a stiff wheel spoke or similar object 5½" long.

Remove h.t. cable and sparking plug.

Remove automatic timing control as already described.

Remove the rocker box side cover.

Turn engine so that both valves are closed (inlet valve opens then closes) then engage top gear.

Insert timing rod through sparking plug hole, feel piston by rocking engine forwards or backwards by turning the rear wheel until it can be felt that the piston is at the extreme top of its stroke with both valves closed.

Refer to Fig. 15, and fit automatic advance control, with the gap formed by the two bob weights in line with the two tapped holes, used to secure contact breaker plate; it should be noted that the peak of the cam, or narrowest part, when correctly positioned is approximately at 12 o'clock.

The two marks on the timing rod is flush with the top face of the sparking plug hole, dependent on the timing method used.

Fit the contact breaker plate with the capacitor at 3 o'clock, lightly tighten the fixing screws. The exact position of contact point separation is best determined by inserting a strip of cigarette paper between the contact points and moving the plate in a clockwise direction until the paper can be pulled away freely.

If a wedge is used to fully advance the unit, scribe a pencil line on the contact breaker plate and a similar line on the plate housing both lines in register. Remove the contact breaker plate, take away the wedge and re-fit the plate with the two scribed lines in register, and firmly tighten the fixing screws.

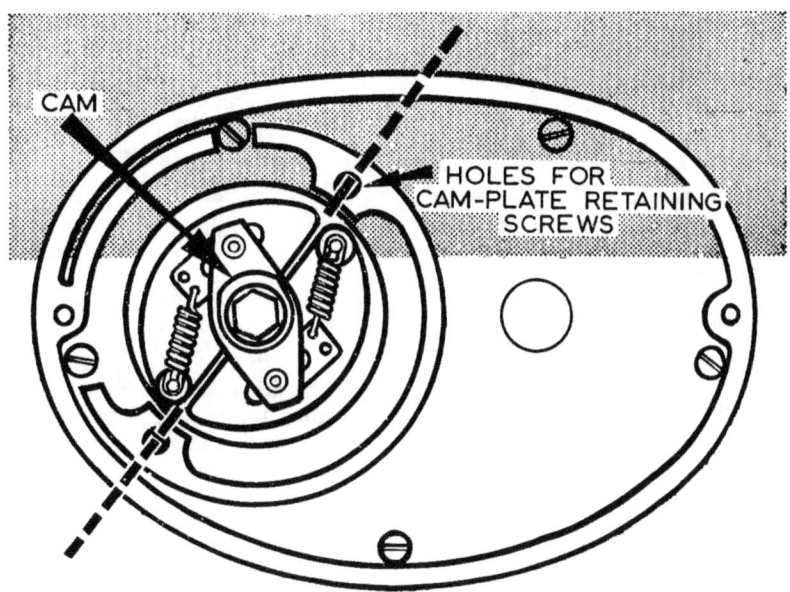

Fig. 15
Setting the ignition timing.

As the ignition timing is important, a re-check should be made, before re-fitting the sparking plug, rocker cover, etc.

350 and 500 cc. HEAVYWEIGHT MODELS

Removing the engine from frame. If the engine has to be removed for dismantling, commence by following the instructions given for removing the cylinder and piston, to facilitate crankcase assembly removal then:

Disconnect two wires from the battery.

Disconnect both oil pipes (watch spanner manipulation at crankcase end) and drain oil tank.

Lever the oil pipes off (tank end) with a screwdriver or a piece of wood.

Disconnect four snap connectors for alternator wires and contact breaker cable, lift off the engine plate cover to expose connectors.

Remove rocker box oil pipe from crankcase. Remove timing cover 027093.

Remove 14 screws securing outer portion of chaincase.

Remove central nut for front chaincase, place a receptacle under chaincase to catch oil.

Remove outer portion, with extreme care, feeding the alternator wires through the rear portion of chaincase.

Remove nuts securing rotor to engine shaft.

Remove clutch springs and clutch pressure plate.

Remove nut on gearbox mainshaft securing clutch. An 'easy to make tool' to prevent the mainshaft moving is shown in Fig. 51.

Remove front chain and take off clutch assembly (use clutch withdrawal tool 040449) (see Fig. 34).

Remove rotor, engine sprocket, watch for distance piece behind it.

Remove three countersunk screws fixing rear portion of chaincase to engine.

Remove crankcase breather pipe.

Remove front engine plate bolts and take away engine plate.

Remove both footrest arms.

Remove three bolts passing through rear engine plate and crankcase.

Release the top and bottom gearbox fixing nuts a few turns.

Move the crankcase assembly forward, lift and take it out of the frame.

Note: If a magneto is fitted, follow details given for removing Scrambler type engine.

Warning: When the engine has to be re-installed connect the two oil pipes at the crankcase end first.

Screw home as far as possible the two nipple nuts by finger application, to avoid the risk of cross threading. Finally tighten without undue force with suitable spanner.

Removing tappet guides. Both guides are a force fit in the crankcase, the guide with its tappet are removed together from inside the timing chest. It is preferable to effect this operation with the engine in a dismantled state, with both halves of the crankcase bolted together to avoid distortion and give additional support.

Heat the crankcase in the vicinity of the guides, sufficiently to enable them to be drifted out. Use the same method to re-fit the tappet and guide. The two dowel pins for the cover can fall out, when the crankcase is heated. When the guide is correctly located, the outside diameter is just flush with the crankcase face.

Dismantling the rocker box (all Single Cylinder Models). The design of the rocker box is basically the same on all single cylinder models. Some Lightweight 250 cc. Models do not use a valve lifter, but a later type rocker box 044034 can be used on this type of engine. Use the following parts for the valve lifter assembly:—

Valve lifter lever 013969.
  ,,   ,,   spring 044035.
  ,,   ,,   ,,   screw 000451.
  ,,   ,,   ,,   washer 000039.
  ,,   ,,   lever ring 014523.
  ,,   ,,   cable 026254.
  ,,   ,,   lever assembly 026239.

The rocker box is supplied with bushes. The existing rockers, etc., can be transferred.

Dismantling the rocker box. It is best to refer to Fig. 21 to understand the assembly sequence of the parts used in the rocker box. To dismantle, place a box spanner (that will fit the nut 000003) firmly in a vice. Invert the rocker box, place one of the two rocker spindle nuts into the box spanner. Using an open end spanner release and remove the rocker axle nut inside the rocker box.

Using a soft drift tap out the axle when the inside rocker will drop off the spindle. The outside rocker with spindle can be pulled out together with the steel sleeve 017292.

Either one or two felt sealing rings used midway between the two rocker axle bushes can be prised out with a sharp pointed tool. As a guide, measure the protrusion of the inner bushes before removal.

Removing the rocker bushes. If the rocker box is slightly heated, the rocker bushes can be drifted out without difficulty.

Refitting the rocker bushes. It should be explained that the location of the rocker bushes controls the end play between the bushes and the rockers. Re-heat the rocker box and fit one of the inner bushes, chamfered end first. The bush should be to the amount measured before dismantling, which usually is approximately $\frac{5}{32}''$. With the four bushes assembled and if new ones are used, they should be reamed to $\frac{5}{8}''+.00075''-.00050''$ *in situ*. Introduce the felt ring(s) into the groove. A taper mandrel inserted into the felt ring is desirable to compress the felt to enable the steel sleeve to pass through. Put the steel sleeve (with some oil on it) over the rocker spindle with the outside rocker attached, carefully work the assembly through the bushes and felt ring.

Refit the inner rocker and using again the box spanner firmly tighten both nuts. If the rocker assembly is tight to move, a light tap on the outer end of the rocker spindle with a light hammer will move the bush and give a free movement. The end play should just be discernible. If the end play is in excess, take out the spindle assembly and tap outwards one of the bushes.

Note: The rocker arm valve end should be central with the valve stem.

Removing the gear box (Heavyweight Single Cylinder Models). If the engine has been removed from the frame it is only necessary to take off all the nuts securing and passing through the right side rear engine plate, disconnect the clutch cable, also the rear chain, and remove the engine plate. It may be necessary also to drive out slightly the footrest rod to enable the plate to come away. The gear box can then be withdrawn.

If the engine is still in position, follow the strip down instructions for removing the chaincase outer portion and clutch assembly, then proceed as detailed.

SINGLE CYLINDER HEAVYWEIGHT MODELS

Separating the crankcase. With the crankcase out of the frame start by:

Removing oil pump guide pin and sleeve (6) (Fig. 1).

Removing four bolts securing cap for oil pump plunger and pull out the plunger.

Removing bottom and front crankcase bolt.

The crankcase can now be separated, as the small timing pinion will pass through the timing side bush; the pinion can be dealt with later.

Separating the flywheels. To do this use the tool and method described for the 250 cc. Scrambler Models.

Removing small timing pinion. The nut securing this pinion has a *left-hand* thread. The pinion is a taper fit on the shaft and usually requires an extractor tool B2151 similar to the one shown in Fig. 16. When using any kind of extractor apply light pressure on the withdrawal part of the tool, then give the end a sharp blow with a hammer, the shock will dislodge the pinion. A new pinion will absorb backlash and cure timing gear rattle.

Removing the drive side bearings. Gently heat the drive side crankcase and drift out both bearings. Check both bearings for roughness caused by pitted race tracks. Renew the bearings at the slightest sign of roughness, the bearing should spin by hand rotation smoothly and quietly. (See paragraph 'Engine noises.')

Removing the timing side bush. Support the half crankcase firmly, press out bush from timing cover end, the locating peg

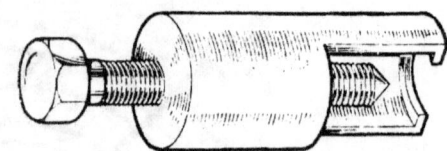

FIG. 16

will come out with bush. If a new bush is used, ream *in situ* to $1.125''+.0005''-.0000''$. Replace locating peg when bush is in position.

Camshaft bushes. These rarely wear, do not be misled by waggling the camshaft supported in the back bush only, the bush is short and some movement will be manifest even with a new bush. Press in new bushes from inside the crankcase with oil holes lined up. Both bushes are located flush with the crankcase. When new they should be reamed *in situ* to $\frac{1}{2}''+.0005''-.0005''$. If new bushes are used assemble the camwheels, fit the timing cover tightly and check camwheel for end float and free movement. Use a shim washer 016847 to absorb end movement. End play can dislodge the metal cap on timing cover by hydraulic. Renew the oil seal (see Fig. 17 for tool used for fitting).

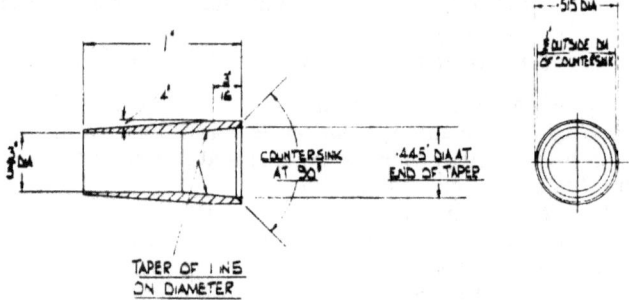

FIG. 17

Reassembling the flywheels. If attention to the big end assembly is needed, it is preferable wherever possible to use a factory serviced con rod, as the big end liner also small end bush is finished ground *in situ* to ensure concentricity. Alternatively, use a lapping tool A 8078 as shown in Fig. 18 for the new con rod liner after it has been replaced. The degree of interference fit between the liner and the con rod controls the contraction of the liner. Although liners issued as spares are finished, ground to a pre-determined size, concentricity cannot be guaranteed, hence the use of a lapping tool in some cases.

Removing the flywheel shafts. Both shafts are a press fit in the flywheels. Remove in turn each shaft nut, support the flywheel and press out with an arbour press, or similar equipment.

Refitting the shaft. The correct location of both shafts is of vital importance. If the drive side shaft is incorrectly located the alternator output will be adversely affected. Looking at the outside of the flywheel the shaft should be inserted with the keyway for the rotor pointing forwards (approximately 9 o'clock).

If the timing side shaft is incorrectly located, the oil supply can be curtailed (with damage to the oil pump plunger), also the valve timing will be deranged. Use a pencil and scribe a line on the shank of the shaft dead central with the oil hole. Offer up the shaft with the scribed line central with the oil hole in the flywheel. Tap the end of the shaft to prevent it moving then press firmly home with a suitable press. To check location of shaft fit the small pinion, the mark on the pinion should be exactly at 12 o'clock.

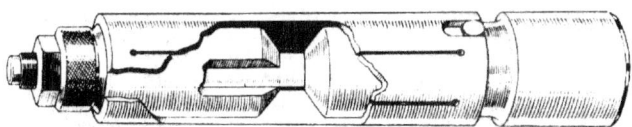

Fig. 18
Lapping Tool

Tighten both shaft nuts with torque spanner set to 190 ft. lbs.

Fitting the crankpin. If the engine has covered considerable mileage prior to dismantling, and a new crankpin is needed, the roller cage should be replaced also. Metal or abrasive can become embedded in the soft metal used for the cage, which with further use can cause abrasive wear. Verify oil holes in the crankpin are clear and clean before fitting. Scribe a pencil line (as described for timing shaft) on crankpin shank, enter the crankpin with the line central with oil holes in timing side flywheel and tap it home. Press the crankpin into the flywheel until it lightly abuts against the crankpin sleeve. Fit the roller cage and fill with rollers (30) that have been checked for uniformity in diameter.

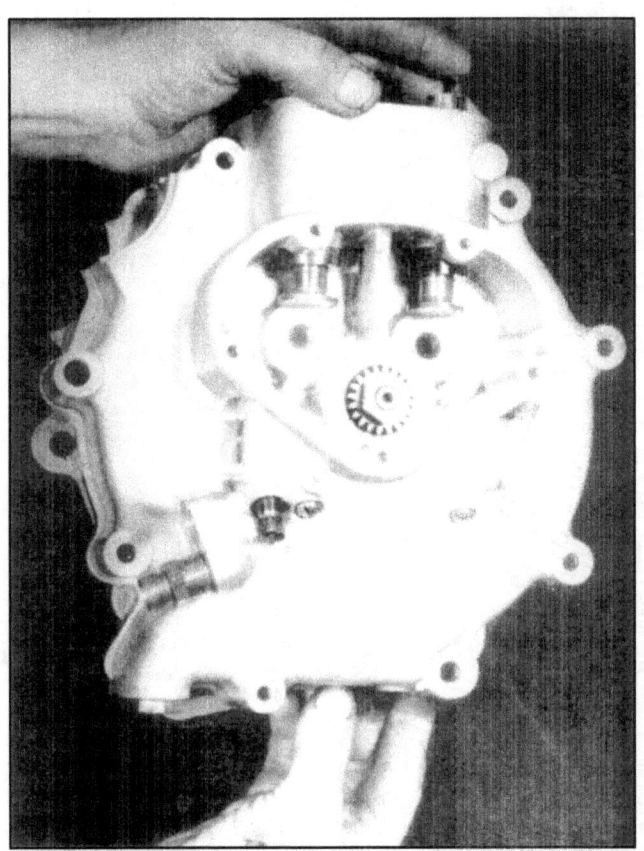

Fig. 19
Separating the Crankcase

Apply some engine oil to the con rod liner, also rollers, or a little Molybdenum Disulphide preparation will provide immediate lubrication. Offer up the drive side flywheel, roughly align both wheels with a straight edge placed on the outside diameter of both wheels. Place both wheels under an arbour press and force each flywheel firmly against the crankpin sleeve. Run down both crankpin nuts evenly (do

Fig. 20

not tighten one nut at a time). Finally tighten both nuts with a torque spanner set to 190 ft. lbs. Set both flywheels with shaft to run true to .001" to .002" error. Commercially made centre used for this purpose is shown in Fig. 24.

Reassembling the engine. When refitting the driving side bearings heat the crankcase, introduce the bearing 026762 squarely with the housing, then washer 021859 followed by bearing 021872. Use a mandrel or old drive side shaft to line up bearings. The inner member of both bearings should rotate independently to avoid end loading. Move outer bearing to free off.

Remove every trace of jointing compound from the crankcase joints, also the cylinder base faces. Apply some jointing compound of the non-flaking type, such as 'Wellseal', to both crankcase faces. Use oil on the crankcase bearings, put both cases together, pass three bolts through the crankcase evenly spaced (as a temporary measure). Set the cylinder base face square and even (the cylinder can be fitted temporary for this purpose) then firmly tighten the three crankcase bolts. The flywheel should rotate by hand application freely without tight places, if the flywheel shafts are running true. Check for end float which should be .012" minimum, between the flywheels and crankcase. **Bearing 026762 is a C3 fit.**

Refitting the oil pump plunger. First renew the paper gaskets on the pump end caps, stick the gaskets to the plates with jointing compound.

Remove burrs or particles of old gasket from crankcase faces. Take up the oil pump plunger, oil it and insert in crankcase. Clean the interior of screwed body (6) (Fig. 1). Oil and insert guide pin (5) as illustrated, the pin should revolve freely. Fit the screwed body and pin with extreme care to ensure the guide pin is located in the annular groove in the pump plunger, using the finger to do so. It may be necessary to revolve the flywheels to locate the pin. The screwed body can be finally tightened with a spanner. *Failure to observe these important instructions can ruin the pump gear beyond further use.* Now fit the two end caps.

Fitting the camshafts. Refer to details on valve timing.

Refitting the timing gear cover. If there is evidence of oil in the contact breaker compartment, the oil seal 024287 should be replaced. To prevent damage to the oil seal during the process of refitting the cover, a guide tool is shown in Fig. 17. The tool is fitted over the shaft for the cam wheel, with a little oil on it to guide the seal over the shaft. The seal should be fitted in the cover with the metal backing facing outwards. Clean the face of the cover and stick a new gasket to it. The cover 024016 can now be put back with three screws 000482.

Resetting the ignition timing. Fit the automatic timing control (make sure the weights move freely, apply a spot of oil on the pivot pins) and the contact plate (Fig. 15), and roughly assemble the timing control as illustrated in Fig. 15.

Set the ignition before fitting the cylinder head as the piston travel can be measured more easily.

Follow details for setting ignition timing previously described.

1962 350 cc. SHORT STROKE ENGINE

The general arrangement of this engine is shown in Figs. 21/22. The standard and sports version are similar in respect of engine design. The bottom part of the engine, excluding the flywheels, is similar to the earlier type engine.

Service details given for the 350 cc. Heavyweight Model apply also to this later type engine.

The push rod tunnels are integral with the cylinder, with oil seals in a recess in the cylinder barrel. Scrambler type valve springs are also used for high r.p.m. The compression ratio is 8.5 to 1.

This engine develops considerably more b.h.p. than the earlier type.

A list of parts that differ from the earlier type are tabulated:

350 cc. G3 16

028106	R/Box steady bolt
029318	R/Box steady bolt
028100	Head gasket
028596	Push rod assy.
022518	Push rod rubber
028104	Cylinder head
026030	Inlet guide
024519	Exhaust guide
026028	Inlet valve
028105	Exhaust valve
026861	Valve spring
026862	Valve spring
028531	Crankcase assd.
028102	Cylinder base stud
028095	Cylinder barrel
028101	Cylinder base gasket

(New Parts)

014044	Valve spring collar inlet and exhaust
014042	Valve spring collet inl.
014039	Valve spring collet exh.
015422	Rocker box
028123	Carburetter
041014	Carburetter O ring
015875	Carburetter spacer
028107	Piston
028114	Piston ring chrome
028115	Piston ring plain
028116	Piston ring scraper
028113	Gudgeon pin
028097	Flywheel T/S
028096	Flywheel D/S
015351	Cylinder stud nut
042157	Cylinder stud washer

SCRAMBLES MODELS CS and TCS

Basically the design of the two above models are identical, with the exception of the bore and stroke.

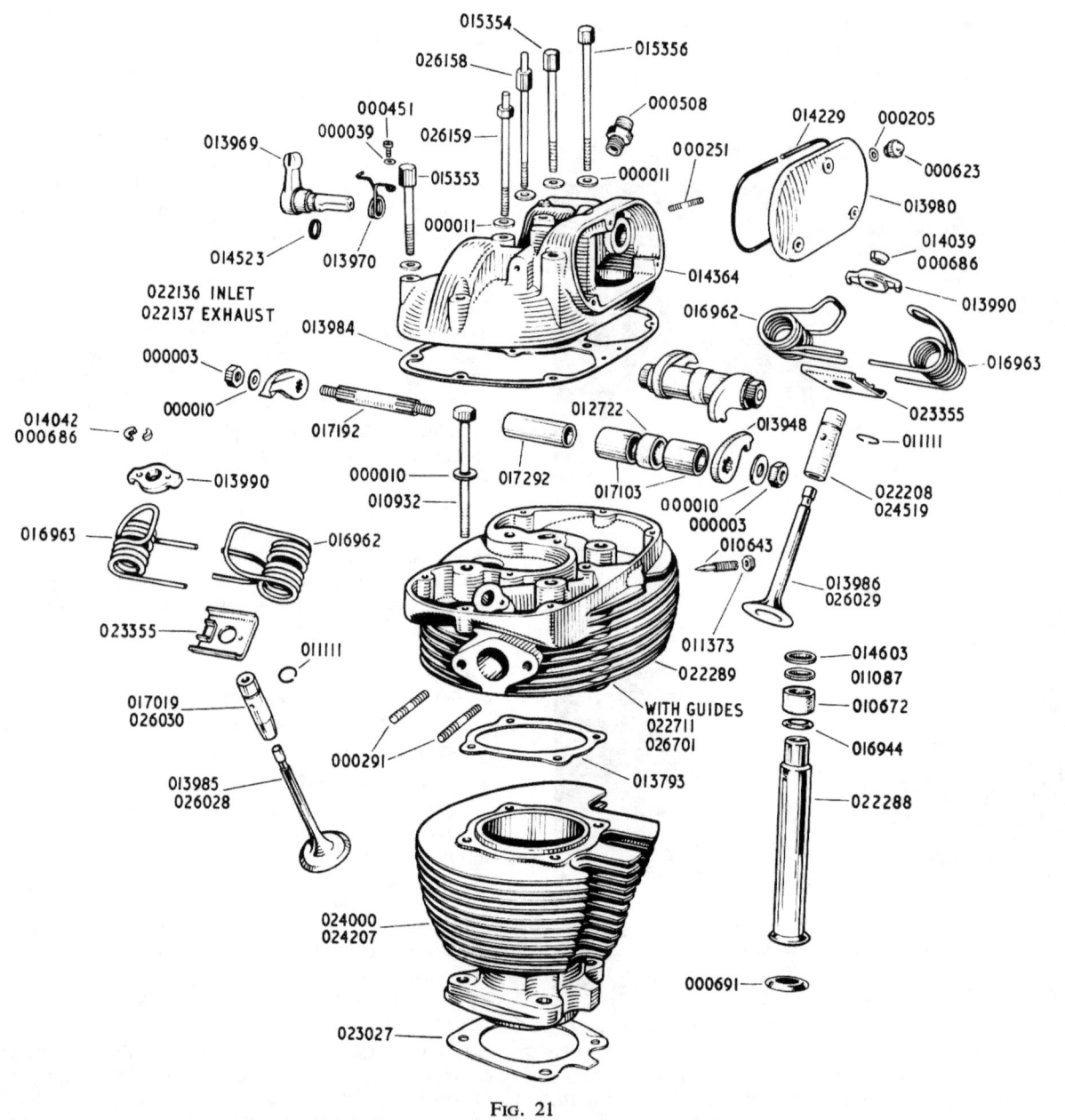

Fig. 21

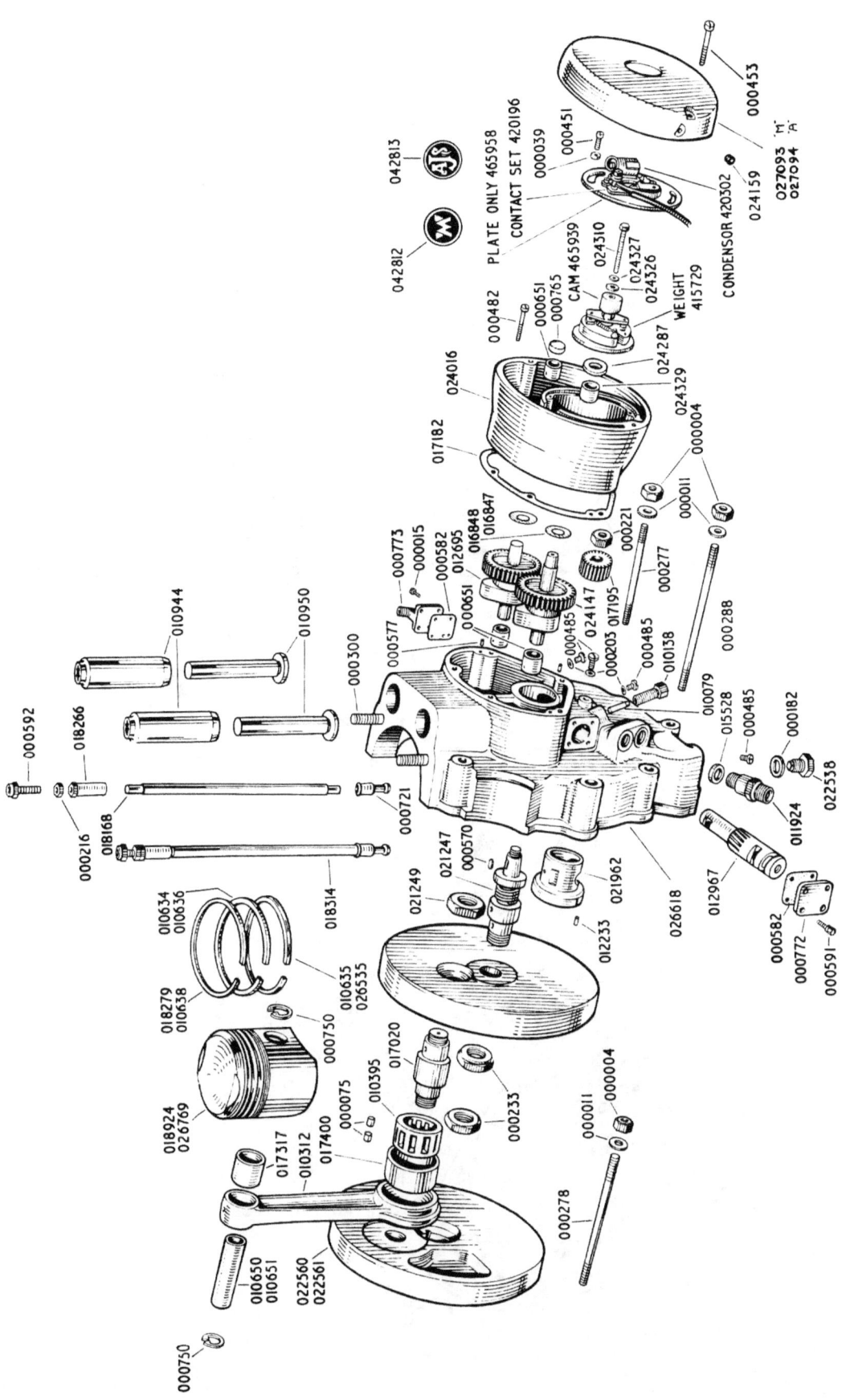

Fig. 22

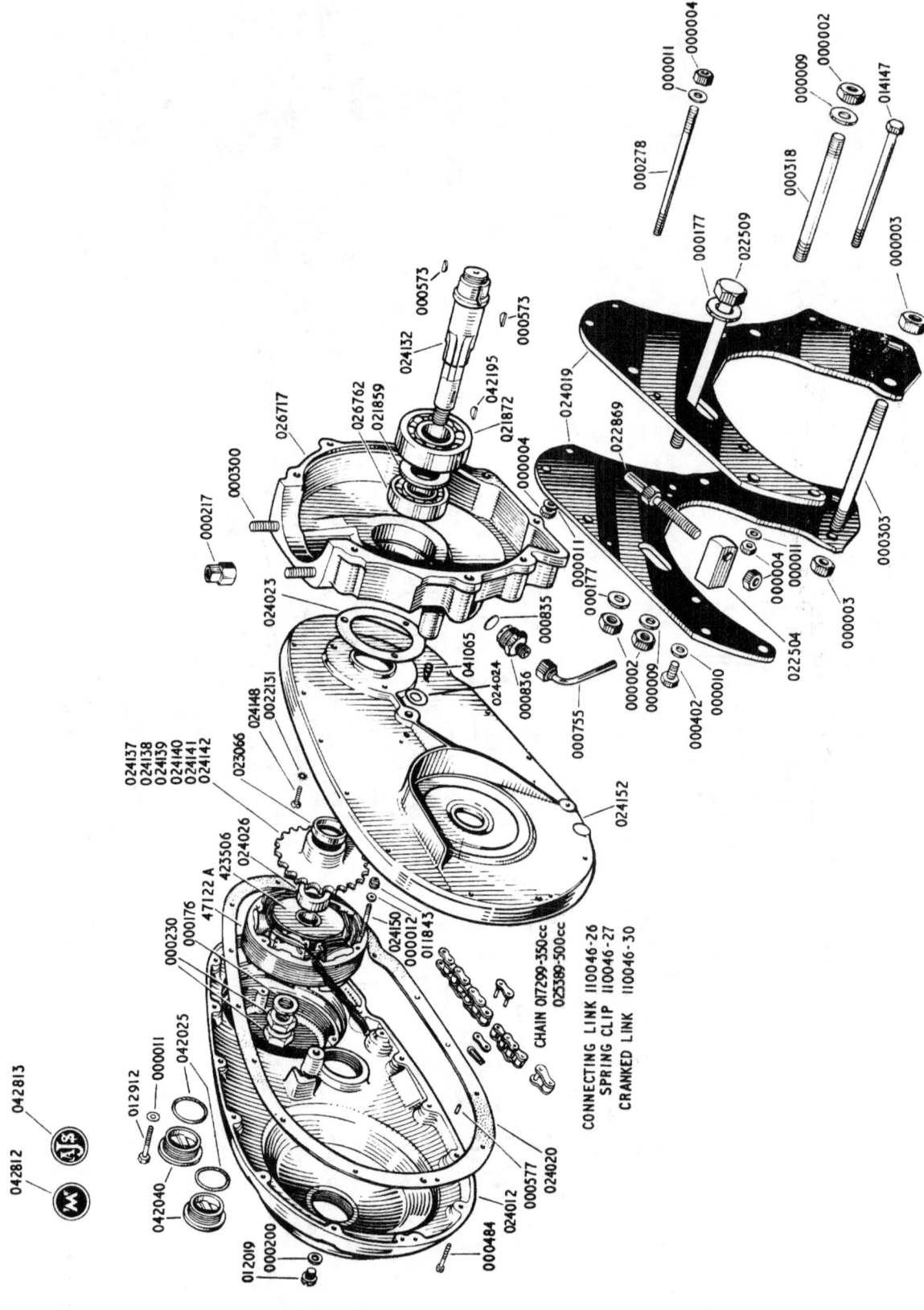

Fig. 23

Fig. 24

The 500 cc. version has a bore size of 86 mm. and 85.5 mm. stroke, as opposed to the 596 cc. engine, which has a bore size of 89 mm. and 96 mm. stroke. The peak r.p.m. of the 500 cc. engine is 6,200, the larger capacity engine peaks at 5,500 r.p.m.

A number of engines were fitted with a Monobloc type carburetter with a bore size of $1\frac{3}{16}''$.

Where a sudden change in diameter between the carburetter outlet, the carburetter spacer and the inlet port occurs, the part or whatever part is affected should be flared out or blended, to overcome any abrupt change in diameter.

The use of G.P. type carburetter with a bore size of $1\frac{3}{8}''$ with a parallel inlet tract will increase the volumetric efficiency of the engine. Attention is drawn to the use of late type camshafts in early type engines, see paragraph on 'valve timing'.

Port polishing. If, during the process of tuning, the ports are polished, the metal removed must be of the smallest amount possible to avoid drastic changes in the port shape. This applies particularly to the metal immediately below the valve inserts, which could cause the inserts to collapse. It is usually considered that a nice bright polished finish to the sphere of the cylinder head and piston crown is essential for best results. This is not so, for the ideal condition of the combustion chamber is when it has reached a nice black or ebony-like finish. This probably explains why it takes a little time for the engine to settle down before coming on 'full song'. Therefore the sphere of the head should not be disturbed, other than to remove soft carbon formed near the exhaust valve. If the engine is 'set up' correctly and under race conditions, the carbon formation should be negligible.

Compression ratio. The normal compression ratio on the CS and TCS engines is 8.7 to 1. An alternative piston giving a ratio of 12 to 1 is available. With this piston the ignition is put back to a maximum of 34°. Straight petrol can be used, octane 100 (research method). A suitable spark plug with a high heat factor is essential.

1957-1959 engines. The cylinder head and piston introduced for the 1960-61 season is more efficient than the earlier type. These new parts can be used together on earlier engines, but not separately.

The big end is robust in construction, the crankpin is materially and dimensionally identical to the G50 race model Matchless. As with the 250 cc. Scrambler Model, it is of paramount importance that the big end is rigidly assembled, to avoid power loss, apart from the risk of breakage. In consequence, if renewals are made, both flywheels must be

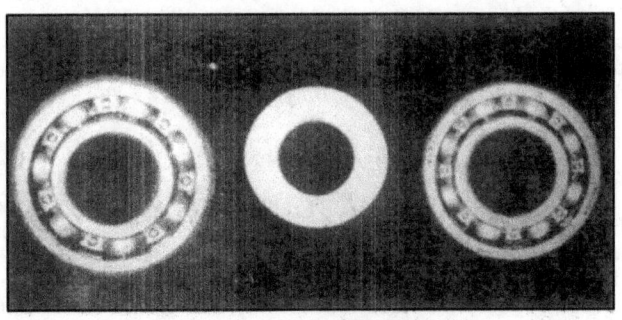

Fig. 25

forced firmly against the two shoulders of the crankpin, by using a press designed for this work. In fact a 12-ton press is used in the factory to assemble the flywheels. An attempt to drive the flywheels together and rely on nut tightness can only lead to mechanical trouble.

Big end wear. Wear on both edges of the crankpin is due to inertia wear, caused by the crankpin cage rubbing on the crankpin. This becomes most acute when the engine is run at high r.p.m. with little or no load. This wear does not affect or cause movement in the big end assembly. Wear on the roller path of the crankpin can be due to abrasive impregnated in the big end cage. In the event of damage to the crankpin, by reason of detonation, due to excess ignition advance, pre-ignition (soft plug), or unsuitable fuel, it is essential to replace the roller cage as well as other big end parts. The crankpin and liner for con rod have a mirror like finish (5 micros) and are made to close limits. To ensure uniformity each roller should be measured by micrometer and selected to a uniform diameter; 1962 big end assembly uses 28 $\frac{1}{4}'' \times \frac{1}{4}''$ rollers.

Timing side shaft. Normally the thread for the small timing pinion is left hand. A number of engines were issued with right-hand threads, these shafts can be identified by the use of a tab, or lock washer, between the pinion and pinion retaining nut. An improved type shaft was introduced for the 1960 models, identifiable by a wider gear. Should wear develop on the oil pump plunger, the new type shaft should be used.

Crankcase bearings. The bearing fitted to the drive side of the crankcase are usually trouble free. If a Scrambler Model is used extensively for racing, or when the power output has been increased by tuning with the fitment of an ultra high compression piston, a heavy duty roller type bearing can be used in place of the ball type. The new bearing is of the Hoffman type RMS 10 ($2\frac{1}{2}'' \times 1'' \times \frac{3}{4}''$) and should be fitted next to the flywheel. When the bearing is pressed into position, the crankcase should be peened alongside the outer bearing sleeve in three equi-distant positions, to keep the sleeve in location.

Timing side bush. It must be mentioned that the outer end (timing gear side) of this bush is swaged out to make it slightly bell mouth, thus preventing the bush from moving inwards towards the flywheel. This means that the bush must be extracted by pressure on the flywheel end of the bush to avoid damage to the crankcase during removal.

Cylinder head and barrel joint. Normally there is an annular space between the spigot on the cylinder barrel and the small face on the cylinder, when the cylinder head is assembled. This space can be eliminated by individual machining, assuming the necessary machining facilities are available. To do this, machine back the wide face on the cylinder head, leaving a gap of .001″ between the small recess in the cylinder head and the narrow spigot on the cylinder barrel. Use grinding paste on the wide face of the cylinder head, also in the small recess. Grind the head on to the cylinder barrel until both faces on the cylinder head are mated to the cylinder barrel to give a gas-tight joint. Should an oil leak develop from the cylinder head face, regrind the spigot *situ* only.

SCRAMBLER ENGINE

Top end strip down. Follow the details given for the Heavyweight Single Cylinder Models, as the sequence is identical with the exception of the cylinder head bolts. Check the cylinder head steady stay for ovality in the bolt holes caused by movement due to looseness, and get the holes built up by weld and re-drill or replace the stay. Engine movement due to torque can cause vibration.

Removing the engine from frame. With the cylinder head and barrel, also piston removed, start by:

Removing magneto case outer cover (see note).
Removing magneto chain with both sprockets.
Removing magneto rocker box oil feed pipe from crankcase.
Removing magneto control cable handlebar end and contact breaker vent pipe and front engine plate.
Removing both oil pipes (be careful with spanner manipulation at crankcase end).
Removing outer portion front chain case.
Removing clutch assembly, engine sprocket and chain (see note).
Removing rear portion front chain case.
Removing crankcase release pipe.
Removing bolts passing through rear engine plates and crankcase, then loosen top and bottom gear box fixing bolts, loosen also footrest rod and central stand pivot bolt which tend to clamp the crankcase.
Removing bottom front engine bolt.
Removing crankcase assembly from frame. When a duplex tube frame is not used, wheel machine off the stand, the frame will open and facilitate removal of crankcase.

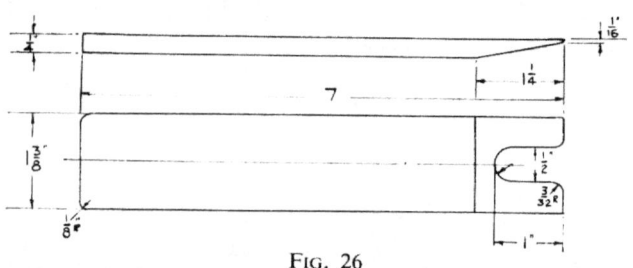

Fig. 26

Note: Use a tyre lever with one end bent at right angle to prise off the lower magneto sprocket. To remove top sprocket, slack off all timing cover screws, use tool B 4018 (see Fig. 26), inserted between magneto sprocket and magneto body. With the armature nut removed, a light tap on the tool will dislodge sprocket. A tool to prevent the engine turning (top gear engaged) whilst unscrewing the gear box mainshaft nut and also engine sprocket nut is shown in Fig. 51, which is easy to fabricate.

Separating the crankcase. Before attempting to separate the crankcase, the oil pump plunger must be removed by taking off the cap at the rear end of the pump plunger housing, then remove the screwed body (No. 6, Fig. 1), and guide pin (5). Insert a piece of stout wire or wheel spoke in the plunger hole and pull out the pump plunger.

Removing the small timing pinion. This pinion is a taper fit on the shaft and needs a tool or puller (B 2151) to extract it from the shaft. Put the tool in position and lightly tighten the draw bolt (do not over tighten), then give the end of the draw bolt a sharp blow with a light hammer, the pinion will then come away from the shaft.

Separating the flywheels. The flywheel separating tool B 2140 as described for the 250 cc. model, can also be used for the Scrambler. As an alternative, use an Arbour press with one flywheel supported by two stout steel bars placed on four blocks, which is the best method if suitable equipment is available.

Removing the timing side bush. Firmly support the crankcase on the timing cover end, press out the bush from inside the crankcase. To fit a new bush, reverse the crankcase, press in the new bush, the inner edge should be flush with the crankcase. This bush is fine bored in production with the bush in position. The new bush should be reamed to .8752″ to .8757″.

Timing side bearing sleeve (022352). This is a press fit on the shaft, the normal outside diameter is 1.2581″ to 1.2585″.

Timing side bearing (022351). To remove bearing sleeve, apply heat to the crankcase, drop the crankcase on the bench, when the bearing sleeve will fall out.

Camshaft bushes. See details given for 'Heavyweight Single Cylinder Models'.

Rocker box. For dismantling instructions refer to 'Heavy weight Single Cylinder Models'.

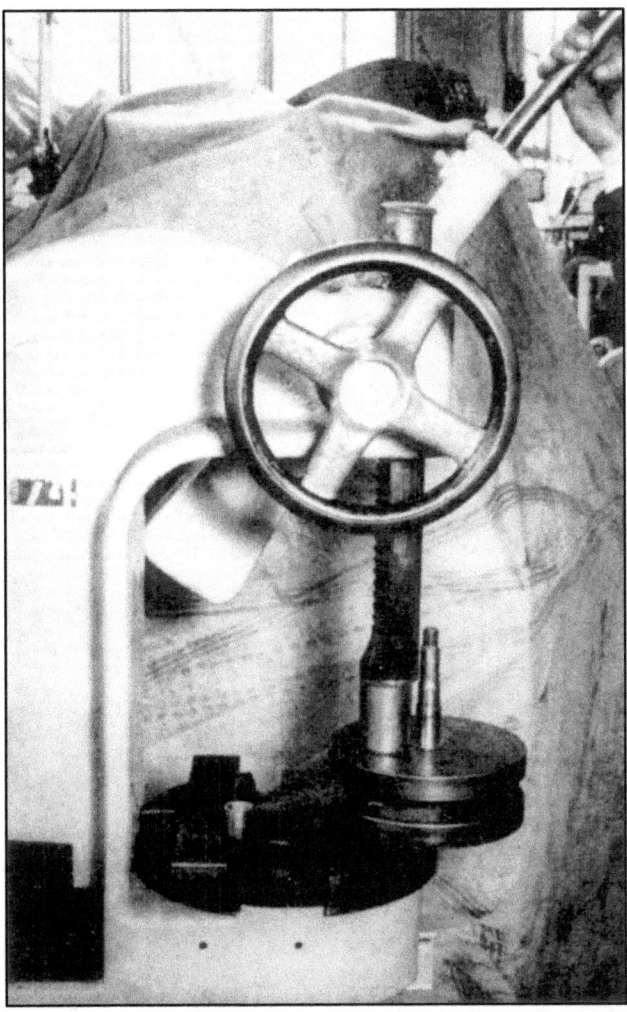

FIG. 27
Arbour Press for Flywheels

Assembling the flywheels. These must be assembled with a suitable hand press. Tighten the crankpin nuts with a torque spanner set to 240 ft. lbs. The shafts should run true to .001″ to .002″.

Cylinder head joint. As a gasket is not used, the joint is remade by grinding the cylinder head on to the barrel by moving the head to and fro through an arc of about 30° and not in a full circular motion. Continue grinding until a full matt surface on both parts is shown.

Valve timing. Up to 1959 cam wheels marked SH were used with part number 018833 and 022567 for the inlet and exhaust respectively. Both cam wheels are marked for correct assembly. Install the inlet cam with the No. 2 mark to register with the mark on the small pinion. Use No. 1 mark for exhaust to also register with mark on small pinion.

The push rod clearance for these cams is *nil* for the inlet and .005″ for the exhaust (engine cold). The inlet push rod should be just free to revolve by finger application. The clearance of .005″ for the exhaust represents one flat on the adjusting screw away from the nil clearance setting. Position the engine for push rod adjustment as described for Touring Heavyweight Models.

The valve timing on average is as follows:

Inlet opens	... ...	59° b.t.d.c.
,, closes	... ...	69° a.b.d.c.
Exhaust opens	... ...	74° b.b.d.c.
,, closes	... ...	48° a.t.d.c.

These readings are taken with the valve .001″ off its seat with running push rod clearance. The valve lift is .375″.

Valve timing—1960. A more efficient type of inlet cam was introduced for and after the 1960 season. The inlet cam is marked C1, Part No. 024534, and is used in conjunction with the 1959 exhaust cam 022567. The valve timing with the new cam allows the inlet to open at 67° b.t.d.c. and to close at 80° a.b.d.c. with a *nil* clearance and the valve .001″ off its seat. The valve lift is .428″.

Fitting new type camshafts. The special inlet cam No. 024534 first introduced in 1960 can be fitted to early type engines providing the crankcase alongside the timing side bush is machined for clearance, as the valve lift is higher. The inlet tappet guide should also be reduced in length (inside the timing cover) to the extent of $\frac{1}{8}$″, also use inlet valve guide 026030.

G80 R Models. Engines for this model use the inlet cam 024534 and a special exhaust cam marked CE Part No. 024535, the exhaust valve opens 83° b.b.d.c. and closes 60° a.t.d.c.

The valve lift is .445″ (use No. 1 mark). This combination is best suited where high r.p.m. is required for short circuit events, or in drag events providing the engine is taken up to 3,500 r.p.m. before take off. Where good torque is needed at comparative low r.p.m. the 1960 set up is the best arrangement.

Valve springs. These springs (which are shot blasted after manufacture) must be free from bruises or blemish, which can cause a spring breakage. The free length (unassembled) taken between the wire centre for the spring leg and the portion which engages with the valve spring collar is $1\frac{17}{32}$.

Valve spring collets. Must be free from burrs and a good tight taper fit in the valve spring collar. Loose fitting collets can cause a valve breakage.

1962 Engines. An improved type of valve operating mechanism is used on current engines, comprising the following parts:

(1) Long push rods	...	...	2 off	028185
(2) Short tappets	...	...	,,	028182
(3) Tappet guides	...	...	,,	028184
(4) Inlet rocker	...	...	1 off	042043
(5) Inlet camshaft	...	...	,,	028191
(6) Exhaust camshaft	...	...	,,	028193

The new type parts can be used on earlier type engines.

LIGHTWEIGHT MODELS

Checking oil circulation. Provision is made to observe the oil circulating, which is visible after removing the oil filler cap on the right side of the crankcase.

ENGINE LUBRICATION SYSTEM

This is by true dry sump system. The oil tank, or reservoir, is integral with the crankcase. The oil pump has only one moving part, i.e., the oil pump plunger, which rotates and reciprocates. Rotation is created by the worm gear on the timing side flywheel axle.

EXPLODED VIEW OF 250 c.c. O.H.V. ENGINE

Reciprocation is caused by engagement of the oil pump guide pin with the profiled groove in the oil pump plunger. The oil pump is designed so that the sump scavenging capacity is greater than the delivery, thus keeping the crankcase sump free of oil during normal running conditions.

Whilst the oil reservoir is integral with the crankcase, oil is fed to the pump by gravity, on the same principle as a machine fitted with a separate oil tank, but without the use of external oil pipes.

ENGINE SERVICE
250 and 350 LIGHTWEIGHT MODELS

To remove the twin seat. Release nuts securing the frame uniting bolt at front of seat, take away two nuts at rear of seat and lift to clear.

To remove petrol tank. Disconnect both petrol pipes. Early types use a bolt through the rear fixing. On new type release rear fixing nut, turn the T bolt 90°, take out front fixing bolts, lift tank clear of frame.

To remove the rocker box. Remove the three nuts and fibre washers securing the rocker box cover, also the sparking plug.

Turn the engine until both valves are closed, i.e., after the inlet valve has opened and just closed.

Remove two nuts and the bolt securing the engine steady bracket to the rocker box and frame. Disconnect valve lifter cable.

Take out the nine bolts securing the rocker box to the cylinder head (one of these bolts is inside the rocker box) (see Fig. 29), the location of these bolts must be noted as they are dissimilar.

Tilt upwards the right side of the rocker box, extract both push rods and identify their location for replacement in their original positions; remove the rocker box from the cylinder head.

To remove the cylinder head. Remove the exhaust pipe and silencer as one unit, then the accessory compartment cover and air filter tube if fitted. Do not rock the exhaust pipe sideways unduly to extract it from the exhaust port which can cause the end of the pipe to close in and result in gas leakage, also movement between the pipe and the port when the engine is hot. Instead, squirt a little paraffin or petrol into the port and try again.

Unscrew the cap on the carburetter mixing chamber, take out both slides, wrap them in a piece of rag and attach it to the frame out of harm's way.

Unscrew the petrol pipe union and take away the petrol pipe. Four sleeve nuts and one bolt retain the cylinder head to the barrel, with these removed the cylinder head with carburetter attached to it can be separated from the cylinder

To remove and replace the valves and guides. The valve springs are removed by inserting the index finger through the coil of the spring and pulling upwards sharply.

A light tap on the valve spring collar will expose the valve split collets (which should be put in a place of safety), then take out the valve.

Both valve guides are located by an external circlip, the cylinder head must be gently and uniformly heated before attempting to remove or replace the guides.

With the head pre-heated, tap the guide upwards out of the port sufficiently to enable the circlip to be prised out of its groove. Re-heat the head and drive out the guides through the cylinder head.

When refitting the guides, pre-heat the head and verify that the oil holes are in alignment with the holes in the cylinder head.

A holder for the valve, when grinding in the valve, can be supplied. The part number is 017482.

Replacing the valves. A valve spring compressor is required to compress the springs, a special tool which is inexpensive can be obtained from dealers or from our spare parts department. The application of this tool is shown in Fig. 13. Before fitting the valve springs, position correctly the valve spring seat—the raised portion on the underside is located with the depression (5) in cylinder head (Fig. 14).

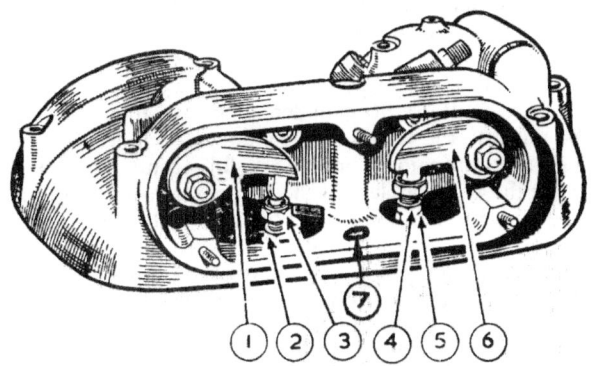

FIG. 29
Tappet Adjustment

1 Inlet rocker arm (tappet end).
2 Nut, locking adjusting cupped screw.
3 Cupped adjusting screw.
4 Cupped adjusting screw and lock nut.
5 Sleeve, to accommodate adjusting screw, on top end of push rod.
6 Exhaust rocker arm (tappet end).
7 Rocker box bolt.

FIG. 30
Fitting Cylinder Barrel

The inlet valve is the larger of the two valves and it is vitally important to locate correctly the two split collets into the grooves on each valve stem.

Clean the valve guide bores with a piece of clean rag, apply a little oil on the valve stems and also inside each guide before assembly.

Removing the cylinder and piston. With the cylinder head removed, the barrel can be raised vertically to clear the holding down studs. Before doing so, position the engine with the piston on the top of its stroke, have available a piece of clean rag. Raise the cylinder sufficiently to enable the rag to be put into the throat of the crankcase (under the piston) as a precaution against a broken ring falling into the crankcase, then lift the cylinder clear of the four studs passing through it.

The gudgeon pin is a sliding fit in both the piston and the connecting rod.

Use round-nose pliers to compress and extract the circlip (it is immaterial which one is removed), then push out the gudgeon pin and lift the piston off the connecting rod.

Do not disturb the piston rings unless absolutely necessary.

If new piston rings are fitted and if they are obtained from our spare parts department, they are ready for fitting, as the ring gap is allowed for during manufacture.

The top compression ring is chromium plated and has a slightly tapered extension.

When new, the word 'TOP' is etched on the ring top to indicate which way it should be fitted. Fit first the scraper or oil control ring, then the two compression rings, to avoid breakage do not expand these rings unnecessarily.

Refitting the piston. Before refitting the piston apply a little oil to the gudgeon pin, also to the bosses for the gudgeon pin in the piston. Place the piston over the connecting rod in the same way as it was removed, or in accordance with the marking made, and then introduce the gudgeon pin through the piston, connecting rod and piston bosses.

It is vitally important to correctly locate the gudgeon pin circlip, and a little extra care and time should be devoted to this most simple and important operation. Use round-nosed pliers to introduce the circlip into its groove, using a rotary motion, then verify that the circlip is correctly located.

Refitting the cylinder barrel. Fit a new cylinder base gasket, after removing broken pieces of the old one. Use a little jointing compound on the base of the cylinder and stick a new gasket to it, no jointing compound should be on the crankcase face. Set the piston ring gaps at 120°, pass the cylinder over the four long studs and lower it gently at the same time compressing each piston ring in turn with the fingers, until the cylinder has passed the scraper ring, when it can be lowered on to the crankcase.

Note: Some clean rag under the piston to fill the throat of the crankcase will safeguard against a broken piston ring falling into the crankcase.

Refitting the cylinder head. The cylinder head gasket also acts as an oil seal for the push rod tunnels, consequently it must be in good order if it is to be used again. To avoid the possibility of subsequent attention a new gasket is desirable. This gasket is neither symmetrical nor reversible, and it must be placed on the cylinder in the correct way.

A study of the cylinder barrel face will show an elongated hole (where the push rods operate).

Just behind is a tapped hole for the cylinder head bolt.

Close to the cylinder bore and to the right of the cylinder head bolt hole is a smaller hole, which is the oil feed passage from the pump to the rocker gear.

Place the gasket on the cylinder so that the oil feed hole in the cylinder registers with the small hole in the gasket.

Put the cylinder head in position, refit the four cylinder head sleeve nuts and the long cylinder head bolt; do not omit the five washers.

First tighten the four sleeve nuts diagonally—not one side at a time—then tighten the long bolt, until all are firmly tightened.

If a torque spanner is available it should be set to 35 ft. lbs. for the *four sleeve nuts only.*

Refitting the rocker box. Before attempting to refit, make sure the piston is on t.d.c. of the firing stroke, with both cam followers down.

Use a new rocker box gasket for this assembly. In the centre portion of this gasket is a projection with a small hole in it. There is also a similar size hole in the cylinder head which is the oil feed passage from the oil pump through the cylinder to the rocker gear. It will be readily seen that if the rocker box gasket is reversed the oil feed passage will be sealed, therefore, ensure that the gasket is properly located before fitting the rocker box.

With the rocker box gasket correctly located, take up the rocker box, pass all the holding down bolts through it, put the rocker box into position.

Take up the two engine push rods, tilt the right side of the rocker box upwards, then introduce the push rods through the head and cylinder. The exhaust push rod operates with the cam follower nearest to the contact breaker.

Locate the rocker arms in the push rod adjusters and first tighten the two central rocker box bolts which have screwed extensions. Tighten the remainder diagonally including the one inside the rocker box.

Washers are fitted under the heads of all these bolts.

It should be remembered that a soft gasket is used between the cylinder head and the rocker box, therefore the degree of tightness for these bolts is a matter of good judgment and commonsense.

Re-adjust the tappets as described elsewhere.

Ignition timing. Before setting or checking the ignition timing, make sure the contact gap, at full separation, is .012". (See details on Contact Breaker.)

Reference to Fig. 31 will indicate the principle used.

To check the timing. Position the engine as detailed for tappet adjustment. Remove the sparking plug, the cover for the contact breaker and engage top gear. Obtain a short length of stiff wire or wheel spoke about 5" long. Insert the wire through the sparking plug hole until it touches the piston crown. By slowly moving the rear wheel backwards and forwards the top dead centre of the piston travel can be ascertained. Keep the wire vertical as far as the plug hole will permit—make a mark on the wire to register with the seating for the sparking plug on the cylinder head. Take out the wire and make a further mark on it $\frac{1}{4}$" *above* the previous mark. Put the wire through the sparking plug hole, then turn the engine *backwards* until the top mark on the wire registers with the seating for the sparking plug, the piston is now $\frac{1}{4}$" before top dead centre.

A $\frac{5}{8}$" hole is drilled in the contact breaker base plate to enable a small screw driver to be inserted, and engaged between the two bob weights for the automatic ignition control. (See Fig. 31.)

Turning the screwdriver clockwise will separate the bob weights to the fully advanced position. If the timing is correct the contact points should be just about to separate.

The exact point of separation can best be found by inserting a piece of cigarette paper between the points, which when pulled lightly will be free when the contact points separate.

To adjust ignition timing. By slackening the two screws in the slotted holes on the contact breaker base plate, the plate can be moved either clockwise or anti-clockwise to adjust the timing as required.

Move the plate clockwise to advance and use the method described for checking to obtain the correct timing.

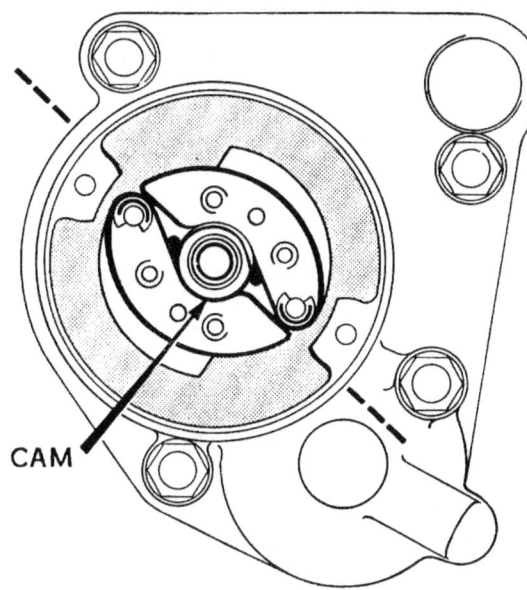

FIG. 31
Automatic Ignition Advance Mechanism.
(Approximate Ignition Setting).

To reset ignition timing. As the ignition advance is limited to ¼" b.t.d.c., this setting is critical and must be carefully carried out. The automatic ignition control unit is a taper fit on the camshaft, retained by a central bolt.

To remove this unit take out the retaining bolt, use in its place a withdrawal bolt, Part No. 042247. Screw home this bolt—do not use undue force—then tap the head of the bolt lightly, which will separate the unit from the shaft.

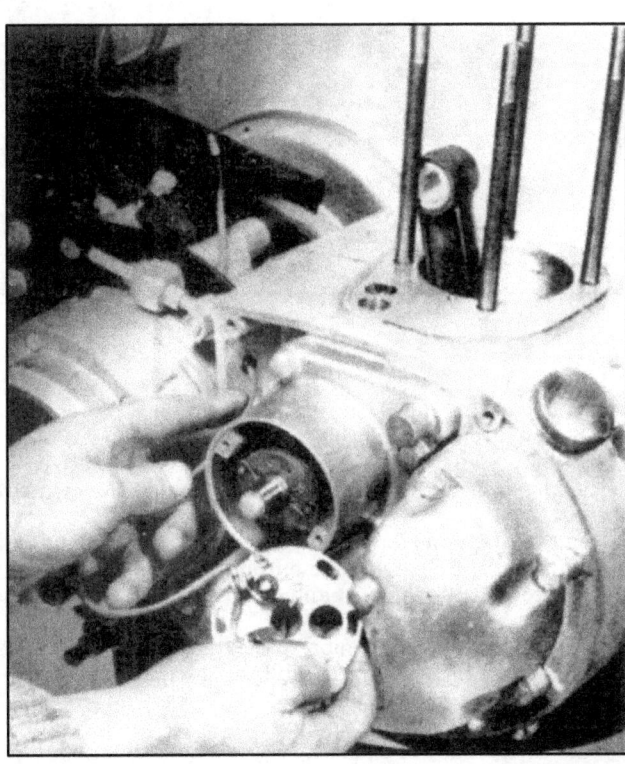

FIG. 32

Note: The contact breaker cam is detachable and if it is inadvertently removed, the timing should be re-checked after refitting the cam, before attempting to start the engine.

Valve timing. The cam wheel, also the small timing pinion which drives it, are both marked to facilitate assembly.

If, for any reason, the cam wheel is removed, to reassemble rotate the engine until the piston is on t.d.c. of the stroke, the mark on the small timing pinion tooth will then be at 11 o'clock. Take up the cam wheel, raise both cam followers, then introduce the cam into the crankcase with the mark on the tooth gap to register with the mark on the small pinion.

These markings have been selected to give the most effective valve timing and best engine performance.

To check the valve timing, as a single piece camshaft is used, it is only necessary to record the inlet valve opening also the exhaust valve closing positions to verify that the valve timing is correct. The average valve timing, taken with .010" rocker clearance is:

Inlet valve opens ... ... 40° b.t.d.c.
Exhaust valve closes ... ... 40° a.t.d.c.

See 'Tappet adjustment' for running push rod clearance.

ENGINE SERVICE

250 cc. and 350 cc. LIGHTWEIGHT MODELS

Removing the engine from frame. *Disconnect battery wires.* The engine, with gear box, can be removed as a unit. It is preferable to remove the gear box first as it makes handling easier.

Strip down as detailed for 'Removing cylinder and piston', then remove drain plug from front chaincase, catch oil in a suitable receptacle.

Remove near side footrest.

Remove rear engine plate cover (two screws).

Remove four snap connectors on alternator cables.

Remove six chaincase screws and inspection cap.

Remove chaincase cover, with care, feeding the alternator cables through back half of case, turn back one of the terminals to allow plastic sheath to pass through metal duct.

Remove three clutch springs and take away pressure plate.

Remove gear box mainshaft nut securing clutch.

Remove nut securing rotor to engine shaft (see Fig. 33).

Remove chain connecting link.

Remove clutch assembly complete.

Remove rotor and key, engine sprocket.

Remove three screws securing rear portion chaincase to crankcase.

Remove kickstarter crank and footchange pedal (see 'Gearbox section').

Remove fairing for timing cover 042053/4.

Pull contact breaker cable clear.

Removing the front chain. A Duplex type chain, which is 'endless', is fitted to the Lightweight 350 cc. Model, also the 250 cc. CSR Model.

To remove the front chain take off the nut securing the clutch to the gear box mainshaft, the nut securing the engine sprocket to the engine mainshaft, then withdraw simultaneously the engine sprocket, together with the clutch assembly with the chain *in situ*.

Reverse this procedure to refit the chain.

Removing the gear box. Disconnect rear chain, clutch cable (gear box end).

Remove gear box adjuster, gear box top bolt 042394, all nuts securing right side engine plate, release gear box clamps.

Remove engine plate with distance pieces behind it, then pull out the gear box.

Turn to engine. Remove five studs passing through the frame and crankcase, raise the rear end of crankcase assembly, pull it backwards and lift out of frame. If difficulty exists, wheel machine off the central stand.

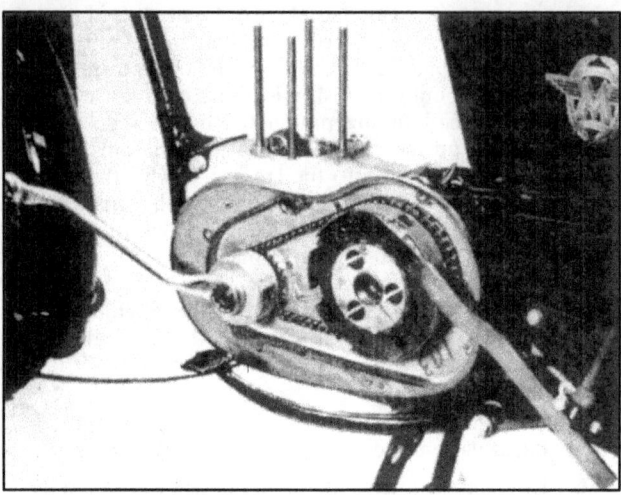

Fig. 33

1961 250 cc. LIGHTWEIGHT MODELS

Exhaust valve modification. A larger exhaust valve stem diameter introduced on engines after No. 10587, which can be fitted to earlier type engines. New parts used:
Exhaust valve 042868   Exhaust valve collets 042870
Exhaust valve guide 042869

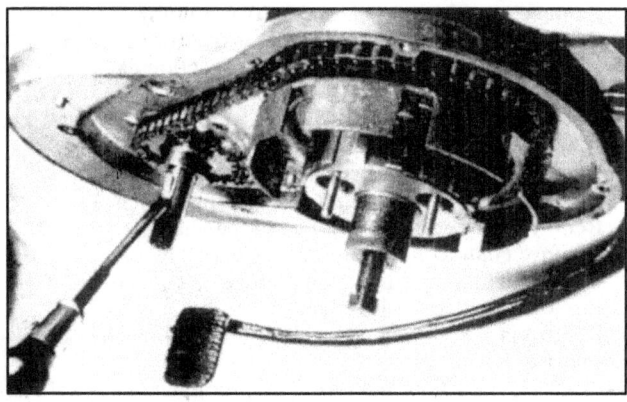

Fig. 34

LIGHTWEIGHT CSR MODEL

Engine section. The engine strip down details given for the Standard, Scrambler and Sports Lightweight Model apply also to the above model. The technical details which differ from the Sports version are listed hereunder.

Compression ratio. This is 8 to 1, the volumetric efficiency has been increased to a marked degree by using an improved inlet tract, in conjunction with a carburetter with a bore size of $1\frac{1}{8}''$.

Flywheels. Made from steel billets as opposed to cast iron for the Sports and Standard type engine.

Inlet valve. The inlet valve head diameter has been increased to $1\frac{19}{32}''$ as a further aid to engine efficiency.

Valve springs. These are similar to those used on the Scrambler type engine (see 'Technical Data' for details). The spring loading is 180 lbs. for each valve at full lift.

Cylinder head. As the inlet valve head diameter is larger a new type cylinder is used, which can also be used on previous 250 cc. engines.

Engine sprocket. Has been increased to 22 teeth.

Push rod adjustment. Refer to details described for the Scrambler and Standard type engine.

Ignition timing. Should not exceed $\frac{1}{4}''$ (32°—34°) b.t.d.c. with ignition control unit fully advanced.

Dismantling sequence for the engine. Before dismantling, study the exploded view of the engine and gear box as shown in Fig. 28.

Special tools required:

(1) Extractor bolt for automatic ignition device, 042247.
(2) Small timing pinion extractor, 043332.
(3) Clutch withdrawal tool, 040449 (used also on Heavyweight gear box).

Fig. 35

With engine removed from the frame:
Remove drain plugs from the crankcase, also oil reservoir, oil in timing chest with spill into crankcase, and drain by tilting the assembly over on the drive side.
Remove contact breaker base plate, the a.t.d. (use extractor bolt, 042247).
Remove four bolts for cam housing, gently tap to remove it.
Remove nine bolts and take off oil reservoir, 042083.
Remove small timing pinion nut, 000230 (right-hand thread).
Remove small timing pinion (use extractor tool, 043332).
Strip down timing gear in the following sequence:
(1) Camshaft.
(2) Camshaft follower distance piece—wide.
(3) Camshaft follower exhaust.
(4) Camshaft follower distance piece—narrow.
(5) Camshaft follower inlet.

Warning: An attempt to separate the crankcase halves without first removing the oil pump plunger, 042104, will result in serious damage.

Remove oil pump guide pin, 010079, and sleeve, 010138.

Remove screwed plug and 'O' ring, 042178.

Remove oil pump plunger, 042104 (use short length of clean ¼″ diameter rod).

Remove felt filter cap, 042058, extract filter.

Remove six crankcase bolts, 042035, one bolt, 042036, also stud, 016103.

The timing side crankcase can now be separated from the drive side.

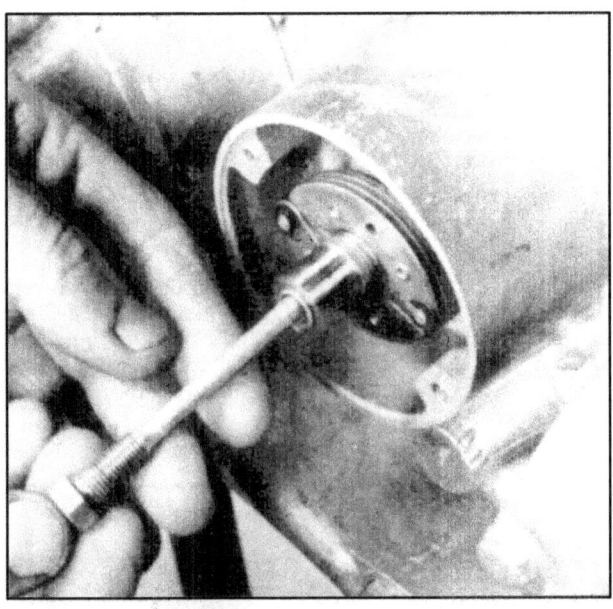

Fig. 36

Remove the crankcase breather tube, 042221 (see *Note*) before proceeding further. The drive side crankcase must be uniformly and gently heated to relieve the interference fit of the drive side bearings, before separating the crankcase from the flywheels. Possibly the outer ball bearing will remain in the crankcase, the two bearing housings are dimensionally different.

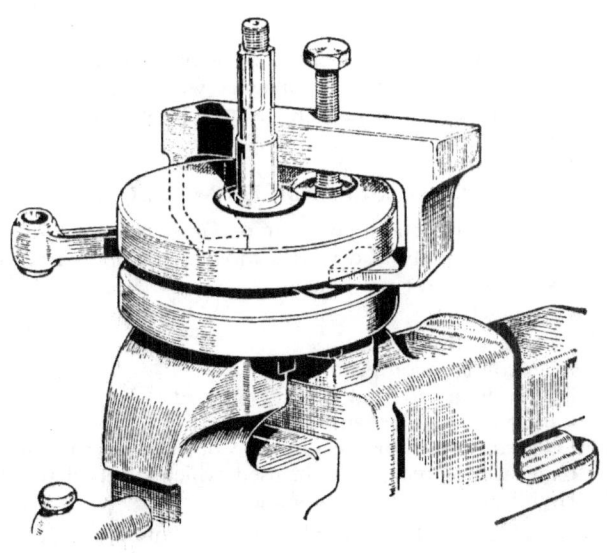

Fig. 37

To remove outer ball bearing, re-heat the crankcase, use a double diameter drift to prevent the bearing tilting during removal. With the flywheels out, take off breather stator, 042220 (this may also remain in the crankcase), and watch for key 017602, when rotor is removed. Remove this key before taking off the inner ball bearing.

Note: On engines after 8979 an improved type of release valve is used. The stator is retained by a short bolt below the bearing housing. When refitting this stator the recess should face the engine sprocket side of the housing. The new valve cannot be adapted to earlier type crankcases.

Dismantling the flywheels. A flywheel separating tool B2140 is shown in Fig. 37. With one crank pin nut removed, place the tool over the flywheel, correctly position the draw bolt, screwing in the draw bolt will pull the flywheel away from the crank pin. Remove the second nut and repeat the process.

Removing the flywheel shafts. Both shafts are a force fit in the flywheels and are pressed out with an Arbour press.

Refitting the shafts. The only precautions required is to ensure both shafts are firmly home against the shoulders, and in particular to correctly locate the driving side shaft, otherwise the alternator output will be affected. As a guide, the keyway for the breather rotor is pointing to the crank pin. The correct shaft location is shown in the engine breakdown (see Fig. 28).

Drive side bearings. Early type engines were fitted with two ball journal bearings, 012542. The bearing nearest to the flywheel is now replaced by a roller type.

Timing side bush. To remove, support the crankcase then press out the bush from inside the case. The bush is chamfered to facilitate fitting, the retaining pin will come out with the bush.

Cam wheel bush (042101). To remove bush, first take out the oil seal, 042183, press the bush out from inside the cover. Gently warming the cover will assist in removal without 'scruffing'. When refitting the rear cam wheel bush locate the slot at 12 o'clock.

Replacing the oil seal (042183). The oil seal should be refitted with the metal backing facing outwards. A simple tool to prevent damage to the seal when refitting is shown in Fig. 17.

Assembling the flywheels. The diameter of the crankpin and bore of the con rod are manufactured to very close limits. It is recommended that each roller is measured individually to ensure uniformity, for if the rollers are mixed, there can be a slight variation in size. The centre portion of the crankpin is made from 85-ton tensile steel, at the same time a rigid flywheel assembly is essential. This can only be obtained by correct assembly, and by using a hand press to force each flywheel firmly against the shoulders of the centre portion of the crankpin. It is fatal to rely only on the tightness of the crankpin nuts, as this will allow the flywheels to flex, which will absorb power and impose an undue strain on the crankpin. It is also essential to use heat treated crankpin nuts with ground faces. If non-standard nuts are used, without ground faces, this will tend to break off the threaded portion of the crankpin. With the flywheels firmly home, tighten nuts with a torque spanner set to 150 ft. lbs. and 190 ft. lbs. for the Scrambler engine, which uses steel flywheels. The flywheels should run true to .001″ to .002″.

Note: If undue force is used in dealing with the flywheel and if the con rods become stiff to rotate, one or both shafts have moved inwards and are fouling the con rod.

Refitting the timing side bush (042239). Carefully line up and press in the bush then fit the locating pin to prevent the bush moving. A new bush is made to a 'spares size', but it should be reamed to .8755" to .8750" *in situ*. The inner side of the bush should be flush with the crankcase.

Refitting the drive side bearings. The dismantling instructions are reversed to refit these bearings. When a roller bearing, 012543, is used the crankcase should be 'peened' alongside the bearing sleeve in three equi-distant places to retain the bearing.

Replacing the small end bush. Make a draw bolt to pull out the old bush, if the engine is not in an assembled state. The same bolt can be used to press in the new bush. Ream to .7505" to .7500" when fitted.

Refitting the piston. The piston ring gap is already allowed for during the process of manufacture, if supplied by our spares department. If the engine is affected with heavy oil consumption, use a Duaflex ring, which will prevent oil reaching the combustion chamber. Fit the piston with the large cut-away in the crown facing the inlet valve. Use a rotary motion to insert the circlips, with round-nose pliers and ensure the circlip is correctly located. A piston ring clamp of the type shown in Fig. 38 is desirable, as the close proximity of the cylinder studs makes it somewhat difficult to refit the cylinder as previously described.

Fig. 38

Rocker box. For dismantling instructions see 'Heavyweight Single Cylinder Models'.

Assembling the crankcase. The flywheel assembly and 'build up' of the crankcase are dealt with in the following sequence:

Have ready the drive side bearings, release valve rotor, stator and shaft key. Heat the drive side crankcase, fit in the following order:

Fit bearing 012542.

Fit stator 043036 or 042220 and locate it with tube or bolt, tighten the tube to 10 ft. lbs.

Fit bearing ring for roller race, peen the crankcase in three places to retain the sleeve.

Fit centre member for roller race on flywheel shaft.

Fit key for rotor 041021.

Fit rotor 042219 with some oil on it.

Fit flywheels to drive side crankcase.

Apply Wellseal jointing compound to the full crankcase joint, then turn to the timing half crankcase, checking all oil passages for cleanliness and obstruction.

Take out the bolt 042046 for plug, for examination, verify the end is unbroken.

If the 'O' ring 042177 has to be renewed, push out the plug 042044 from the oil pump shaft aperture. The 'O' ring fits into the widest of the two grooves. Re-insert the plug chamfered end first and locate it properly with the pin 042046. Apply jointing compound to the entire crankcase joint and put the two crankcase halves together. Pass the seven crankcase bolts through the crankcase and tighten.

Fitting the crankcase plugs. The reservoir drain plug 042160 is fitted into the front hole with a fibre washer.

The magnetic filter 042201 uses a steel washer.

Fitting the oil pump plunger. If there is evidence of bad tooth marking the plunger should be replaced. Examine also the hardened guide pin 010079, a flat worn on the extreme end will curtail oil supply to the rocker box.

Put some clean oil on the oil pump plunger, insert it into the crankcase to a depth of $1\frac{11}{16}$" from the end of the plunger to the face for the washer 042178. Fit the screwed body (using the fingers only) with extreme care to locate the guide pin in the annular groove in the pump plunger. A spanner to tighten must not be used until it is certain that the guide pin is correctly located. Omission to observe these instructions can damage the pump gear beyond further use.

Fit the housing plug 042045 with its washer and firmly tighten.

To assemble timing gear. Follow dismantling instructions in reverse order.

Fitting gaskets. To avoid subsequent attention to the engine after dismantling all gaskets should be renewed during assembly.

Oil filters. The location and assembly of the crankcase oil filter is shown in Fig. 39. The fabric filter must be clean and undamaged to filter impurities in the oil during circulation. Make sure the cap 042062 at the end of the filter is positioned correctly. If the cap is canted this will restrict the oil returning to the reservoir.

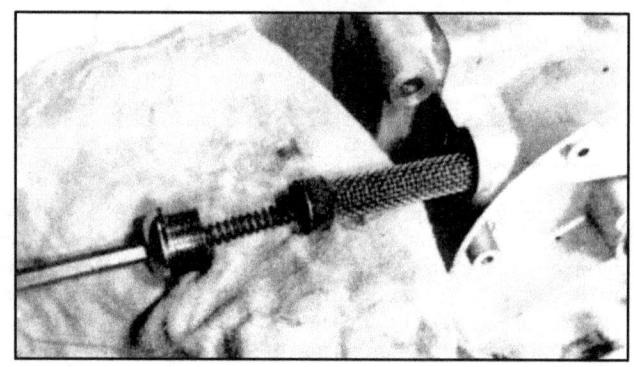

Fig. 39

Magnetic filter. This filter 042201 is fitted in the rear hole in the crankcase. Wipe the magnet with a greasy rag to remove adhesions and keep it clear of large metal objects when not in use.

250 cc. SCRAMBLER MODEL

The technical details given in previous chapters for the 250 cc. model apply also to this model. Engine parts that differ are as follows:

(1) Steel flywheels.
(2) Stronger valve springs.
(3) High compression piston.
(4) Larger diameter crankpin and con rod.
(5) Larger diameter exhaust valve stem ($\frac{11}{32}$").
(6) Differently machined centre line of crankcase to enable larger section rear tyre to be used, which affects chain line.
(7) High heat factor sparking plug.

The engine in its standard form develops approximately 21 b.h.p. at 7,200 to 7,500 r.p.m. It has been found by experiment that a maximum compression ratio of 10.5 to 1 is best suited for this engine.

Exhaust pipe. The best open pipe length is 41", measured on the inside bend.

Flywheel assembly conversion. The 1961 type flywheel assembly can be used on earlier models. As the connecting rod is larger dimensionally and to clear the flange on the timing side and drive side axle, modified shafts are also used. The new assembly comprises the following parts:

Flywheel bare timing side	… …	043026
,, bare drive side	… …	043027
,, axle timing side	… …	043023
,, axle drive side …	… …	043025
,, crankpin … …	… …	044020
Flywheel crankpin cage	… …	020232
,, con rod with liner	… …	043021
,, crankpin nuts (2)	… …	043022
,, crankpin washers (2)	… …	044070
,, crankpin rollers (28) …	… …	000075

If machining facilities are available the existing flywheels can be modified by enlarging the crankpin orifice in each flywheel to .878" to .877". After machining, restore the keyway depth to dimension shown in Fig. 40. The alteration to the flywheel shaft for clearance with the new con rod is shown in Fig. 40.

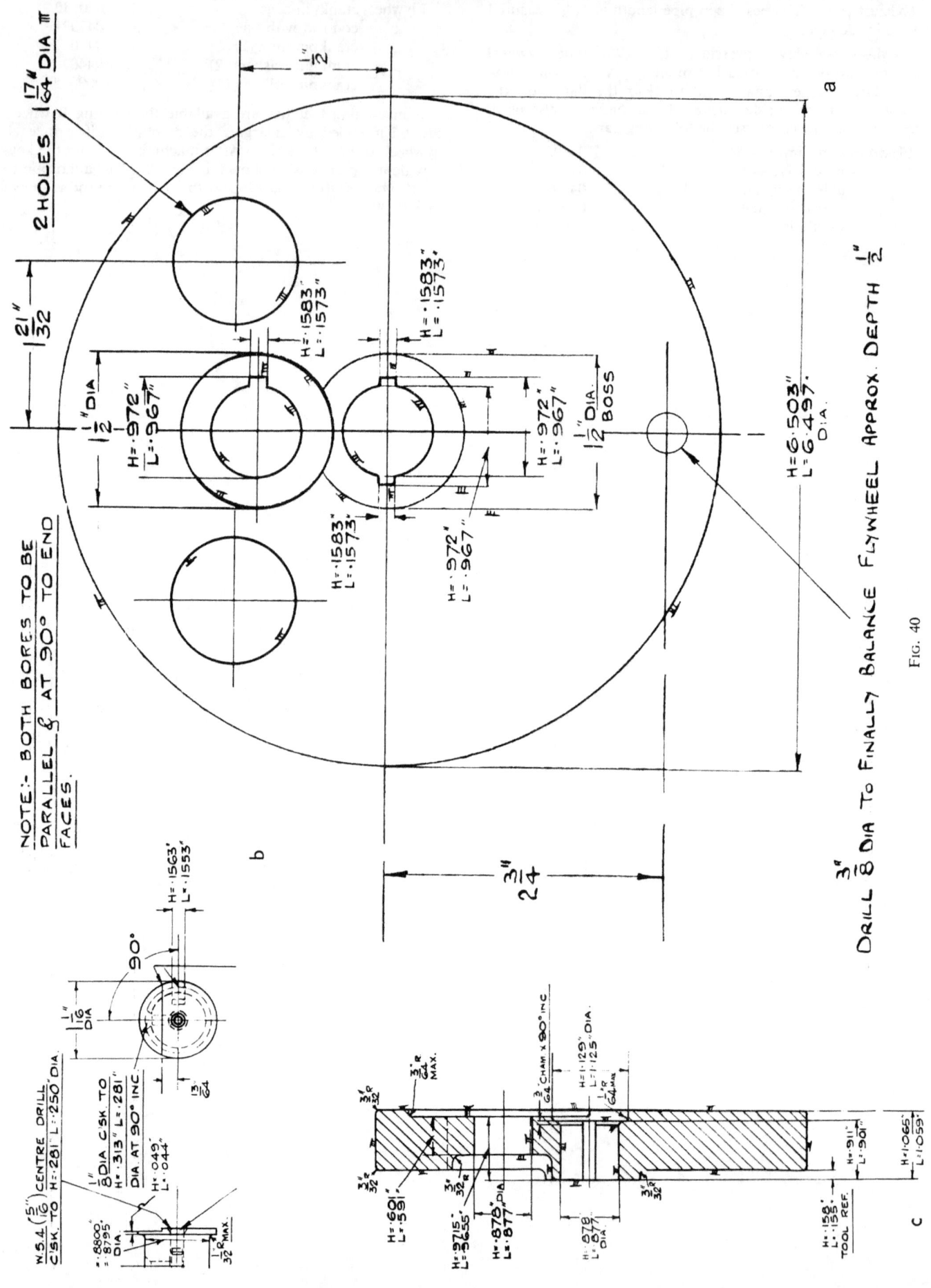

Fig. 40

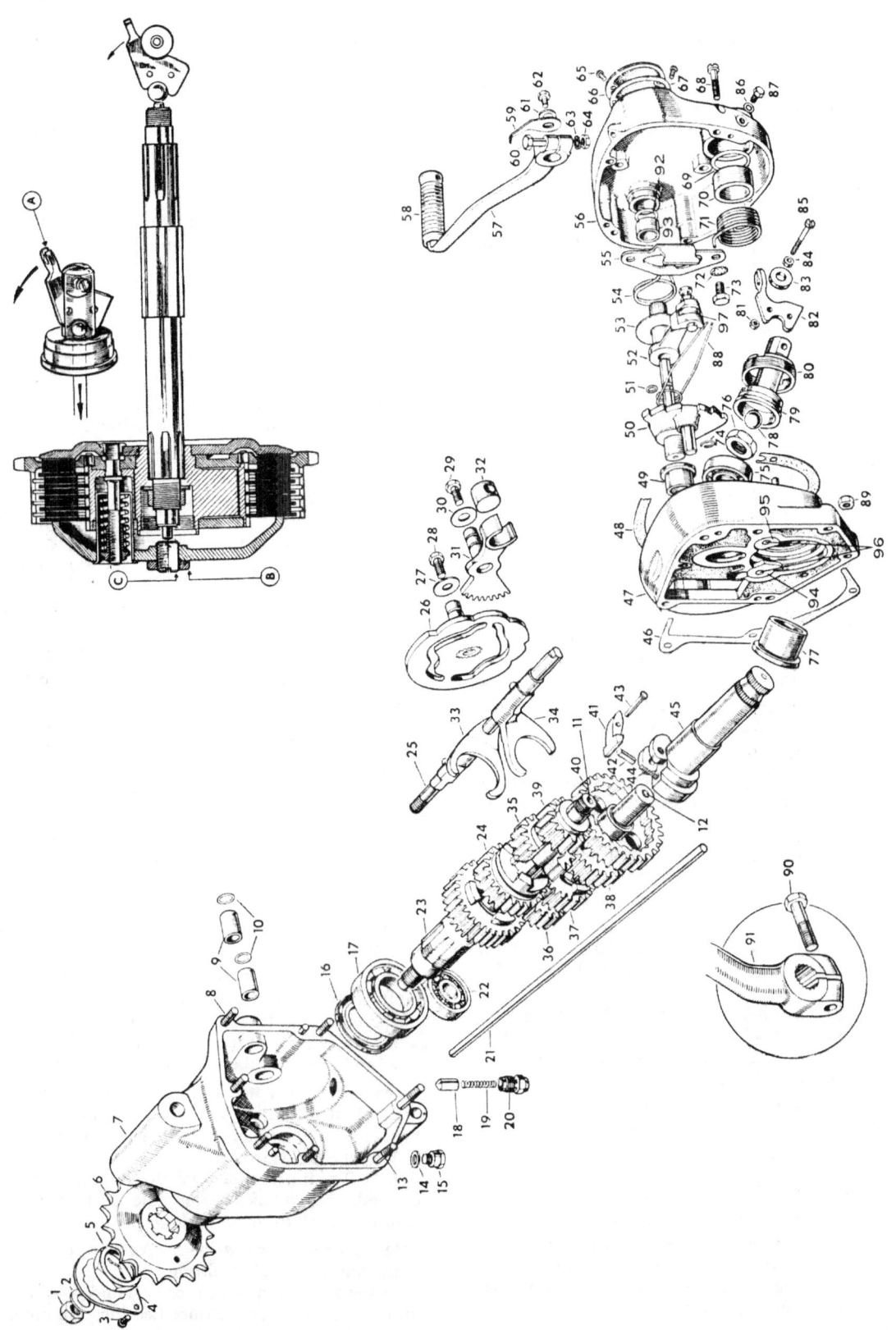

Fig. 41

THE GEAR BOX: HEAVYWEIGHT MODELS

Gear box faults. If difficulty in changing gear from top to third and where it has been ascertained that the clutch is not dragging, the fault can be rectified by attention to the gear change stop plate (55). Take out the plate bolts (73), disconnect the pawl spring. Draw out the two plate holes by elongation to the extent of $\frac{1}{32}$" to enable the plate to go upwards towards the top of the case. The plate must be retained in this position whilst retightening the two bolts. Should the fault occur when changing into a higher gear, elongate the holes in the opposite direction to the same amount, so that the plate can be moved downwards.

To summarise, if the fault is in changing *down* move the plate *upwards*, conversely if the fault is when changing *up*, move the plate *down*.

If gear selection is generally uncertain, first verify the location of the pawl spring (88). If this spring is distorted or fitted upside down, gear selection will be uncertain. The correct position is with the straight leg of the spring uppermost.

Oil leaks from kickstarter axle. Check oil content by removing level plug (87), normal content one pint, or 20 fluid ozs., if normal. Renew the 'O' ring (69) see details 'removing bushes'.

Wear on kickstarter pawl (41). Usually due to a weak kickstarter return spring, causing the crank to depress by inertia over bumpy road surfaces. If the crank is too far away from the vertical position the inertia will increase.

Position the crank approximately 20° left of the vertical position.

Damaged kickstarter stop plate (94). Can only be due to violent backfire causing excessive ignition advance, or too much throttle when starting. Drill the rivet head to remove swaging and push out the pin.

Kickstarter spring disengages. This is due to the end of the spring taking 'a set' where it is located in the cover. Usually it is preferable to fit a new spring.

Gear box noises. First check oil content. After considerable mileage check layshaft bearing for wear, also layshaft fixed gear pinion (36).

Removing the kickstarter axle (45). Lever out the kickstarter return spring from its anchorage in the cover, the opposite end of the spring will come out easily, then pull out the axle.

To replace kickstarter assembly. Fit kickstarter axle, with pawl assembled in cover, turn the axle so that the hole in it for the return spring is at 12 o'clock.

Fit return spring on the axle, insert the end of the spring, which is turned down vertically into the hole drilled in axle. Using tool recommended for spring removal, hooked in opposite end of spring, pull the spring sufficiently to enable the turned in end to enter hole drilled in the cover.

Replace inner and outer cover as detailed previously.

HEAVYWEIGHT MODELS

Dismantling the gear box. (Figures in parenthesis apply to Fig. 41.) If the gear box is to be completely dismantled, first remove the clutch as detailed for 'removing engine from frame', including the rear portion of the front chain case. Have available a new set of gaskets.

Removing the outer cover (56). Remove drain plug (15), catch oil as it drains.

Remove inspection cap (66) and disconnect clutch cable inner wire.

Remove bolt for indicator (62) leave pedal in position.

Remove kickstarter crank bolt (90) and take off the crank.

Remove five cheese-headed screws securing cover (68).

Remove cover by pulling on the gear change pedal.

Removing the inner cover (47). Remove ratchet plate and spindle (5).

Remove clutch operating arm and roller (82).

Remove lock ring (80), take away the body and ball.

Remove mainshaft nut (74).

Remove seven nuts (89) securing the cover.

Remove cover by tapping the rear portion until it is clear of the dowels.

Removing gear box internals. Remove low gear on mainshaft (39).

Remove striker fork (25) by unscrewing.

Remove striker forks (33 and 34).

Remove clutch push rod.

Remove mainshaft (11) with the gears on it.

Remove layshaft and gears; it may be necessary to rock the shaft sideways to extract from bearing.

Removing the cam plate (26). Remove the dome nut (20) and take out the spring and plunger.

Remove two bolts (28 and 29) over the plunger housing.

Remove the cam plate and quadrant.

Removing the sleeve gear (23). Remove screw fixing lock plate (4).

Remove sleeve gear sprocket nut (5), which has a *left-hand* thread.

Use a good fitting ring spanner across the flats and refer to method of removing this type of sprocket nut described for Lightweight gear box.

Remove sleeve gear sprocket which is splined; also distance piece.

Remove sleeve gear by tapping it through the bearing (17).

Removing sleeve gear bushes. Two thin bushes of the oilite type are used as a bearing for the mainshaft.

Note the location of these bushes *in situ*, before they are pressed out. As the material is somewhat brittle, exercise extreme care in pressing in the new bushes.

The internal diameter of both bushes *in situ* is .81325" to .81200".

Removing sleeve gear bearing (17). Remove by prising out the oil seal (16) and sleeve for seal.

Remove bearing after first heating shell and drift out.

Alternatively drop the shell face downwards on a clean bench, when this bearing, also the layshaft bearing (22), will drop out.

Removing the bearings. Pre-heat the inner cover and press out from inside the case the mainshaft bearing (77).

If desired the kickstarter axle bush can be extracted at the same time. To do this, firmly support the inside face of the cover and press out the bush from *outside* the cover.

Removing the footchange spindle bush (99). This is fitted into a blind aperture. Pre-heat the case and screw in a coarse threaded tap to extract. Use the same method to remove the bush in the kickstarter axle.

Note: The footchange bush does not require reaming when renewed. If the kickstarter axle bush 040146 is renewed, ream to .6875" to .6865" *in situ*.

Re-assembling the gear box. *Note:* Apply some clean oil to all moving parts before fitting.

Fit the sleeve gear ball race (17) and layshaft bearing (22), pre-heat the shell and ensure bearings are entered squarely; apply a little clean oil.

Fit sleeve gear through bearing, and oil the sleeve or distance piece for oil seal.

Fit sleeve gear sprocket and firmly tighten left-hand sprocket nut.

Fit lock plate and screw.

Refitting the cam plate (26). The cam plate must be correctly positioned on assembly, otherwise the four gears will not be indexed properly.

(1) Fit the quadrant (31) also its bolt and washer.
(2) Raise the lever portion of the quadrant, with the radius of the lever in line with the top right hand cover stud (top gear).
(3) Insert the cam plate so that the first two teeth of the quadrant can be seen through the slot in the cam plate, then fit the bolt and washer (27).

FIG. 42
Fitting Internals

Fitting the internals:

(1) Insert the mainshaft and fit to it the third gear (24).
(2) Fit the second gear (35) with the striker fork (33) in the pinion groove, then insert the projection of the striker into the groove in the cam plate.
(3) Fit the first gear (39).
   Assemble the layshaft by:
(4) Fitting the fixed gear (36), third gear (37) and second gear (38) with the striker fork (34) in the slot for second gear.
(5) Insert the projection of striker fork into cam plate slot, with layshaft in the bush.
(6) Line up the two holes in the striker forks and pass through the spindle (25) and firmly tighten.
7) Fit the first gear (40).

To complete the assembly. Insert the roller (32) into the quadrant in position to receive the spindle for the footchange. Examine the gasket (46) for blemish, locate it and refit the inner cover. Before finally tightening the clutch body lock ring (80) verify the operating lever (82) is in line with the clutch cable entry, to ensure a straight pull on the inner wire. Do not use force, if the cover does not go home easily, take it off and find out why. Check the position of the pawl spring (88) and refit the outer cover. Refill one pint of SAE 50 oil.

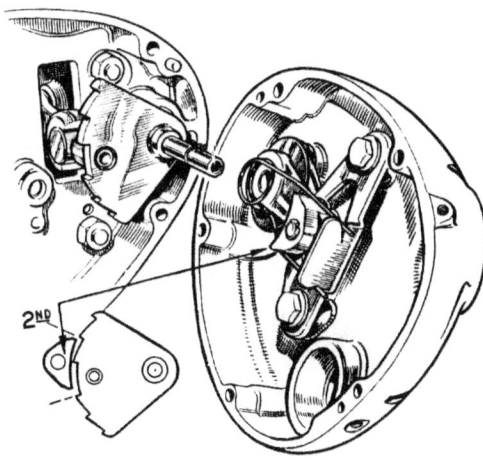

FIG. 43

Replacing the footchange pedal spring. With the outer cover removed, take out the quadrant (50) and the pawl spring behind it. Tap out the footchange sleeve (52) and its washer (53). Remove two bolts (73) and lift away the plate.

The position of the pedal spring assembled is shown in Fig. 44.

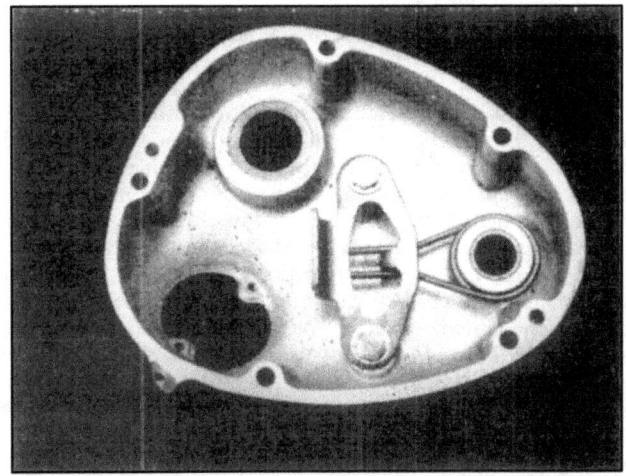

FIG. 44

THE CLUTCH

Three types of clutches have been used since 1957. The original design had loose friction inserts in the clutch sprocket, also in the friction plates. This type of clutch was used on all Heavyweight Models up to 1959, with the exception of the CSR Models, which were equipped with the bonded type clutch.

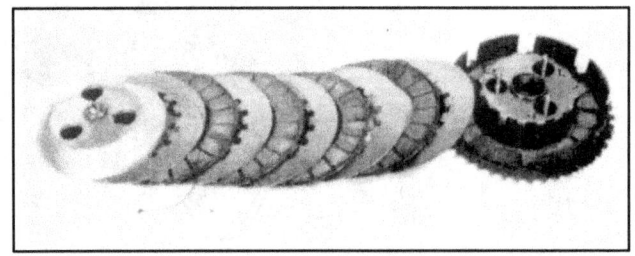

FIG. 45
Early Type Clutch

All 1960-61 Models use bonded type clutches.

For the 1962 season a heavy duty five-plate type clutch was introduced for 650 cc. CSR Models, which can be used on any earlier model.

FIG. 46
1962 Type Clutch

The early type clutch can be converted by using the following components:

1 Back plate 040584.
1 Clutch sprocket 040359.
4 Steel plates, plain 043191.
4 Friction plates 043192.
1 Friction plate 043193.

Clutch slip. The clutch operating mechanism is shown in Fig. 41. To enable the clutch to function satisfactorily it is essential to have clearance between the clutch push rod and the thrust stud (C). The fact that there is play, or lost motion, at the handlebar lever end does not guarantee there is clearance between the push rod and thrust stud.

To obtain the correct adjustment run down, as far as possible, the clutch cable adjuster. Remove the chain case cap for the clutch. Release the nut (B) using a screwdriver screw in the thrust stud until it just touches the clutch push rod.

Unscrew the thrust stud half a turn then retighten the lock nut with care to avoid the stud moving during this process. Now reset the cable adjustment by unscrewing the adjuster, leaving $\frac{1}{8}''$ to $\frac{3}{16}''$ free movement between the outer cable and the adjuster.

If the fault prevails, take down the clutch and check the steel plates for buckle. Put all these plates together and hold up to the light, which will indicate if one or more of the plates are buckled, which reduces the friction area.

New type steel plates are 'dimpled' to prevent buckling. Replace buckled plates with the new type.

An excess of oil in the front chaincase will adversely affect the clutch. Friction plates so affected should be de-greased as they are usually serviceable. Avoid the use of petrol or paraffin and use trichloroephylene. Alternatively, copiously dust the inserts with Fullers Earth to absorb the oil.

Check also the clutch spring cups, which may be fouling the holes in the alloy pressure plate, preventing the spring from exerting maximum pressure. Apply a little grease to the cups before refitting.

Clutch springs. If the clutch has been slipping for any length of time, the heat generated is calculated to weaken the springs, which should be renewed. The correct free length is $1\frac{25}{32}''$. The five plate clutch spring free length is $1\frac{11}{16}''$. Discard springs which have collapsed to the extent of $\frac{3}{16}''$.

Clutch spring adjusting screws. If there is a tendency for the springs adjusting screws to become unscrewed, take out the spring, lift up the end of the spring with a pen-knife and file the end of the spring to give a square abutment of $\frac{1}{8}''$ or get rid of the feathered end. The abutment will then come up against the indentation at the back of the adjuster and prevent it unscrewing. The correct location of the adjusting screws is with the head of the spring stud just flush with the face of the adjusting screw.

If the machine is a combination and heavy loads are carried, and the early type clutch is used, convert the clutch to the bonded type as already described.

Clutch drag. This is due to torque on the gear box mainshaft and creates noisy gear engagement. The cause is due to the clutch plates not separating when the clutch is operated. The fault may be due to:

(1) Excessive play in the operating mechanism (see clutch slip).
(2) Uneven adjustment of the clutch springs.
(3) The steel plates are buckled.
(4) The clutch plates are gummy.

In the case of (2), take off outer portion of chaincase, operate the clutch lever and note if the outside plate is withdrawn parallel with the plate behind it. If the gap between the two plates is uneven, manipulate the spring adjuster until the gap is equal and evenly between the two plates, with a preference for screwing in the adjuster to balance.

In the event of (4), treat the clutch plates as recommended for clutch slip to get rid of the gumminess.

Needless to say, continual use with clutch drag can cause damage to the gear box pinions.

Clutch nut works loose. If the mainshaft nut securing the clutch to the mainshaft works loose, this is due to damage to

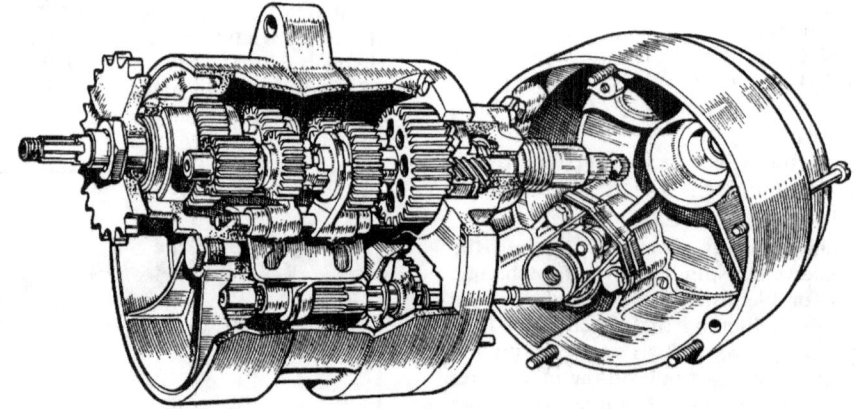

FIG. 47
Gearbox with End Cover Removed.

the splines in clutch centre for the shock absorber 040354. To remedy, replace the centre and avoid over-tightening the mainshaft nut.

Clutch shock absorber. Refer to details given for the Lightweight clutch.

To remove a clutch control cable. Remove the oil filler cap from the kickstarter case cover.

Screw right home the clutch cable adjuster that is located in the top of the kickstarter case cover.

Disengage, from the operating lever, the clutch cable inner wire by operating through the oil filler cap opening.

Completely unscrew the clutch cable adjuster.

Disengage, from the handlebar operating control lever, the clutch inner wire.

Pull cable, by its lower end, till removed from the machine, easing it through the frame cable clips while doing so.

250 cc. and 350 cc. LIGHTWEIGHT MODELS

The gear box. It will be seen in Fig. 47 that the gear box internals are situated above the centre line of the gear box shell. It is for this reason at least three pints of engine oil must be filled and maintained for satisfactory lubrication.

Possible gear box faults

Top gear disengages. This is most likely to occur on early type gear boxes before 7988 (250 cc.) and 2300 (350 cc.).

To rectify, discard the sleeve gear 041273 and sliding gear 041276 as shown in Fig. 28. Replace the sleeve gear with modified type 044075, also sliding gear 044076, which use undercut dogs for positive engagement. Should the fault develop on a later type gear box, the plunger 042835 may be damaged on the extreme end, or the spring for plunger 040045 is weak allowing the gear to disengage. Both gears must be changed to convert.

Third gear only disengages. The only remedy is to renew the two third gear pinions 041276 and 041277. Usually this is due to bad gear changing and possibly clutch drag.

Bottom gear only disengages. This can only be due to end play between the first gear pinion and kickstarter bush.

To remedy, use a shim washer .020" thick placed over the layshaft between the pinion and kickstarter bush.

Difficulty in selecting the gears. Usually due to a distorted pawl spring 041327 preventing the pawl from rocking.

Gear pedal does not centralise. The footchange pedal spring is broken. Replace with improved cross over type 043453. Separate the legs as shown in Fig. 48 when fitting.

First gear modification. In gear boxes made before number G8603 (250 cc. Model) and M2701 (350 cc. Model) a plain layshaft first gear 041291 was used. This is superseded by a bushed pinion 044080. The new first gear can be used with the existing second gear pinion.

Wear on kickstarter axle bush. Only likely to occur on early models with gear box numbers before G6014. This can happen if the kickstarter return spring 040043 is overwound, which tends to pre-load the kickstarter bush against the first gear pinion. Gear boxes after the above number are fitted with a circlip 042900 encircling the kickstarter axle 042130 with a thrust washer 042901 to prevent pre-loading also wear on the axle bush. The new parts can be fitted to earlier type gear boxes.

Oil leaks. Two metal discs or core plugs are used to seal the aperture for the layshaft and quadrant spindle. These discs are a press fit in the gear box shell.

To rectify an oil leak from this part of the gear box it is necessary to take away the primary drive and rear portion of the front chaincase as described in removing the engine. Take out the gear box internals to drive out the discs and use replacements. Clean all traces of oil from the two apertures, apply jointing compound and tap the new discs into position. Allow plenty of time for the jointing compound to set before refilling gear box with oil.

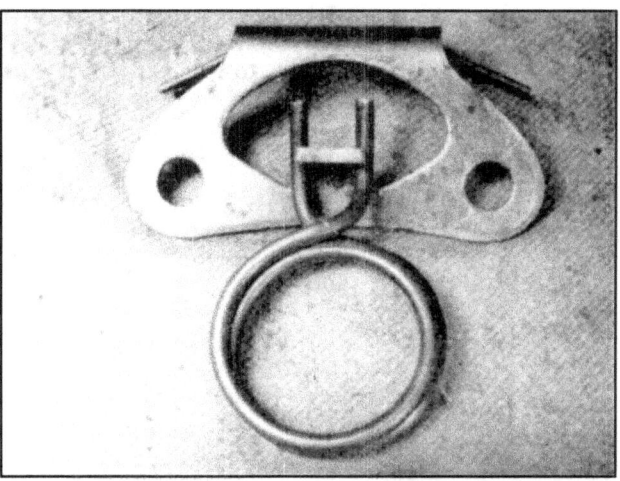

FIG. 48

Oil leaks from end covers. Can only be due to a broken or deformed gasket. Stick the gasket with jointing compound to the gear box shell before refitting the cover.

Dismantling the gear box. (All nuts are right-hand, except rear chain sprocket nut 041271). With the gear box in the frame and clutch removed:

Remove exhaust pipe and silencer in one piece.
Remove right side footrest arm.
Remove gear indicator bolt 040137.
Remove gear change pedal, by releasing the pinch bolt.
Remove kickstarter crank bolt and nut, pull off the crank.
Remove four screws securing the fairing and take it away.

FIG. 49

Gear box end cover.

Take out the gear box drain plug, catch oil in a suitable receptable.

Remove ratchet nut 041340 and ratchet 041283.

Remove six screws securing end cover, take off cover then remove ratchet and nut. The ratchet cannot be removed without taking off the cover. See Fig. 49.

Gear box inner cover. Remove clutch inner cable from lever.

Remove, by unscrewing clutch body lock ring 041280, use a soft drift and hammer.

Remove clutch operating body 042141 (watch for $\frac{3}{8}''$ ball inside).

Remove mainshaft nut 041265.

Remove ratchet nut 041340 and washer.

The cover can now be removed exposing internals as shown in Fig. 53.

Fig. 50

Removing gear box internals. Remove footchange quadrant 041334 with spindle assembled.

Remove, by unscrewing selector fork shaft 041345 (use a spanner on the two flats).

Remove gear cluster with mainshaft, layshaft and two striker forks.

See Fig. 54 for sequence of gear assembly.

The plunger 042835 together with its spring 040045 will remain in the gear box shell.

Removing sleeve gear and sprocket. Remove the rear chain.

The sleeve gear sprocket nut 041271 has a *left-hand* thread.

As the sprocket on the sleeve gear is subjected to reversal by accelerating and decelerating the sprocket nut must be positively tight. In consequence the sprocket 041269 must be firmly held during the process of unscrewing, or tightening the nut. A chain bar (easy to fabricate) in use is shown in Fig 52. Use a short length of $\frac{1}{2}'' \times .305''$ chain attached to a bar of suitable length, which is the best medium of holding the sprocket.

Turn back or flatten the tab washer between the nut and sprocket. Use a well fitting ring spanner $1\frac{1}{2}''$ across the flats to release the nut.

Removing the sleeve gear. With the sprocket removed, press or gently tap the gear into the gear box shell.

Removing sleeve gear bearing. Prise out the oil seal, note the way it is fitted. Use a suitable drift to drive out the roller bearing. The distance piece 041391 will remain in gear box shell.

Fig. 51

Remove bearings from gear box shell. Push out the two metal caps 041394/5 then drift out the layshaft bush 041289 and bush for footchange spindle 041307.

It is most unlikely that the spindle bush will be affected by wear.

Note: The roller bearings for the sleeve gear are self-aligning and can be waggled about when unsupported by the mainshaft. This can give an erroneous impression that the bearing is badly worn.

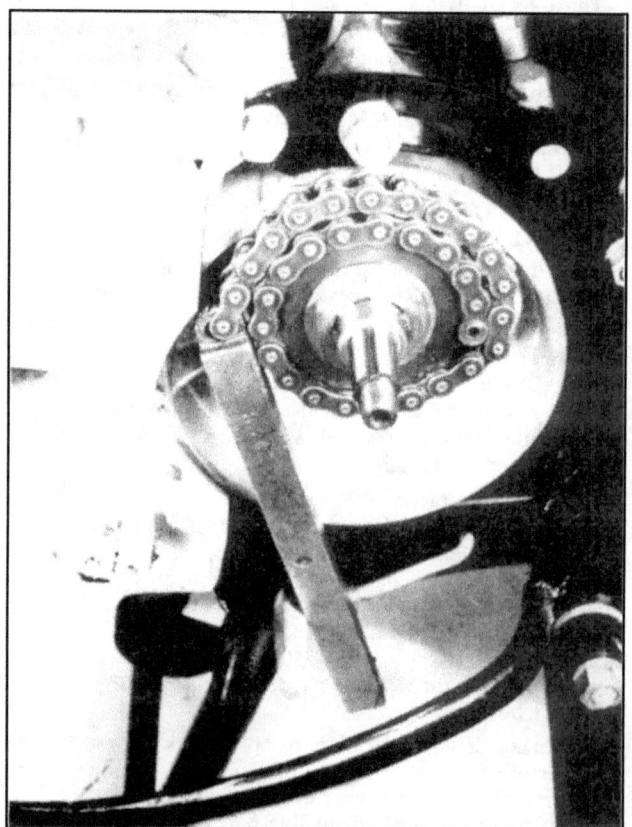

Fig. 52

Removing bearing from inner cover. Support firmly the cover and press out the bush 041299. The kickstarter axle bush 041298 goes into a blind hole. Screw a coarse thread tap into the bush, and pull out the bush.

There is a peg to locate the clutch body 042141, watch this, when using a drift to extract the ball bearing 012545 for the mainshaft.

Two oilite bushes 042145 are used for footchange spindle. Carefully note their location before driving out. An 'O' ring 040006 is used between the outer bush and the cover, which should be discarded before fitting new bushes.

Removing sleeve gear bushes. Support the gear in a vice (note the location of the two bushes), then drift out.

Refitting the bearings. The oilite bushes in the outer cover are made to size and do not require reaming.

Ream the layshaft bush in gear box .6260" to .6255".

Refitting sleeve gear bushes. These two bushes are thin and somewhat brittle. Oil the outside diameter of each bush, insert them squarely in the gear and gently press into position.

Ream both bushes .689" to .688" *in situ*.

Refitting the sleeve gear sprocket. The flat side of the sprocket should face outwards (away from the gear box) see instructions on removing sprocket nut.

Refitting the oil seal. The metal backing faces outwards. Gently and squarely tap the oil seal into position.

Assembling the gear box internals. The assembly sequence of the various pinions are clearly illustrated. Ensure the plunger and spring are in position in the gear box shell.

Fig. 53

Fig. 54

For clarity, assemble in the following order:
(1) Fit footchange spindle and quadrant.
(2) Take up the mainshaft fit first, second and third gear, enter shaft through sleeve gear.
(3) Fit mainshaft selector fork and locate it in quadrant.
(4) Take up layshaft fit second and third gear, enter shaft in bush.
(5) Fit layshaft selector fork and locate.
(6) Pass selector fork shaft through both selectors and screw home.
(7) Fit low gear pinion.

Precautions during assembly of gear box.
(1) Make sure the selector forks 041341/3 are correctly indexed.
(2) If the end cover does not go back properly, do not use force, take off the cover and find out what is wrong.
(3) Make sure all gaskets are undamaged, stick them on to the gear box and covers some time before they are refitted.
(4) Make sure the small peg inside the ball race housing has not fallen out. This locates the clutch operating body.
(5) Insert the pin 042143 for clutch body from the *top* end. If this pin is a loose fit, give the top end a few light blows with a hammer to deform it and make it fit tight.
(6) Put a little clean oil on *all* moving parts.

DO NOT OMIT TO FILL THREE PINTS (1.8 LITRES) OF SAE 50 OIL.

The kickstarter axle. Should it be necessary to dismantle the kickstarter, take off the gear box end cover as described elsewhere. The ratchet pinion 041300 is in tension by the ratchet spring 041358. To relieve this tension temporarily, fit the kickstarter crank, and depress it which will release the pinion and enable it to be taken away.

Remove the circlip encircling the shaft, should one be fitted, prise out the end of the return spring 040045, the shaft can now be extracted.

250 cc. CSR MODEL

Gear box section. The actual gear ratios are detailed in the table of gear ratios.

Clutch. This is identical to the assembly fitted to the Lightweight 350 cc. Model.

LIGHTWEIGHT GEAR BOX
THE CLUTCH

Dismantling the clutch. Remove the drain plug with a tray underneath to catch the oil.

Remove three clutch adjusting screws 040389. Take out the springs and spring cups.

Remove clutch plates and note the order in which they are fitted.

Remove clutch body from mainshaft using a box key measuring $\frac{23}{32}''$ across the flats for shaft nut.

Use the clutch plate tool shown in Fig. 51, to hold the clutch with top gear engaged. Alternatively, apply pressure on the rear brake pedal.

If the clutch is difficult to remove, use extractor tool, Fig. 34.

The clutch friction segments are bonded to the plate and are not detachable. When new, the segments protrude $\frac{3}{64}''$.

Check the plain steel plates for buckle by placing them together when, if held against light, any distortion can readily be seen. The plain plates on late type clutches are 'dimpled' to prevent buckling.

Check the clutch springs for free length which should be $1\frac{3}{4}''$.

Refitting clutch plates. The clutch plates are fitted in the following order:

250 cc. Model	250 cc. Scrambler	350 cc. Model
1 Thick steel back plate chamfer inwards	1 Thick back plate	1 Thick back plate*
2 Plain steel plate	2 plain steel plate	2 Friction plate (double sided)
3 Friction plate (double sided)	3 Friction plate (double sided)	3 Plain steel plate
4 Plain steel plate	4 Plain steel plate	4 Friction plate (double sided)
5 Friction plate (double sided)	5 Friction plate (double sided)	5 Plain steel plate
6 Plain steel plate	6 Plain steel plate	6 Friction plate (double sided)
7 Friction plate (single sided)	7 Friction plate (double sided)	7 Plain steel plate
	8 Plain steel plate	8 Friction plate (double sided)
	9 Friction plate (single sided)	9 Plain steel plate

*(Recess for back plate inwards).

Fig. 55

Dismantling the clutch shock absorber. With the clutch removed, take out the three countersunk screws, prise out the cover plate 043187.

Use an old gear box mainshaft held in a vice and put the clutch body on the shaft. Use the tool shown in Fig. 56; then compress the large rubbers, by leverage, use a pointed spoke to pick out the thin rubbers. The thick ones will come out without difficulty.

Use the same method if the gear box is still in the frame, with top gear engaged and pressure on the brake pedal. Very firmly tighten the plate screws and centre pop between the screw head and the plate.

Fig. 56

The clutch bearing. The bearing race plate 043196 is shown in Fig. 28, alongside the bearing cage and rollers. With the clutch removed, remove the three stud nuts 040356, take off the plate 043195. The clutch sprocket can be lifted to expose the rollers and roller cage. It will be observed that the closed end of the roller race faces the plate 043195.

To remove clutch control cable. Remove the oil filler cap from the kickstarter case cover.

Screw right home the clutch cable adjuster (adjacent to the handlebar lever).

Disengage, from the operating lever, the clutch cable inner wire by operating through the oil filler cap opening.

Disengage, from the handlebar operating control lever, the clutch inner wire.

Pull cable, by its lower end, till removed from the machine, easing it through the frame cable clips while doing so.

Clutch spring adjustment. In the event of clutch slip, first ascertain that the operating mechanism is correctly adjusted (see 'Clutch adjustment').

After dismantling the clutch, when refitting the clutch spring adjusting nuts, they should be screwed on until the spring stud just protrudes through the bottom of the recess in the adjuster nut.

Clutch adjustment. Attention to the clutch is usually confined to adjustment of the operating mechanism. To avoid clutch slip or clutch drag, it is essential to have $\frac{3}{16}$" free movement between the clutch outer casing and the clutch cable adjuster. Without such movement the operating mechanism will be pre-loaded causing wear on the operating parts, also clutch slip. Conversely, excessive movement in the clutch cable will prevent separation of the friction plates and cause the clutch to drag, thus making the gear selection difficult.

As the clutch inserts tend to settle down, this has the effect of lengthening the clutch push rod, as the width of the friction inserts are slightly reduced. To deal with clutch drag, or clutch slip, first unscrew the clutch cable adjuster lock nut which is located at the handlebar end, run down the adjuster as far as it will go. Remove the clutch inspection cap, unscrew one or two turns the adjuster lock nut 040376, shown in Fig. 28.

With a screwdriver, screw in the adjuster until contact with the push rod can be felt, unscrew the adjuster exactly half a turn and retighten the lock nut, taking care the adjuster does not move. Complete the adjustment by unscrewing the clutch cable adjuster until there is $\frac{3}{16}$" movement between the outer casing and the adjuster, tighten the lock nut. Replace the inspection cap.

Clutch slip should be dealt with promptly otherwise the friction plates will be damaged and the clutch springs affected by heat. The normal free length of the clutch springs is $1\frac{3}{4}$", the clutch push rod length is 10".

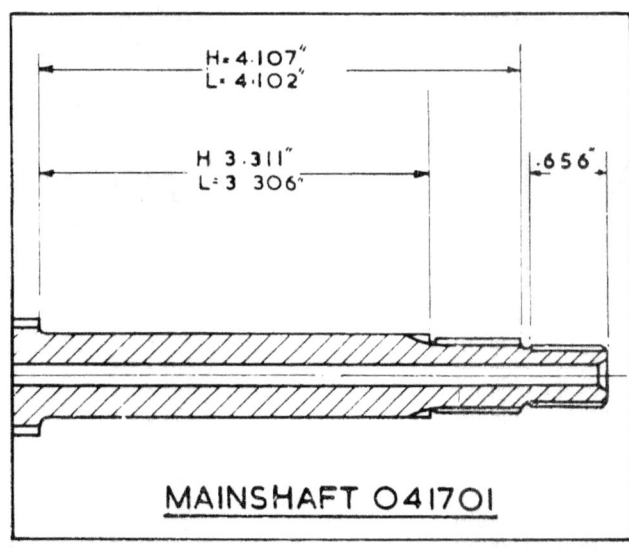

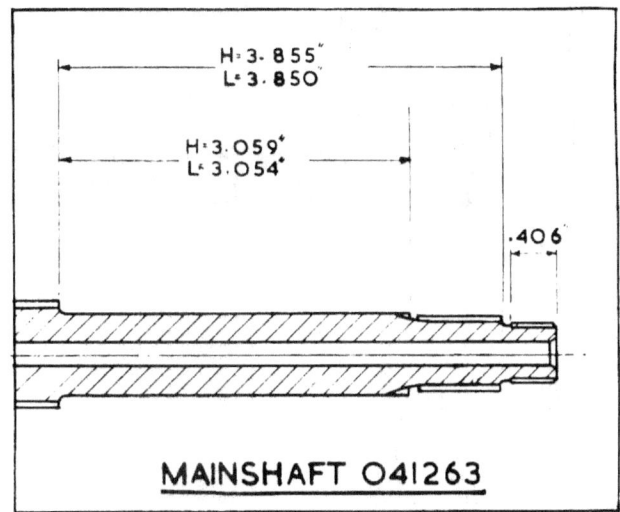

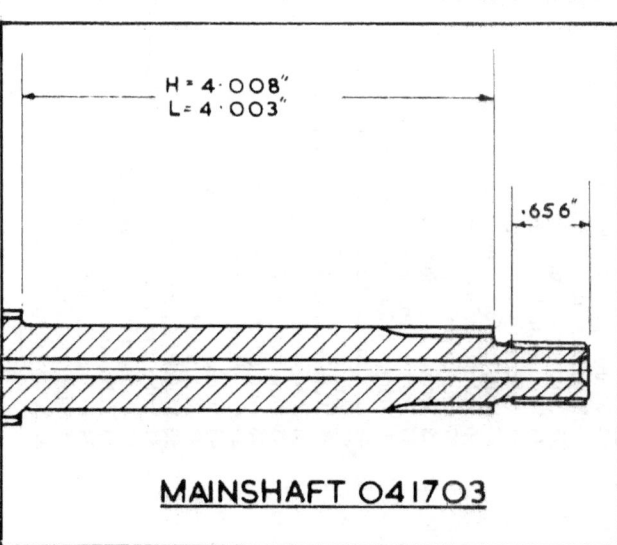

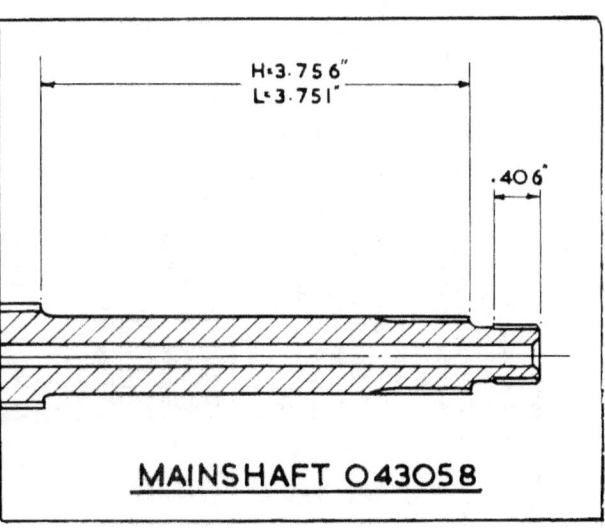

Fig. 57

Fig. 58

FIG. 59
Exploded View of Teledraulic Forks.

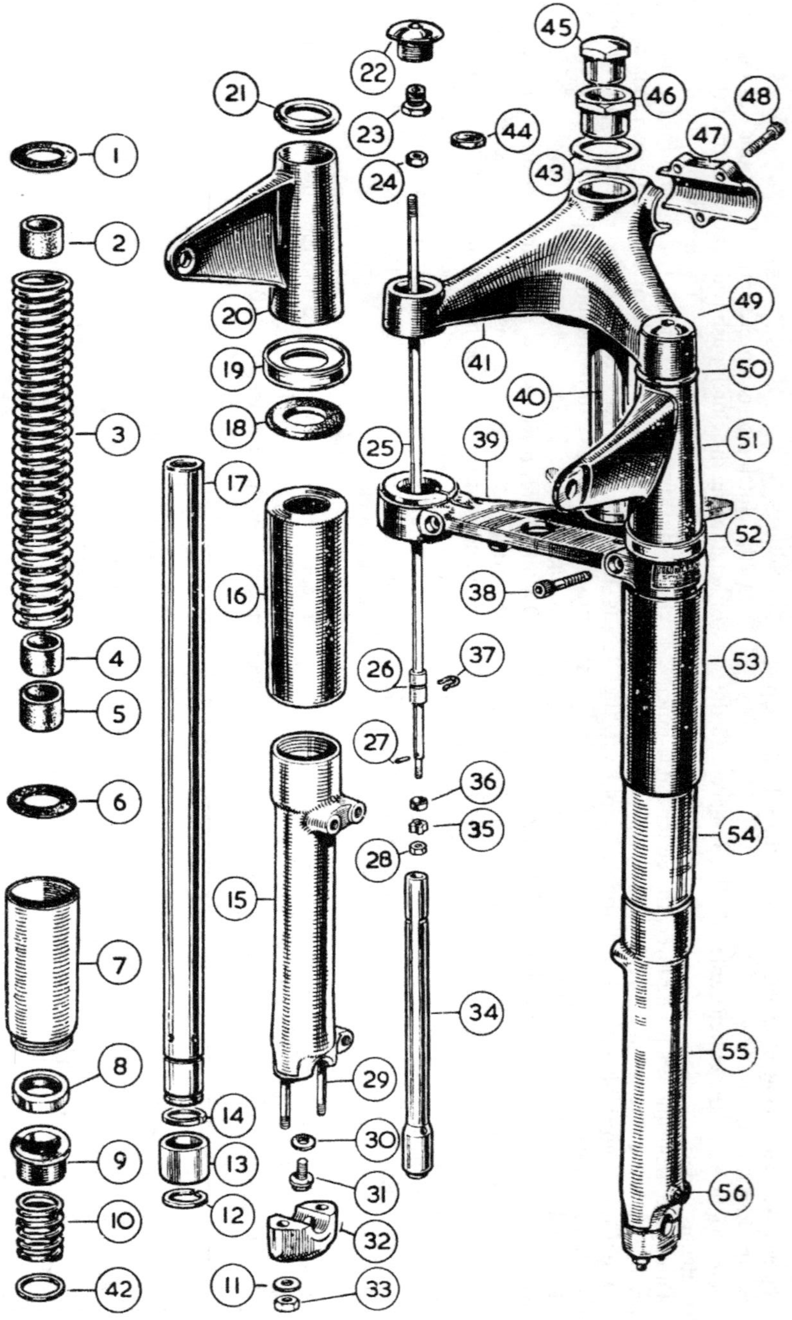

Ref. No. Description.
1 Washer, leather, for fork spring top seating.
2 Buffer, rubber, for fork inner tube.
3 Spring, main, for front fork.
4 Buffer, rubber, for fork inner tube.
5 Buffer, rubber, for fork spring bottom seating.
6 Washer, leather, for fork spring bottom seating.
7 Extension for fork slider.
8 Oil seal, for fork inner tube.
9 Bush, top, plastic, for inner tube.
10 Spring, buffer, for front fork.
11 Washer, plain, for fork slider cap securing stud.
12 Circlip, locating fork inner tube bottom bush.
13 Bush, bottom, steel, for fork inner tube.
14 Circlip, locating, fork inner tube bottom bush.
15 Slider, for fork, with studs (right side)
16 Tube, fork cover, bottom.
17 Tube, fork, inner.
18 Rubber ring for top cover tube housing ring.
19 Housing ring, top cover tube.
20 Tube, fork cover, top, right, with lamp lug.
21 Spigot ring top cover tube.
22 Bolt, top, for fork inner tube.
23 Adaptor.
24 Nut, lock, for top end of damper rod.
25 Rod, for fork damper.
26 Sleeve, plunger, on fork damper rod.
27 Pin, stop, for fork damper valve.
28 Nut, lock, for damper valve seat.
29 Stud, securing cap to fork slider
30 Washer, fibre, for damper tube bolt.
31 Bolt, fixing damper tube to slider.
32 Cap, for fork slider.
33 Nut, for fork slider cap securing stud.
34 Tube, for fork damper.
35 Seat, for fork damper valve.
36 Valve, for fork damper.
37 Clip retaining damper rod sleeve.
38 Screw, pinch, for fork crown.
39 Fork crown, not sold separately.
40 Stem, for fork crown, not sold separately.
41 Lug, for handlebar and steering head.
42 Collar for buffer spring.
43 Washer for fork stem adjusting nut.
44 Ring, rubber, sealing, for inner tube top bolt.
45 Nut, lock, for fork stem.
46 Nut, adjusting, for fork stem.
47 Clip (half only), for handlebar lug.
48 Screw, pinch, for handlebar clip.
49 Bolt, top, for fork inner tube.
50 Spigot ring top cover tube.
51 Tube, fork cover, top, left, with lamp lug.
52 Housing ring top cover tube.
53 Tube, fork cover, bottom.
54 Extension, for fork slider.
55 Slider, for fork with studs (left side).
56 Screw, plug, with fibre washer, for fork slider oil drain hole.

N.B.: Washer (43) deleted from assembly.

LIGHTWEIGHT GEAR BOX MAINSHAFTS

350 cc. Lightweight. Mainshaft 041701 was fitted to gear boxes with numbers from zero to 3757.

An improved type mainshaft 041703 was first used in gear boxes 3758 and onwards.

250 cc. Lightweight. Mainshaft 041263 is used on gear boxes from zero to 9974, also to gear boxes between numbers 10064 to 10128 as a temporary measure.

A modified shaft type 043058 is used in gear boxes with numbers 9975 to 10063 inclusive, which is now the current type.

The dimensions affecting the various mainshafts are given in Figs. 57-58, the drawings are to scale.

Note: The shaft dimensions affect the vaned shock absorber centre. For mainshafts 041263/041701 use shock absorber centre 043186. For mainshafts 043058/041703 use shock absorber centre 043509.

FRONT FORKS

(HEAVYWEIGHT, 350 cc. LIGHTWEIGHT and 250 cc. SCRAMBLER MODELS)

(The figures in parenthesis refer to Fig. 59)

Stiff fork motion. First try the effect of releasing the two bolts securing the front mudguard to the fork slider (15). If normal movement is restored use washers between the mudguard and the slider to relieve side strain, or remove the guard and spread the sides. Try also releasing the four cap nuts (33) and work the forks violently to line up the inner tube and retighten the nuts.

If the fork motion is unduly stiff, and assuming the fork tubes are not bent by impact, it is possible that the black bushes (9) have swollen and are a tight fit on the tubes.

To rectify, dismantle the forks and ease down the inside diameter of the bush with emery cloth, until it is an easy sliding fit. Oil the fork tube, or use graphite before assembly.

Fork noise on full deflection. Check the bottom cover tube (53) for contact with the slider extension (54), the cover tube may be deformed or canted. Remove the cover tube and set the tube face where it abuts against the fork crown (39) so that it is at complete right angles to the axis of the tube. The tube should be concentric with the slider extension. Usually there are score marks on the slider, under these circumstances.

Rattle in forks. One of the damper rods (25) may be detached from the top anchorage. A low oil content will have the same effect.

Fork spring rattle. Three neoprene rubber sleeves (Nos. 2, 4 and 5) are placed over the fork inner tubes, near the top, bottom and centre of the fork spring. If these sleeves have piled up at the bottom of the spring, the spring can rattle against the fork tube. Reposition or renew the sleeves to rectify. Apply some grease to the fork springs before refitting.

Lateral fork movement. If the steering head bearing adjustment is correct and if there is a juddering effect when the front brake is applied, this can be due to lateral movement caused by wear on the black fork bushes. The movement can be detected also by jacking up the front wheel clear of the ground when, by raising and lowering the front wheel, the movement will show up. Replace the bushes to rectify.

It is rare for the steel bushes to be affected, providing the fork oil content is not contaminated by abrasive. When replacing the bushes make sure the inside of the fork tubes is perfectly clean.

Indifferent steering. If the machine is inclined to steer in an elongated figure of eight, this denotes unwanted friction in the steering which can be due to:

(1) Steering head bearing over tightened.
(2) There is friction, which cannot be released if a steering damper is used.
(3) The steering head bearing is unduly loose and the fork stem is rubbing against the inside of the ball race.
(4) The ball races are pitted, as a result of driving with a loose bearing adjustment (see 'Steering head adjustment').

In the case of (2) take out the bolt securing the steering damper plate to the frame. If the friction is removed, use washer(s) between the plate and the lug on the frame.

Handlebars oscillate at low road speed. This trouble is not associated with the front forks, or wheel alignment. If the handlebars oscillate or 'wobble' at low road speed and stops as the road speed increases, this is due to either one or both tyres not running true with the wheel rim and invariably becomes manifest after the tyres have to be changed. In the main the front tyre is responsible.

Oil leaks from forks. First try the effect of tightening the slider extension (7) to compress the oil seal against the bush. If the leakage persists, replace the oil seal (8).

Should the leak take place at the lower end of the fork slider (15) check the damper tube bolt (31) and its washer for security.

Loose head lamp brackets. The top fork cover tube (20) with lamp bracket incorporated is compressed between the handlebar lug (41) and the fork crown (39) with a rubber packing ring (18) interposed. If the rubber ring deteriorates or collapses, the tension on the tube will be reduced. Usually the trouble can be rectified without completely dismantling the front forks, by using a fork spring leather washer 021116 for each cover tube as packing.

Release the two nuts (45 and 46).
Tap upwards the handlebar lug (41).
Make a cut across one side of the washer and feed it round the fork tube, between the rubber and the fork crown. A little soapy water will assist the washer to slide over the rubber.
Re-align the head lamp and tighten the two nuts.

Head lamp beam. If the lamp beam is out of parallel to the machine, thump the head lamp shell with the heel of the hand in the required direction.

Bent fork inner tubes (17). The fork tubes can be straightened providing the set does not exceed 10° out of true.

Support the tube in 'V' blocks and use an Arbour press.

Note: The fork tubes must be smooth and free from bruises and blemish, particularly in the part where the oil seal operates, otherwise the seal will be damaged beyond further use, with serious oil leakage.

Fork damper conversion (Scrambler Models). For the 1962 season an improved type of fork damping was introduced in the Heavyweight forks fitted to Scrambler Models.

Earlier type forks can be converted by:

Dismantling the forks.
Dismantling the damper tubes (34).

Seal off, by welding, the small hole below the slot for the circlip (37).
Drill a $\frac{1}{16}"$ diameter hole 2" from the top of the damper tube.
Drill a $\frac{3}{32}"$ diameter hole 3" from the top of the damper tube.
Reduce the overall length of the top cover tube (16) to $1\frac{1}{16}"$.
Reduce the overall length of the slider extension (7) to $3\frac{7}{8}"$.

Use fork springs 016782.
Discard the buffer springs (10).
Fit two gaiters (dust protectors).
Fit four gaiter clips 042775.

If new parts are required, instead of converting, use:

2. Bottom cover tubes ... 028046
2. Slider extensions ... 028051
2. Damper tubes ... 028048
2. Main springs ... 016782
2. Gaiters ... 020463
4. Gaiter clips ... 042775

Removing the front forks. Remove the two drain plugs (56) in turn and catch oil in a container.

Raise the front wheel with boxes under footrests.

Remove handlebars (use padding on the petrol tank to avoid damage).

Remove head lamp and disconnect speedo drive cable.

Remove front wheel, mudguard and stay.

Remove steering damper plate to frame (if fitted).

Remove rubber grummets from tube bolts (22), also the two bolts. Use spanner 018667.

Remove lock nuts (24) and adaptor to release damper rods (25).

Remove domed nut (45) and adjusting nut (46).

Tap off the handlebar lug (41) using a rawhide mallet, until the lug clears the fork stem (40) and tubes, the forks can then be taken away as a unit. Watch for steering race ball bearings, 56 in number.

Dismantling the forks. Hold the fork stem in a vice.

Remove slider extension (7) from the slider (15) by unscrewing from the slider.

Remove slider by giving it a sharp jerk downwards. The oil seal is a close fit in the top of the slider. If there is resistance in separating the slider, apply a little heat to the top part, which will expand and enable the slider to come away with ease, with the damper assembly attached.

Remove two Allen screws (38) then pull out the fork tubes.

To remove steel bush. Prise out the circlip (12) and pull off the bush. If the circlip becomes distorted during removal, replace it with a new one.

To dismantle the damper tube. Use a thin wall box key to take out bolt (31) in the slider recess $\frac{1}{2}$" across the flats, pull out the damper tube, with damper rod assembled.

Pull out the circlip (37), extract the damper rod with valve assembled. If the valve is taken off the rod, watch for small pin (27).

Table of fork springs used

250 cc. Scrambler Model and Lightweight 350 cc.

Part No. 014950 ... Free length 11" Wire gauge .207"

350 cc. Trials Model

Part No. 014950 ... Free length 11" Wire gauge .207"

Heavyweight Scrambler Model

Part No. 021790
(CSR) ... ... Free length $11\frac{1}{4}$" Wire gauge .222"
Part No. 016782
1962 (CS) ... Free length $12\frac{3}{4}$" Wire gauge .212"

Heavyweight Touring Model

Part No. 022369 ... Free length 11.90" Wire gauge .212"

Heavyweight Sidecar Model

Part No. 021789 ... Free length $12\frac{3}{4}$" Wire gauge .222"

Buffer springs

All Models except 350 cc. Trials

Part No. 022079 ... Free length $2\frac{23}{32}$" Wire gauge .192"

350 cc. Trials, 250 cc. Scrambler and 350 cc. Lightweight

Part No. 010360 ... Free length $2\frac{21}{32}$" Wire gauge .187"

To remove one fork tube. If attention to one fork tube only is necessary, the fork tube and components can be extracted by:

(1) Taking out the front wheel, mudguard and stays.
(2) Remove the domed nut (22), disconnect the damper rod and release the Allen screw (38).

Usually the fork tube is a close fit in the two top members (39 and 41), thus to avoid damage to the internal thread in the fork tube, a draw bolt is required, which is also used to pull back the tube. The tools for the large, also small, diameter fork tubes are shown in Fig. 60.

Insert the tool into the fork tube which can now be driven out.

If at this stage the slider has to be removed, and if the tube is held in a vice, use a suitable clamp and hold the tube at the top and away from the oil seal travel.

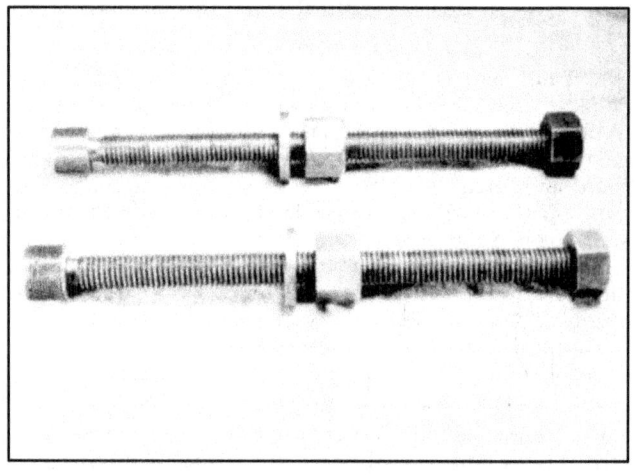

FIG. 60

Assembling the forks (without a draw bolt). Hold the fork crown in a vice.

Assemble a fork tube with its components as described in 'Assembling the forks with a draw bolt'.

Push the fork tube into the fork crown (see Fig. 61).

Insert the key 018667 in the Allen screw.

With one hand pull up the tube until it protrudes $6\frac{1}{2}$" and quickly tighten the Allen screw.

Then assemble the second tube in a similar manner.

Fit the crown races with bearings as previously described and pass the fork stem through the frame.

If assistance is available hold the forks in position, assemble the top frame race and bearings.

Alternatively, place a box under the forks to support.

Assemble the two top cover tubes and handlebar lug, connect the damper rods to the top bolts.

Engage the top bolts as far as possible, then release the clamp screws.

Firmly tighten the top bolts then the clamp screws. (See 'Special precautions').

Adjust the steering head bearings and fill oil to each fork tube.

Steering head adjustment. The steering head frame races are of the floating self-aligning type and have spherical seats. Therefore they do not fit tightly in the head lug.

Occasionally test the steering head for correct adjustment by exerting pressure upwards from the extreme ends of the handlebars.

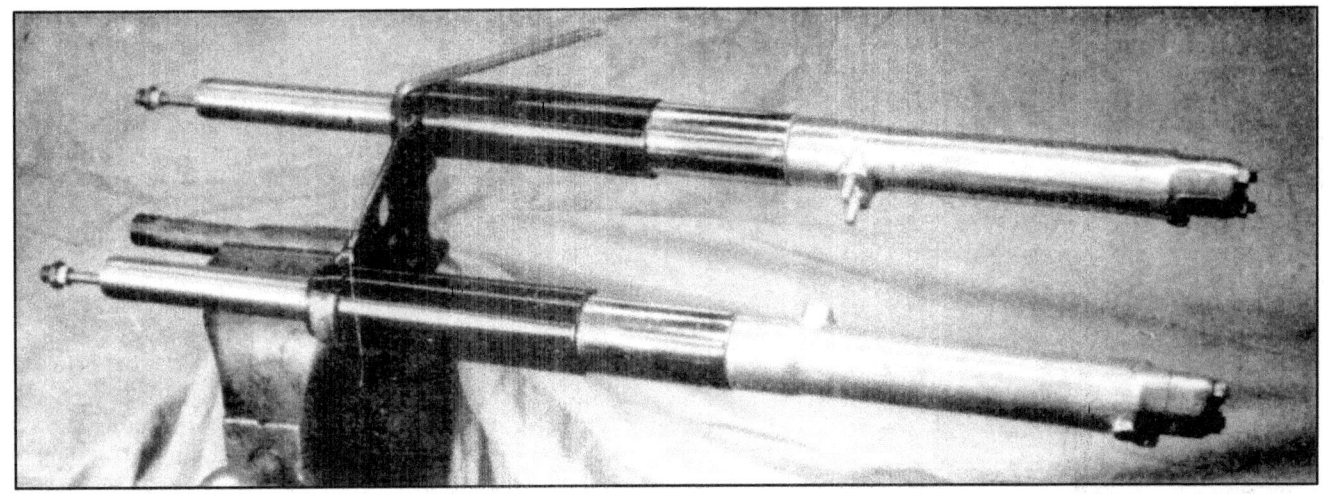

Fig. 61

It is particularly important that the adjustment is tested after the first 100 miles because of the initial settling down that always occurs in that period.

Should any shake be apparent, adjust the steering head bearings.

Adjust steering head bearings by: Jacking up the front of the machine so that all weight is taken off the front wheel. (A box under each footrest serves that purpose).

Slacken the two fork crown Allen screws.

Slacken the domed nut at top of the steering column.

Screw down the nut underneath the domed nut a little at a time and while doing so, test the head assembly for slackness by placing the fingers over the gap between handlebar lug and frame top lug, at the same time exerting upward pressure by lifting from the front edge of the front mudguard. Tested in this manner the slightest slackness is discernible.

Continue to tighten the lower adjusting nut until no perceptible movement can be felt and yet the steering head is perfectly free to turn, then tighten down the domed nut in order to lock the adjustment.

Securely tighten the two fork crown Allen screws (this is very important).

Remove packing from under footrest.

Special Precautions: It is vitally important to firmly and positively tighten the two Allen screws (38) which clamp the fork tubes.

Movement between the tubes and the fork crown (39) will cause 'fretting' which can weaken the tube.

Never attempt to repair a fork slider after damage by impact, by welding. Where serious damage has occurred after frontal impact, carefully examine the slider for latent cracks.

Steering angle. When the Duplex tube frame was introduced in 1960, a slight alteration to the steering angle was made to improve steering, also road holding. The parts affected are the fork crown and stem and the handlebar lug.

Whilst the difference between the old and new parts is exceedingly small, it does affect interchange of the fork parts individually, viz., whilst both the new type handlebar lug with fork crown can be used on early models (with the exception of CSR models with siamesed exhaust pipes) as a pair, they cannot be used separately.

As the new parts are virtually identical in appearance, they can be identified by the figure 6 stamped on each part.

Fitting a sidecar. To accommodate the extra load the solo fork springs should be exchanged for a stronger type (see 'Table of fork springs'). In the case of a heavy type sidecar, the rear suspension springs must be exchanged also. Fit a steering damper to offset heavy steering and stop handlebar wobble.

See 'Technical data' for engine sprocket.

To re-assemble the forks (using a draw bolt). Check steering head races for pitting or damage. Pack the lower crown race with grease and fill with 28 steel bearings, put the lower frame race over the stem to retain the bearings. Pack the top frame race with grease, fill with 28 bearings and place it in the frame.

Take up the fork crown and pass it through the frame, fit the handlebar lug and hold these two members together by fitting the nut (46).

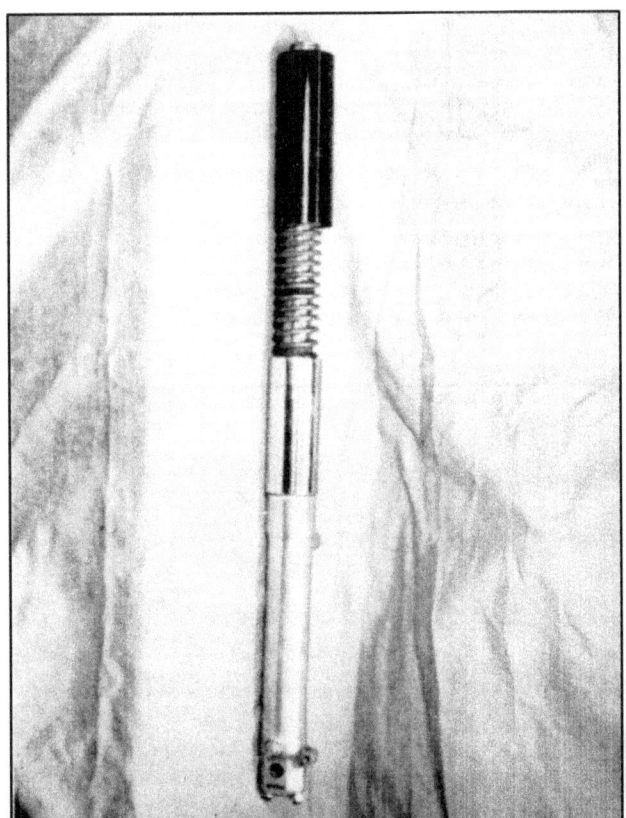

Fig. 62

Assemble the top cover tubes in the sequence shown in Fig. 59 and fit them between the fork crown and handlebar lug. It may be necessary to release the nut (46) to do this, then retighten this nut to clamp the cover tubes. The steering head adjustment can be dealt with later.

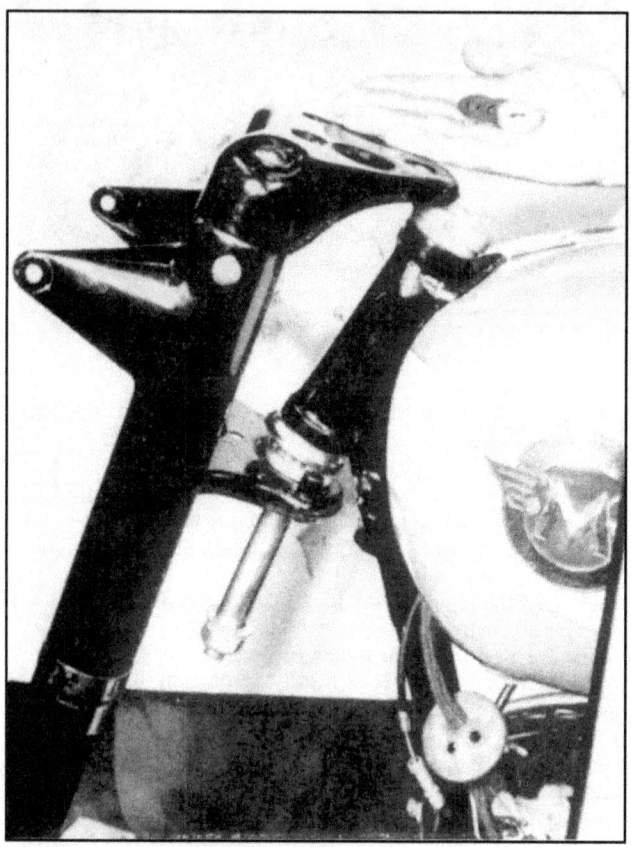

Fig. 64

Assembling the fork tube. With the fork tube horizontal apply a little oil to the bottom end of the tube.

Fit the oil seal, metal backing towards the top, use a rotary motion at the bottom end of the tube.

Fit the black bush, flange upwards, buffer spring and collar (42).

Fit one circlip, the steel bush and second circlip.

Fit from the top end, slider extension, leather washer (6).

Take up the fork slider, with damper rod assembled, pass it over the fork tube from the bottom end, engage the slider extension.

Fit rubber sleeves, spaced over fork spring length.

Fit main spring, leather washer and top tube (16).

Fit the tube assembled into the two top members, as far as it will go, tighten the clamp screw lightly to hold the tube in position.

Fit the draw bolt, well engaged in the tube and pull the tube home.

Firmly tighten the clamp screw to stop the tube from moving and take away the tool.

Fit damper rod (see 'Changing fork springs') to top bolt and firmly tighten. Fill each tube with 6½ ozs. (186 cc.) SAE 20 oil.

Changing the fork springs. The fork springs can be examined, or exchanged, without entirely dismantling the forks, as shown in Fig. 65. The draw bolt, as illustrated, is necessary for this operation.

First detach the front brake cable at the handlebar end.

Take out the two fork tube nuts (49), disconnect damper rods.

Release the two Allen screws (38), clamping the fork tubes.

As the front wheel spindle is attached to the forks, it is obvious that the fork tubes are extracted simultaneously. To do so, engage the fork tool in the tube (a fair way down) and drive the tube downwards a small amount.

Transfer the tool to the other fork tube and treat it likewise.

Repeat the operation, transferring the tool from one tube to the other, until they are clear as depicted.

To reassemble. Refit the assembly and enter the tubes as far as they will go. The tubes should be parallel with the covers. Run back the large nut on the tool and engage it in one of the tubes. Run down the tool nut and tighten, to pull the tube back a slight amount, thus reversing the method used for extracting the tubes.

An old engine push rod, with the adjusting cup taken out can be used to bring up the damper rods. Alternatively, use a loop of copper wire. Assemble the damper rods to the top anchorage and firmly tighten the lock nuts. Refit the tube top bolts, firmly retighten the two clamping screws.

Front forks (250 cc. Model). An exploded view of the front forks is shown in Fig. 67-68.

Dismantling the forks. Remove the front wheel as described in 'Wheels and brakes section'.

Take off the head lamp front and detach bulb holders.

Disconnect the speedometer drive cable.

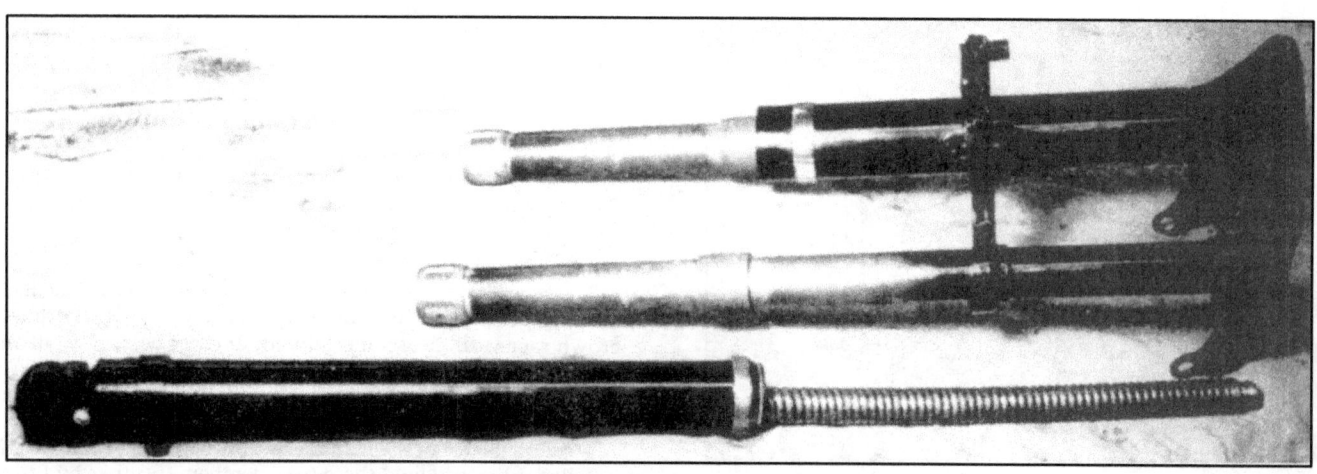

Fig. 63

Detach the black and blue cable plugs.
Detach ammeter wires and dip switch cable.
Detach handlebars.
Detach front mudguard by taking out the two clip bolts, expand the clip a trifle to avoid damage to enamel.
Detach drain plugs (7) and catch the oil.
Detach head stem nut (24), watch for three shim washers.
Detach steering head stem and support the forks (see Fig. 64). Watch for head bearings (29), set of 39 and take away forks. Support the forks in a vice (Fig. 63), take out screw (2), and pull off the bottom slider extension (13) with fork spring attached.
Detach two screws securing top cover tube, and take tube away.
Detach bolt (15), pull out fork spring and damper. The spring is screwed on to the damper, also the top spring anchor.

Removing the oil seal. The oil seal will come away attached to the slider.

Secure the slider in a suitable clamp fixed in a vice.

Bring the mudguard clip up to the oil seal body, using a series of light blows with a hammer directed on to the ears of the clip. Move the clip round the seal body whilst doing this to remove it squarely.

Re-assembling the front forks. The work involved is straightforward with the following precautions:
(1) After fitting the cover tubes leave the two fixing screws loose. When the forks are assembled and working correctly, retighten the screws.
(2) Assemble the oil seal to the slider squarely.
(3) When refitting the slider bring the seal up to the bush. Use a small radio-type screwdriver or similar tool, insert the tool between the oil seal rubber and the fork bush. Use a rotary motion pressing gently against the slider, the seal will go over the bush without damage.

Refill with 70 cc. of SAE 30 oil.

Note: The fork tube bushes are silver soldered to the tubes $5\frac{3}{4}''$ apart.

Steering head adjustment. With the machine on the stand, need for adjustment of the steering head bearings may be detected by trying to rock the forks with hands holding the fork legs. The bearings should be tested for slackness after the first 200 miles and subsequently every 1,000 miles. Two spanners should be used, one turning the adjusting nut (34), the other to slacken and retighten the lock nut when the adjustment has been carried out.

Adjustment should be such that no play be felt, yet the bearings are free to rotate and are not over tight.

Adjusting the bearings too tightly will ruin them and induce heavy steering.

Note: It is important that adjusting and locking nuts are tightly locked together.

Front forks (350 cc. Lightweight Model, CSR, also 250 cc. Scrambler). The front forks fitted to these Models are virtually identical in design to those fitted to the Heavyweight Models. The difference is confined to the diameter of the fork inner tubes. Therefore, the assembly and maintenance details given for the Heavyweight Models apply also to the Lightweight counterpart (see page 59).

Rear suspension units. These are sealed units. Maintenance is confined to greasing the outside diameter of the springs should a grating noise develop during movement. The damper fluid filled is sufficient to outlast the life of the unit. Should an oil leak develop, the damper unit must be exchanged.

Removing the units. Simply take out the top and bottom fixing bolts, the unit will come away.

Removing the top cover tube. To do this the spring is compressed to extract the split collets. Without the aid of a

Fig. 65

Fig. 66

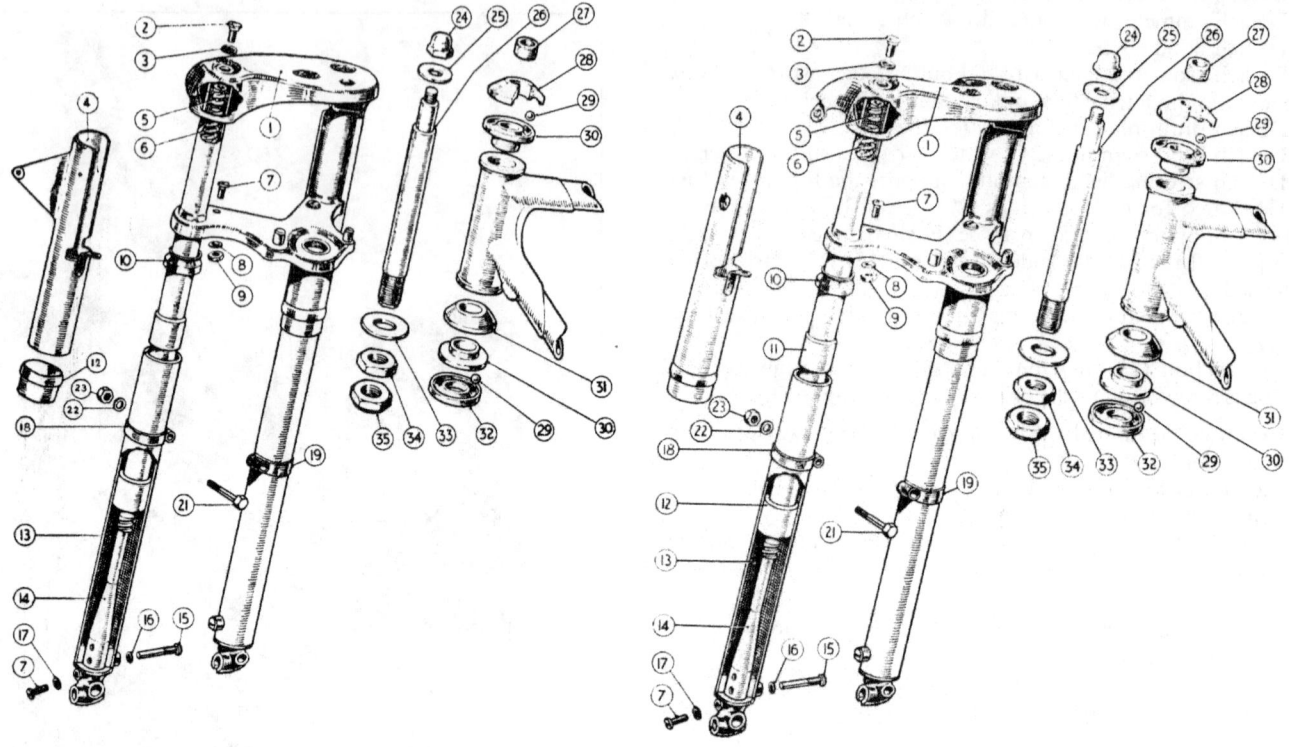

Fig. 67
1960-1962 Type.

1	043343	Fork "H" member.
2	043245	Screw, inner tube, top.
3	000201	Washer, fibre, inner tube top screw.
4	043345-6	Tube, cover, top, left and right.
5	043246	Adaptor, inner tube top screw.
6	043259	Spring, main.
7	043251	Screw, top cover tube and drain plug.
8	021579	Washer, shakeproof top cover tube screw.
9	000005	Nut, top cover tube screw.
10	043253	Seal, oil, fork tubes.
12	043344	Sleeve, end, top cover tube.
13	043347	Extension, slider.
14	043256	Tube, damper.
15	043257	Screw, retaining damper tube.
16	043258	Washer, fibre, damper tube retaining screw.
17	000203	Washer, fibre, drain plug.
18	043260	Clip, mudguard attachment, left.
19	043261	Clip, mudguard attachment, right.
21	000373	Bolt, mudguard attachment clip.
22	000011	Washer, Mudguard attachment clip bolt.
23	000004	Nut, mudguard attachment clip bolt.
24	043262	Nut, domed, head stem, top.
25	043263	Washer, head stem top domed nut.
26	043235	Stem, head.
27	043236	Spacer, head stem.
28	043240	Race, adjusting top.
29	000021	Bearings, ball, head races.
30	043238	Race, frame head lug, top and bottom.
31	043241	Cover, dust, bottom ball race.
32	043239	Race, fork crown, bottom.
33	043244	Washer, head stem bottom nuts.
34	043242	Nut, adjusting, head stem, bottom.
35	043243	Nut, lock, head stem, bottom.

Fig. 68
Exploded View of Teledraulic Forks—1959

1. Fork, H.
2. Inner tube top screw.
3. Inner tube top screw fibre washer.
4. Top cover tube.
5. Inner tube top adaptor.
6. Main spring.
7. Drain screw.
8. Top cover tube shakeproof washer.
9. Top cover tube fixing screw nut.
10. Oil seal.
11. Assembled part.
12. Assembled part.
13. Slider extension.
14. Damper tube.
15. Damper tube retaining screw.
16. Damper tube retaining screw fibre washer.
17. Drain screw fibre washer.
18. Mudguard clip left.
19. Mudguard clip right.
21. Mudguard clip bolt.
22. Mudguard clip bolt washer.
23. Mudguard clip bolt nut.
24. Nut, domed top.
25. Washer top domed nut.
26. Head stem.
27. Spacer for head stem.
28. Adjusting race.
29. Balls steering.
30. Frame race top and bottom.
31. Dust cover for ball race.
32. Crown race.
33. Washer head stem bottom nuts.
34. Head stem adjusting nut, bottom.
35. Head stem lock nut, bottom.

spring compressor tool, the collets can be removed with the unit attached to the frame. The assistance of a second person is required to press down the cover tube (compressing the spring) and smartly prise out the collets. It may be necessary to deal with one collet at a time. Alternatively, hold the top end of the unit in a vice and use the first method.

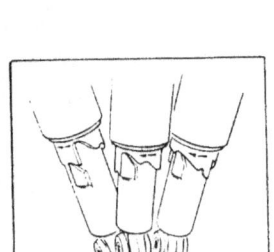
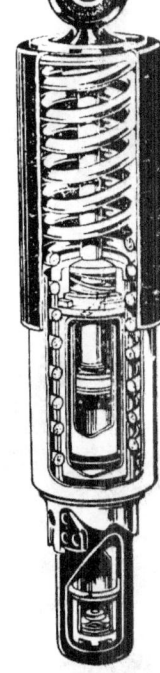

Fig. 69
"Ghost" View of Rear Suspension Unit.

Removing the rubber bushes. These are a press fit and can be extracted without difficulty. To refit use a little water on the rubber, which will facilitate entry without deterioration of the rubber.

The cam ring adjuster. By applying less than half a turn to the stepped cam (use spanner 023284) the suspension is corrected and retained to suit the change of load. This also enables the head lamp beam to remain unaltered.

Table of rear suspension springs

Model	Part No.	Free length	Colour marking
250 cc. Scrambler	043178	$8\frac{1}{4}''$	Green/Yellow/Green
350 cc. Trials Model	043312	$8\frac{1}{2}''$	Red/Red/Red
Heavyweight Scrambler	024443	$8\frac{7}{8}''$	Green/Green/Green
,, Touring Model	023373	$8\frac{1}{4}''$	Red/Pink/Red
,, Sidecar Model	023372	$8\frac{1}{4}''$	Blue/Yellow/Blue
250 cc. Touring Model, CSR	043312	$8\frac{1}{2}''$	Red/Red/Red
350 cc. Lightweight Model	043179	$7\frac{3}{4}''$	Green/Blue/Green

THE FRAME

Lightweight Models. Details for removing the engine and gear box, the forks and wheels, have been described elsewhere. The further dismantling of the frame is self evident.

The swinging arm (Fig. 70). If movement develops between the swinging arm and the main frame, this does not necessarily indicate that the two spindle bushes are worn.

First try the effect of releasing the nut fixing the cotter pin on the left side of the arm. Tap the cotter pin upwards, then knock together the two tubular members and drive back the cotter pin and retighten. This will absorb end play, which is often associated with wear in the bushes.

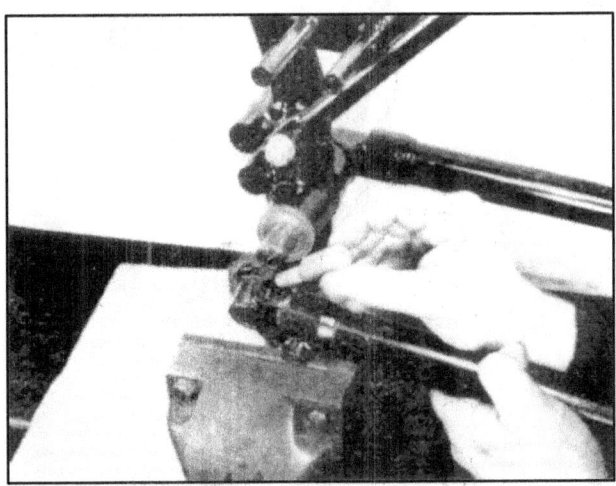

Fig. 70

To remove the bushes. Both bushes are a press fit in the frame. They can be removed by using a tubular drift passed through one of the bushes. The finished size of the bush *in situ* is $\frac{3}{4}'' +.0075'' -.005''$. Pack the spindle orifice with graphite grease before fitting swinging arm.

The accessory compartment. The ignition coil and electric horn are exposed after removing the accessory cover on the left side of the machine, by unscrewing the knurled knob then taking out the two $\frac{1}{4}''$ diameter bolts and nuts at the bottom of the compartment.

Tool box compartment. Fitted to the right side of the machine. Remove the knurled knob, the tools are located in a second compartment, the lid is secured, also by a knurled knob. To remove the compartment, take out two $\frac{5}{16}''$ bolts and nuts which are visible when the lid is opened.

The central stand. The central stand pivots on the footrest rod. To remove the stand, take the footrest arms and with no load on the stand, drive out the footrest rod. There is a

Fig. 71

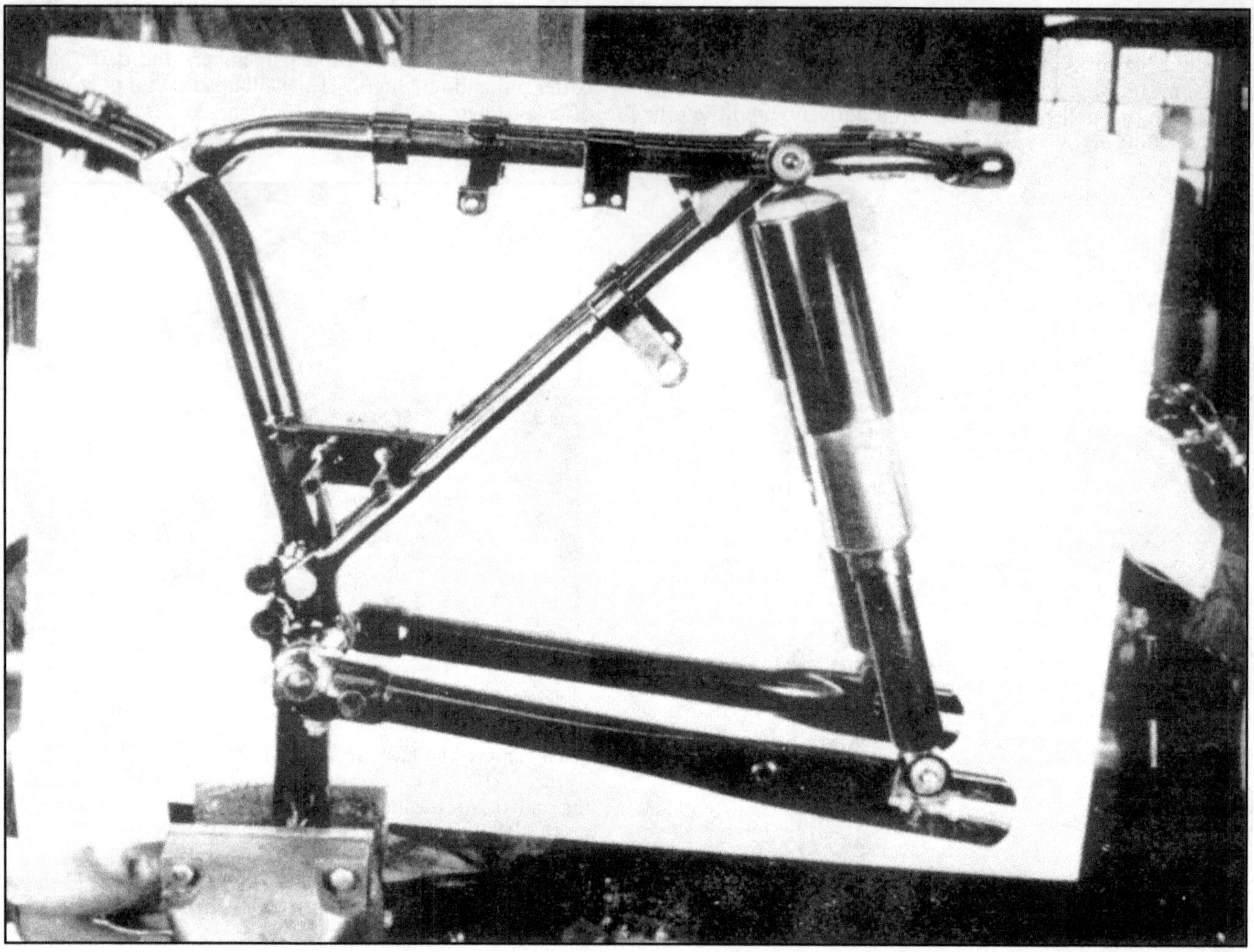

Fig. 72

distance piece together with a stop plate each side of the engine support channel.

The stand spring (Fig. 71). Usually trouble free. The spring is anchored between the operating rod and a spacer. The spacer is secured by a recess in the channel. Spring the channel apart, the spacer will fall out.

The stand stop. Is fitted between the right side pillion footrest arm and the frame channel.

A rubber grummet, which is detachable, goes through the bracket to prevent metallic contact.

Frame strip down (Heavyweight Model). Strip down as detailed for removing the engine and gear box.

Take out both wheels, also take off the head lamp and loom by:

Disconnecting the battery wires and removing the twin seat.

Disconnecting horn, coil and rectifier cables (if alternator model).

Disconnecting control box cables (if fitted) and take it out of the tool box.

Disconnecting stop light switch and rear lamp wires.

Release screw on head lamp rim and take it away with reflector assembly. Disconnect main and pilot bulb wires; also speedo lamp wire. Place the reflector in a safe place.

Disconnect speedo drive cable, pass the cable through the head lamp and fork crown.

Remove dipper switch with cables.

Remove head lamp bolts, release clips on frame, take the head lamp away with the loom.

Remove the front forks as described in 'Fork section'.
Remove frame cover, secured by two slotted screws.
Remove oil tank by taking out the top front fixing bolt.
Remove air cleaner (two bolts).
Remove tool box attached to rear frame loop by two ¼" bolts.
Remove both rear suspension units.

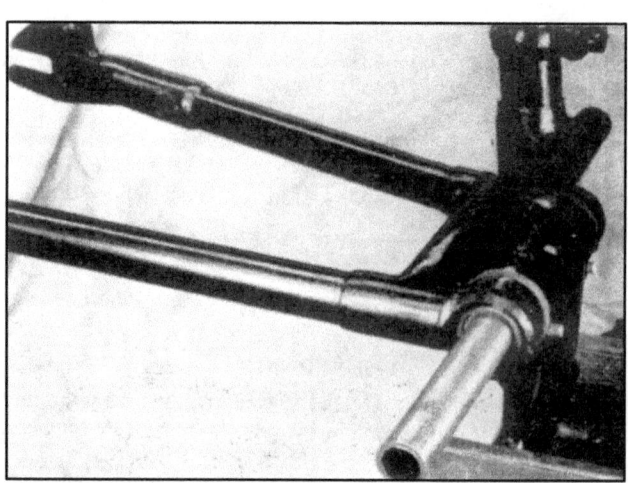

Fig. 73

Removing the rear mudguard. Remove ¼" bolt securing gear guard to frame loop.

Remove 5/16" stud fixing bottom front of the guard to the frame lug.

Remove bolt (3) and spacer (see Fig. 74), and chain guard.

Remove bolt fixing rear chain guard at front.

To remove the rear loop. Remove stud uniting rear loop to seat lug.

Remove nut for stud on right side of rear loop.

Remove this stud with brake pedal attached, take away the rear loop.

Remove screw for plate in swinging arm.

Release the two cotter pin nuts which locate the bearing tube. Push out the bearing tube as shown in Fig. 73.

Swinging arm bushes. The two flanged bushes are housed in steel sleeves which are not supplied separately. The bushes are of the oilite type, but provision is made for lubrication via the centre plate screw (use heavy duty oil). If lateral movement develops at the wheel end this could be due to end float between the arm and the frame lug, particularly after long mileage, with a sidecar attached.

Taking up side play. When it has been ascertained that end play is manifest, it is extremely difficult to absorb this movement by moving the bushes with the arm assembled in the frame, even with a sturdy support on one side of the arm. Whilst the bush in the opposite end is drifted in, there is always a certain amount of spring in the two extremities of the arm. It is therefore preferable to take the swinging arm away from the frame.

To decide if the bearing tube or the bushes are worn, the spindle diameter is .9995"/.9990", the bush diameter *in situ* is 1.001". At the factory a pilot reamer 1" diameter is used for these two bushes, for correct alignment.

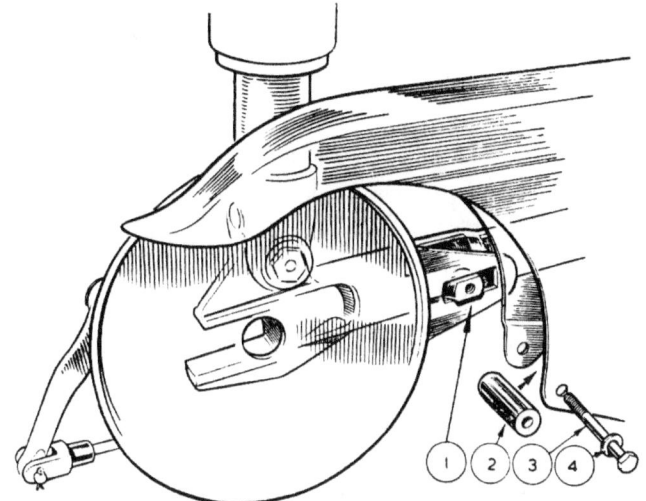

FIG. 74 **Brake Anchorage**
1 Break anchorage boss. 3 Fixing bolt.
2 Spacer. 4 Washer.

WHEEL BEARINGS
(Heavyweight Models)

The break down of the front wheel bearings is shown in Fig. 75. It is vitally important to avoid tightly adjusting bearings of the taper roller type, as a crushing action takes place, the rollers will be damaged beyond further use. Should excessive movement suddenly develop, the bearing should be dismantled for inspection, for with correct adjustment and constant lubrication, these bearings will last indefinitely.

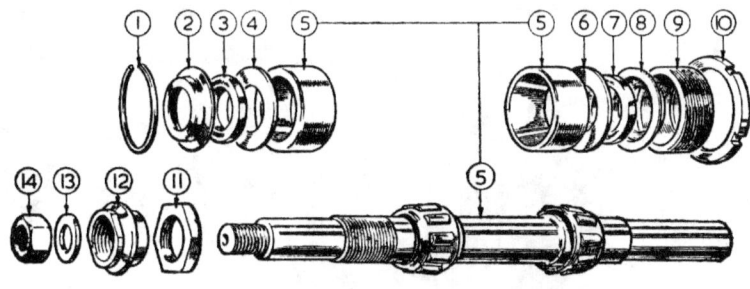

FIG. 75
Front wheel bearings

1 Circlip.
2 Oil seal cup.
3 Oil seal.
4 Washer retaining seal.
5 Wheel spindle complete.
6 Washer retaining seal.
7 Oil seal.
8 Oil seal cup.
9 Adjusting ring.
10 Adjusting ring locknut.
11 Nut locating brake coverplate.
12 Nut securing brake coverplate.
13 Spindle end washer.
14 Spindle end nut.

To dismantle the bearing. Remove the front wheel.
Remove nut securing brake cover plate (12).
Remove locating nut (113) and washer.
Remove locking ring (10) and cover disc.
Remove adjusting ring (9).
Press out the spindle from the threaded end which will push out items 6-7-8 and bearing ring 5.
The bearing ring will remain in the left side of the hub.

To extract the bearing ring. Press in the washer (4) sufficiently far enough to permit the circlip (1) to be extracted. Use a piece of steel tubing passed through the hub and drift out the bearing sleeve, which will also eject the washer (4), oil seal (3) and collar (2).

Avoid using heavy hammer blows when taking the spindle out, as this action can cause indentations in the bearing sleeve.

Adjusting the front wheel bearing. Release the locking ring (10), screw in the adjusting ring (9) until the bearing is devoid of end movement, unscrew the adjusting ring half a turn only, give the opposite end of the spindle a light blow to move the bearing ring away from the bearing.

Position the cover disc and firmly retighten the lock ring.

There should be approximately .002" side rock at the wheel rim if the adjustment is correct. The friction of the oil seals can create a false impression that the bearing is tight.

Dismantling rear wheel bearing (Fig. 76). Before removing the rear wheel, release the speedo drive fixing nut (16), disconnect speedo cable and take out the wheel.

Remove the nut (16) and speedo gear box, release the lock ring (13).

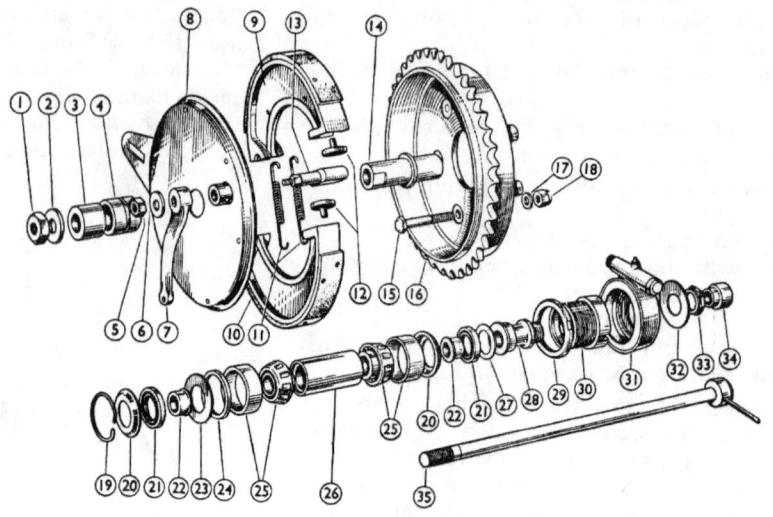

Fig. 76
Non-quick-detachable Wheel Assembly.

1 Nut for wheel solid spindle.
2 Washer, for wheel spindle nut.
3 Spacer, for wheel spindle nut.
4 Spacer, for cover plate, outer.
5 Nut, for expander lever.
6 Washer, for expander lever nut.
7 Lever, expander.
8 Plate, cover.
9 Shoes, brake, with linings.
10 Linings, for brake shoes.
11 Spring, for brake shoes.
12 Pin thrust, adjusting brake shoes.
13 Expander, for brake shoes.
14 Spacer, for cover plate, inner.
15 Bolt, retaining, sprocket to hub shell.
16 Sprocket and brake drum.
17 Washer, sprocket retaining bolt.
18 Nut, sprocket retaining bolt.
19 Ring, spring, locating bearing.
20 Cup, for bearing oil seal.
21 Oil seal, for bearing.
22 Spacer, on spindle, for oil seal.
23 Ring, retaining hub bearing, large.
24 Spacer, between bearing and oil seal.
25 Bearing, roller.
26 Spacer, between bearings.
27 Ring, retaining hub bearing, small.
28 Spacer, on spindle, for speedometer gearbox.
29 Nut, lock, bearing adjusting ring.
30 Ring, adjusting bearing.
31 Speedometer gearbox.
32 Washer, outside, speedometer gearbox.
33 Nut, locking, speedometer gearbox.
34 Spacer, on spindle, speedometer gearbox side.
35 Spindle, rear wheel solid.

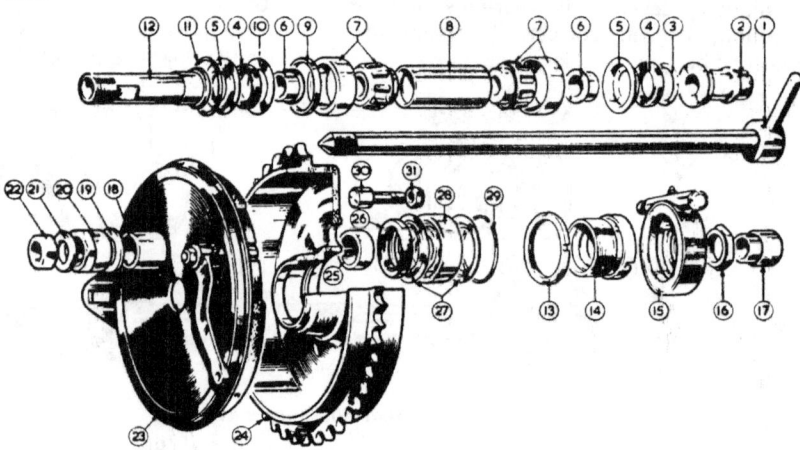

Fig. 77
Rear Brake and Wheel Bearings, De-luxe Models.

1 Withdrawable wheel spindle.
2 Speedometer gear box sleeve.
3 Ring retaining oil seal (small).
4 Oil seal.
5 Cup for oil seal.
6 Oil seal distance piece.
7 Taper roller bearing complete.
8 Spacer between bearings.
9 Bearing spacing collar (brake side).
10 Ring retaining oil seal (large).
11 Circlip.
12 Brake drum dummy spindle.
13 Lock nut for adjusting ring.
14 Adjusting ring.
15 Speedometer gear box complete.
16 Speedometer gear box fixing nut.
17 Spacer for withdrawable spindle.
18 Outer spacer for brake cover plate.
19 Washer for cover plate fixing nut.
20 Brake cover plate fixing nut.
21 Spindle end washer.
22 Spindle end nut.
23 Brake cover plate complete.
24 Rear brake drum.
25 Inner spacer for brake cover plate.
26 Brake drum bearing oil seal.
27 Brake drum oil seal washers.
28 Brake drum ball bearing.
29 Circlip retaining bearing.
30 Driving peg (5 off).
31 Nut securing driving peg (5 off).

Remove adjuster sleeve (14) and speedo gear box sleeve (2), and cover disc.

Remove the washer (3), oil seal (4) and oil seal cup (5); also distance piece (6).

Turn to the brake side of the hub, when with the use of a short steel rod or tubing, with an external diameter of $\tfrac{7}{8}''$ drift out the hub internals, leaving the bearing ring (7) *in situ*.

Fig. 78

To remove the bearing ring. Press inwards the steel cup washer (5) to permit extraction of the circlip (11), take out the cup washer, oil seal and spacer (6). Drift out the bearing ring with a length of steel tubing.

Note: When refitting the circlip press back the bearing ring. See 'Wheel bearing adjustment'.

Brake drum bearing (Fig. 78). With the brake drum away from the frame, to dismantle:

Remove dummy spindle (12).

Remove circlip (11) and cup for oil seal (5).

Remove bearing by drifting out, with second cup.

Remove oil seal (4) and distance piece (6).

Refit the oil seal with metal backing towards the inside of brake drum. Use a little anti-centrifuge grease for the bearing.

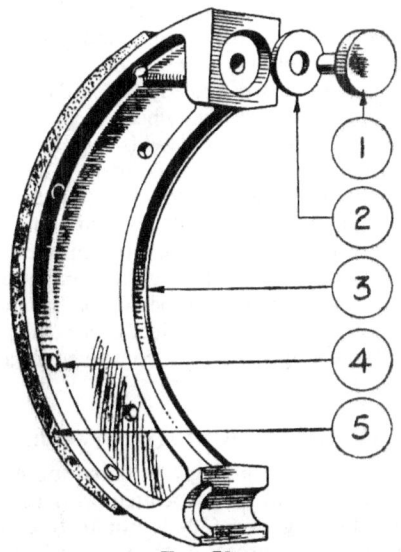

Fig. 79

1 Brakeshoe thrust pin.
2 Thrust pin packing washer.
3 Brake shoe.
4 Rivet, securing brake shoe lining.
5 Brake shoe lining.

BRAKES

(Lightweight Scrambler and 350 cc. Trials Model)

The front brake. The front brake is dimensionally the same as the rear brake, see page 71.

The rear brake. The brake drum diameter is 5.5″ as opposed to 7″ for the front brake.

Brake adjustment to compensate wear on the linings is effected by finger adjustment on the rear brake rod and front brake cable.

After considerable mileage, brake lining wear will adversely affect the leverage of the brake shoe expander as indicated in Fig. 81.

To restore the leverage without relining the brakes, packing washers 000174 are used under the heat treated thrust studs. The washers used must be uniform in thickness, to ensure both brake shoes make contact with the drum simultaneously (Fig. 79.)

(Heavyweight Models)

Front brake. The front brake drum is cast in the hub and is machined after the wheel has been built, thus ensuring concentricity. During the process of lacing the wheel spokes, slight distortion can take place. If a wheel is rebuilt and brake efficiency is impaired, the brake drum should be skimmed to restore efficiency.

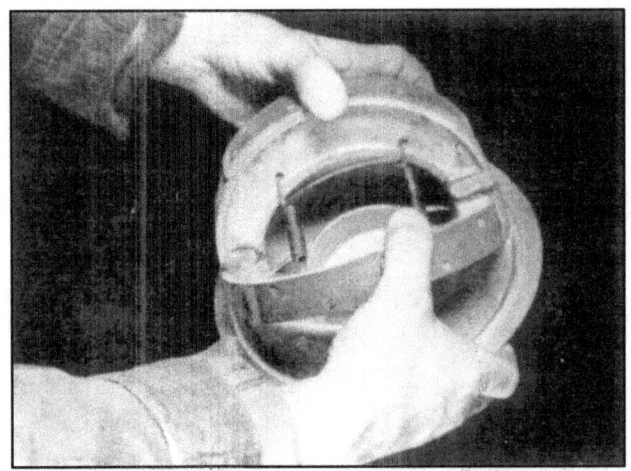

Fig. 80

Front brake cover plate. The brake cover is located by a nut 021931 at the back of the plate. This nut is adjusted so that the plate when assembled is flush with the edge of the hub shell. The plate lock nut 018071 is fitted with the hexagonal side against the plate.

Water enters the brake. Check the location of the cover plate for correct position.

Centralising the brakes. For maximum brake efficiency both brake shoes must contact the drum simultaneously when the brake is applied. Release the spindle nut, also the cover plate lock nut. Closely adjust the brake cable and put pressure on the brake lever. Whilst maintaining the pressure, retighten the lock nut and spindle nut, this action will allow close adjustment of the brake shoes, without binding.

In exceptional cases the hole in the plate for the wheel spindle can be enlarged a slight amount.

Removing the plate lock nut. If there is difficulty in releasing this nut and a vice is not available, put the wheel spindle into one of the fork slider caps, with wheel outside the forks and tighten the clamp nuts, which will act as a temporary vice, see Fig. 82.

Rear brake. The rear brake drum is detachable. The front and rear brake shoes are interchangeable. See details for Scrambler brake for brake shoe adjustment.

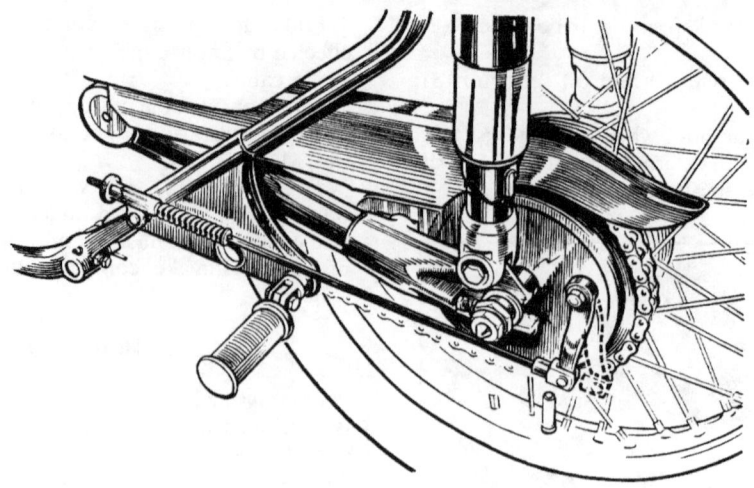

Fig. 81
Showing break rod adjustment exhausted, indicating the need for break thrust pin adjustment.

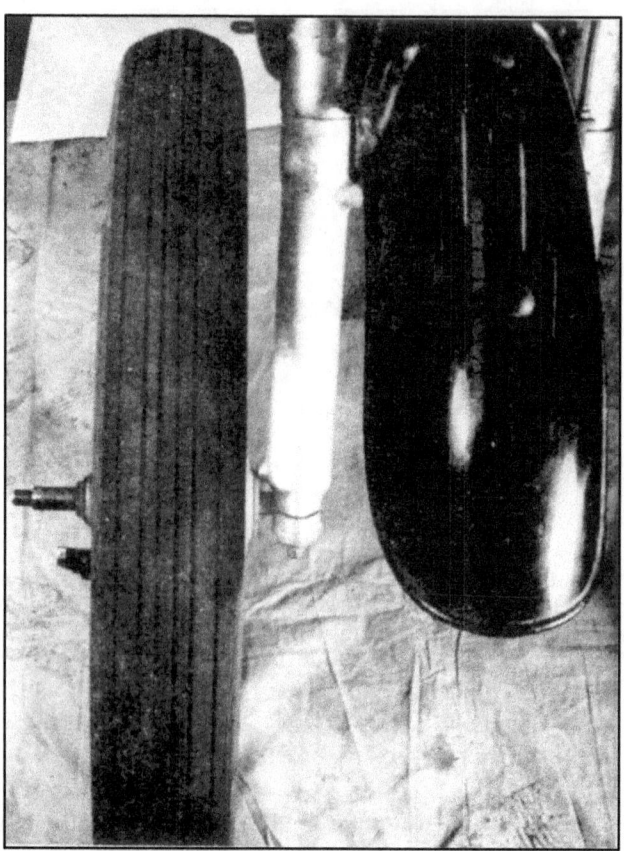

Fig. 82

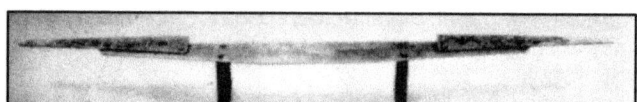

Fig. 83

Balancing the wheels. At high speeds, if the tyres are out of balance, the steering can be affected and in extreme cases the front forks can 'flap' at maximum speed. As oil seals are used on both wheel spindles, the wheel cannot be accurately balanced until the friction caused by the seals is removed. The courses open are:
(1) Remove the oil seals.
(2) Obtain two ball races with an internal diameter sufficiently large enough to take the wheel spindle, mount the wheel on two boxes as shown in Fig. 86.

If the wheel is correctly balanced, it should remain stationary in any position in which the wheel is placed. The most likely out of balance position will be where the valve is situated or where a security bolt is fitted. The heaviest part will of course come to rest at 180° or 6 o'clock. To counter-balance, use thin strips of lead twisted round the spoke. Special weights for this purpose are supplied by the tyre makers. When the wheel is in perfect balance, secure the strips of lead with insulating tape which should be painted with jointing compound. The effect of a balanced wheel has to be tried to be appreciated if continued high speeds are permissible.

SPEEDOMETER DRIVE (Heavyweight Models)

Should the bearing lock ring (29) come loose and unscrew the bearings, this could be associated with the speedo gear box. If the adjusting ring (30) is not truly concentric with the speedo drive, the tightness of the lock ring can be affected.

A modified adjusting ring 021583 is recommended, or if machining facilities are available, existing part is altered to the dimensions shown in Fig. 85. The old part number is still used for the modified type. The new dimensions are ringed, also indicated by arrow.

WHEELS AND BRAKES
(Lightweight Models)

To remove front wheel (1959 type). With front wheel clear of the ground, run back the brake cable adjuster, disconnect the cable.

WHEEL ALIGNMENT

A tool to check wheel alignment, which is inexpensive and easy to fabricate, is shown in Figs. 83-84. Alternatively a long wooden batten with a straight edge can be used. With the road wheels on a level surface, place the batten alongside both sides of the rear tyre. Straighten the front wheel, when, if the alignment is correct, both sides of the front tyre should make contact with the batten.

Adjust the wheel alignment by manipulating the rear chain adjuster, with an eye on the adjustment of the rear chain. Make allowance when the front tyre is smaller in section to the rear tyre.

FIG. 84

Release the two nuts securing the guard stay.
Give both nuts a sharp tap to centralise the stays.
Take off both spindle nuts, the wheel will come out of the sliders.

To remove front wheel (1960-1961 type). A pull out spindle is used on these models. Follow instructions for earlier type wheel, then remove the right side spindle nut and pull out the spindle. A tommy bar can be used in the spindle hole provided.

To remove front wheel (250 cc. Scrambler). Refer to details given for the Heavyweight Models as the wheel arrangement is identical.

To remove front wheel (350 cc. Lightweight Model). Disconnect brake cable, take off nut securing brake torque arm to brake.
Release the spindle nut, take off the two caps on the slider ends, the wheel will come out.

To remove rear wheel (Lightweight Model). Remove rear chain guard.
Remove speedo drive cable.
Remove chain connecting link.
Remove rear brake rod adjuster.
Release both wheel spindle nuts, pull the wheel clear of the fork ends. Standing on the left side lean the machine to the left and take out the wheel.
When refitting, take care to carefully locate the dogs for the speedo drive into the slots in the hub.

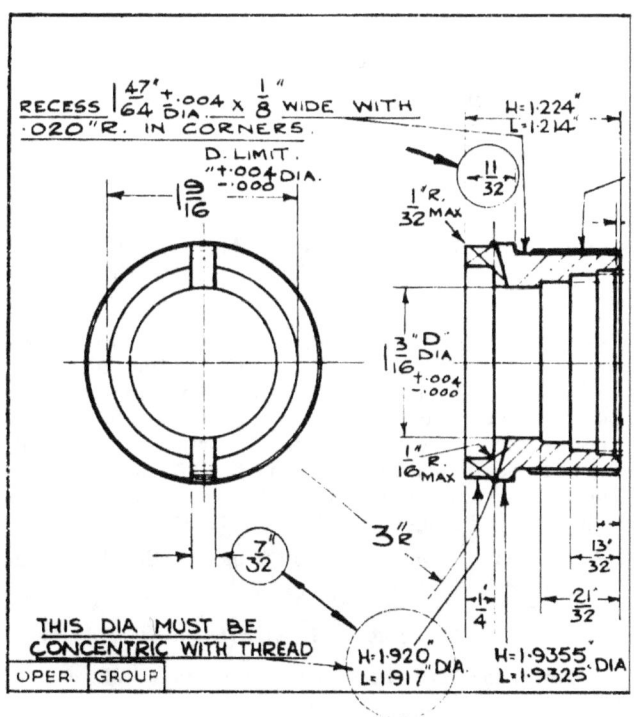

FIG. 85

Fig. 86

To remove rear wheel (Scrambler Model). Remove rear chain connecting link.

Remove rear brake rod adjuster.

Remove speedo cable.

Release wheel spindle nuts, pull the wheel to the right to clear the brake anchorage and pull back the wheel.

Take the wheel out on the right side of the machine.

TO DISMANTLE FRONT WHEEL BEARINGS

(Lightweight)

Front wheel (1959 Model) (Fig. 87). Remove the brake cover plate assembled, then knock out the wheel spindle which will eject the bearing (18), the oil seal (16) and cup (14).

Front wheel (1960-62 Models) (Fig. 88). It will be seen in Fig. 88 that the outside diameter of the spacing tube (13) is nearly the same as the inner member of the bearing (12). In consequence the projection into the spacing tube is small.

Use a steel rod with a square end, inserted through the inner member of nearest bearing and 'feel' for the projection. One or two blows on the rod with a light hammer will dislodge the bearing and bring with it the oil seal and cup.

Rear wheel (all Models). Use the method detailed for the 1959 front wheel bearing.

250 cc. CSR MODEL

Removing the front wheel. Disconnect front brake cable at wheel end.

Disconnect brake torque arm by removing bottom fixing bolt.

Remove front wheel spindle nut.

Remove four nuts securing fork slider clamps.

Remove both clamps, the wheel can now be removed.

Front brake. The air vent slots are intentionally sealed to prevent entry of water. For competition work the metal seal can be removed by a penknife passed through the vent slots.

Front wheel bearings. These are journal type and no adjustment is necessary. The bearings are pre-packed with grease on assembly.

Bearings should be cleaned and re-greased at five to eight thousand miles.

Bearing assembly. The assembly sequence is in the following order:
  Oil seal cap.
  Oil seal felt washer.
  Oil seal collar.
  Oil seal thin washer.
  Bearing SKF 6302 (02).

A spacing tube separates the two bearings, both assemblies are identical.

Removing front wheel bearings. Use a steel rod or bar with a section of $\frac{1}{4}''$.

Insert this tool half-way inside the hub and lever it sideways, which will move the bearing spacer tube.

Place the tool on the bearing ring and drift out, moving the tool from one side of the bearing ring to the other.

Brakes (Lightweight Models). The front and rear brake shoes are identical and interchangable.

When new linings are required and when possible, service exchange brake shoes should be used.

Factory serviced shoes are ground on a fixture, so that the linings will be concentric with the brake drum, with immediate efficiency, providing the brake drum is not badly scored.

The brake drums are not detachable.

If braking efficiency is impaired by reason of over greasing the wheel hub, the brake shoes should be de-greased and not treated with petrol or paraffin, which only tends to make the grease more fluid.

Contrary to general belief, a smooth surface on the brake linings gives the best braking.

Centralizing the brake shoes. If the rear wheel and the brake cover plate has been disturbed, when the wheel is refitted leave the spindle nut 043303 and lock nut 043305 slightly loose.

Press hard on the rear brake pedal, tighten the lock nut whilst pressure is maintained.

The fact of opening out the spindle hole in the cover plate to the extent of $\frac{1}{32}''$ will ensure centralization.

Brake squeal. Check linings and drum for dust from linings. Centralize brake shoes or fit new type rear brake expander lever 043419, which will also improve braking efficiency.

Wheel bearings (Lightweight Models). Two journal bearings at each end of the hub are a press in fit. The bearings are greased when assembled. The bearings should be cleaned and re-greased every 4,500-5,000 miles. Use grease of the anti-centrifuge type for these bearings.

If wear develops on the right-hand front wheel bearing, entry of water is the cause. Fit the new water excluder 043420 to shroud the bearing.

Discard cover 043282 and spacer 043358.

Wheelbearings (250 cc. Scrambler). Taper roller bearings similar to those used on the Heavyweight Models are fitted to both wheels. The outer cups are pressed into the hubs.

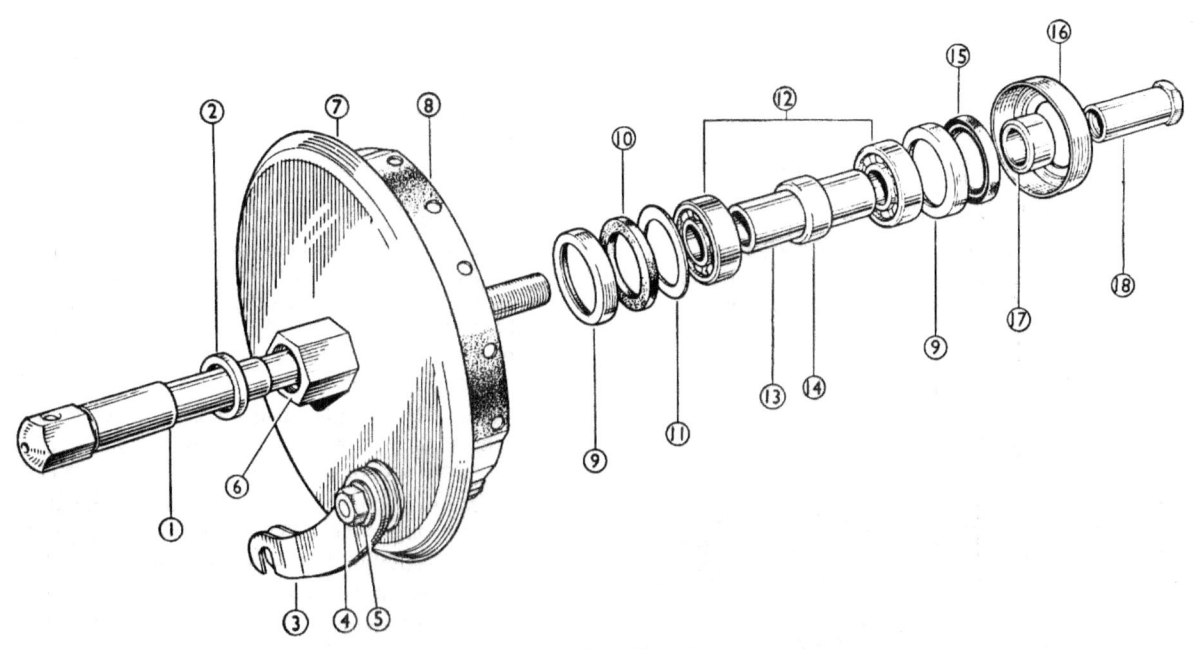

Fig. 87
Front Hub Assembly 1960-1962 Type.

1 Spindle, front wheel.
2 Washer, front wheel spindle (350 cc. only).
3 Lever, brake shoe expander.
4 Nut, brake shoe expander lever.
5 Washer, brake shoe expander lever.
6 Spacer, hexagon, front cover plate.
7 Cover, front brake plate.
8 Brake shoes, pair.
9 Enclosure cup, oil seal.
10 Seal, felt, for bearing.
11 Washer, bearing felt seal.
12 Bearing, for hub.
13 Spacing tube, bearing.
14 Pressing, spacing tube.
15 Seal, rubber, for bearing.
16 Enclosure cap.
17 Spacer, front spindle.
18 Nut, front spindle.

These bearings rarely need adjustment, providing grease is applied via the nipples on the hub, say every 1,000 miles.

For service details see Heavyweight Models.

The assembly sequence is shown in Fig. 90.

FIG. 90

Spoke breakage (early type Lightweight Models). In the event of spoke breakage in the rear wheel of the above models, replacement of the broken spokes is not recommended as the spokes adjacent to the broken ones will be unduly strained and subsequently break.

It is preferable under these circumstances to rebuild the wheel with an improved type of spoke lacing. The old, also new method, are depicted in Fig. 91. It will be seen that the inner spokes only are affected.

OLD TYPE   FIG. 91   NEW TYPE

Speedometer gear box lubrication. Where a grease nipple is not fitted, periodical lubrication is not necessary as the drive parts are made from self lubrication material. A little oil on the seal is beneficial when the drive is removed from the wheel.

TRANSMISSION

(Heavyweight Models)

Front chain adjustment. The general arrangement for adjusting the chain is shown in Fig. 92.

The Scrambles Models use a chain adjuster on each side of the gear box, to prevent the gear box from moving.

Remove the engine plate cover, also inspection cap on chaincase.

Slack off the nut at the end of bolt (5).
Slack off the nut at the end of bolt (3).
To tighten the chain: Screw down the bolt (1). Press down the rear chain to pull the gear box backwards.

Check the chain tension, which, if correct, should have a whip of $\frac{3}{8}''$.

If the chain is too tight, unscrew the bolt (13) a little at a time, until the adjustment is correct.

Check the tension in several places. Chains do not always stretch evenly. Retighten the nuts (3) and (5).

Now check the rear chain adjustment.

Chain case oil level. With the machine vertical and on both road wheels, the bottom run of the chain should just touch the oil.

Rear chain adjustment (quickly detachable wheel). To take up slack or tighten the rear chain and with the machine on the central stand:

Release slightly the spindle nut (22) and the dummy spindle nut (20).

Run back the lock nuts on the two chain adjusting bolts through fork ends, unscrew each adjusting bolt a trifle at a time, also an equal amount, until the chain whip taken in the centre of the bottom chain run is $1\frac{1}{8}''$. Check the tension in one or more places.

As an alternative and possibly the best method is to have this adjustment made with the machine on its road wheels and the rider seated, when the chain whip should be $\frac{1}{2}''$. Retighten the released nuts when the adjustment is correct, then check the rear brake adjustment, which will be affected when the wheel position is altered.

Rear chain adjustment (non-quickly detachable wheel). Release the spindle nut (1) and adjust the chain as already described.

Removing the front chain. Follow details for removing engine from frame. When refitting the chain the closed end of the spring line should face the direction of rotation.

Removing the rear chain. The rear chain is closely shrouded by the chain guard, which leaves little room to operate, other than releasing the chain guard from its fixings. If a new chain is to be fitted, disconnect the connecting link in the fitted chain and connect it to the new chain at the top run. Select a neutral position in the gear box then with the left hand holding the bottom chain run and the top with the right hand, the new chain can be pulled into position until the chain joint is accessible, when the connecting link can be fitted.

Note: The closed end of the spring link should face the direction of rotation.

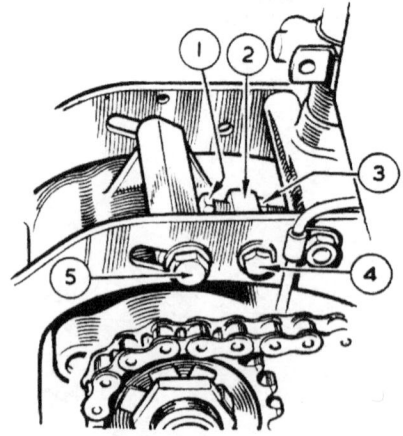

FIG. 92
Front Chain Adjustment.

1 Adjusting bolt.   5 Engine plate bolt.
3 Adjusting bolt lock nut.

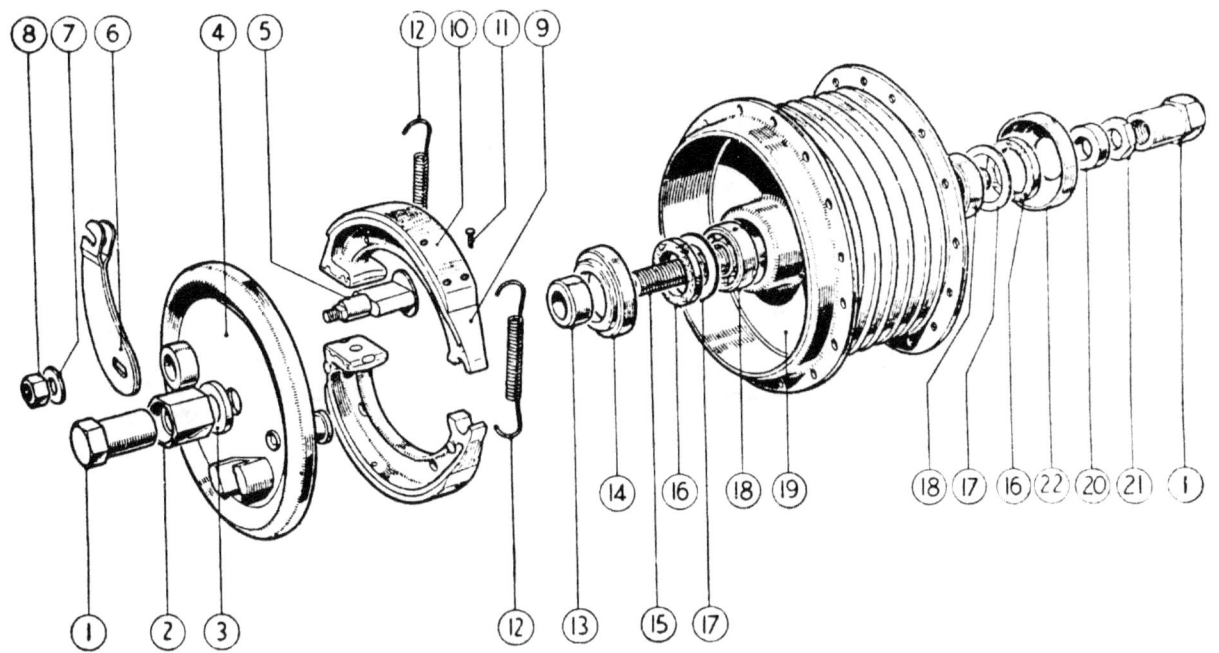

FIG. 88 Front Hub Assembly 1959 Type

1 Spindle end nut.
2 Recessed locknut.
3 Plain washer.
4 Brake cover plate.
5 Expander cam.
6 Brake expander lever.
7 Lever washer.
8 Lever nut.
9 Brake shoe.
10 Brake lining.
11 Lining rivets.
12 Brake shoe spring.
13 Spindle distance piece.
14 Felt seal cup.
15 Spindle.
16 Felt seal.
17 Felt seal washer.
18 Hub bearing.
19 Hub shell and brake drum.
20 Spindle distance piece.
21 Spindle Lock nut.

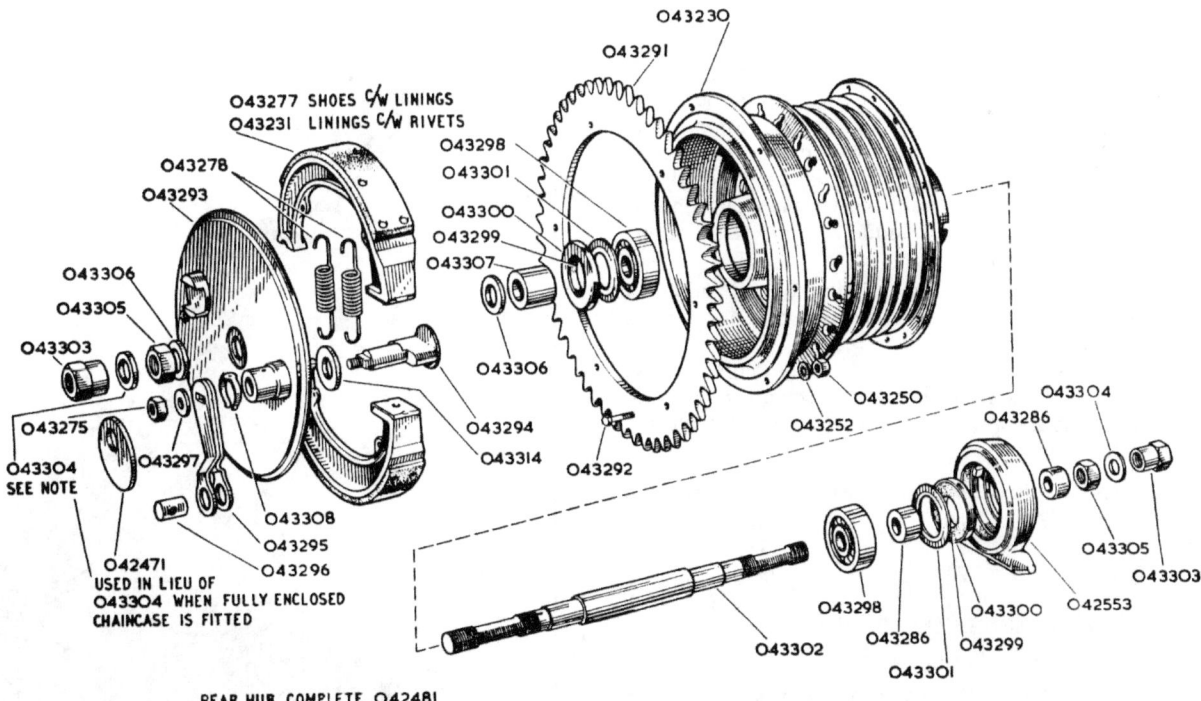

FIG. 89
Rear Hub Assembly

If a second chain is not available, use a piece of string 10 ft. long, take out the connecting link and pass one end of the string through the link hole. Pull on the string until both ends meet and tie them together.

Pull on the bottom run of the chain, with one hand, keeping the string taut with the other hand.

As the chain leaves the gear box sprocket, the string will be each side of the sprocket teeth.

When the chain is well clear, cut one piece of the string about one foot from where it passes through the chain.

Detach the chain, leaving the string in position.

To refit the chain. Pass the longer end of the string through the chain and tie the ends together. Now pull on the string, guiding the chain until it encircles the gear box sprocket. Continue pulling until the top run encircles the rear wheel sprocket and fit the connecting link.

THE CARE OF CHAINS

The primary chain. This chain operates under ideal conditions as it is totally enclosed and runs in a bath of oil. Nevertheless, periodical attention is necessary to verify the oil level is maintained, also that the adjustment is correct. As this chain is not readily visible, this maintenance can unintentionally be overlooked.

The rear chain. With the exception of the Lightweight Model this chain is not so favourably situated. Each chain joint is in fact a plain bearing of steel to steel on a hardened surface. To prevent metal to metal contact, it is essential to maintain a film of lubricant between the bearing surfaces, which will minimise friction and prolong the life of the chain.

If lubricant is applied with the chain *in situ*, oil should be diverted firstly to the joint formed by the roller and link edges (a Wesco gun is best suited for this purpose). Apply oil whenever the chain has a dry appearance.

When the machine has been used frequently during inclement weather it is preferable to remove the rear chain for attention. All traces of road grit should be removed with a wire brush and the chain thoroughly washed in paraffin. Wipe the chain dry.

Use a shallow tray sufficiently large enough to accommodate the chain, fill it with a quantity of anti-centrifuge grease, heat the grease until it reaches a state of fluidity and immerse the chain. Agitate the chain sideways to assist penetration of the fluid and leave for about ten minutes. When cool, remove the chain and take off surplus grease. After refitting and adjusting, and with short use, the chain will slacken off slightly, when the surplus grease has been squeezed out of the joints and will need further adjustment.

Checking the chain for wear. A simple and practical method to decide if the chain has reached the rejection limit is shown in Fig. 93.

The chain should be washed in paraffin so all joints are free. Use a flat board and anchor one end of the chain with a nail, using a foot rule as shown, measure the elongation from the following table.

Chain pitch.	Pitches measured.	Rejection limit or over.
$\frac{5}{8}"$	16	$10\frac{7}{32}"$
$\frac{1}{2}"$	23	$11\frac{3}{4}"$
$\frac{3}{8}"$	24	$9\frac{3}{16}"$

TRANSMISSION SERVICE

(Lightweight Models)

Front chain adjustment. Remove inspection cap from front chaincase; remove the two securing screws on the rear engine cowling; lift the cowling to expose the gear box adjuster bolt. Slacken nut on left-hand side of gear box top fixing bolt. Slacken two clamping strap bolts.

Adjust chain by means of adjuster eye-bolt 043938 and two nuts. (The correct chain whip is $\frac{3}{8}"$.)

Check the adjustment in several positions and adjust at tightest part of chain.

Tighten two clamping strap bolts, top gear box fixing bolt.
Refit rear engine cowling and securing screws.
Replace chaincase inspection cap.

Note: After adjusting front chain, check rear chain adjustment.

Removing the front chain (350 cc. and 250 cc. CSR Models). The front chain fitted to this model is duplex and endless, which means that the clutch sprocket, also the engine sprocket must be withdrawn simultaneously if the front chain is to be removed. To proceed, follow the instructions given for dismantling the clutch, as far as removing the gear box main axle shaft nut. Then remove the nut and washer retaining the rotor to the driving side engine shaft, take out the key for the rotor from the shaft. The engine sprocket and clutch, together with the chain in position, can then be withdrawn.

Note: One or more shim washers may be fitted at the rear of the engine sprocket, which must be replaced during assembly.

Rear chain adjustment. Prior to adjusting rear chain, check front chain and adjust if required.

Loosen both nuts on the rear wheel spindle.

Loosen lock nuts on the adjusters and turn the adjusters until correct chain adjustment is obtained, taking care to move both adjusters exactly the same amount to maintain wheel alignment.

While on the stand the chain whip should be $\frac{3}{4}"$ to ensure $\frac{1}{2}"$ whip when rider is seated.

Check the adjustment in several positions and adjust at tightest part of chain.

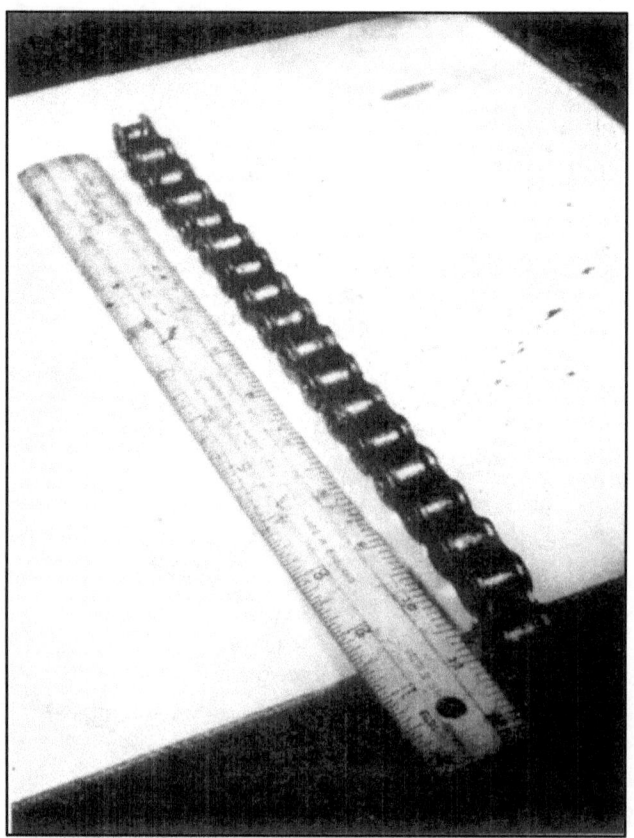

Fig. 93

Remove the rubber cap on the totally enclosed chain guard to check chain tension.

Retighten wheel spindle nuts, and adjuster lock nuts.

Note: After chain adjustment rear brake should be checked and re-adjusted as necessary. See 'Brake adjustment'.

Removing and refitting rear chain. To protect the rear chain from mud and water it is very closely shrouded by the chain guard and removing the chain without first detaching the chain guard, can present considerable difficulty. A simple procedure, however, is as follows:

First obtain a piece of thin string about 10 ft. long.

With cycle on the stand turn the rear wheel until the chain connecting link is at a position near the rear sprocket, and remove the connecting link.

Now pass the string through the centre hole of the end link of the top run, draw the two ends of the string level and tie together.

Then pull the bottom run of the chain backwards with one hand while keeping the string taut at the rear end with the other hand.

As the end of the top run of the chain disengages with the gear box sprocket it will leave the string attached lying one strand each side of the sprocket teeth.

When the chain is well clear cut the string one side only at a point about one foot from where it is looped through the chain link.

Leave the string then *in situ* awaiting chain refitting.

To refit the chain: pass the longer cut end of the string through the centre hole of the end chain link and then tie the two loose ends of the string together. Then pull the string from the rear end, at the same time guiding the chain up to engage with the gear box sprocket.

Continue pulling until the chain encircles the sprocket. Remove the string, refit the connecting link with the spring clip closed end facing direction of rotation.

To remove the rear chain guard (fully enclosed type). Remove bottom fixing nut on left-hand rear suspension unit, and slide the lower end of the unit off the stud, slacken the left-hand wheel spindle nut. Remove the two chaincase securing bolts. The large spindle washer is used outside the guard.

The top and bottom halves of the chaincase can then be removed.

Open chain guard. Remove bottom fixing nut on left-hand rear suspension unit and slide the lower end of the unit off the stud. Remove rear brake rod adjuster nut, rear chain and speedometer cable, slacken wheel spindle nuts. Remove the two chain guard securing bolts, lift the rear of the chain guard and slide the rear wheel out of the forks ends. The rear chain guard can now be removed.

Reverse this procedure for reassembly.

Front chaincase oil seal. The felt washer in the rear half of the chaincase, for the gear box mainshaft is fitted before the plates are spot welded. If this seal is unserviceable, take a new felt ring and using a razor blade, cut the new one into two. The ring half its normal thickness can be pressed between the steel plates.

CARBURETTER SERVICE

Carburetter function. The petrol level is maintained by a float and needle and in no circumstances should any alteration be made to these parts. In the event of a leaky float, or a worn needle valve, the part should be replaced with new. (Do not attempt to grind a needle to its seat.)

The petrol supply to the engine is controlled, firstly, by the main jet and, secondly, by means of a taper needle (see Fig. 94), which is attached to the throttle valve and operates in a tubular extension of the main jet.

The main jet controls the mixture from three-quarters to full throttle, the adjustable taper needle from three-quarters down to one-quarter throttle, the cut-away portion of the intake side of the throttle valve from one-quarter down to about one-eighth throttle, and a pilot jet, having an independently adjusted air supply, takes care of the idling from one-eighth throttle down to the almost closed position. These various stages of control must be kept in mind when any adjustment is contemplated (see Fig. 94 for location of the pilot jet air adjustment screw). The pilot jet, unlike on earlier models, is now detachable for cleaning.

The size of the main jet should not be altered save for some very good reason. See 'Data' for details of standard sizes of jet, throttle valve and jet taper needle.

With the standard setting it is possible to use nearly full air in all conditions, except perhaps when the engine is pulling hard up hill or is on full throttle, when some benefit may be obtained by slightly closing the air control.

Weak mixture is always indicated by popping or spitting, at the air intake.

A rich mixture usually causes bumpy or jerky running and in cases of extreme richness, is accompanied by the emission of black smoke from the exhaust.

Carburetter adjustment. With the taper needle projection, main jet size and type of throttle slide specified, correct carburation, except at idling speed is assured. In the event of difficulty being experienced look for cause under heading 'Useful information'.

To check for correct idling mixture, first run the engine until it is just warm, but not too hot, when with the throttle nearly closed and air fully open it should fire evenly and slowly. If it fails to do so, first of all make certain that the sparking plug is clean and the point setting correct. Having done this and idling is still uneven try resetting the pilot jet air screw.

Adjustment of this air screw is not unduly sensitive and it should be possible to obtain the correct setting for even firing in a few seconds.

In the event of even firing at idling speed being unobtainable by adjustment of the air screw, look for obstruction in the pilot jet.

Having obtained even firing, all that remains is to adjust if necessary the position of the throttle stop screw until the desired idling speed is obtained.

Air Filter. In locations, such as the United Kingdom, where the roads and atmosphere are particularly free from dust, it is not considered necessary to have an air filter fitted to the carburetter, but in countries where the atmosphere contains a very heavy dust content, an air filter is essential in order to prevent abrasive wear.

The filter available (optional extra) for the conditions mentioned above is of the 'Oil Wetted' type, and this requires periodical servicing.

When servicing the air filter, withdraw the filter element. Thoroughly wash this in petrol, paraffin or other suitable solvent and allow to dry. Then re-oil, using one of the light oils (SAE-20) and allow to drain before replacing in the filter case. Clean at intervals of 2,500 to 5,000 miles according to road conditions and renew the element every 10,000 miles.

Scrambles Models. It is worth while to coat the inside of the metal container with heavy grease to trap foreign matter. Service the filter after each event.

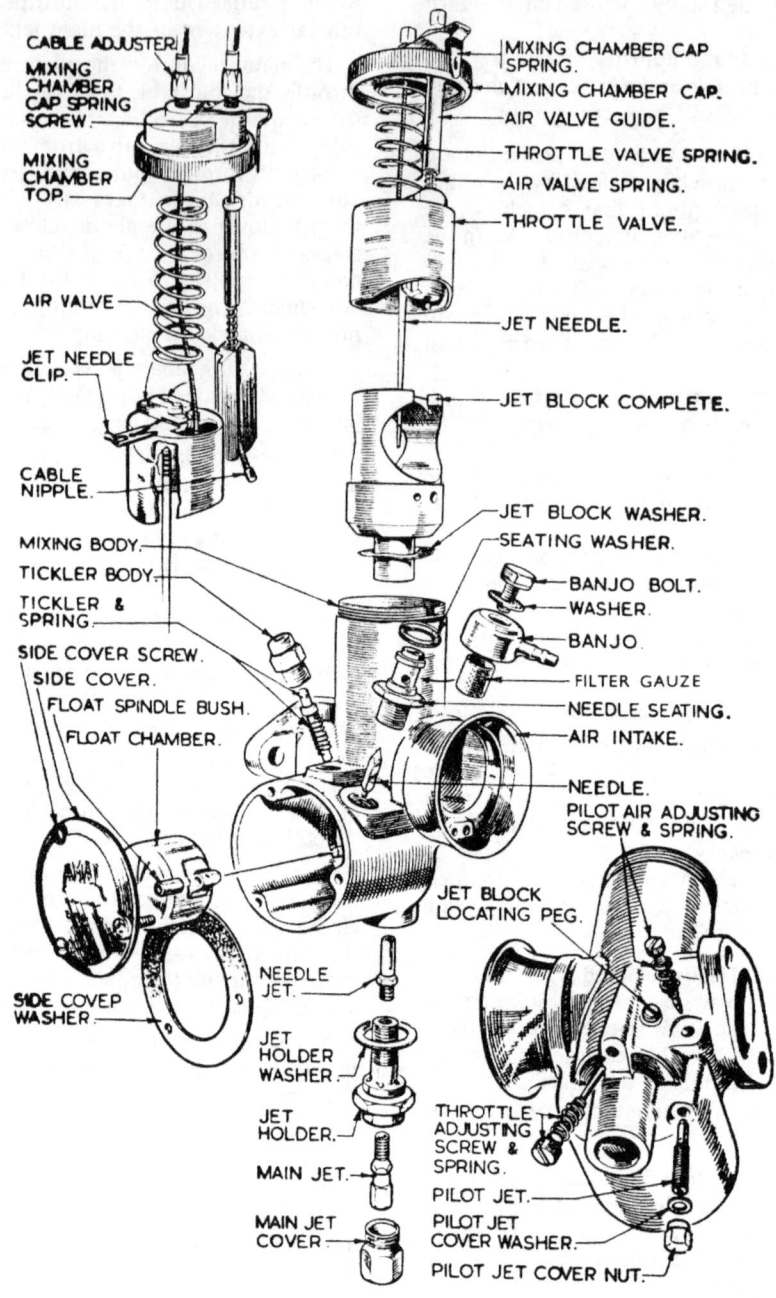

Fig. 94
Carburetter details in Assembly Order.

FITTING TWIN CARBURETTERS 1960-1962 MODELS (650 cc.)

Special carburetter distance pieces for use in place of the manifold are available for the above models. The original carburetter can be retained for use with the additional parts, as detailed.

Discard the original main jet, pilot jet and throttle slide, locate taper needle fourth notch from the top.

Setting the Slow Running. Start by using two clean spark-ing plugs with a plug gap of .020″ to .022″. Set the slow running on each cylinder separately by starting the engine with the ignition slightly retarded (Magneto Models) then remove the H.T. plug cable from the left side cylinder. Manipulate the slow running adjustment screw in conjunction with the throttle slide stop screw, until the tick over is slow, also positive. Repeat the process to deal with the other cylinder.

Note.—The throttle inner cables must be of equal length to ensure both throttle valves move the same amount when the twist grip is operated, by manipulating the cable adjuster.

Parts Required
1. 028232 Carburetter type 389/49.
1. 376/140 Jet Holder, long.
1. 376/141 Banjo, single.
2. 376/074 Fibre Washers.
1. 389/064 Mixing Chamber top cap.
2. 4/035 Cable Adjusters.
1. 376/076 Pilot jet size 25.
1. 376/100 Main jet size 280.
1. 389/060 Throttle valve size 3.
1. 028219 Spacer.
1. 028221 Spacer.
4. 018873 Allen screws.
2. 041014 'O' Rings.
2. 024308 Spacers.
4. 010624 Studs.
4. 000004 Nuts.
2. 028236 Air cables, carburetter end.
1. 028237 Air cable, lever end.
2. 028238 Throttle cables, carburetter end.
1. 028239 Throttle cable, twist grip end.
2. 019824 Junction boxes for cables.

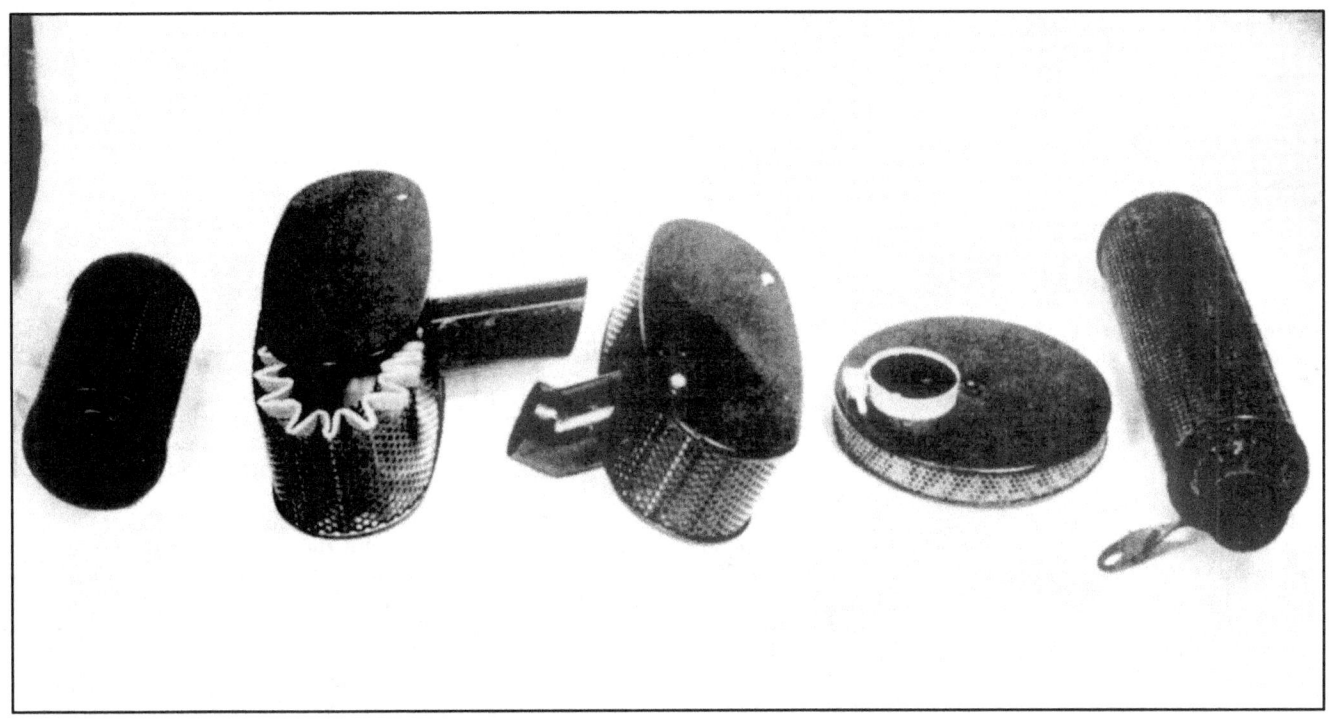

250 cc. Twin Single Trials 500 cc. Scrambler

Carburetter tuning information

Poor idling may be due to:
  Air leaks either at junction of carburetter and inlet manifold, or by reason of badly worn inlet valve stems or guides.
  Faulty engine valve seatings.
  Sparking plug faulty, or its points set too closely.
  Ignition advanced too much.
  Contact breaker points dirty, pitted, loose or set too closely.
  High-tension wire defective.
  Pilot jet not operating correctly. Partially choked or incorrect air supply.
  Rockers adjusted too closely.

Heavy petrol consumption may be due to:
  Late ignition setting.
  Bad air leaks. Probably at carburetter or manifold joints.
  Weakened valve springs.
  Leaky float (causing flooding).
  Taper needle extension insufficient.
  Poor compression, due to worn piston rings or defective valve seatings. (Test compression with throttle wide open.)

Carburetter flooding. If the carburetter is flooding, the float spindle bush (Fig. 94) may be pinched between the float swivel and the float chamber cap.

Reduce slightly the width of the tube or renew the gasket for the cover.

Exercise care to avoid over tightening the pilot jet which can deform its seating in the mixing chamber. A defective jet block fibre washer will allow fuel to leak across the choke.

Notes on carburation. The main jet originally fitted is deemed to be the most suitable. There should be no necessity to alter the main jet size without good reason, i.e. by fitting an air filter, running with an open exhaust pipe system or at specified altitudes.

Riders with considerable experience can, after driving at full throttle for at least a third of a mile decide, after 'reading' the sparking plug if the main jet size is suitable or otherwise.

Without such experience it is preferable to drive at full throttle and close the air lever ¼". If the engine speed increases, the main jet is small. Conversely, if the engine speed decreases, the main jet is larger.

Jet alterations should be made in stages of 10 cc. increase in jet size, viz. size **200** to **210**.

TORQUE SPANNER SETTINGS

Twin Models

Cylinder head bolts	16 ft. lbs.
Twin cylinder head bolts (⅜ studs)	25 ft. lbs.
Centre web clamp	20 ft. lbs.
Con rod nuts	22 ft. lbs.
Centre web studs (6 off)	7 ft. lbs.

Heavyweight Models

Cylinder head bolts	35 ft. lbs.
,, ,, ,, Scrambler and Short Stroke	40 ft. lbs.
,, ,, ,, (all singles) (1964)	40 ft. lbs.
Crankpin nuts	190 ft. lbs.
,, ,, Scrambler	240 ft. lbs.
,, ,, (all singles) (1964 models)	240 ft. lbs.

Lightweight Models

Cylinder head bolts (250 cc. and 350 cc.)	35 ft. lbs.
,, ,, ,, Scrambler	42 ft. lbs.
Crankpin nuts	140 ft. lbs.
,, ,, Scrambler	190 ft. lbs.

SPECIAL TOOLS

Lapping tool for con rod liner	A8078
Extractor for tappet guides	B152
Chain bar	B2139
Flywheel separating tool	B2140
Fork inner tube tool (small)	B2141
,, ,, ,, ,, (large)	B2141A
Pinion extractor	B2151
Magneto and dyno sprocket tool	B4018
Oil pressure gauge	B4108
Shaft locating tool	B5761
Extractor bolt contact breaker	042247
Pinion extractor	043332
Valve spring tool	018276
Extractor mag. and timing pinion	015273
Extractor cam gears	015374
Extractor bolt contact breaker	024328
Clutch extractor tool	040449
Timing disc	022011

Piston ring clamps obtainable from Elms Garage (Birmingham Ltd.), Birmingham 31.

IMPROVISED WORKSHOP TOOLS

Several useful workshop tools can be fabricated from worn or scrapped parts, for example: a tool to fit on the gear box mainshaft splines (where the clutch is fitted) to prevent the shaft from turning whilst tightening the shaft nut 041265, can be made from an old first gear pinion 041279 (250 cc. gear box) with a length of strip steel 12″ × 1″ × 3/16″ welded to the pinion.

Similarly for the A.M.C. Heavyweight gear box, an old Burman clutch sleeve for mainshaft G-35-2 with a clutch washer 12-10-4 welded, or something similar, together with a steel strip of above dimensions, can be used for the same purpose.

A tool to turn the engine during overhaul, to set tappets, ignition, etc., is invaluable. A suitable handle for this purpose can be made up from an old shock absorber cam, 000830, for single-cylinder models, and cam 016584 for twin-cylinder models. A short length of steel strip welded to the cam with an old crankcase bolt through the end of the strip, completes the handle. This tool in position and used as a sprag against the bench, will hold the engine from turning whilst tightening or unscrewing the small timing pinion nut, camshaft nuts, etc.

If a gear box, either the Lightweight or Heavyweight type, is completely dismantled, or for attention to the main sleeve gear bearing and oil seal, it is not an easy matter to secure the sleeve gear whilst tightening the rear chain sprocket nut. A mainshaft third gear pinion 040012, welded or brazed on to an old mainshaft 040001, is the tool for this job. With the mainshaft held in a vice, invert the gear box shell over it and engage the third gear pinion into the sleeve gear. The chain sprocket nut can then be firmly tightened, without stress on the sleeve gear or the gear box shell.

Use pinion 041276, and shaft 041263, Lightweight gear box, for the same purpose.

A bent or damaged single-cylinder engine push rod with the adjuster removed, can be screwed on to the fork damper rods to 'fish-up' the rod for attachment to the fork tube bolt.

WIPAC ALTERNATOR TESTING INSTRUCTIONS

The Series 114 Alternator consists of a six pole Stator ring 5″ in diameter with six coils and a six pole permanent magnet rotor. There are three main leads coloured white, light green and orange. Three coils are connected in series to white and light green, the other three coils are connected in series to white and orange. The output from these coils is a.c. converted to d.c. by means of a bridge-connected metal rectifier. The output of the alternator is controlled through the switch on the headlamp and connects three or six coils according to its position.

Emergency starting. The emergency position is intended for starting when the battery is discharged. This position is marked 'EMG' on the ignition switch.

In this position the two groups of alternator coils are connected in parallel, and if the lights switch is in the 'OFF' position the full output of the alternator goes into the battery. This will raise the voltage of a discharged battery to a level sufficient to start the engine. In the EMG position the charge rate is high—the engine should not be run in EMG too long. The boost charge thus provided may be used to restore a discharged battery. Switch over to IGN after ten minutes.

Rotor demagnetised. Although the WIPAC Rotor is robustly built and holding a very high magnetic charge, it can become demagnetised if the machine is run with battery connections reversed, or if the rectifier breaks down. A demagnetised rotor should be returned to WIPAC for satisfactory remagnetisation.

Testing. Testing of component parts can be carried out if the following instruments are available:

0-12 d.c. Volt Meter.

0-15 a.c. Volt Meter.

1 ohm Resistor (capable of carrying 8 amps.).

10-0-10 d.c. Ammeter.

High grade moving coil instruments must be used and accurate. The 1 ohm. resistor must also be accurate, otherwise correct readings cannot be obtained. *Engine speed* when testing should be in the region of 2,500 r.p.m. Tests should not be attempted at speeds below 2,000 r.p.m. A few revs. above or below 2,500 will not affect the readings of an alternator in good condition.

Charge rate test:

(1) First check the battery voltage which, if fully discharged, should be substituted for one that is in good condition.

(2) Disconnect the brown negative lead from the double connector.

(3) Connect the d.c. ammeter in series with the battery wire and the double connector.

(4) Run the engine at 3,000 r.p.m., the minimum permissible readings are shown in the following table:—

Ignition switch.	Lights switch	Minimum charge rate.
Ignition on	Off	1.0a
Ignition on	Low	1.3a
Ignition on	High	1.0a
Emergency on	Off	6.0a

The rate of engine speed and condition of the battery will affect the charge rate recorded. The figures shown in the table in comparison with the recorded figures indicate if the system is functioning correctly.

N.B.: If the charge rate is down with lights on HIGH check the main bulb wattage.

Low or no charge rate test. Check the alternator output by:

(1) Disconnect the white, orange and light green wires from the four-way connector. If a maroon colour lead is also used, leave this in position.

(2) Using the a.c. voltmeter with the one ohm. resistor across the terminals (parallel) join one wire from the voltmeter to the white wire, the other meter wire to the orange wire. Run the engine at a speed equivalent to 30 m.p.h. in top gear, the voltage reading should be between 6.2 and 6.8 volts.

Transfer the meter wire from the orange wire to the light green and repeat the test. A low reading on one of these tests indicates a fault in the coils. A low reading on both tests can be due to a partially demagnetised rotor.

If no reading is shown in both tests, the alternator is defective (see test 3).

(3) A short circuit to earth on one or more coils will affect the a.c. voltage output.

To check, with the front chain case in position, use the d.c. voltmeter in series with a battery in good condition, Connect the wire from the meter to the white wire, the battery wire to a good and convenient earth on the engine. If a reading is shown on the meter, one or both coils are shorting to EARTH.

Note: The white wire is common to all coils.

Remove the outer portion of the chain case, check the alternator wires for damaged insulation, also coil connections before discarding the alternator.

When the fault is located, repeat the tests previously described.

Rectifier tests. Before testing, verify the earth connection is clean and secure. Check also the wires attached to the rectifier for loose connections. Take out the white, green and brown wires from the rectifier.

For this test use a 6 volt battery connected to a 3 watt bulb and holder. Connect the battery and bulb holder wire across the rectifier as shown in diagram (A) (Fig. 95).

Test in the following sequence:

Positive wire to Light Green ⎫ Bulb earthed. Bulb lights.
  ,,   ,,   ,, White   ⎬   Rectifier O.K.
                              ⎭ Bulb on Green. No light.
  ,,   ,,   ,, Brown   ⎫   Rectifier
  ,,   ,,   ,, Brown   ⎬ ,, White. No light.
                              ⎭   Rectifier faulty.

Reverse the battery connections with:

Negative wire to Light Green ⎫ Bulb earthed. No light. Rectifier O.K.
  ,,   ,,   ,, White   ⎬ fier O.K.
                              ⎭ Bulb on Green. Bulb lights.
  ,,   ,,   ,, Brown   ⎫ ,,   ,, White. Rectifier
  ,,   ,,   ,, Brown   ⎬   faulty.

Note: The common cause of rectifier trouble is invariably due to reversed battery connections, which can also demagnetise the rotor, if the engine is run with these connections reversed. The battery positive terminal is connected to EARTH (translucent), the negative is the feed line (brown).

Ignition and lighting switches. Both switches in the head lamp are mechanically identical and will interchange, the switch knobs being differently marked. If one switch is suspect, take off the lamp rim and glass. Pull off the cable plugs and reverse their location. A further check will indicate

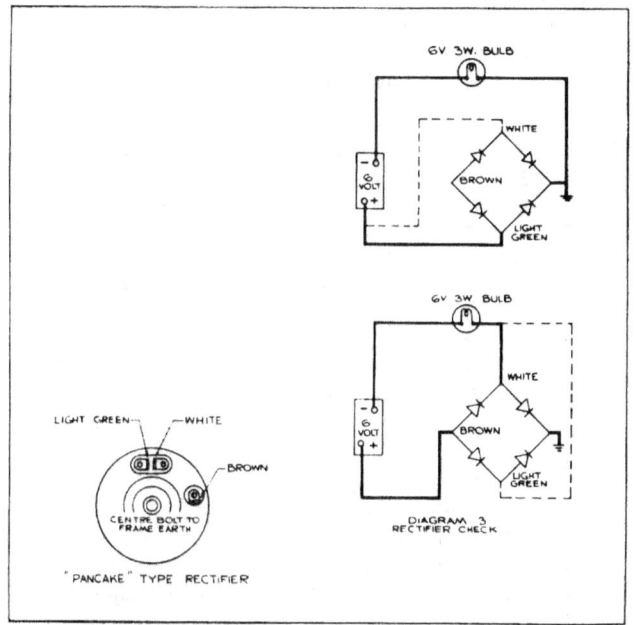

FIG. 95 A

if the switch is defective or otherwise. Replace the cable plugs in correct position after changing the switch.

Replacement switches should be of the improved type which can be identified by a NYLON post for the switch knob. Old type switches use a steel post.

Plug location. The blue plug is for the lighting system and the black for ignition.

WIPAC ELECTRICAL SERVICE

Lamp bulb 'blowing'. Premature bulb failure involving all or many of the light bulbs at one time on a full d.c. battery system is caused by a defective connection in the battery 'line'.

This 'line' starts at (1) the frame end of the translucent lead from the positive battery terminal and proceeds:

(2) Positive battery terminal.
(3) Negative battery terminal.
(4) Brown wire from battery negative to 4-hole connector (bullet terminal).
(5) Brown wire from 4-hole connector to ammeter (bullet terminal).
(6) Ammeter terminal with brown wire.
(7) Ammeter terminal with blue wire.
(8) Both ends of short insulated link wire in the ignition switch plug, which joins blue ammeter wire to brown wire going to lights switch.

Should the ammeter develop internal open circuit, bulbs will blow, also should the battery have little or no electrolyte, this is a partial or complete open circuit with the same results. There is finally the remote possibility of one of the actual wires in the battery 'line' being broken—again, bulbs will 'blow'.

For quick checking, test connections in this order:

(1) Both battery terminals.
(2) Both ammeter terminals.
(3) All brown wires into 4-hole connector.

Speedometer bulb. On models made before 1961, the speedometer bulb is in circuit during daylight running and fails from filament fatigue. Transfer the wire attached to the speedometer bulb holder and connect it to the light switch as shown in wiring diagram for 1962 models, to illuminate the speedometer when lights are in use.

Ignition system.

Special Note: The star-shaped washer for contact breaker pivot is not detachable. If the engine fails to start and there is no spark at the sparking plug points, examine the contact breaker by:

Check the gap at full separation .012" and reset if necessary (ensure feeler gauge is free from oil).

Check condition of contact points which should have a grey frosted condition. The presence of oil or grease in the contact breaker compartment will cause a black matt condition.

Clean points with an abrasive strip or alternatively fine grade emery cloth. Pass a strip of clean paper, or rag soaked in petrol, across the points after cleaning.

Check free movement of contact breaker arm on its pivot.

Adjusting contact breaker gap. This adjustment is effected by altering the position of the plate for the fixed contact point by:

(1) Releasing slightly the locking screw.
(2) Adjust the gap by turning the eccentric screw (close to the fibre pad) in the required direction, with the fibre pad on the rocker arm on the cam lobe (maximum separation) .012". Retighten the lock screw when adjustment is correct.

Lubrication. The felt pad should be impregnated with H.M.P. grease. Use sparingly, an excess can affect contact points surface.

Before replacing the contact breaker cover, check the condenser fixing for security.

If attention to the contact breaker fails to produce a spark, check the circuit by:

Switch on the ignition, rotate the engine very slowly until the contact points close. A discharge between three to four amps will be shown on the ammeter if current is passing.

As the ammeter is not closely calibrated, a more accurate check can be made by using the d.c. ammeter in between the brown battery wire and its connector.

If a discharge is not shown on the ammeter with contact points closed, this indicates current is not passing through the primary windings in the h.t. coil.

With ignition switch on check the dark green wire attached to the coil by:

Removing this wire from the coil terminal.
Connect one side of the d.c. voltmeter to the end of the dark green wire, the other side of the meter to earth.
If there is no reading on the meter, check the ignition (black) plug in the headlamp.
If the internal insulated wire bridge across two of the plug terminals (see wiring diagram) is fractured or disconnected, this will allow the engine to start with the switch on either emergency or ignition, but not in both positions, as one switch connection is out of circuit.

Renew the bridge connection.

Ignition coil test.

(1) Use a battery with one wire attached to the d.c. voltmeter with a short length of wire attached to the other voltmeter terminal.
(2) Disconnect the two wires attached to the coil, also the h.t. cable.
(3) Use a further wire on the second battery terminal. Connect the free end of this wire, also the meter wire across the coil terminals. If there is continuity, a reading will show on the meter indicating the primary winding is in order.
(4) Transfer one wire from the coil terminal to the centre h.t. connection, if there is continuity a lower voltage reading will show by reason of the higher resistance of the secondary winding.
(5) Place one of the test wires on to one of the two coil terminals, the other to the coil case. No reading should show. Use the test wires on the h.t. connection and the case. No reading should show.

A meter reading on one or both tests means the windings are earthed, the coil should be replaced.

Usually a defective primary winding will produce a weak spark, conversely, an intermittent spark is associated with a faulty secondary winding. Where doubt exists, test by substitution.

The condenser (see 'Ignition system'). If the condenser is suspect, use a sound condenser with two crocodile clips attached to it.

Remove contact breaker cover, attach one clip to the connection on the contact breaker terminal, the other to a convenient earth position.

Running the engine with the external condenser in use will prove if the condenser is faulty or otherwise.

Vivid blue arcing at the contact points is indicative of a faulty condenser.

Where the orthodox electrical testing gear is not available, improvisation can be made by using the following equipment:

(1) A 6 volt 36 watt bulb and holder.
(2) A 6 volt .04 amp bulb and holder (this bulb is used on cycle rear lamps).
(3) A fully charged 6 volt battery.
(4) A short length of wire to join the battery to one side of the bulb holder. Also two test wires about 24" long connected to the other battery and bulb holder terminals.

Test to ensure the bulb lights then proceed by:

Disconnecting the alternator wires from the connector.
Join one test lead to the white cable, the other test wire to the green cable.
Run the engine at a fast tick over speed when the bulb should show a fairly bright light.
Transfer the test wire from the green cable only to the orange cable and repeat the test.

Conclusions from test

(1) If the lamp bulb is not uniformly lighted on both tests, there is a fault in the alternator (see 'Earth test').
(2) Should the bulb fail to light, the alternator is defective.
(3) A dull light on both tests indicates a partially demagnetised rotor, due to battery connections being reversed at some time or other. Use a.c. voltmeter to check voltage output.

Alternator coils earthed. Use the test set with the 6 volt .04 bulb.

Connect one test wire to a convenient earth position on the engine.

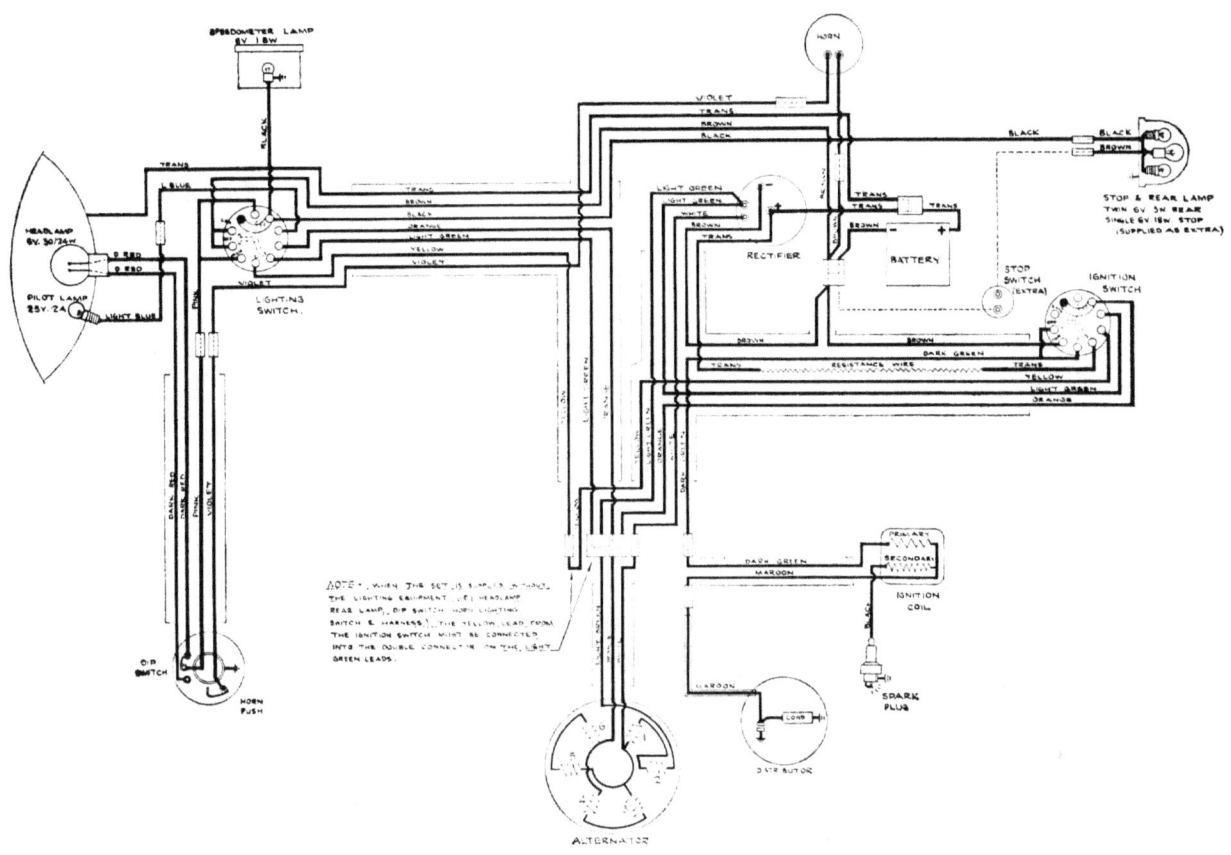

Fig. 96
Wiring Diagram, 250 cc. Scrambler.

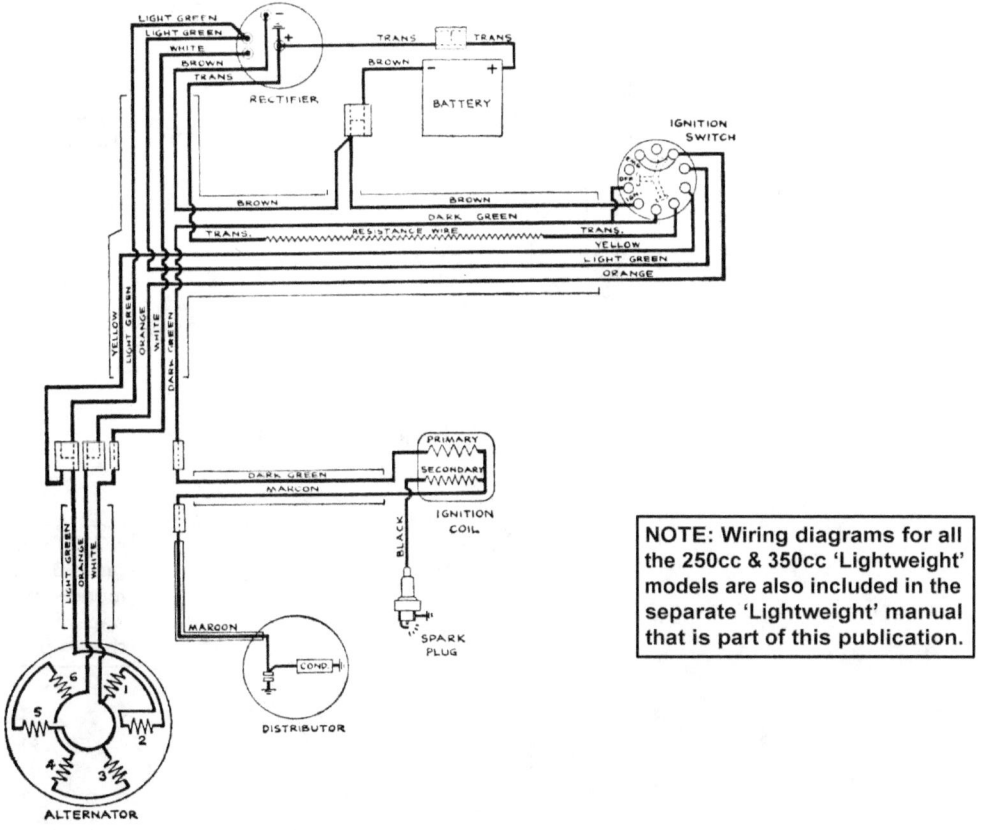

Fig. 97
Wiring Diagram, 250 cc. Scrambler (with lights removed).

NOTE: Wiring diagrams for all the 250cc & 350cc 'Lightweight' models are also included in the separate 'Lightweight' manual that is part of this publication.

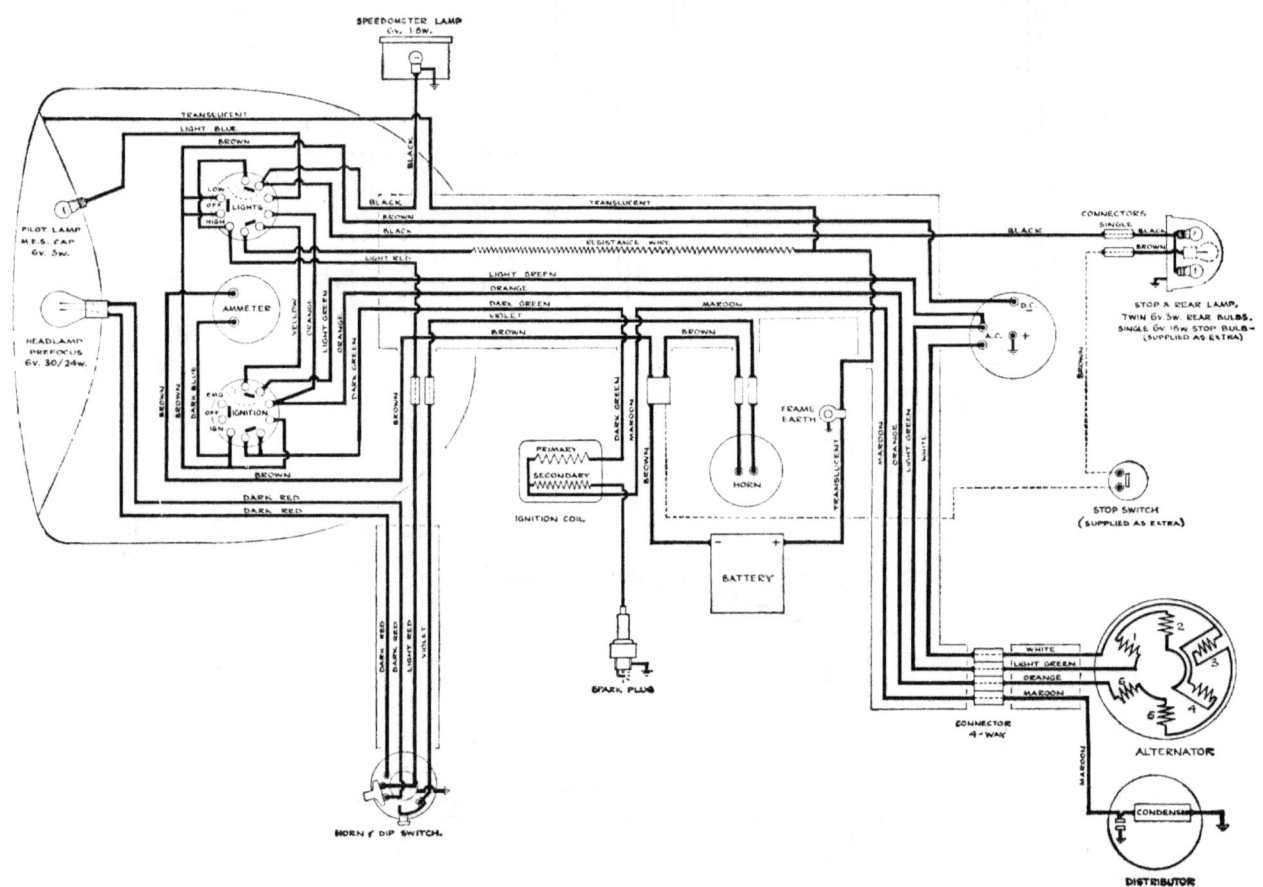

FIG. 98
Wiring Diagram 250 and 350.

NOTE: Wiring diagrams for all the 250cc & 350cc 'Lightweight' models are also included in the separate 'Lightweight' manual that is part of this publication.

Connect in turn, the other test wire to the white, green and orange wires.

Should the bulb light on any of these tests, the coils are shorted to earth.

Rectifier (forward flow test). With the ignition and lights switches 'OFF', use the 36 watt bulb for this test, then:

Disconnect the wire from the brown connector on the rectifier (keep the wire end clear of the frame and engine).

Connect one test lead to rectifier brown terminal, the other test lead to earth.

Switch on to EMG and run the engine at tickover when, if the rectifier is O.K. the bulb will light brightly (six coils in circuit).

Repeat the test with the switch at IGN (three coils in circuit), the bulb will light, but not so brightly if rectifier is O.K.

Warning: Do not attempt to run the engine with an open circuit for the rectifier. The brown wire or the test set must be connected to prevent high voltage which will cause damage.

Rectifier (reverse flow test). With the light and ignition switches 'OFF' test by:

Taking off one of the battery wires from the battery.

Connect the test set with the .04 amp bulb between the battery terminal and the battery wire.

If the reverse flow is normal, the bulb will light dimly, a bright light indicates a defective rectifier.

Alternative rectifier tests. An alternative method of testing can be effected by using the following equipment:

(1) A moving coil ammeter, scale 10-0-10.
(2) A fully charged 6 volt battery.
(3) A 6 volt 30 watt lamp bulb and holder.
(4) A 6 volt 0.040 amp bulb and holder.
(5) Three short test wires.

Forward flow test. Make a series circuit as shown in diagram B (Fig. 95B). The bulb will light with a reading of approximately 4.5 amps on the meter.

Take off the wire from the positive battery terminal, connect the third test lead to the positive battery terminal, also to the brown terminal on rectifier (d.c. negative).

Take up the wire taken from the battery and connect in turn to the green, then white, terminals (a.c. side).

In each test the bulb should light with a reading of 4.5 amps on the meter.

For clarity, remove test wires from rectifier, remake the series circuit B.

Next remove the battery negative wire, connect the third test wire to the negative battery terminal, also to the rectifier earth bolt or case.

Connect in turn the wire removed from the battery to the green and white terminals. Again, in each test the bulb should light with a reading of 4.5 amps.

If the meter readings on these tests are above 3 amps, the rectifier is satisfactory. Discard the rectifier if the readings are below 3 amps.

Note: Whilst a new rectifier will show 4.5 amps, this value will decrease after considerable service.

Reverse flow test. Make the circuit shown in diagram C (Fig. 95C) for this test.

A rectifier that is normal will have a reverse flow which should not exceed 0.040 milliamps, by using the 0.040 bulb with a current consumption of 40 milliamps it can be established if the reverse flow is abnormal by:

Removing the positive lead from the battery.

Join the third test wire to the battery positive, also to the rectifier earth bolt or case.

Connect the wire removed from the battery, in turn, to the white and green terminals.

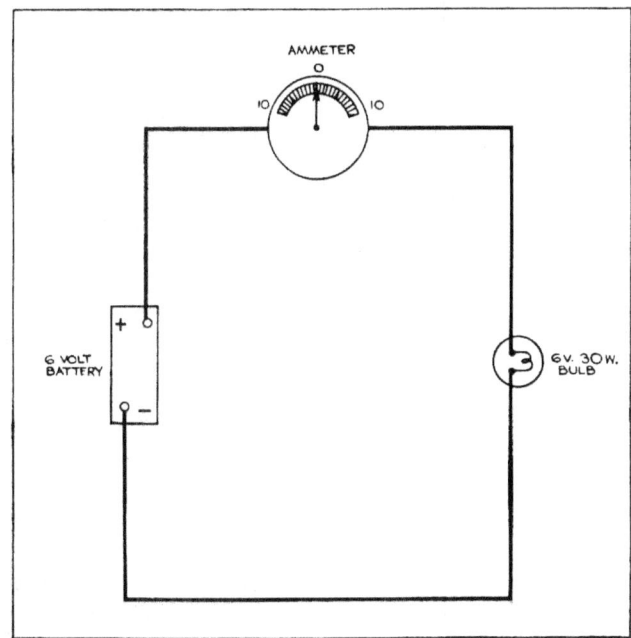

Fig. 95 B

If the bulb lights in these two tests the rectifier is defective.

Take off the test wires from rectifier and remake the circuit C.

Remove the negative wire from the battery.

Join the third test wire to the battery negative terminal, also to the brown rectifier terminal.

Connect the wire removed from the battery in turn, to the green and white terminals.

Should the bulb light in either of these tests the rectifier is defective.

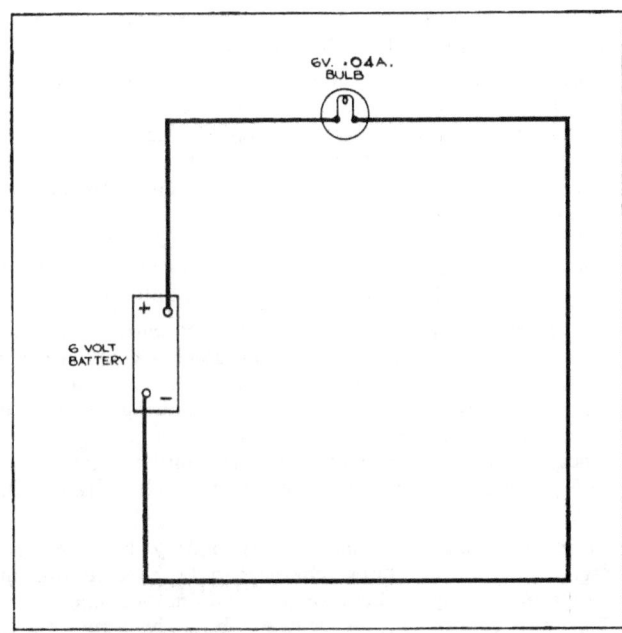

Fig. 95 C

LUCAS ELECTRICAL SERVICE

SINGLE CYLINDER AND ALTERNATOR TWINS
LUCAS A.C. LIGHTING-IGNITION UNIT

ALTERNATOR MODEL RM15

The alternator consists of a spigot-mounted 6-coil laminated stator bolted to the outer portion of chaincase with a rotor carried on and driven by an extension of the crankshaft. The rotor has an hexagonal steel core, each face of which carries a high energy permanent magnet keyed to a laminated pole tip. The pole tips are riveted circumferentially to brass side plates, the assembly being cast in aluminium and machined to give a smooth external finish.

Thus there are no rotating windings, commutator, brush-gear, bearings or oil seals and consequently the alternator requires no maintenance apart from occasionally checking the snap connectors in the three output cables are clean and tight, which are located behind the frame cover which is located by two knurled screws.

(1) Disconnect the green and yellow and green and black connectors.
(2) Reconnect the green and black to the green and yellow.
(3) Do not interfere with the green and white cable.

It is stressed that this is a temporary measure, prolonged use will adversely affect the battery.

Rectifier. The rectifier is a device to allow current to flow in one direction only. It is connected to provide full-wave rectification of the alternator output. The rectifier is mounted on the tool box under the twin seat.

The rectifier requires no maintenance beyond checking that the connections are clean and tight. **The nut clamping the rectifier plates together must not under any circumstances be slackened, as it has been carefully set during manufacture to give correct rectifier performance.** A separate nut is used to secure the rectifier to the frame of the motor cycle.

Note: It is important to check periodically that the rectifier is firmly attached to its mounting bracket.

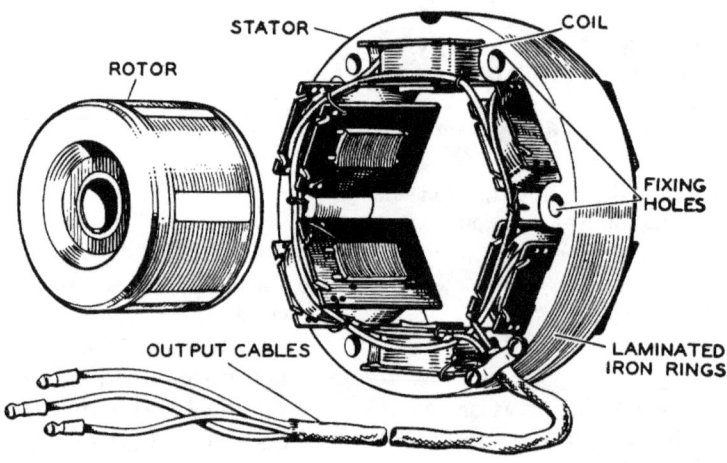

FIG. 99
Alternator.

If it is necessary, for any purpose, to remove the rotor, there is no necessity to fit keepers to the rotor poles. When the rotor is removed wipe off any metal swarf which may have collected on the pole tips. Place the rotor in a clean place.

Normal running. Under normal running conditions (i.e., ignition switch in IGN position) electrical energy in the form of rectified alternating current passes through the battery from the alternator—the rate of output depends on the position of the lighting switch. When no lights are in use, the alternator output supplies the ignition coil and trickle-charges the battery. When the lighting switch is turned, the output is automatically increased to meet the additional load of the parking lights and again when the main bulb is in use.

Emergency starting. An EMERGENCY starting position is provided in the ignition switch for use if the battery has become discharged. Under these conditions, the alternator is connected direct to the ignition coil, allowing the engine to be started independently of the battery.

Once the engine is running, turn the ignition switch back to the normal running position, otherwise misfiring will occur.

Emergency charging. Should the battery become discharged a temporary boost charge can be effected during daylight running, by an alteration to the alternator connections.

The snap connectors are located behind the frame plate, which is secured by two knurled screws.

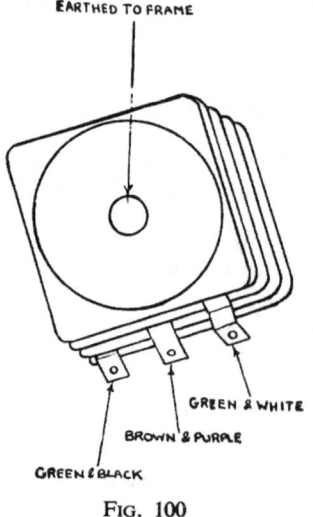

FIG. 100
Rectifier.

LUCAS COIL IGNITION (SINGLES)

The coil is clipped to the front frame top tube underneath the petrol tank.

The ignition equipment comprises a model MA6 ignition

coil and a model CA1A contact breaker unit. The contact breaker, together with an automatic timing control, are located in the engine timing case.

The automatic timing control is centrifugal operated and varies the firing point according to the speed of the engine.

Lubrication. To be carried out every 6,000 miles.

No grease or oil must be allowed to get on or near the contacts when carrying out the following procedure.

Smear the surface of the cam very lightly with Mobilgrease No. 2, or, if this is not available, clean (SAE 30-40) engine oil may be used.

Squeeze a little grease into the felt wick.

Place a spot of clean engine oil on the contact breaker pivot.

Remove the central fixing bolt and inject a small amount of clean engine oil into the hole thus exposed. When the fixing bolt has been replaced and the engine run for a few minutes, the oil will be forced out over the automatic advance mechanism by centrifugal force.

Cleaning (every 6,000 miles). Examine the contact breaker. The contacts must be free from grease or oil. If they are burned or blackened, clean with fine carborundum stone or very fine emery cloth, afterwards wiping away any trace of dirt or metal dust with a clean petrol moistened cloth. Cleaning of the contacts is made easier if the contact breaker lever carrying the moving contact is removed.

To remove the moving contact, unscrew the nut securing the end of the spring and remove the nut, spring washer and bush. Lift the contact breaker lever off its pivot.

After cleaning, check the contact breaker setting.

Contact breaker setting. The contact breaker gap should be checked after the first 500 miles running and subsequently every 3,000 miles. To check the gap, turn the engine over slowly until the contacts are seen to be fully open, and insert a feeler gauge between the contacts.

The correct gap setting is 0.014″—0.016″.

If the gap is correct, the gauge should be a sliding fit. (Make sure the gauge is clean and oil free before use.)

To adjust the gap, keep the engine in the position giving maximum contact opening and slacken the screws securing the fixed contact plate. Adjust the position of the plate until the gap is set to the thickness of the gauge, and tighten the securing screws.

LUCAS COIL IGNITION (ALTERNATOR TWINS)

The ignition equipment comprises a Model MA6 coil with a Model 18D2 distributor assembly. The contact breaker with automatic advance mechanism is mounted in the distributor body.

The distributor has a flange fitting retained to the crankcase by one bolt and two nuts.

The drive is by gear pinion on the distributor shaft which is located by a parallel pin passing through the distributor shaft and the pinion. The parallel pin is retained by a circlip encircling the boss on the pinion.

An efficient oil seal encircles the distributor shaft to prevent oil entering the contact breaker compartment with an 'O' ring on the body for oil retention. A bronze thrust washer is fitted between the pinion and the distributor body. A clamp incorporated in the flange mounting, when released, will allow the distributor to be moved for ignition timing. The rotation is anti-clockwise.

Cleaning. To be carried out every 6,000 miles. Remove and clean the distributor cover, which must be handled with care. Pay particular attention to the spaces between the metal electrodes in the cover, and check that the small carbon brush moves freely in its holder.

Lubrication. Lift off the rotor arm, and unscrew the two screws securing the contact breaker base plate. Remove the base plate and lubricate the automatic advance mechanism with clean engine oil, paying particular attention to the pivots.

Re-fit the base plate and rotor arm.

Examine the contact breaker. The contacts must be free from grease or oil. If they are burned or blackened, clean with fine carborundum stone or very fine emery cloth, afterwards wiping away any trace of dirt or metal dust with a clean petrol-moistened cloth.

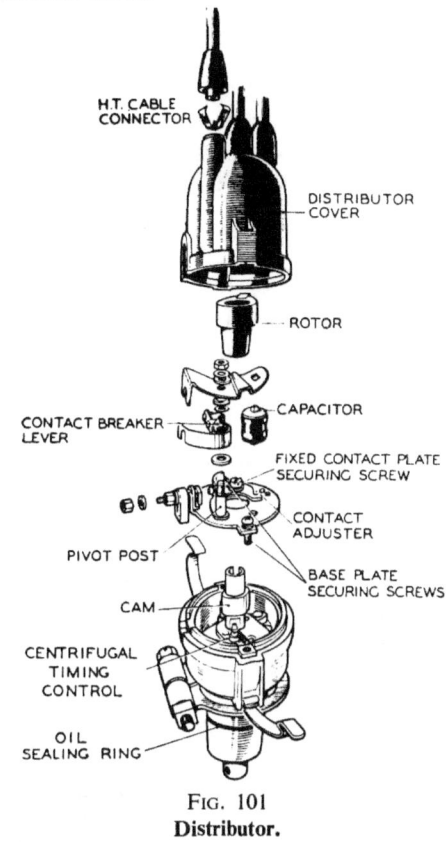

Fig. 101
Distributor.

Contact cleaning is made easier if the contact breaker lever carrying the moving contact is removed. Before re-fitting the contact breaker lever, lightly smear the cam and pivot post with clean engine oil.

No grease or oil must be allowed to get on or near the contacts.

After cleaning, check the contact breaker setting.

Contact breaker setting. The contact breaker gap should be checked at the first 500 miles and subsequently at every 6,000 miles. To enable the engine to be rotated freely and slowly, remove both sparking plugs and distributor cover. Turn the engine slowly until the heel for the moving contact is on the peak of the cam (maximum separation). Check the gap by introducing a feeler gauge (which must be clean) between the points which should be a sliding fit with the correct gap, the correct setting is .014″—.016″.

To adjust the gap, ensure maximum separation, slacken slightly the screw securing the fixed contact plate.

Insert the screwdriver between the two projections on the base plate and the notch in the fixed contact plate and adjust to obtain the correct gap.

Re-tighten the fixed contact screw and re-check the gap.

IGNITION COIL (ALTERNATOR TWINS)

The coil, Type MA6, requires no attention whatsoever beyond keeping its exterior clean, particularly the terminals and occasionally checking that the connections are tight.

When the high tension cable shows signs of perishing or cracking it must be renewed, using 7 mm. p.v.c.-covered or neoprene-covered rubber ignition cable.

To remove the old cable from the ignition coil, pull the cable together with its connector from the moulded terminal socket. It is advisable to fit new connectors when renewing ignition cables.

The coil is clipped to the front-frame top tube underneath the petrol tank.

CAPACITOR (ALTERNATOR MODELS)

The capacitor is now attached to the base plate by a screwed extension. Take away the base plate to remove capacitor. Fig. 102 shows the early type.

MAGNETO MODELS

ELECTRICAL EQUIPMENT

Lucas electrical equipment is fitted and this comprises three independent electrical circuits, as follows:

(1) IGNITION—Magneto, High-tension wires, Sparking plugs and Cut-out switch.
(2) CHARGING—Dynamo compensated voltage control unit and Battery.
(3) LIGHTING AND ACCESSORIES—Lamps, Horn, Switches and Wiring.

To remove contact breaker. Take out the hexagon-headed screw from the centre of the contact breaker, then pull the assembly off the tapered shaft. When refitting, ensure the projecting key on the assembly engages with the keyway cut in the armature shaft. Incorrect assembly will affect ignition timing.

Adjustment every 3,000 miles. Remove the contact breaker cover and turn the engine until the contact points are fully opened. Check the gap with a gauge having a thickness of .012" (spanner 015023 has a gauge of this thickness as an integral part of it). If the setting is correct the gauge should be a sliding fit, but if the gap varies appreciably from the gauge it should be adjusted by releasing the fixed contact plate securing screw and using a screwdriver as shown in Fig. 102.

Cleaning every 5,000 to 6,000 miles. Take off the contact breaker cover and remove the contact breaker. If the contact points are burned or blackened, clean them with a fine carborundum stone or with very fine emery cloth, and afterwards wipe away any dust or dirt with a petrol-moistened cloth. After replacing the contact breaker check the point gap and, if necessary, re-set it.

Remove the high tension pick-ups (held by swinging spring clips), wipe clean and polish with a fine dry cloth. The high tension pick-up brush must move freely in its holder.

If it is dirty, clean with a cloth moistened with petrol. If

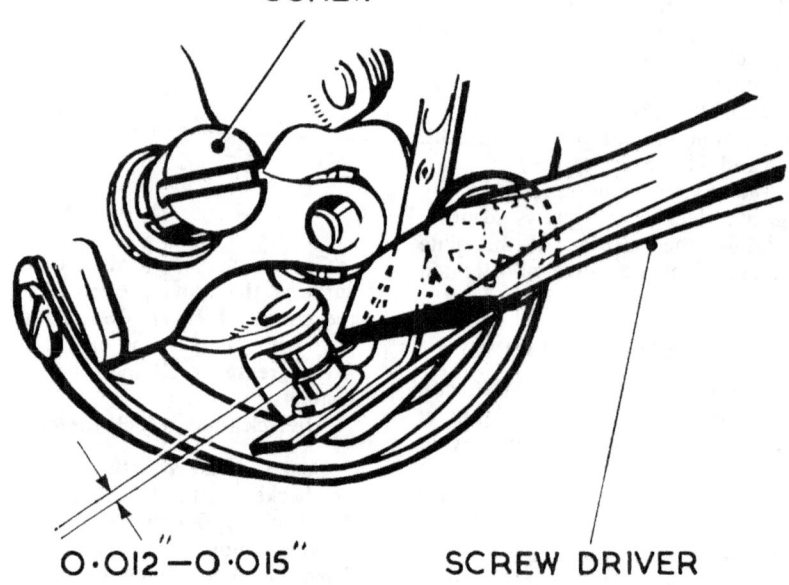

Fig. 102

IGNITION

A Lucas type K2F magneto is fitted. The replacement part number is 42230-A and the part number of the complete contact breaker is 492854.

Lubrication and adjustment is required every 3,000 miles, cleaning is required every 5,000 miles and every 10,000 miles the complete unit should be handed to a Lucas Service Station for dismantling, replacement of worn parts, cleaning and lubrication.

Lubrication every 3,000 miles. Smear the cam ring inside and out with Mobilgrease No. 2. Apply a spot of clean engine oil to the tip of the pivot post. **No oil must be allowed on or near the contacts.**

the brush is worn to within $\frac{1}{8}$" of the shoulder it must be renewed. Treat both pick-ups and their brushes.

While the pick-ups are removed, clean the slip ring track and flanges by holding a soft cloth on the ring by means of a suitably shaped piece of wood, while the engine is slowly turned.

If, on inspection, the high tension cable shows signs of perishing or cracking, it must be replaced by a suitable length of 7 mm. p.v.c.-covered, or neoprene ignition wire.

Magneto removal and fitting. The magneto is 'spigot fitting' and is retained to the crankcase by two studs and one bolt.

To remove the magneto it is necessary to:

Take away the timing gear cover.

Withdraw the driving gear from the magneto shaft. (Already described in the 'Engine Section').

Disconnect the high tension wires from the sparking plugs.

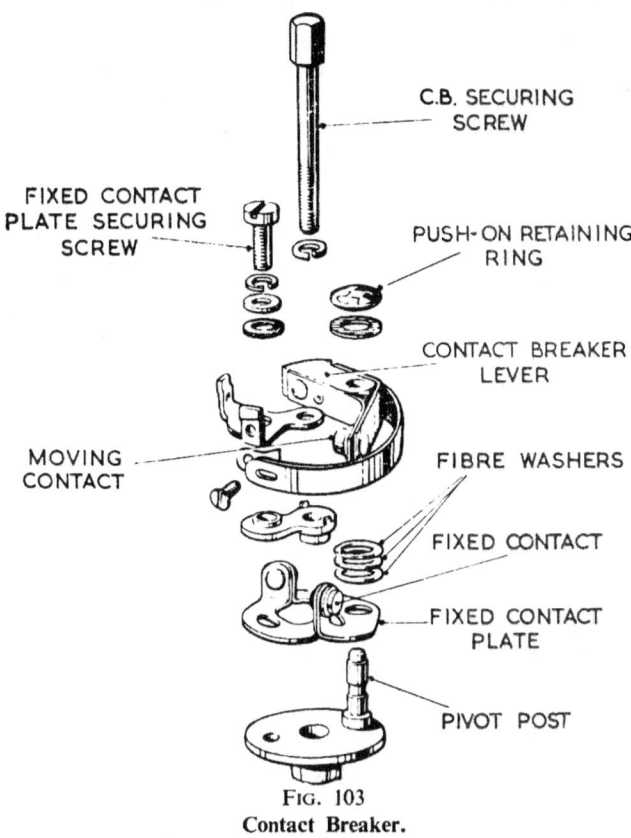

Fig. 103
Contact Breaker.

Disconnect the ignition control cable.

Remove the nuts from the two studs and one bolt that secure the magneto body to the crankcase and the unit is free to be taken away.

The re-fitting is done by the above procedure reversed and the method of timing has already been described in the 'Engine Maintenance Section'.

DYNAMO

A Lucas type E3L-L1-O dynamo is fitted. It is anti-clockwise in rotation. The cutting in speed is 1,050—1,200 r.p.m. at 6.5 volts and at 1,850 to 2,000 revolutions per minute it gives an output of 8.5 amps at 7 volts. The positive brush is earthed. The two exterior terminals are marked 'D' and 'F', indicating the respective terminals for the output and field wires that lead to similarly marked terminals on the regular unit.

Inspect commutator and brush gear every 5,000 to 6,000 miles (maker's recommendation).

Remove the cover band to inspect commutator and brush gear.

The brushes are held in contact with the commutator by means of springs. Move each brush, see they are free to slide in their holders, if dirty, or if sticking, remove and clean with a cloth moistened with petrol. Take care to replace brushes in their original positions, otherwise they will not 'bed' properly on the commutator.

If, after long service, the brushes have become worn to such an extent that the brush flexible wire is exposed on the running face, or if the brushes do not make good contact with the commutator, they must be replaced by genuine Lucas brushes.

The commutator must be free from any trace of oil or dirt and should have a highly polished appearance. Clean a dirty, or blackened, commutator by pressing a fine dry cloth against it while the engine is slowly turned over by means of the kickstarter. (It is an advantage to remove the sparking plugs before doing this.) If the commutator is very dirty, moisten the cloth with petrol.

At every 10,000 miles the complete dynamo should be handed to a Lucas Service Station for dismantling, replacement of worn parts, cleaning and lubrication.

Electrical breakdown of the dynamo is most unusual and therefore before assuming this unit is defective, it should be tested as follows:

Check that the dynamo, regulator and battery are correctly connected.

Test dynamo in position by:

(*a*) Remove the two wires from the dynamo terminals and connect the two terminals with a short length of wire.

(*b*) Start the engine and set to run at normal idling speed.

(*c*) Connect the negative lead of a moving coil voltmeter (calibrated not less than 0 to 10 volts) to either of the two dynamo terminals and connect the positive lead to a good earth point on the dynamo or engine.

(*d*) Gradually increase the engine speed, when the voltmeter reading should rapidly rise and without fluctuation.
Do not allow the voltmeter reading to rise above 10 volts. Do not race the engine in an attempt to increase the voltage. It is sufficient to run up the engine to a speed of 1,000 r.p.m.
If the above reading is obtained the dynamo is in order.
If there is no reading, check the brush gear.
If there is a low reading of approximately ½ volt, the field winding may be at fault.
If there is a low reading of approximately 1½ to 2 volts, the armature winding may be at fault.

If the tests, mentioned above, clearly indicate the dynamo is not charging, it is then desirable to remove the dynamo from the machine in order to make further tests and repairs or replacements.

To remove and re-fit dynamo. The dynamo rests on a cradle forming part of the crankcase and is retained by a band having an adjustable clamping action and one stud passing through timing gear case.

It is rotated by a gear meshing with the timing gear wheel on the exhaust cam shaft.

Upon merely slackening the clamping strap and removing the sleeve nut on the outside of timing cover, the dynamo, complete with its driving gear, can be withdrawn from the crankcase. The two wires from dynamo to regulator unit are retained by an insulated bridge secured by one screw and, upon removing that screw, the bridge, with the two cables, can be taken away from the dynamo.

Control box. The regulator is set to maintain a pre-determined dynamo voltage at all speeds and regulate the output of the dynamo to the battery according to the state of charge of the battery. The charge rate is at its maximum when the battery is discharged, automatically tapering off to a minimum as the battery becomes charged and its voltage rises.

Normally, during day-time running, when the battery is in good condition, the dynamo gives only a trickle charge, so that the ammeter reading will seldom exceed 1 to 2 amperes, i.e., half to one division of scale.

If, under normal running conditions, it is found that the battery is continually in a low state of charge, or is being constantly overcharged, then the regulator setting should be checked by a qualified electrician and, if necessary, re-set. Whenever possible, this should be carried out by a Lucas Service Depot or agent.

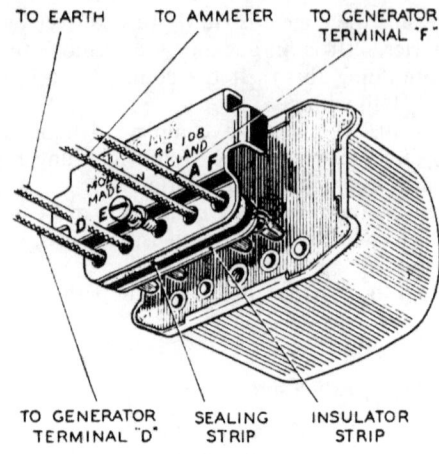

Fig. 104
Control Box Connections.

To remove control box. The A.V.C. unit is held in sponge rubber and housed in a partition at the rear top corner of the tool box. To remove it, open the box lid, grasp the unit between the fingers and thumb of one hand, and gently and firmly pull it out. Re-fit with cover outwards.

The four terminals of the control box are plainly marked by the letters D.E.A.F. Wires from F and D go to similarly marked terminals on the dynamo. The A terminal is connected to one of the ammeter terminals and the E terminal is 'earthed'.

We specially warn against unskilled meddling with the settings of the regulator and the cut-out contacts.

Battery—All Models (MLZ9E). A lead-acid battery Lucas type is used on all models.

The voltage is 6, the capacity is 12 ampere hours, at the 10 hour rate.

Machines are issued with dry charged batteries, the acid is filled by the dealer.

All models have the POSITIVE battery terminal connected to 'EARTH'.

Battery unit (all Models). The battery is housed in the front portion of the tool box and retained in position on its platform by a stout rubber strap.

To remove the battery, grasp the rubber strap with the fingers between the strap and the battery case. Push the strap downwards sufficiently to release the metal toggle from the strap retaining clip. The battery can now be lifted out.

Fitting the battery. The battery must be inserted with the negative terminal on the right side of the battery compartment.

Topping up the battery. Fortnightly or more often in warm climates, check if the electrolyte in each cell is level with the top of the separators. Top-up, if necessary, with distilled water. Do not allow distilled water to come into contact with metals—always only use a glass or earthenware container and funnel.

If a battery is found to need an excessive amount of topping-up, steps should be taken to find out the reason. If one cell in particular needs topping-up more than another, it is likely the case or container is cracked, in which event the battery must be replaced and arrangements made to clean up the battery carrier. Metal parts should be well cleaned and, if possible, washed with a solution of ammonia or bicarbonate of soda, in water.

LIGHTING AND ACCESSORIES

Headlamp. A pre-focus main bulb, also a pilot bulb are mounted in the lamp reflector. The reflector and lamp glass are made up as one assembly and are not sold separately.

To remove the head lamp rim, release the screw retaining the lamp rim with one hand and support the light unit with the other.

The light unit can then be taken off the lamp.

To refit. Engage bottom tag on lamp rim with the small slit in the shell and gently force the top of the rim back into the shell, after which re-tighten the retaining screw on the top of the lamp body.

The main bulb is secured by a bayonet fixing holder, which is removed by turning anti-clockwise.

The pilot bulb is a plug-in or push fit.

The headlamp rim is detachable from the light unit by removing six spring clips.

Main bulb

Home Models ... Lucas No. 373 6-volt
30/24 watt prefocus (left hand dip).
General Export Models Lucas No. 312 6-volt
30/24 watt prefocus (vertical dip).
Continental Models ... Lucas No. 403 6-volt
35/35 watt prefocus duplo (vertical dip).
French Export Models Lucas No. 379 6-volt
36/36 watt 3-pin duplo (vertical dip).
Parking Bulb ... ... Lucas No. 988 3-watt M.C.C.

Setting. The headlamp should be set so that when the machine is carrying its normal load the driving beam is projected straight ahead and is parallel with the road surface.

Dipper switch. Every 5,000 miles the moving parts of the dipper switch should be lubricated with thin machine oil.

Headlamp (Alternator Models). A separate ignition switch is incorporated in the right side of the headlamp body.

Lucas stop tail lamp (Model 564). The correct size of bulb to be used in rear lamps is based on the cubic capacity of the engine. The replacement bulb for this lamp is Lucas No. 384, 6-volt, 6/18 watt. Small bayonet cap.

Lucas horn (Model HF1441). Horns are pre-set to give their best performance and, in general, no further adjustment is necessary.

If the horn becomes uncertain in its action, giving only a choking sound, or does not vibrate, it does not follow that the horn has broken down—the trouble may be due to a discharged battery, a loose connection, or short-circuit in the wiring of the horn.

In particular ascertain that the horn-push bracket is in good electrical contact with the handlebars.

It is also possible that the performance of a horn may be upset by its mounting becoming loose.

Terminals. All models have the POSITIVE battery terminal connected to 'EARTH'.

The earth connection, for the electrical system, is connected to the frame, on top of the seat lug tube.

Remove the twin seat for access.

ALTERNATOR

Model RM15

The following data applies to three versions of Model RM15, namely, 540, 210, 18, fitted to magneto ignition machines, 047, 534, fitted to coil ignition machines, and 540, 210, 05, fitted to two-way radio equipped machines.

Test equipment required

(1) First-grade moving coil a.c. voltmeter. 0-20 volts.
(2) First-grade moving coil d.c. ammeter. 0-25 amps.
(3) One ohm load resistor (capable of carrying 20 amperes without overheating).

Test No. 1. For this test, the battery must be in good condition and more than half charged.
(1) Connect the d.c. ammeter between the battery negative terminal and the battery main cable.
(2) Start the engine and set it to run at approximately 3,000 r.p.m.
(3) Observe the ammeter readings in each of the positions of the lighting switch.

The figures given in the following table are the minimum acceptable battery input currents. If the readings obtained are lower than the figures quoted, proceed to Test No. 2.

Minimum acceptable battery charging currents.

Switch Position	Despatch number of unit.			
	540, 210, 18	047, 534	540, 210, 05	
			Boost switch Open	Boost switch Closed
Off	2.75	2.5	4.0	9.0
Parking	2.0	1.5	2.5	7.0
Head	2.0	2.5	3.5	3.5

Unsatisfactory readings can be due to defective wiring or connections.

Ensure that all snap-connector joints and earth connections are in good condition before proceeding to Test No. 2.

If considered necessary, check the rectifier by substitution.

(1) Disconnect the three alternator output cables.
(2) Start the engine and set to run at approximately 3,000 r.p.m.
(3) Connect the one ohm load resistance in parallel with the a.c. voltmeter and check the voltage between the alternator output cables.

Minimum acceptable voltage readings.

Voltmeter and Resistor connected between	Despatch Number of unit		
	540, 210, 18	047, 534	540, 210, 05
White-with-Green and Green-with-Black cables	4.0	4.0	9.5
White-with-Green and Green-with-Yellow cables	6.5	6.5	13.0
White-with-Green and Green-wht-Black (with Green-with-Yellow connected to Green-with-Black)	8.5	9.0	15.5
Each cable in turn and earth	Zero	Zero	Zero

(4) Conclusions to be drawn from results of above tests:
  Demagnetised rotor magnets indicated by all readings being low.
  Short-circuited coil indicated by individual reading being low.
  Open-circuited coil or coils indicated by aero reading(s).
  Earthed coil or coils indicated by voltage reading between any output cable and earth.

Alternator, Model RM15, with rotor, withdrawn (REC 728).

BATTERIES

Model:	PU7E	SC7E
No. of plates per cell	7	7
Ampere-hour capacity:		
At the 10-hour rate	12	22.5
At the 20-hour rate	13.5	26
Electrolyte to fill one cell (approx.):		
Pint measure	1/5	$\frac{1}{2}$
Cubic centimetre measure	115	280
Initial-charge current in amperes (not applicable to 'dry-charged' batteries)	0.8	1.5
Re-charge current in amperes	1.5	2.5
Examination of electrolyte level	Fortnightly	Weekly

Notes for putting battery into service. It is necessary to use different filling-in specific gravities, according to shade temperature, when preparing electrolyte solutions. When filling batteries for the home trade and in climates having shade temperatures ordinarily below 80° F. (26.6 C.) add one part (by volume) of acid (1.835 S.G.) to 2.8 parts of distilled water, to obtain a filling-in solution having a specific gravity of 1.270 at 60° F. (15.5 C.).

For use in climates where shade temperatures are frequently over 80° F., the acid-to-water ratio must be 1 : 4 to give a specific gravity of 1.210 at 60° F. Specific gravity readings taken at electrolyte temperatures other than 60° F. can be corrected to this reference temperature by deducting 0.002 from the observed reading for every 5° F. (2.7° C.) that the temperature is below 60° F. Conversely, 0.002 must be added to the observed reading for every 5° F. that the temperature exceeds 60° F. The temperature of the filling-in solution should be 60° F. to 80° F. When applicable, allow battery to attain room temperature before filling. Fill to the top edge of separators or separator guards in one operation with acid of appropriate strength. Then initial-charge uncharged batteries and if time permits, give 'dry-charged' batteries a four-hour charge at the appropriate re-charge rate.

Maintenance. At the intervals given in the above table, remove the battery lid, unscrew the filler plugs and if necessary, add distilled water carefully to each cell to bring the electrolyte just level with the separator guard or, if visible, with the top edges of the separators. *Do not use tap water.* Wipe away all dirt and moisture from the top of the battery.

If the motor-cycle is to be laid up for a while, give the battery a fortnightly freshening charge at the appropriate re-charge rate until the electrolyte in the cells is gassing freely, in order to replace the energy lost during standing.

CONTRACT BREAKER UNITS AND DISTRIBUTOR

Model:	18D2	CA1A	CA1A	CA1A
Part No.	40589	47578	47579	47595
Contact Gap Settings:				
Inch measure	0.014-0.016	0.014-0.016	0.014-0.016	0.014-0.016
Centimetre measure	0.356-0.406	0.356-0.406	0.356-0.406	0.356-0.406
Centrifugal Advance Curve	ECM 667	ECM 674	ECM 675	ECM 748
Contact Breaker Spring Force (Measured at contacts)—				
In ounces	18-24	18-24	18-24	18-24
In grammes:	511-680	511-680	511-680	511-680
Capacity of Capacitor in microfarads:	0.14-0.20	0.18-0.23	0.18-0.23	0.18-0.23

CONDENSER CHECK

When investigating a misfire, and where the condenser is suspect, the use of an external condenser will prove if this component is defective.

Use a sound condenser with two crocodile clips attached.

Attach one clip to the low tension terminal on the distributor, the other to a convenient earth position.

A short test, by running the engine, will indicate if the condenser is defective.

In the case of Single Cylinder Models, remove contact breaker cover, fit one clip to terminal for contact breaker pivot post, the other to earth.

Maintenance. Check the contact breaker gap setting after the first 500 miles (800 km.) running and subsequently every 6,000 miles (9,660 km.).

Every 6,000 miles examine and clean the contacts and also the moulded cover of Model 18D2.

At this period carry out the following lubrication procedure:

(1) *Cam.* Smear the surface of the cam very lightly with Mobilgrease No. 2 or clean engine oil.

(2) *Cam bearing.* Model 18D2. Inject a few drops of thin machine oil into the rotor arm spindle.

Model CAIA (every 3,000 miles, 4,830 km.). Remove the central securing bolt and inject a few drops of thin machine oil (this will also lubricate the timing control mechanism).

(3) *Contact breaker pivot post.* Apply a spot of clean engine oil to the exposed tip of the contact breaker pivot post.

(4) *Centrifugal timing control mechanism.* Model 18D2. Lift off the rotor arm and unscrew the two screws securing the contact breaker base plate to the body. Lubricate with clean engine oil the centrifugal timing control mechanism thus exposed, paying particular attention to the pivots.

Model CAIA. See (2).

High tension cable. Renew as required, using 7 mm. p.v.c.-covered or neoprene covered rubber insulated ignition cable.

Oil seal replacement (Model 18D2 only). The oil sealing ring which is fitted in a groove round the shank is simply replaced, but the oil seal fitted inside the shank requires the use of a suitable extractor to remove it from its housing.

Bearing replacement. Use a hand press to remove the old bush from the shank of the unit.

Before fitting the replacement bush (Part No. 425498), allow it to soak in medium viscosity engine oil for at least 24 hours. In cases of extreme urgency, this period of soaking may be shortened by heating the oil to 212° F. (100° C.) for two hours and then allowing the oil to cool before removing the bush.

A shouldered mandrel must be used to press the new bearing into the shank. This mandrel must be hardened and polished and be 0.0005" (0.013 mm.) greater in pin diameter than the distributor shaft. To prevent subsequent withdrawal of the bush with the mandrel, a stripping washer should be fitted between the mandrel shoulder and the bush.

MAGNETOS

Models K2F and NC1

Endurance test. With the contact breaker cover in place, run the magneto for one hour at 3,000 r.p.m. with the high tension cable (or cables) connected to an 8-kilovolt annular spark gap.

Inspection. After the above run, disconnect the magneto and examine it as follows:

Remove the pick-up brush (or brushes) and check for signs of sticking movement, of flashover or of fouling against the slip ring moulding. Examine the slip ring for signs of flashover, burnt or rough track, presence of swarf or of eccentricity. Examine the contact breaker. The contacts must be in line and have a maximum opening setting of 0.012"—0.015" (0.305-0.381 mm.).

The contact breaker arm must be free to turn on its pivot. Remove the earthing brush and check that it is free to move in its holder. Check the armature for excessive end float or binding. Up to 0.005" (0.127 mm.) end float is permissible. Shims of 0.005" and 0.003" (0.075 mm.) thickness are available for correcting excessive end float.

High speed test. Connect the high tension cable (or cables) to a rotary gap set to spark at 8 kilovolts. A loading resistor must be connected in parallel with the spark gap to simulate 'leaky' sparking plugs.

With model K2F magnetos use a 1.5-micromho load. With model NC1 use a 2.5-micromho load. Remove the contact breaker cover and run the magneto over the speed range 1,000—3,000 r.p.m. No missing must occur. Observe the contact breaker for excessive sparking.

While running at 3,000 r.p.m., the primary winding should be short circuited at least six times, by touching the contact breaker spring with an earthed cable.

Low speed test. Connect the high tension cable to a 3-point spark gap set to 5.5 mm., using independent spark gaps for the two cables of twin-cylinder magneto model K2F. Not more than 5 per cent missing must occur under the following conditions of speed and ignition timing:

Magneto model.	NC1	K2F
Part No.	423, 47	422, 30 and 422, 64
Maximum speed (r.p.m.):		
Ignition advanced ...	130	150
Ignition retarded ...	170	180

Maintenance. Every 3,000 miles check and (if necessary) reset the contact breaker gap to 0.012"—0.015".

Apply a spot of clean engine oil to the exposed tip of the contact breaker pivot post.

Every 6,000 miles clean exterior and interior of magneto. Renew earthing and pick-up brushes if worn to within ⅛" of shoulder. Clean contacts with carborundum stone, silicon carbide paper or very fine emery cloth.

CHECKING THE RECTIFIER

If a spare rectifier known to be in good condition is available, the simplest check is that of substitution. (In this connection, Lucas rectifier 47132 is used with alternators 540, 210, 18 and 047, 534, while rectifier 47142 is used in conjunction with alternator 540, 210, 05.)

When a satisfactory substitute is not available, the rectifier is best checked by removing it from the machine and bench testing it as detailed.

Test equipment required

(1) Two first-grade moving coil 0-20 direct current voltmeters.
(2) One-ohm load resistor (capable of carrying 12 amperes without overheating).
(3) Fully charged 12-volt battery of about 50 ampere-hours capacity at the 10-hour rate, e.g., any typical nine-plates-per-cell car battery, as fitted to medium-sized cars.

N.B.: When testing, it is essential that the battery terminal voltage (as indicated by voltmeter V2) is at least 12.

When testing, it is essential to make the individual tests as quickly as possible to avoid overheating of the rectifier plates.

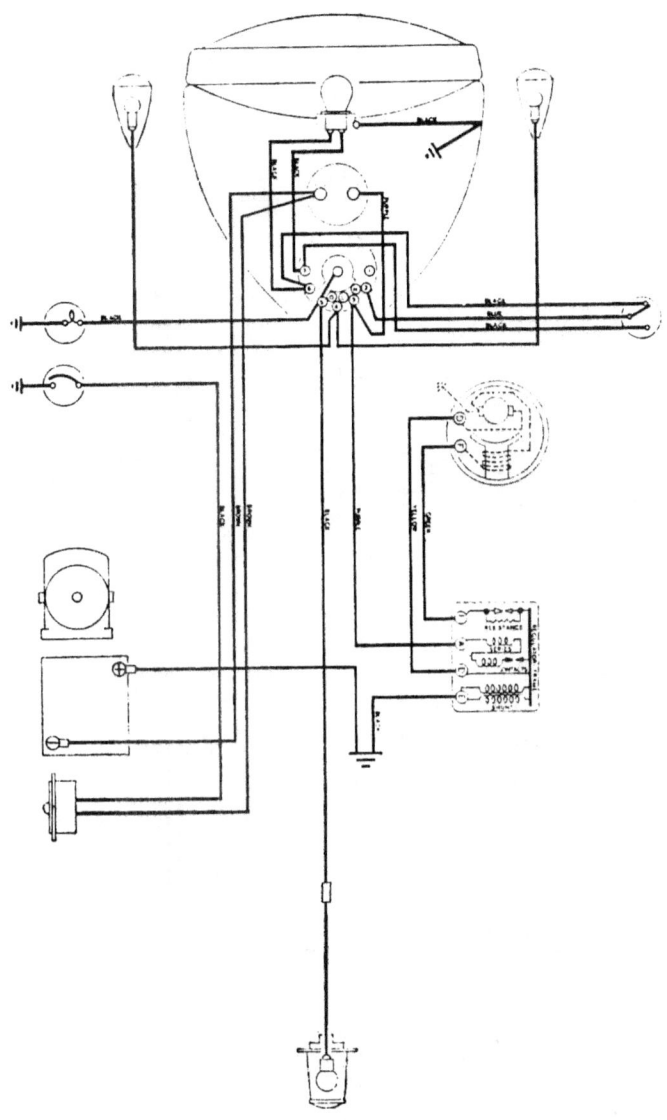

Fig. 105
1957 Single and Twin Models.

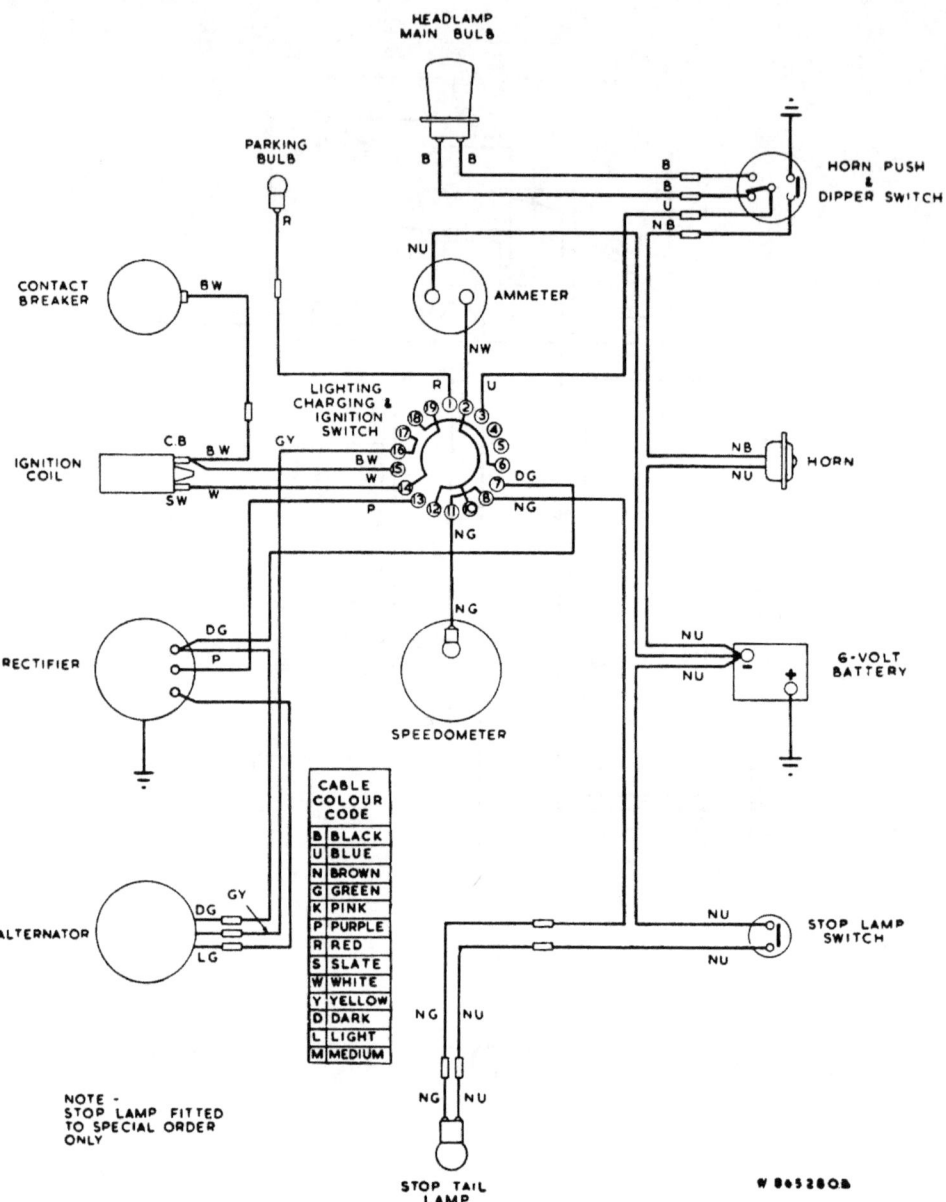

Fig. 106 Wiring Diagram, Singles, 1958-59.

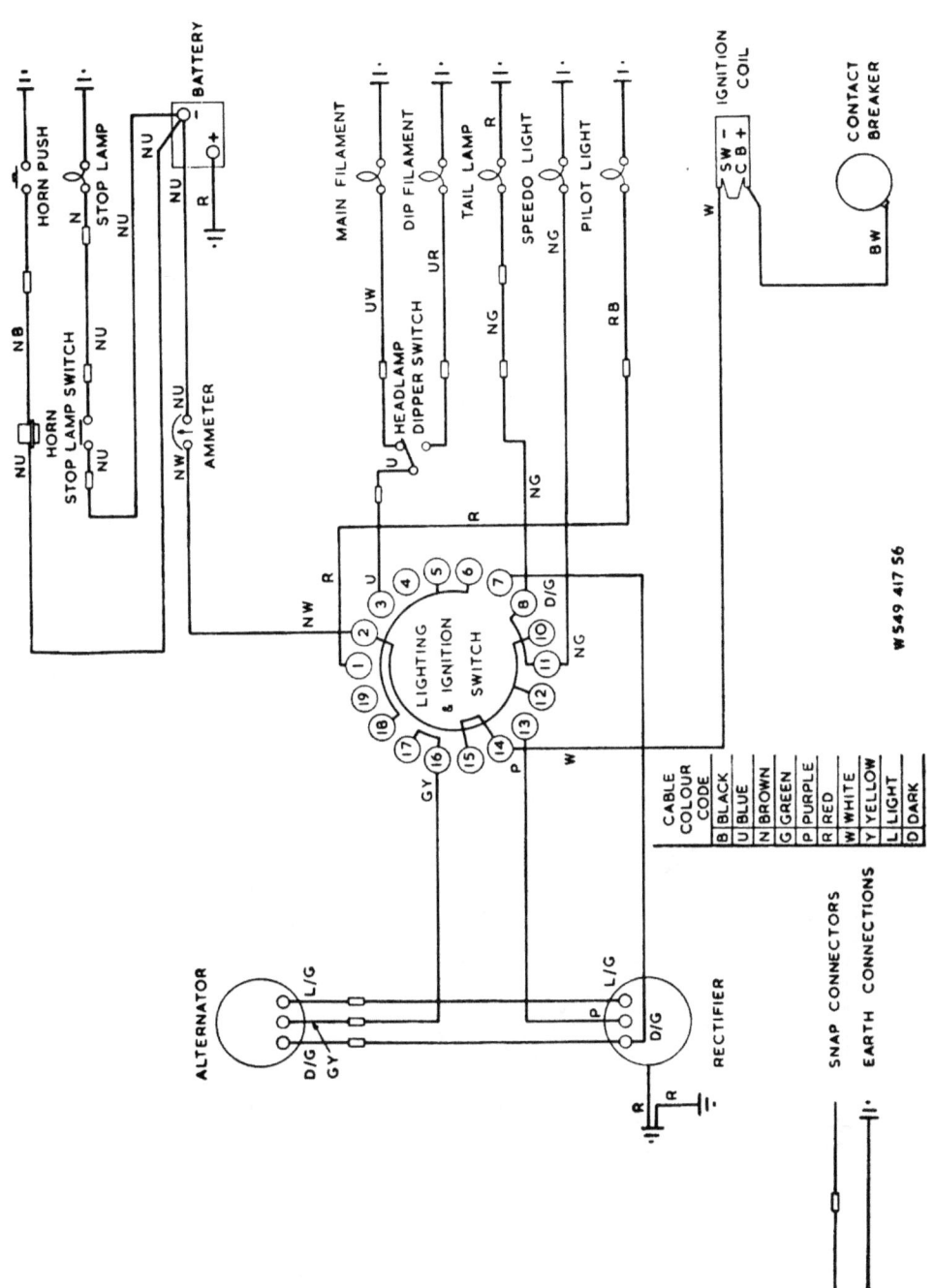

Fig. 107
Wiring Diagram, Standard Twins, 1959.

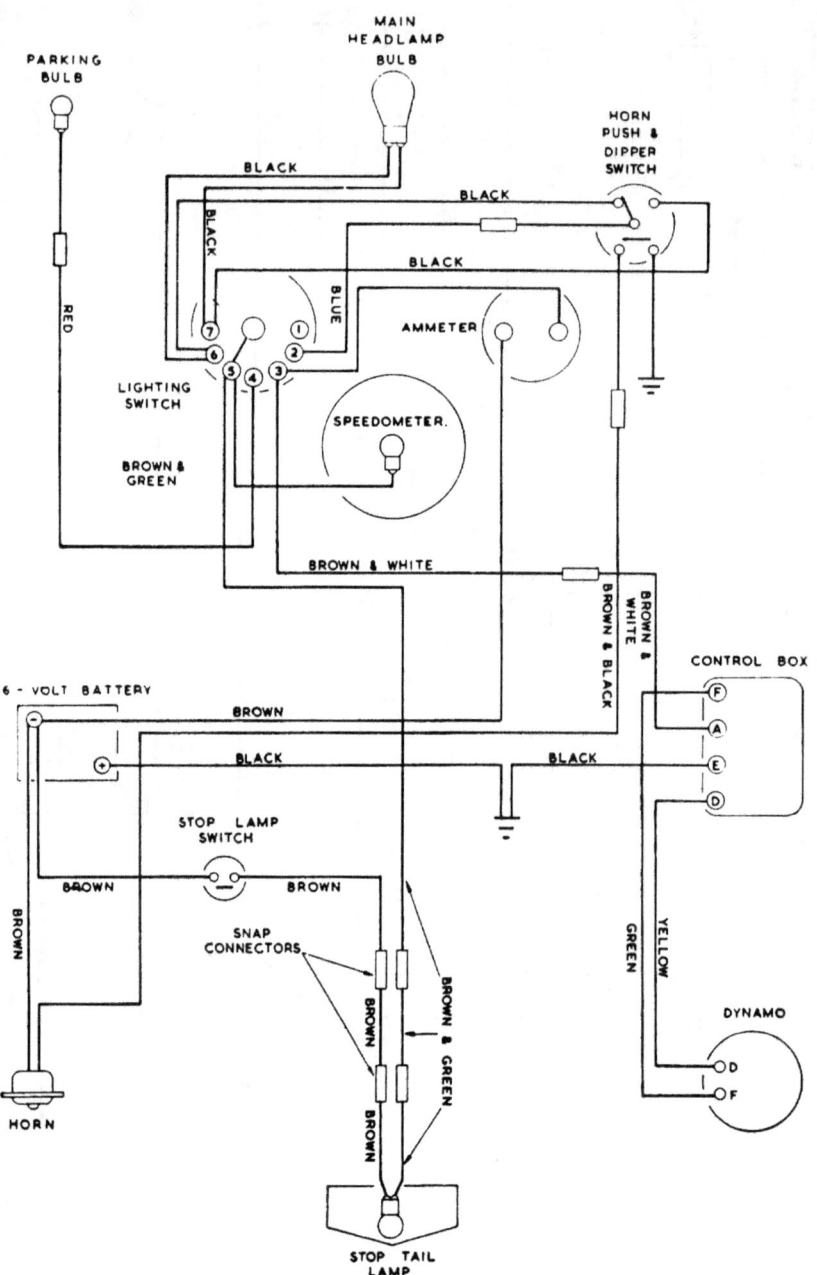

FIG. 108
Wiring Diagram, Magneto Twins, 1960-61.

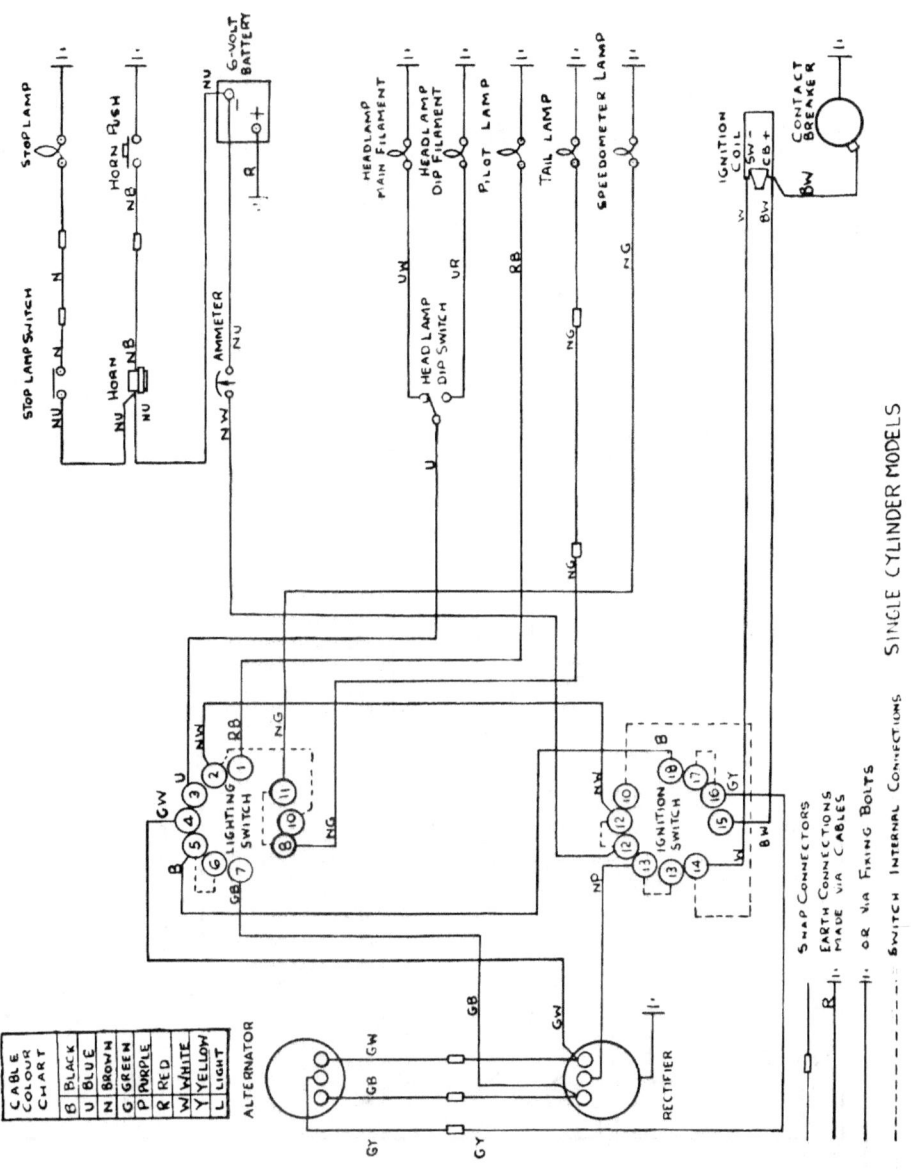

Fig. 109
Wiring Diagram, Singles, 1960-61.

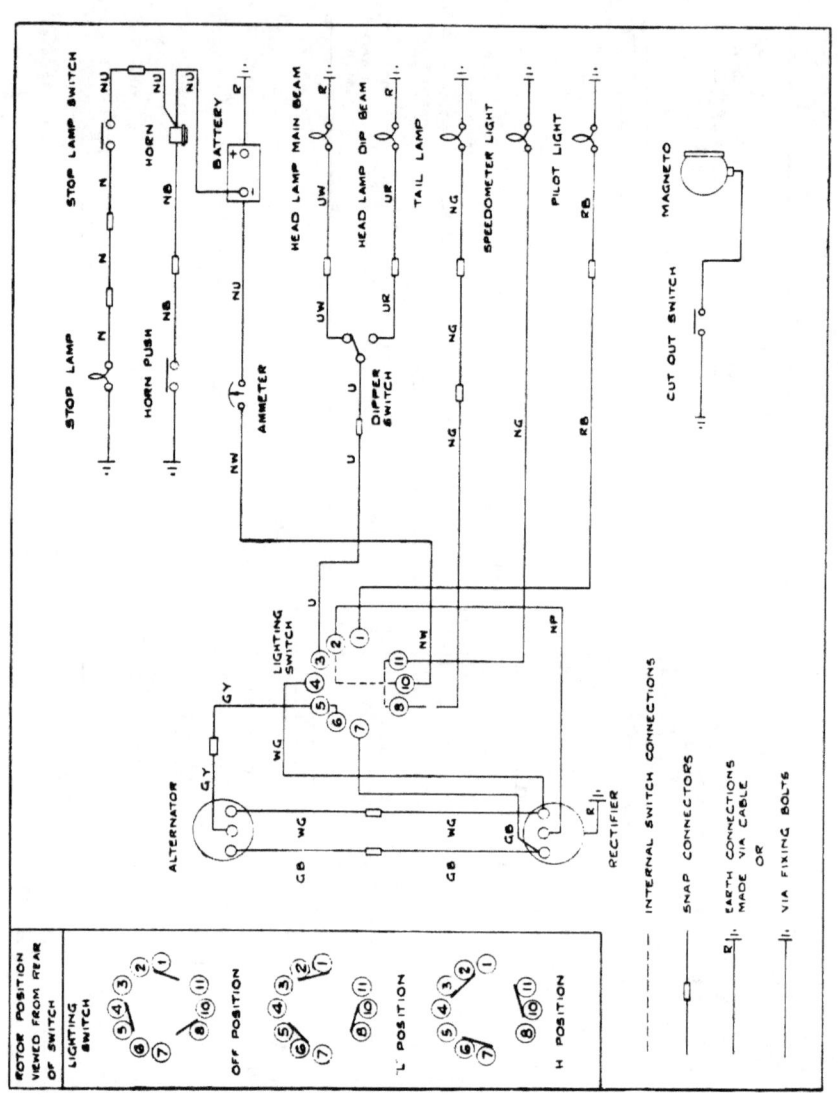

Fig. 110
Wiring Diagram, Magneto Twins, 1962.

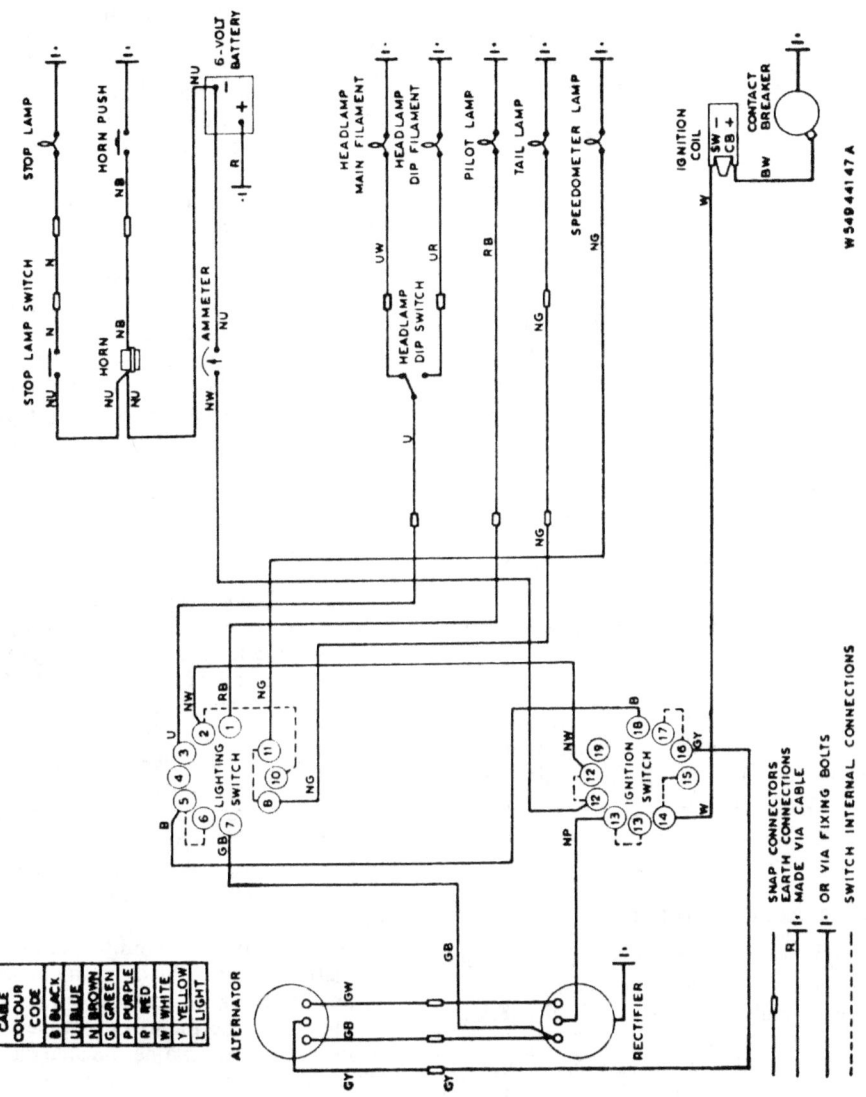

FIG. 111
Wiring Diagram, Alternator Twins.   FRAME NOS. AFTER 79800

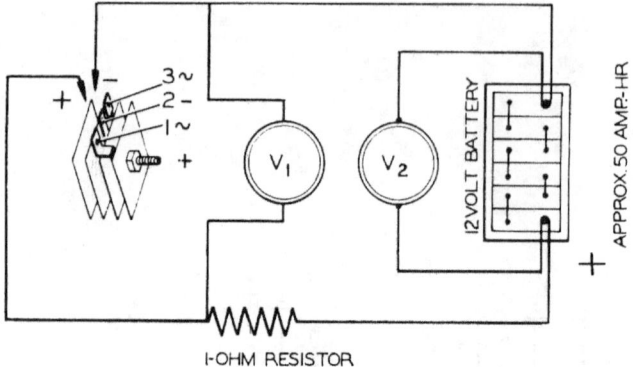

V_1 — WILL MEASURE THE VOLT DROP ACROSS THE RECTIFIER PLATE
V_2 — MUST BE CHECKED WHEN TESTING THE RECTIFIER PLATE TO MAKE CERTAIN THE SUPPLY VOLTAGE IS THE RECOMMENDED 12 VOLTS ON LOAD

Fig. 112

Forward resistance test. With the test equipment connected as shown in the illustration, proceed as follows to check in turn each of the four cells which form the rectifier:

In sequence, connect the
+ve test prod to terminal '2' and the −ve to terminal '1'
+ve test prod to terminal '2' and the −ve to terminal '3'
−ve test prod to centre bolt and the +ve to terminal '1'
−ve test prod to centre bolt and the +ve to terminal '3'

In each check, not more than 2.5 volts should be shown by voltmeter V1.

Back leakage test. With the test equipment connected as before, proceed as follows:

In sequence, connect the
−ve test prod to terminal '2' and the +ve to terminal '1'
−ve test prod to terminal '2' and the +ve to terminal '3'
+ve test prod to centre bolt and the −ve to terminal '1'
+ve test prod to centre bolt and the −ve to terminal '3'

In each check, the voltage shown by voltmeter V1 should be within 2 volts of that shown by voltmeter V2.

LUCAS 88SA SWITCH

General. Model 88SA switches have superseded the equivalent versions of model 63SA as initial equipment on motor-cycles, and will eventually replace the model 63SA in service.

Unlike the model 63SA, which has terminals crimped directly to the cable harness, the model 88SA consists of a switch fitted with contact pins that engage with a specially designed socket. In this latter case it is the socket that is permanently connected (resistance brazed) to the cable harness. This plug-in feature of the 88SA switch simplifies disconnection for replacement, or test purposes.

There are three versions of the 88SA switch which are as follows: Lighting switch, ignition switch knob operated and ignition switch key operated. Alternative positions of the ignition switch are ignition off, ignition on and emergency. The emergency position on the key operated model is obtained by *pressing the key inwards* and then turning it in an anti-clockwise direction.

For service purposes sockets pre-wired with 4″ of cable are to be made available.

Rectifier output—circuit simplification. With the improved characteristics of modern rectifiers the possibility of battery discharge due to rectifier leakage can be discounted. The 88SA switch therefore, does not make provision for disconnecting the rectifier from the battery because, first, it is not necessary, and, secondly, its omission permits a degree of switch standardisation.

THE EFFECTS OF MODERN ENGINES AND FUELS ON SPARKING PLUGS

The growing trend these days is for engines to produce more power with improved economy, thus giving more of a sports car performance to the family saloon. As a result of this it is usual for touring engines to employ much higher compression ratios than was the custom a few years ago. Fuels with higher octane ratings have been developed to accommodate the more severe conditions, which have brought in their train many difficult problems for both petroleum chemists and automotive engineers.

The improved high octane fuels are complex blends of petroleum fractions with various additives including tetra-ethyl lead in greater or lesser degree. In addition to soot and carbonised oil residues certain products of combustion, including lead and sulphur compounds, settle on the surfaces of combustion chambers, piston crowns, valves and sparking plugs. Unfortunately some of these deposits, although effectively non-conducting when cold, become electrical conductors at high temperatures, and their formation on a plug insulator offers a leakage path to earth for the high tension current. This can cause weak sparking and mis-firing, particularly at wide throttle openings when maximum compression pressures demand a higher voltage to spark the electrode gap. The problem is accentuated by the higher compression ratios now employed which require in any case a greater voltage to produce a spark across the plug gap than was necessary with earlier, low compression engines.

Whilst higher performance engines are now commonplace, present day traffic conditions compel many vehicles to spend a large proportion of their running time at low duty, especially in city congestion. Such prolonged slow driving can allow an accumulation of lead fouling to form on plug insulators, although the symptoms may not manifest themselves under low duty operation. A spell of open road driving, however, with wider throttle openings, may well cause the temperature of the plugs to rise sufficiently to render the deposits electrically conductive, thus shorting out the spark and producing misfiring.

This condition is common to, and can occur in, any brand of sparking plug. We have on the one hand better automotive engines with highly developed fuels and oils to suit them, and on the other the increased problem of combustion chamber deposit. Do not blame the sparking plug—it can only work efficiently when clean. Regular cleaning not only prevents heavy deposit formation, it makes it easier to remove, for when plugs start shorting the deposits are virtually baked on, making them difficult to clean satisfactorily.

The higher temperatures reached in modern engines under fast driving conditions cause the sulphur compounds produced when petrol is burnt to have a more corrosive action on plug electrodes. Where corrosion and reduced plug life result from habitual hard driving, the use of a cooler running plug type will be beneficial in minimising the attack.

Careful tuning of carburetter and ignition settings will retard the formation of fuel deposits. Contact breaker points, which make and break four times as often as each plug fires in a four-cylinder engine, are bound to be worn by the time new plugs are needed. When the points become pitted and burned, they cannot supply the correct current to the coil to enable the latter to deliver an adequate output to the plug to produce a good spark. In severe cases this can also have a retarding effect on ignition timing.

No plug is any better than the electrical system backing it up. Examine the contact breaker points and if necessary reface them or renew, making sure their gap is set to the engine maker's specification by using a K.L.G. ignition gauge. Check also that the insulation of the high tension plug leads is sound, and is not frayed or cracked.

INSTRUCTIONS FOR CLEANING

For maximum efficiency a sparking plug operating under normal conditions should be cleaned and have its gap(s) reset several times during its life. In average motor car conditions this should be at approximately 3-5,000 mile intervals and proportionately less in other engines where running conditions may be more severe. Similarly more frequent attention may be necessary in oily engines. It is sometimes possible to avoid the effects of over-oiling by fitting a softer plug, but if the oiling is due to engine damage or wear, this is only a palliative and should not replace the proper corrective action. Where sustained hard driving is involved it may be necessary to reset gaps more frequently, as the high temperatures cause more rapid erosion of the electrodes, and cleaning at the same time will be amply repaid.

K.L.G. plugs should be cleaned on a reputable sand-blast cleaner. If plugs are oily on removal from the engine, they should be washed out with petrol and blown dry with an air gun prior to sand-blasting to reduce the tendency for sand to stick inside the body.

When sand-blasting, the plug should be slowly rotated and slightly tilted from side to side to allow the sand full access to the inside. It should be done in several short bursts, removing the plug each time for examination and carried on long enough only to effect the desired cleaning. Excessive blasting may damage the electrodes and insulator.

Finally, the plug should be well blown out with air to remove all particles. A final examination should be made for any particles tightly lodged inside and these removed by some pointed object, preferably non-metallic, but if metallic, care should be taken not to abrade metal on to the ceramic, as this could cause shorting.

With overhead earthwire plugs which still have considerable life left in them, it is advantageous before re-setting the gap to file the underside of the earth wire and the end of the centre electrode lightly to restore the sharp edges which existed when the plugs were new. Only the minimum of metal should be removed, but the resultant lower sparking voltage will be of benefit in giving starting, idling and cruising performance approximating more closely to that of new plugs.

Detachable K.L.G. plugs can be cleaned easily and efficiently by hand if preferred or if a sand-blast cleaner is not available. The following instructions are for cleaning a plug by hand:

To dismantle the plug for cleaning, the gland nut (B) must be unscrewed from the body (D), so that the insulated electrode assembly (A) may be withdrawn. This is best accomplished by using two close fitting box spanners, one fitting the gland nut hexagon (B) and the other the body hexagon (E); the box spanner holding the gland nut should itself be gripped in a vice, whilst the other box spanner is utilised for unscrewing the body. Alternatively, the hexagon of the gland nut may be held gently in a vice, care being taken not to distort by over-tightening. *Never* grip the body hexagon in a vice as this will distort it sufficiently to lock the gland nut in position, making it impossible to take the plug apart.

If the insulator is oily, first wash it in an oil solvent such as petrol or paraffin and dry; then, with fairly coarse glass paper, remove the carbon deposit and wash again. Do not scrape with a knife or other metallic object, as metal will be abraded on the ceramic and leave a potential short-circuiting path.

The firing point (F) should be cleaned with a fine emery cloth.

The plug body (D) should be scraped clean internally with a knife or wire brush after removing the old internal gasket, paying particular attention to the earth electrodes. With overhead earth plugs which have a considerable life still left in them, the electrodes should be lightly filed as already described, but this can be done if preferred before re-assembly.

Finally rinse in petrol or a cleaning spirit.

A new internal washer (H) should be lightly smeared with thin oil. Make sure that it is properly seated in the plug body before re-inserting the central electrode assembly.

Screw up the gland nut and tighten sufficiently to give a gas-tight joint.

Before refitting the plugs to the engine adjust the gaps to .020" to .022". Coat the threaded portion with oil Dag or graphite paste.

Always remember the golden rule—never try to move the central electrode. It is surrounded by insulation which cannot bend. Move the earth electrodes only.

Sparking plug tightening torque: 22 ft. lbs. (3.05 M/KG).

REPAIRS AND SERVICE
REPAIRS

The instructions regarding repairs should be clear and definite, otherwise the cost may be greater than that expected. We shall be pleased to give estimates for repairs if parts are sent to us for that purpose. If the estimate is accepted, no charge is made for the preliminary examination, but, should it be decided not to have the work carried out, it MAY be necessary to make a charge to cover the cost of whatever dismantling and re-assembly may have been done to prepare the estimate.

Customers desiring that old parts which are replaced with new during the course of overhaul or repair be retained must make the fact known prior to the work being put in hand because, normally, such parts, having no further useful life, are scrapped upon removal.

Parts sent to us as patterns, or for repair, should have attached to them a label bearing the sender's full name and address. The instructions regarding such parts should be sent under separate cover.

If it is necessary to bring a machine, or parts, to the works for an urgent repair, **it is essential** you **make an appointment** beforehand to **avoid disappointment**. This can be done by letter or telephone.

CORRESPONDENCE AND ORDERS

Our routine is organised into different departments, therefore delay cannot be avoided if matters relating to more than one department are contained in one letter.

Consequently, it is desirable, when communicating with more than one department, to do so on **separate sheets**, each of which should bear your name and address.

When writing on a technical matter, or when ordering spares, it is essential to quote the **complete engine number**. Some numbers have one, or more, letters incorporated in them and these letters **must be quoted**, otherwise model identification is not possible.

Orders should always be sent in list form and not as part of a letter.

Owners are strongly advised to purchase a Spare Parts List so that correct part numbers can be quoted. Most parts are clearly illustrated in this list which makes it very easy to recognise the part or parts required.

PROPRIETARY FITTINGS

No expense is spared to secure and fit the most suitable, and highest quality, instruments and accessories for the standard equipment of our machines.

Nevertheless, our Guarantee does not cover such parts and, in the event of trouble being experienced, the parts in question should be returned to, and claims made, direct on the actual manufacturers who will deal with them on the terms of their respective guarantees.

Those manufacturers are:

Carburetters: Messrs. Amalgamated Carburetters Ltd., Holford Road, Witton, Birmingham 6.

Chains: The Renold & Coventry Chain Co. Ltd., Didsbury, Manchester.

Electrical Equipment: Messrs. Joseph Lucas Ltd., Great King Street, Birmingham 19.

Sparking Plugs: K.L.G. Sparking Plugs Ltd., Putney Vale, London, S.W.15.

Speedometers: Messrs. S. Smith & Sons (M.A.) Ltd., Cricklewood, London.

Tyres: Messrs. Dunlop Rubber Co. Ltd., Fort Dunlop, Birmingham.

Rear Suspension: Girling Ltd., King's Road, Tyseley, Birmingham 11.

All the above manufacturers except S. Smith & Sons (M.A.) Ltd., issue instructive literature regarding their products which is obtainable by writing to them.

SPARE PARTS

Genuine spare parts purchased from an authorised dealer, or from the factory, are identical with the parts originally built into your motor cycle. By using them you are assured that they will fit accurately and give satisfactory service.

SPARES STOCKISTS

For the convenience of owners spares stockists are appointed for most districts. To prevent delay and save the delivery surcharge, customers are recommended always to apply to their nearest spares stockist.

CORRESPONDENCE AND SPARES ORDERS

Always quote the complete engine number, including all the letters in it. This will enable us to identify the machine.

Each series of frames is numbered from zero upwards, therefore, the quotation of a frame number only does not facilitate identification.

SPARES LIST

An illustrated spares list covering the models described is available on application.

PART NUMBERS

If there is any doubt about the names of parts required, or their part numbers, please send the old parts as patterns.

REMINDER

Do not forget to include your name and full postal address. We do receive orders without this very necessary information.

PAYMENT

(1) Cash with order.*
(2) Cash against pro-forma invoice.
(3) Approved ledger account.

We do not send C.O.D. (Cash on delivery).

*Add 5 per cent of total value for carriage and packing. Minimum 1s.

GUARANTEE

1. In this Guarantee the word 'machine' refers to the motor cycle, scooter, motor cycle combination or sidecar as the case may be purchased by the Purchaser.

2. In order to obtain the benefit of this Guarantee, the Purchaser must correctly complete the attached registration form and return it to us within fourteen days of the purchase.

3. We will supply, free of charge, a new part in exchange for, or, if we consider repair sufficient, will repair free of charge any part proved within six months of the date of purchase of any new machine or within three months of its renewal or repair in the case of a part already renewed or repaired to be defective by reason of our faulty workmanship or materials. We do not undertake to bear the cost of fitting such new or repaired part or accessory.

4. Any part considered to be defective must be sent to our works, carriage paid, accompanied by the following information:

   (a) Name of purchaser and his address.
   (b) Date of purchase of machine.
   (c) Name of dealer from where the purchase was made.
   (d) Engine and frame numbers of machine.

5. This Guarantee shall not extend to defects or damage appearing after misuse, neglect, abnormal stress or strain, or the incorporation or affixing of unsuitable attachments or parts and in particular:

   (a) Hiring out.
   (b) Racing and competitions.
   (c) Adaptation or alteration of any part or parts after leaving our works.
   (d) The attaching of a sidecar in a manner not approved by us or to an unsuitable motor cycle.

This Guarantee shall not extend to machines whose trade mark, name or manufacturing number has been altered or removed, or in which has been used any part not supplied or approved by us, or to tyres, saddles, chains, speedometers, revolution counters and electrical equipment or to parts supplied to the order of the Purchaser and different from our standard specification.

6. Our liability and that of our dealer who sells the machine, shall be limited to that set out in paragraph 3, and no other claims including claims for consequential damage or injury to person or property, shall be admissible.

All other conditions and warranties statutory or otherwise and whether expressed or implied are hereby excluded and no guarantee other than that expressly herein contained applies to the machine to which this Guarantee relates or any accessory or part thereof.

REPAIRS GUARANTEE

1. Whilst the highest standard of workmanship and materials is aimed at, we cannot accept liability for any defects appearing more than three months after the machine, assembly or component has left our works after being repaired.

2. We will repair or replace at our option free of charge any defective work, materials or parts relating to the repairs carried out by us appearing within that time but shall not be under any further or other liability for any other loss or damage whether direct or consequential and our liability shall be limited to the cost of so making good.

3. We do not accept liability in respect of parts of proprietary manufacture, e.g. tyres, saddles, chains, speedometers, revolution counters and electrical equipment which may be used by us in effecting a repair. All other conditions and warranties statutory or otherwise expressed or implied are hereby excluded.

1963/64 TWIN CYLINDER MODELS

TWIN CYLINDER LUBRICATION

Oil pumps. Engines with a number after 8084, are fitted with large capacity oil pumps, which increase the oil flow by 100 per cent. The new pumps can be fitted to earlier models by using also new type timing cover 029610 together with 10 screws 028492, as the new pumps are wider. The part number for the new feed pump is 028521, the return pump is 028522.

Pressure relief valve. This valve was located in the base of the filter tunnel, and is now transferred to the plate carrying the oil pumps, on engines after 8912. The valve needs no attention and consists of a plunger and spring, which are retained by a split pin.

Crankcase fabric filter. The filter element is now separate from the non return valve, and uses a blow off plunger, which will lift, if there is obstruction in the felt filter, to prevent oil being cut off to the engine (see Fig. 113).

The wire frame supporting the filter element is overlapped to avoid collapse when the oil pressure is high, with a cold engine.

Where machines are used frequently for short journeys, particularly in winter, the filter should be cleaned at monthly intervals, in preference to a fixed mileage.

Cam followers. Unbreakable forged steel cam followers, with stellite pads, are a standard fitting on the 1963/64 twin engines, which can be used on earlier type twin engines. The part number for these new parts is 029936.

Cylinder base gasket. Cylinder base gaskets, of an improved type material (W.B.1) are available which should be used if persistent oil leakage takes place from the cylinder base, and crankcase joint. Jointing compound is not needed with this type of gasket.

Cylinder holding down studs. The long cylinder studs passing though the cylinder barrel was originally $\frac{5}{16}$" in diameter, which have now been increased to $\frac{3}{8}$" in diameter, with larger nuts, and washers to suit.

This alteration is entirely machining, the conversion can be carried out if first class machining facilities are available. These new studs were first fitted to engine number X9712. To tighten the stud nuts use a torque spanner set to 25 foot lbs. New gaskets will also be needed to complete the conversion.

Race kit pistons. These pistons give a ratio of 10.25 to 1 for use with super grades of fuel. When fitted, the ignition timing must be reset to a maximum of 29°, with the ignition in the fully advanced position. Serious damage can result if this adjustment is not effected.

Use also super-sports sparking plugs, such as the K.L.G. F.E. 220 type.

Race kit cams. See diagram on page 9. Use .012" running clearance.

TWIN CARBURETTERS

Carburetter Data.   Bore size, 1⅛"
Main jet size, 280
Pilot jet size, 25
Needle jet size, .106"
Slide No. 3
Needle position 4

CHAIN DATA

1963/64 models fitted with 18" wheels use an engine sprocket with one more tooth than those shown in the table of chains and sprockets given on pages 6 and 7. The difference in sprocket size affects the chain lengths shown in the following table.

1963/64 Models

Front		Rear	
350 cc. Single	... 68 links	350 cc. Single	... 98 links
500 cc. Single	... 69 links	500 cc. Single	... 99 links
650 cc. Twin	... 69 links	650 cc. Twin	... 96 links
650 cc. C.S.R.	... 68 links	650 cc. C.S.R.	... 97 links

1964 SINGLE CYLINDER MODELS

1964 350 cc. and 500 cc. SINGLE CYLINDER MODELS and 500 cc. SCRAMBLER MODEL

Lubrication. A gear type oil pump driven by the worm gear on the timing side axle is retained by two studs, and secured by two nuts. A conical shaped heat resisting rubber seal is attached to the pump body, where it abuts against a drilling in the timing cover.

From here oil is fed to the big end via a steel quill, which enters the timing side axle, lubricating the big end assembly. A by-pass from the main feed, taken from the timing cover conveys oil to positively lubricate the rocker gear. The oil supply is regulated in a manner described for the earlier type engines.

The oil seal. It is important that the oil seal is under light pressure when the timing cover is fitted, for a reason that is self evident. When both valves are closed and the timing cover fitted, the pressure of the seal should move the cover outwards, making a gap of about .010". If pressure does not exist, use packing shims, provided for this purpose, between the seal and the pump body. Conversely too much pressure can mutilate the seal and cause oil leakage.

The oil pump. The face of the oil pump body, where it joins the crankcase, must be perfectly flat also free from bruises and blemish; otherwise the oil "pick up" from the pump will be curtailed, as the pump will suck air at this point. Use a little Wellseal as jointing compound on the pump body when fitting.

There are more than one type of oil pump worm nut and pump pinions. If at any time new parts are fitted, check the new ones against the old ones before they are installed. The pump pinions are of the three start type. If the pump is dismantled, on assembly make sure the end plates do not protrude over the pump body; they should be just below the pump body.

The bearing oil seal. A thin bronze bush is used in the timing side crankcase, this does not constitute a bearing as it is simply an oil seal to stop oil leaking past the roller bearing.

Fig. 113

Crankcase bearings. The design of the driving side bearings is unaltered. Details for removal as described for earlier models still apply. A flanged type roller bearing is now used in the timing side of the engine on all single cylinder engines. The bearing sleeve is an interference fit in the crankcase, to take it out the crankcase must be gently heated, then the action of dropping the case on to a flat wood bench will dislodge the sleeve.

Separating the crankcase. First take off the oil pump worm drive nut which has a *left hand thread*. Take off the oil pump, retained by two nuts. Remove the small timing pinion, which now has a parallel bore. With all the bolts passing through the crankcase taken out the case can be parted, the inner member for the roller bearing will remain on its shaft.

The flywheels. To take off the inner member for the roller bearing use two taper steel wedges behind the bearing, once a gap is formed a puller can be used to extract the bearing member from its shaft.

Tappets and guides. The timing side crankcase tappet guide *in situ* has two locating diameters ¼″ wide at the top and bottom of the guide housing. The guides are located by a grub screw in register with a vee shaped groove machined circumferentially on the outside diameter of the guide. As the tappet foot is larger than the outside diameter of the guide, the tappet must be taken out from *inside* the timing chest, after removing the guide.

Removing the tappets. With the push rods, timing cover, oil pump, and cam gear removed, take out the grub screws, warm the crankcase, then push the tappet and guide upwards until the guide is clear, then take out the tappet from inside the timing chest. The short interference fit makes it easier to remove the guides.

Fitting tappets and guides. Warm the crankcase, pass the tappet up the guide hole and put on it the tappet guide. Press the guide home until the edge of the large diameter is just flush with the crankcase face, the vee shaped groove should now register with the grub screw hole, fit the screws.

Timing gear. The cam contour on all single cylinder models for 1964 is the same as shown in the diagrams on page 9; they will not interchange with 1963. Single marking is used on all cams, and for identification each cam wheel is marked with the factory part number. The 500 cc. scrambler inlet cam is 030124, exhaust 030125. Inlet cam for the 350 cc. is 030121, the exhaust is 030123. For the 500 cc. standard engine the inlet cam is 030122, and for the same engine the exhaust is 030123 (same as the 350 cc.).

500 cc. Scrambler Model. The alternative piston to give a ratio of 12 to 1 is suitable for the new engine, for use with octane 100 fuel. When this piston is used the ignition timing must be put back to 33° to 34° full advance. For long distance events, the use of a compression plate .050″ thick should be used, to maintain engine efficiency.

Ignition timing all 1964 singles.

    Maximum advance 350 cc.   34° (8.9 mm.)
               ,,   ,,   500 cc.   38° (10.98 mm.)
               ,,   ,,   500 cc. Scrambler 38° (10.98 mm.)

All with the ignition unit fully advanced.

On coil ignition models the ignition unit can be advanced by using a tool in the slot provided in the end of the cam.

Carburetter settings.

    1964 350 cc. models

Type No. 389/208
Main jet, 260 (with or without air filter)
Slide, 3
Pilot jet, 25
Needle jet, .1065
Needle position, central notch

    1964 500 cc. model

Type No. 389/209
Main jet, 290 (with or without air filter)
Slide, 3.5
Pilot jet, 25
Needle jet, .106
Needle position, central notch

    1964 500 cc. Scrambler

Type No. G.P.5 (1⅜″ choke)
Main jet, 310 (with air cleaner 290)
Air jet, .125″
Slide, 6
Needle, G.P.6, 5th notch.

1963/64 250cc MODELS

Engine modifications. Numerous alterations to the engine were introduced for the 1963/64 season. The oil supply to the engine is increased by lengthening the stroke of the oil pump plunger, which entails a modified timing side half crankcase. The dismantling also assembly sequence is unaltered. The flywheels are made from steel billets which to not flex under load, giving a rigid bottom end assembly. A larger diameter crankpin not subject to premature wear, is used in the big end assembly. The oil filter has been increased in length to prevent oil accumulating in the sump at high speed. A shorter spring goes with this filter. This alteration is most beneficial when used on the Lightweight 350 c.c. engines. New part No. 042061.

Valve springs. Valve springs similar to those used on the scrambler models, with a spring loading of 90 lbs.(valve fully opened) are a standard fitment. The free length of these springs is $1\frac{1}{2}''$ between wire centres.

Inlet valve. The valve head diameter has been increased to $1\frac{13}{32}''$, this valve is the same as used on the Lightweight 350 c.c. engine, with the valve seat opened out to suit. This in conjunction with a larger inlet port improves the volumetric efficiency of the engine. It is possible to use a cylinder head of the 350 lightweight type for improved performance.

Carburetter settings.
> Type No. 389/82
> Main jet, 200 (with or without air filter)
> Needle jet, .106
> Slide, 3
> Pilot jet, 25
> Needle position, central notch

Sprockets.
> Engine   22 teeth
> Clutch   46 teeth
> Gear box   18 teeth
> Rear wheel 54 teeth

Gear ratios.
> Top   6.51
> Third   8.46
> Second 12.03
> First   19.00

Chain size.
> Front 72 links (duplex) .315X .628
> Rear 124 links

Transmission. See page 73 (350 c.c. and 250 c.c. C.S.R. models).

Clutch. See details for 350 c.c. model on page 54.

Front wheel bearings. An improved front hub and brake are used on the above model. The wheel bearings are pre-packed with grease on assembly, and need no further attention until the machine has covered 8,000 miles when the journal bearings should be cleaned and packed with fresh grease.

To remove bearings. The journal bearings are separated by a spacing tube, use a length of $\frac{1}{4}''$ diameter steel rod half way through the hub and lever sideways to move the spacing tube to one side.

Place the end of the rod on the inner member of the bearing and drift out, the bearing will bring with it hub parts in the assembled sequence.

> Oil seal cap
> ,, ,, felt washer
> ,, ,, collar
> ,, ,, thin steel washer
> The bearing S.K.F. 6302(02)

Similar parts are used in the other side of the hub.

Front forks. See details for Lightweight 350 c.c. model on page 57.

WHEELS AND BRAKES

For the 1963 season all models, excluding the model C.S.R., were fitted with journal type wheel bearings, as opposed to the taper roller type previously used. No adjustment to these bearings is possible, or necessary; the only attention needed is to renew lubricant and clean every 10,000 miles, the bearings being lubricated on initial assembly.

A strip-down of both hubs is shown in Fig. 114, please note the grease nipple, on the speedometer gear box, is no longer used.

The front wheel (excluding models CS-CSR-Trials). Two journal bearings type RMS 6 are used in the front hub with a pull-out wheel spindle. A super oil seal is fitted against the bearing on the brake drum side to prevent grease entering the brake drum.

A similar oil seal is used in the bearing retaining sleeve at the opposite end of the hub, also a felt sealing ring.

The hub is packed with grease during assembly, subsequent lubrication should not be necessary until the machine has covered 10,000 miles, when the bearings can be re-greased if necessary. (See table of lubricants.)

To remove the front wheel. With the machine on the centre stand, disconnect the front brake cable from the brake expander lever, then remove the bolt (securing the torque stay) from the brake plate and release the spindle nut 000001.

Remove the four nuts securing the detached fork slider caps, take off both slider caps, when the front wheel can be removed.

Dismantling the front hub. Both wheel bearings are a press fit into the hub.

To avoid "scruffing" the bearing housings in the hub during the process of removing and refitting the bearings, the hub must be gently heated to cause the hub material to expand and relieve the interference fit. Have available a new oil seal 029263.

With the front wheel removed, take off the spindle lock nut 029246, pull out the spindle and brake plate.

Remove oil seal collar 029262.

Prise out the oil seal 029263.

Gently heat the hub in the vicinity of the wheel bearing 029264 (do not concentrate the applied heat in one place) drop the hub on to a flat wood bench, when the bearing will move away from the centre of the hub. Invert the hub, use a suitable drift to drive out the bearing, placing the drift on opposite sides of the bearing so that it is extracted parallel with its housing.

Pull out the bearing spacing tube 029266.

Remove the lock ring *lefthand thread* 029238, also the hub disc.

Unscrew the bearing retaining sleeve 029269.

Re-heat the hub and drift out the second bearing as described for the first one.

To assemble the front hub. Gently heat the right side of the hub, insert the bearing and press it fully home by screwing in the bearing retaining sleeve (*lefthand thread*). Invert the hub and pack some grease against the bearing just fitted. Insert the bearing spacing tube and fill some more grease to the hub. Re-heat the brake side of the hub, insert the bearing and press it fully home.

Fit the oil seal (metal backing outwards) flush with the hub.

Fit the hub disc and secure it with the lock ring.

Insert the oil seal collar into the oil seal, put the spindle through the brake plate and the hub and tighten the spindle fixing nut.

Refitting the front wheel. Refit in the reverse sequence given for removal, with the following precautions: Ensure the bolt fixing the brake torque arm to the brake plate is securely tightened. Do not over tighten the four nuts securing the two fork slider caps.

Front wheel hub assembly.

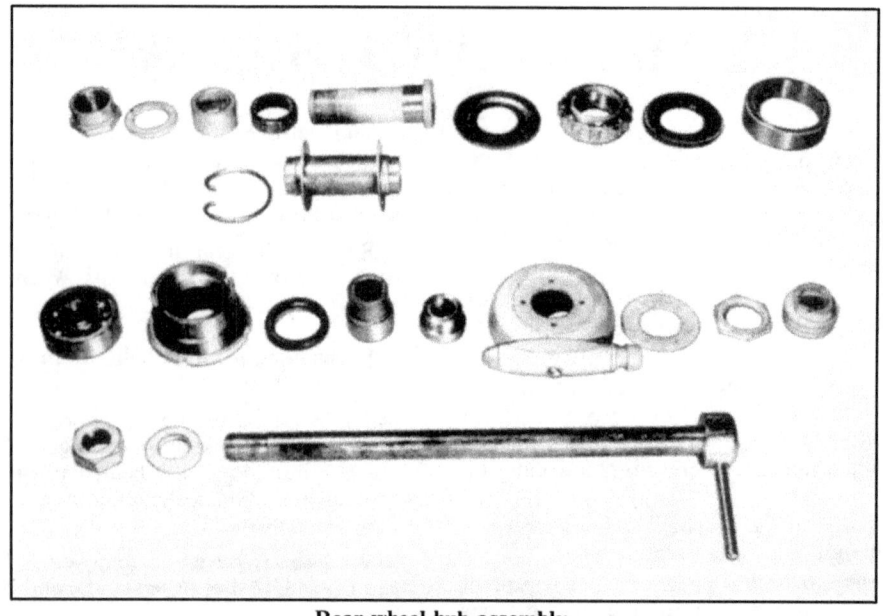

Rear wheel hub assembly.

Fig. 114

The rear wheel (excluding models CS-CSR-Trials). A journal type bearing RMS 5 is used in the right side of the rear wheel hub, also a roller type bearing CRL 8 in the brake drum. The pull-out spindle passes through both bearings and the hub.

The wheel is detachable from the brake drum.

To remove the rear wheel. Using the box key 029385 (supplied with the tool kit) remove the five extended nuts 029235.

Remove the wheel spindle nut 014869, pull out the wheel spindle, when the speedometer drive will come away from the hub with the drive cable attached.

Slide out and towards the rear the spindle distance piece 029243, the wheel will now come away from the brake drum.

If the machine is leaned over on the right side, the wheel will come out under the brake drum. Alternatively, detach the right side silencer.

To re-fit the rear wheel. Put the wheel back, insert the spindle through the frame and hub (without the distance piece of speedometer drive), which will help to line up the wheel.

Fit the five extended nuts and screw home lightly.

Take out the wheel spindle, fit the distance piece, put back the spindle with speedo drive through the hub and frame.

Position the speedometer drive and cable, re-fit and tighten the wheel spindle nut. Now firmly re-tighten the five extended nuts.

Re-fit the silencer, if removed.

Dismantling the rear hub. With the rear wheel removed, unscrew the bearing retainer sleeve 029236 (*lefthand thread*) together with the oil seal and distance piece, which will come away with the retainer. Invert the hub, extract the circlip 029234 (use round-nose pliers) take out the distance piece 029231.

Gently heat the hub in the vicinity of the bearing 029233, drift out the bearing.

Removing the oil seal 029237. Tap the oil seal distance piece out of the bearing retainer, which will dislodge the oil seal.

Rear brake drum. To remove the roller bearing, use a suitable drift or a piece of steel tube to drift out the roller bearing. Invert the brake drum and press out the oil seal.

1964 MODELS

WHEELS AND BRAKES

To remove the front wheel. With the machine on the central stand: Detach the brake cable from the expander lever. Detach the brake cable adjuster from the brake plate. Detach the right hand spindle nut. Release the pinch stud in left fork slider end. Take the weight of the wheel by the left hand, pull out the wheel spindle. The wheel can be taken out of the forks.

To refit the wheel. Reverse the procedure described for removal, with the following precautions. Remove traces of rust from the spindle and grease. Exercise care to correctly locate brake plate in the fork slider. Do not tighten unduly the slider pinch bolt, overtightening can cause a fracture.

Note. If the fork motion is stiff after refitting the wheel, slack off the spindle nut and work the forks up and down (the fork tubes will take up alignment), then retighten the spindle nut.

To remove the rear wheel. The rear wheel is detachable from the brake drum. With the rear wheel clear of the ground: Take out the three rubber grummets (4). Remove the sleeve nuts (8) which retain the wheel to the brake drum. Unscrew the wheel spindle (20) and remove it. Take away the distance piece, between the speedometer drive, which will come away also, there is no need to separate the cable from the drive. Pull the wheel away from the driving studs in the brake drum. Incline the machine to the right side, then pass the wheel under the left side silencer, clear of the machine.

To remove the brake drum. With the rear wheel removed: Take off the brake rod hand adjuster, then remove the rear chain connecting link. Release the nut securing the dummy spindle, pull back the brake drum clear of the fork ends.

To dismantle front hub. The wheel hubs are packed with grease during initial assembly, and should not need further lubrication for at least 10,000 miles, when the hubs should be dismantled for cleaning and fresh grease used. To dismantle the front hub, with the wheel removed take away the brake plate with brake shoes.

Unscrew bearing lock plate on left side of hub, holes are provided for a peg spanner or use a punch. If the plate resists removal use a little heat which will facilitate removal, take out felt sealing washer and distance piece.

To eject the bearing use a drift through the brake side (the front wheel spindle can be used for this purpose) when a few light blows from a mallet will drive out the bearing until it is clear of the hub, and no more, as the other bearing goes into the hub during this process.

Take out the spindle, or drift, invert the wheel and repeat the process to eject the double bearing which will bring with it the large steel washer, the felt washer, also the thin steel washer.

Assembling the hub. Clean and repack both bearings with fresh grease (see table of lubricants). Press into the left side of the hub the single bearing, fit the distance washer (flat side against the bearing), then the felt washer and secure with the lock plate.

Invert the hub, insert the distance tube (small end first) against the bearing.

Enter the double bearing square with the hub, use the drift through both bearings and drive home until the bearing abuts against the distance tube.

Fit the smallest of the two washers, the felt washer, then the large steel washer.

With a suitable punch peen the hub material, where it joins the washer in three equi-distant positions to retain the washer.

Rear hub dismantling. With the wheel removed, remove the speedometer drive lock ring (this has a *lefthand thread*), take out felt washer and distance piece. To eject the bearing use the wheel spindle with its washer also the distance piece that goes between the speedometer drive and the frame placed on the spindle. Partially drive out the bearing until it abuts against the reduced diameter inside the hub. Take out the spindle, use a short length of steel tubing with the outside diameter slightly smaller than the inside diameter of the bearing and drive out the bearing.

Invert the wheel, then drift out the other bearing, which will take with it the steel cup, felt washer and the thin steel washer.

Assembling the hub. Deal with the bearings as already described and assemble by first fitting the single row bearing, in the reverse order described for dismantling, with the following precaution: when tightening the *left hand* lock ring avoid damage to the slots for the speedometer drive. Finally "peen" the hub dished washer to the hub. The hub assembly sequence is shown in Fig. 115.

Dismantling the brake drum. A bearing is not used in the brake drum; when the spindle nut is removed together with the spacer and washer, the spindle can be taken out.

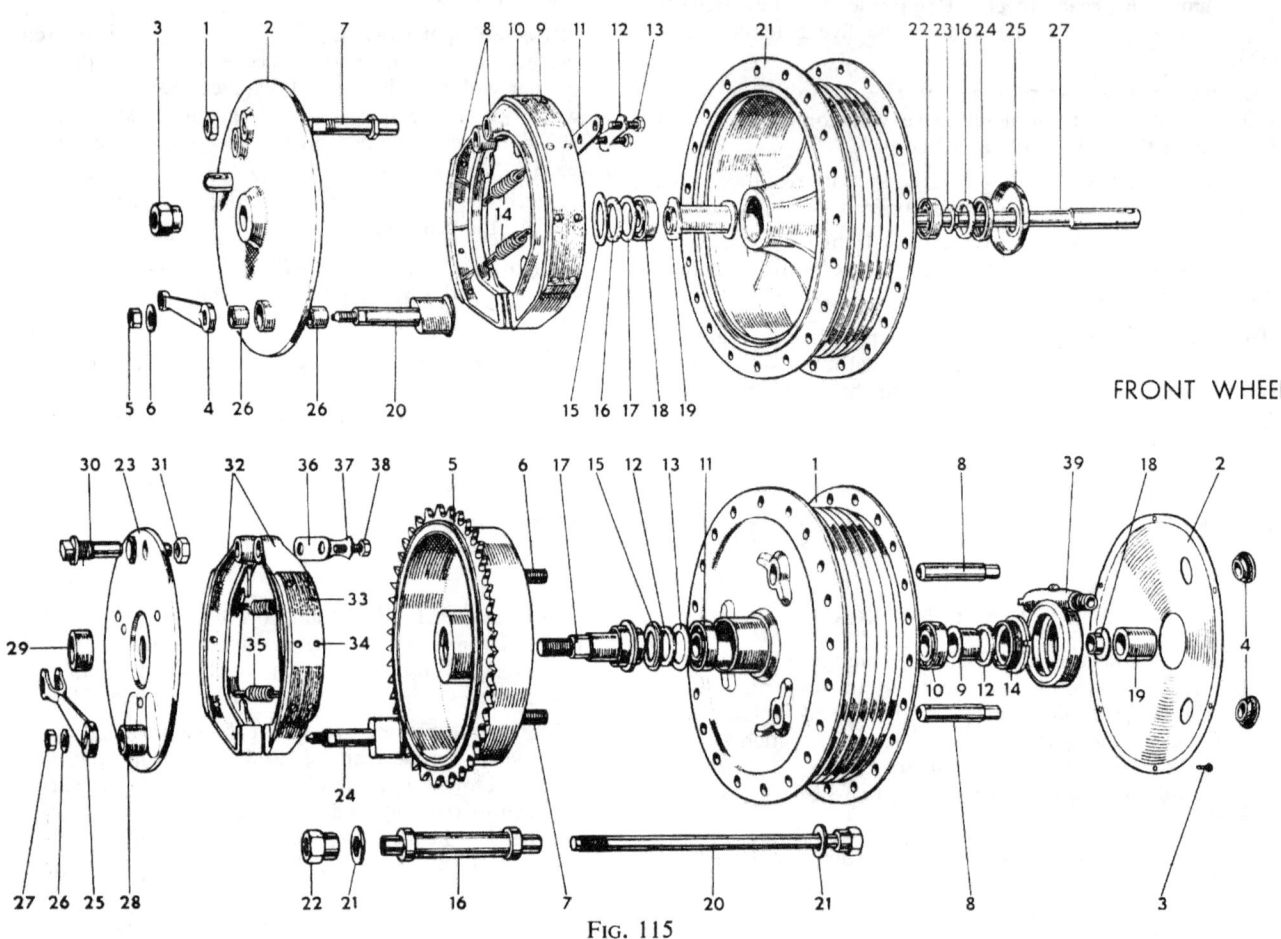

FIG. 115

FRONT FORKS

Lubrication. Use one of the grades of oil, S.A.E. 20 as shown in the table of lubricants. The normal oil content is five fluid ozs. (142 cc.). Attention is only necessary at the first 1,000 miles and again at 10,000 miles when the oil should be changed by draining. An exploded drawing of the front forks is shown in (Fig. 116) from which it will readily be seen that the fork springs abut against the filler plugs (34), before removing these plugs weight must be taken off the front wheel, by placing the machine on its central stand to avoid the forks collapsing.

To drain the forks. With the machine on the central stand: Unscrew the two filler plugs (34). Have available a container to catch oil drained, then remove the drain plug screw (7) with its washer, with the container under the fork leg. If the wheel is inclined to one side, draining will be more complete. Deal with the other fork leg in a similar manner.

Filling oil. It will be seen that the air space between the fork spring, and the inside of the tube is very close; therefore fresh oil must be filled with extreme care, to avoid losses by spilling. Use a measured container for the correct content of 5 ozs. Replace the drain plugs before filling, also firmly tighten the filler plugs after.

Steering head adjustment. On a new machine the filler plugs (34) should be checked for tightness due to settling down, check as well the steering head bearing at the first 100 miles, and then occasionally, as the mileage increases. Using the machine with movement in these bearings will damage the races. Movement in these bearings can usually be detected when the front brake is applied. To check, raise the front wheel well clear of the ground, with a box under the crankcase. Try to raise or lower the front wheel with one hand and use the fingers of the other hand encircling the handle bar lug where it meets the frame, when movement can be felt. To adjust bearings a thin open ended spanner 1⅜" across the flats is needed. First release the tube clamping stud nut (28), unscrew the stem nut (37) slightly. Use the thin spanner on the sleeve nut (30) and manipulate as necessary. The bearing should be devoid of play with free movement. Retighten the column nut, also the clamping stud nuts.

Steering lock. The lock is pressed into the handle bar lug, and can be removed by driving it out from underneath. A number is stamped on the bottom of the lock for key identification.

1964 Front Fork Assembly

1. Fork main tube
2. Main tube bush
3. Main tube bottom bush
4. Main tube bottom bush circlip
5. Fork end left hand
6. Fork end right hand
7. Fork end drain plug
8. Washer for plug
9. Oil damper tube
10. Oil damper rod
11. Oil damper tube bolt
12. Washer for bolt
13. Washer for tube
14. Nut for rod top
15. Nut for rod bottom
16. Damper tube cap
17. Piston locating peg
18. Oil damper valve cup
19. Oil damper valve cup slotted ring
20. Main tube lock ring with cup
21. Main spring
22. Main spring locating bushes
23. Spring cover tube
24. Spring top cover tube securing plate
25. Screws securing plate
26. Crown lug complete with column
27. Pinch stud for crown lug
28. Nut for stud
30. Fork head race adjuster nut
31. Top cover left hand
32. Top cover right hand
33. Main tube top cover ring
34. Fork main tube filler and retaining plug
35. Washer for plug
36. Fork head clip
37. Fork crown and column lock nut

Fig. 116

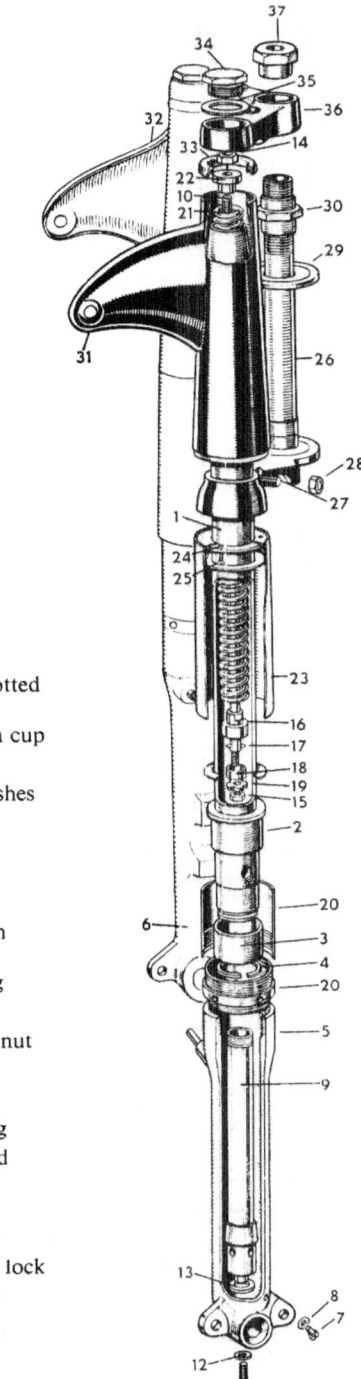

Dismantling the forks. The forks can be removed as a unit, or the fork legs can be removed individually. To take out one fork leg remove the front wheel as described elsewhere. Take off the front mudguard with stays. Release nut for pinch bolt (28). Remove filler cap plug (34), disconnect it from the damper rod, by using two spanners.

The fork inner tube can now be drawn downwards clear of the handlebar lug and fork crown. If the tube resists removal fit back the filler plug without being connected to the damper rod, screw in a few turns, then give it a few sharp blows with a soft faced mallet to separate the tube from its taper fixing in the handlebar lug.

To remove the forks as a unit. Follow the instructions given for removing a fork leg, as far as disconnecting the filler plugs from the damper rods. Proceed by taking off the headlamp leaving it suspended by the loom. Separate the control cables from the levers, and remove handlebars. Remove the column nut (37) then give the underside of the handlebar lug one or two blows with a mallet until it is clear of the fork tubes. At this stage support the ends of the forks, for after removing the sleeve nut (30) the forks will drop out. Watch for the steel balls for the races, there are 18 in each race (36 in all) if a steering damper is fitted detach the fixed plate from the frame.

To dismantle a fork slider. Remove from the fork slider the bolt fixing damper tube (11). Unscrew the bottom cover (23), holes are provided for a C spanner. Take away the fork slider (5).

The damper tube with the fork spring can be extracted from the tube. To dismantle further, take off nut securing fork spring, unscrew the damper tube cap (16) with a tommy bar through the holes in the damper tube, for if this is held in a vice it will distort and become useless. The damper assembly sequence is clearly depicted in Fig. 116.

Note. When removing the oil seal, sealing washer and flanged bush pass them along the fork tube and take off from the top end past the taper end, if the oil seal is to be used again.

Assembling the forks. It will be apparent from the dismantling instructions given that there is nothing complicated in the fork assembly and if the reverse sequence is used, no difficulty should occur with the following precautions.

The fork tube, where the oil seal operates, must have a smooth finish and free from blemish.

The oil seal is fitted from the top of the tube, with the visible spring facing downwards against the flange for the bush.

The damper tube cap also the damper tube fixing bolt must be properly tightened.

Finally tighten the bottom cover (23) when the front wheel has been put back.

Fill 5 ozs. of S.A.E. 20 oil to each fork leg.

ELECTRICAL SECTION

12 volt system. This improved form of lighting was first introduced for the 1964 models. The heat sink plate, to which the Zener diode is attached, must be kept in the air stream for heat dissipation. Two 6 volt batteries in series are mounted in the battery compartment. It is most important to ensure that the battery cables, as well as the link cable, are securely tightened. A wiring diagram is shown on page 108.

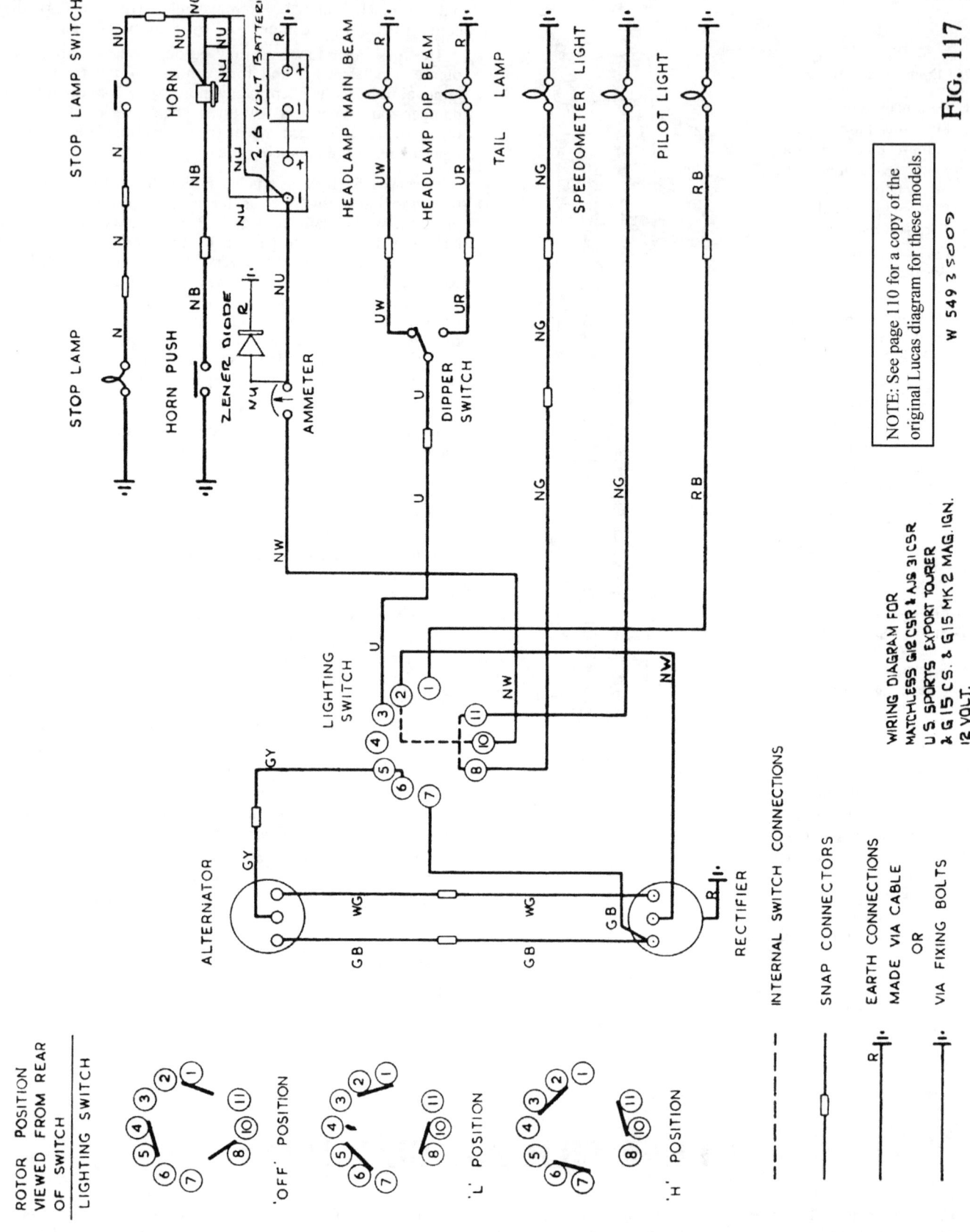

FIG. 117

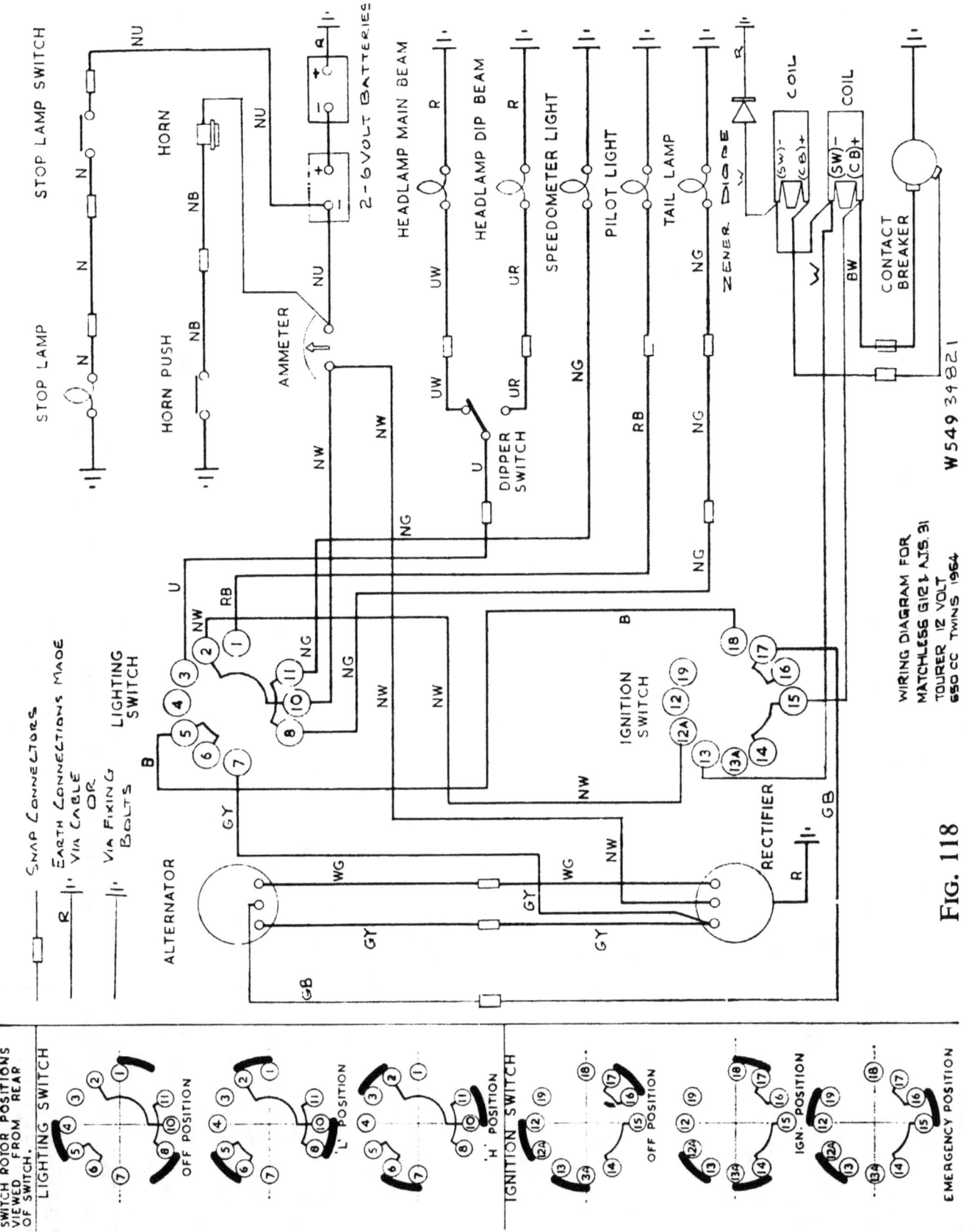

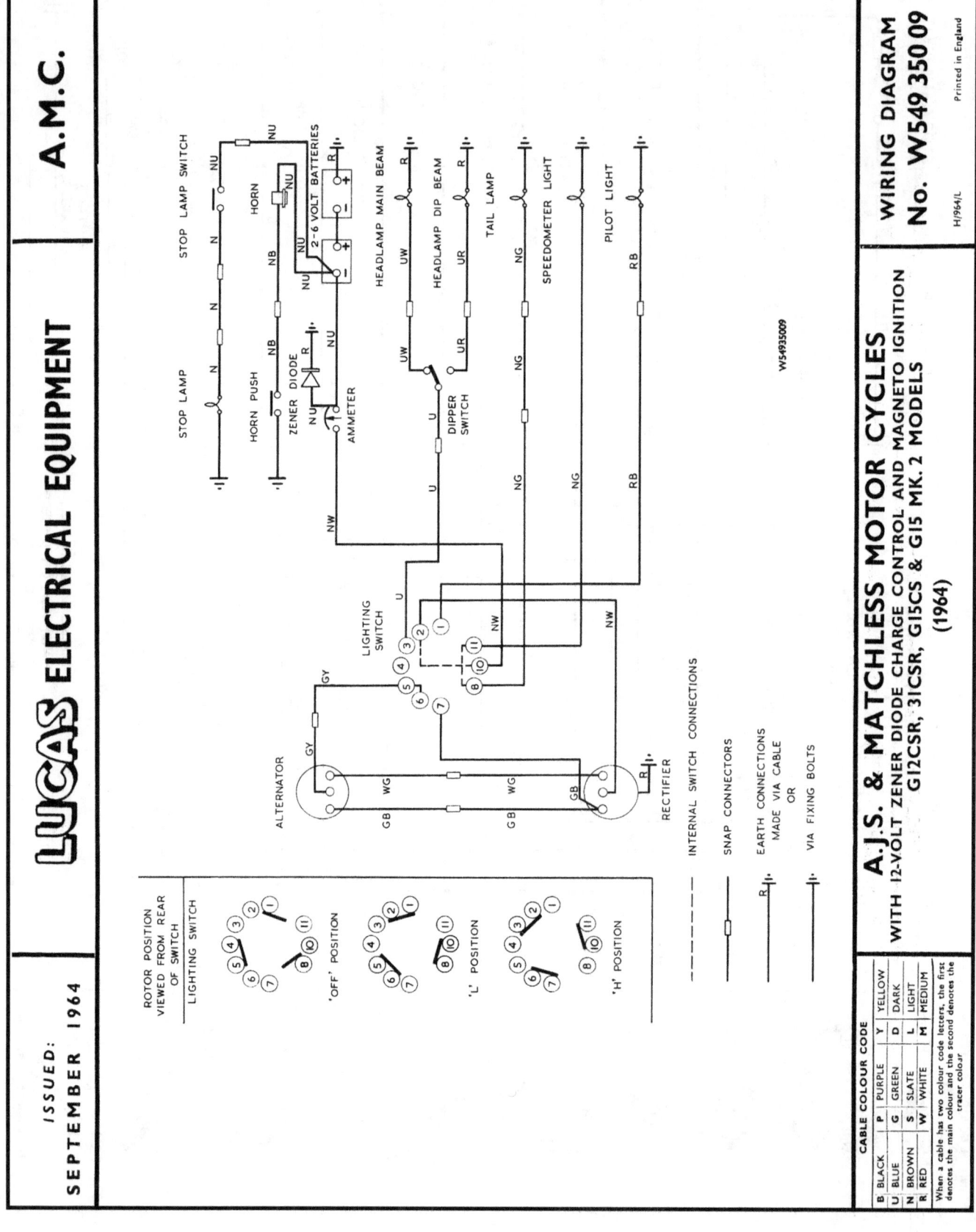

Supplementary Instruction Book for Competition Models

~~~

Associated Motor Cycles Ltd.
Plumstead . London . S.E. 18

Introduction

Sports twins, scrambles and trials models, are fitted with engine sprockets which are considered to be best suited for competitions.

Owners, who intend to use a machine of this type for normal road work, should fit a standard type engine sprocket, for reasons that are obvious.

Where prolonged full throttle driving is desired, the use of sparking plugs with a reasonably high heat factor, also with a good oil factor are recommended. (See *Technical Data*.)

Machines of the above type are usually acquired by experienced motor-cyclists and with this in mind elementary details are not included in this supplement.

For those without previous experience, elementary details for decarbonisation, etc., are detailed in the normal Instruction Book, which is issued with each new machine.

TECHNICAL DATA.
SPORTS TWINS.

Engine capacity	592 cc.
Bore and Stroke	72 × 72.8 mm.
Compression ratio	8.5
Carburettor AMAL Monobloc	Type 376/78
Carburettor bore size	1 1/16 ins.
Main jet size	280
Main jet size with Air Filter	240
Throttle slide	376/3 1/2
Pilot jet	30
Needle position	Third position
Needle jet	.106
Petrol Tank capacity	2 gallons
Oil Tank capacity	4 pints
Front chain	66 links 1/2 in. × .305 in.
Rear chain	97 links 5/8 in. × .380 in.
Engine sprocket normal. (Competition)	19 teeth
Engine sprocket standard. (Touring)	22 teeth
Gear ratios	See page 12
Sparking plugs	K.L.G. FE. 80
Sparking plugs. Competition type	FE. 220

SUPPLEMENTARY INSTRUCTIONS FOR TRIALS AND SCRAMBLES MODELS.
(To be used in conjunction with normal Instruction Book).

TECHNICAL DATA.
TRIALS MODELS.

Capacity	347 cc.
Bore	69 mm. (2.7187 ins.)
Stroke	93 mm.
Compression Ratio	6.5
Carburettor Type	376/59T Monobloc
Carburettor Bore	$1\frac{1}{16}$ ins.
„ Main Jet	210
„ Slide	3
„ Needle Jet	107 T
„ Pilot Jet	30
Ignition Setting	Maximum advance $\frac{1}{2}$ in. (free wire control)
Magneto Type	NR—1 (Lucas 42179E)
Sparking Plug	K.L.G. FE. 80
Petrol Tank capacity	2 gallons
Oil Tank capacity	4 pints
Ground clearance	10 ins.
Tyre Sizes	Rear 4.00 × 19 ⎫ Trials Universal
Tyre Sizes	Front 2.75 × 21 ⎭
Contact Breaker Gap	.012 ins.
Chain Sizes and Length: Primary Chain	$\frac{1}{2}$ × .305 66 links
Rear Chain	$\frac{5}{8}$ × .380 97 links
Brakes	7 ins. × $\frac{7}{8}$ ins.

TECHNICAL DATA.
SCRAMBLES MODELS.

	Model 350	Model 500
Engine capacity	348 cc.	497 cc.
Bore and Stroke	72 × 85.5 mm.	86 × 85.5 mm.
Compression Ratio	9.9	8.7
Carburettor AMAL Monobloc	389/18	389/12
Choke Diameter	1⅛ in.	1 3/16 in.
Main Jet No.	270	440
Pilot Jet No.	30	30
Slide No.	3	3
Needle Position	Centre Notch	Centre Notch
Needle Jet	.106	.106
Petrol Tank capacity	2 gallons	2 gallons
Oil Tank capacity	4 pints	4 pints
Brakes	7 ins. × ⅞ ins.	7 ins. × ⅞ ins.
Rear Chain	⅝ ins. × 0.380 ins.—97 links	97 links
Primary Chain	½ in. × 0.305 in.—66 links	67 links
Sparking Plug. (For Running-in)	FE. 80	F.E 80
Sparking Plug. (For Racing)	FE. 220	FE. 220

ENGINE SERVICE.

Instructions in this supplement apply only to parts that are dissimilar to the Touring Models.

TRIALS MODELS.

This model closely resembles the standard type engine, with the exception of the alloy cylinder barrel and the method of retaining the cylinder and head to the crankcase. A ground joint is used for the cylinder head and cylinder barrel, jointing compound is not to be used as a seal.

To remake the joint, apply a little fine grinding paste on to the wide face of the cylinder barrel, put the head on to the cylinder. Using both hands, move the head in an oscillating motion through an arc of about 90 degrees, with a slight downwards pressure. Raise the head from time to time to get a fresh "bite" on the grinding paste. Continue this process until (after wiping both joint faces) a continuous matt surface is obtained.

Note: The head joint is made on the wide face only and not on the spigot of the cylinder.

SCRAMBLER MODELS.

Instructions for cylinder head grinding for Trials Models apply also to the scrambler type engine. The two sealing rubbers surrounding the top of the push rod tunnels must be removed, before grinding takes place.

VALVE GRINDING.

Both valve seats are inserts cast in the cylinder head, and are not replaceable. Unnecessary, or prolonged valve grinding should be avoided, which can only cause the seat to become saucer shaped with an ineffective gas seal.

If the valve seat is pitted it should be recut with a valve seating cutter, the valve angle is 45°.

PORT POLISHING.

If the ports in the cylinder head are ground, or polished, avoid removing metal immediately below the valve seat insert, which will weaken the support of the insert and may cause it to move.

DECARBONISING.

The engine should only be decarbonised when there are definite signs of a loss of power, increased petrol consumption, or difficult starting, assuming the ignition system is in order.

The competition type engine runs at a low temperature, and providing the oil consumption is not excessive, a heavy formation of carbon on the piston crown and sphere of the cylinder head is unlikely to occur.

If the cylinder barrel is removed to examine the piston rings, the rings should not be disturbed unless it is absolutely necessary. Gas leakage past the rings is indicated by brown patches on the ring surface.

PISTON REMOVAL.

Trials models are fitted with a split skirt piston, if the piston is removed it must be replaced with the split in the skirt facing the front wheel indicated by FRONT stamped on the piston crown.

Scrambles models are fitted with a solid skirt piston, and although the recesses for valve clearance on the piston crown are symmetrical, the piston should be suitably marked before removal, so that it can be refitted in its original position.

PUSH ROD ADJUSTMENT. SCRAMBLER ENGINE.

Special racing camshafts (marked SH) are a standard fitment for the Scrambler models, and for engine efficiency correct push rod adjustment is of considerable importance.

Make this adjustment when the engine is cold, with the piston on T.D.C. of the firing stroke. Clearance for the inlet valve is Nil, the push rod should be just free to rotate by finger application with no up and down movement.

The exhaust valve clearance is .005 inches, obtainable by first adjusting the push rod with a Nil clearance, the adjusting screw is screwed down to the extent of one-sixth of a turn, or one flat on the hexagon for the adjusting screw.

PUSH ROD ADJUSTMENT. TRIALS ENGINE.

Follow details given for the Standard models.

To avoid "losing the engine", or spitting back through the carburettor when tuning for "Plonk" the push rod adjustment can be made with the engine cold, or the inlet push rod clearance increased slightly.

TO RETIME THE IGNITION. TRIALS MODELS.

The normal ignition advance is 39° or ½ inch.

First check contact breaker gap, .012 inch; leave off contact breaker cover.

Remove magneto chain case cover, and slacken the nut securing the lower magneto drive sprocket, two or three turns. Lever the sprocket loose on its taper shaft.

Refer to the normal instruction book and follow the dismantling instructions then set the piston ½ inch before T.D.C. as recommended.

Place the ignition control lever in the fully advanced position, rotate the sprocket on magneto, anti-clockwise, until the contact points are just about to separate. The precise point of separation can be found by inserting a piece of tissue paper between the points, when by rotating the magneto sprocket and with a light pull on the paper until it is released, the exact contact separation point will be indicated.

With care that the magneto does not move, tap the lower magneto sprocket back on its shaft and tighten the fixing nut.

Recheck this setting before refitting the parts removed.

Replace contact breaker cover.

TO RETIME THE IGNITION. SCRAMBLER MODELS

The normal ignition advance is between 39 to 41 degrees or ½ inch vertical measurement for both the 350 cc. and 500 cc. model. Follow details given for Trials models.

VALVE TIMING. SCRAMBLER AND TRIALS MODELS.

Both cam wheels, also the small timing pinion are marked for correct assembly. Use No. 2 mark for inlet cam, No. 1 for exhaust cam.

TO REFIT CAM WHEELS.

With both cam wheels removed, turn the engine until the marked tooth on the small pinion is in line with the centre of the cam wheel bush for the inlet cam.

Insert the inlet cam into its bush with the No. 2 tooth gap mark in mesh with the mark on the small pinion.

Turn the engine *forward* until the marked tooth on the small pinion is in line with the centre of the cam wheel bush for the exhaust cam.

Insert the exhaust cam into its bush, with the No. 1 tooth gap mark in mesh with the mark on the small pinion.

Note: The mark on the small pinion is central with the key way and if obscured release the pinion nut which has a LEFTHAND THREAD one or two turns to expose the mark.

AVERAGE VALVE TIMING FIGURES. SCRAMBLES MODELS.

Inlet Valve opens: 59° B.T.D.C.   } Nil clearance.
Inlet Valve closes: 69° A.B.D.C.
Exhaust Valve opens: 69° B.B.D.C.   } .005 in. clearance.
Exhaust Valve closes: 48° A.T.D.C.

Taken with valve .001 inches off the valve seat.

TRIALS MODELS.

Inlet Valve opens: 26° B.T.D.C.
Inlet Valve closes: 53° A.B.D.C.
Exhaust Valve opens: 64° B.B.D.C.
Exhaust Valve closes: 25° A.T.D.C.

Readings taken with .016 inches rocker clearance and valve .001 inches off its seat.

SPORTS TWINS.
REMOVING THE TWO-PIECE EXHAUST PIPE.

Slacken the bolt securing the clip, where the short pipe joins the long pipe.

Remove nut and washer on front engine plate.

Pull out the short pipe from the exhaust port and the long pipe simultaneously.

Remove both the nut and washer on the front frame uniting bolt.

Slacken the silencer clip bolt.

Pull out the long pipe from the exhaust port, leaving the silencer attached to the frame.

Refit in reverse order.

Note: Do not unduly rock the exhaust pipes sideways during removal, which tends to distort the exhaust pipe and cause gas leakage.

PETROL TANK REMOVAL. COMPETITION TYPE.

Where a competition type petrol tank is fitted the method of attachment differs from the standard fitting as shown on page 30 in the Instruction Book.

The front attachment for the petrol tank is made by two cylindrical-shaped rubbers attached to the tank support rail and engaged in two tubular steel extensions, the rubbers are expanded, when the two bolts securing the rubbers are tightened.

To remove this type of petrol tank:

Disconnect both petrol pipes.

Remove the bolt passing through the tank and frame tube at the rear end of the tank.

Release the two front attachment bolts and lift up bodily the tank, with care not to misplace the two separating rubbers for the rear attachment.

When refitting do not unduly tighten the front attachment bolts.

REAR WHEEL REMOVAL.

With the machine on its central stand:

Disconnect: Rear chain.
             Rear brake rod.
             Speedometer drive cable.

Remove the bolt which passes through the rear chain guard, and the rear brake cover plate anchor lug.

To avoid disturbing the wheel spindle distance pieces, leave the spindle in position and remove both spindle nuts only, twist the wheel to the right, until the cover plate is clear of its anchorage and withdraw the wheel.

FRONT CHAIN ADJUSTMENT.

Refer to Illustration 27 in the Instruction Book for location of adjuster.

Scrambler models have two chain adjuster bolts.

Trials and Sports Twin models use one chain adjuster bolt.

For front chain adjustment follow details on page 56 of the Instruction Book.

Where two chain adjusters are used, both bolts must be moved an equal amount, when this adjustment is carried out.

TO REMOVE FRONT CHAINCASE.

To remove outer half of front chaincase:

Place tray under chaincase to catch oil.

Remove screw binding chaincase metal band at its rear.

Remove metal band.

Remove endless rubber band.

Remove nut and washer, in centre of chaincase front.

Take away outer half of chaincase.

Fit outer half of front chaincase by:

Ensure faces of both halves of chaincase are clean.

Ensure the rubber and metal bands are clean and undamaged.

After carefully positioning the outer half so that its exterior edge exactly coincides with that of the inner half, apply the endless rubber band.

Fit the metal band, starting at the front end of the chaincase and drawing together the two free ends with the fingers of one hand while with the other hand insert the binding screw.

Whilst slowly tightening this binding screw apply at the same time light taps all round the band exterior using a small rubber mallet.

These light taps will cause the metal band to creep on the rubber to ensure an even all-round pressure.

Remove the inspection cap from the chaincase and pour in engine oil to the level of the bottom edge of the inspection cap orifice and then replace the cap.

Do not overtighten the clamping screw.

TO REMOVE THE DYNAMO.

Remove the left side footrest arm.

Place a tray under primary chaincase to catch the oil.

Remove chaincase band binding screw and remove metal band and also endless rubber band.

Remove nut and washer in centre of chaincase when outer half can be taken away.

Remove spring circlip, locking plate and nut securing dynamo sprocket and withdraw sprocket with a suitable tool. (Use spanner 017254 to hold sprocket while nut is being slackened, this relieves the dynamo shaft of all bending strain).

Detach dynamo cables and loosen dynamo clamping bolt to fullest extent.

Twist dynamo by hand until the locating strip on its body is in line with the keyway cutaway in the rear engine plate housing the dynamo, in which position same can be withdrawn tilting upwards to clear gear box while doing so.

To re-fit the dynamo, reverse the foregoing taking care to accurately locate the dynamo sprocket key when applying the sprocket. See separate instructions for correct dynamo chain adjustments. Ensure that dynamo sprocket securing nut is well tightened before refitting locking plate and retaining circlip.

DYNAMO CHAIN ADJUSTMENT.

The dynamo armature shaft is eccentric to the body of the dynamo.

Therefore, by partially revolving the dynamo in its housing the distance between the two dynamo driving sprockets can be varied, thereby allowing latitude for chain adjustment.

Tighten dynamo chain by:

Remove inspection cap from front chaincase.

Slacken dynamo clamping strap bolt.

With the fingers turn dynamo bodily in an anti-clockwise direction till, by passing a finger through the inspection cap opening, it can be felt the chain tension is correct.

The chain whip should be about $\frac{1}{4}$ inch. Ensure, when feeling tension, the front driving chain is not confused with the dynamo chain which lies behind the front driving chain.

Tighten dynamo clamping strap bolt.

Re-check chain tension.

Replace chaincase inspection cap.

MAGNETO CHAIN ADJUSTMENT.

The magneto platform hinges on one of its fixing bolts. This provides sufficient movement for adjustment to the magneto driving chain.

Tighten magneto chain by:

Remove magneto chain case cover.

Slacken nut on rear bolt supporting magneto platform.

Insert a screwdriver under that end of the magneto platform and lever upwards until the chain tension is correct.

The chain whip should be about $\frac{1}{4}$ inch.

Tighten nut on platform supporting bolt.

Re-check chain tension.

Place a supply of grease on magneto driving chain and using a broad pen knife blade or thin strip of metal work well into the interior of the auto ignition advance unit a generous quantity of either Mobilgrease No. 2 or Esso Fluid Grease.

Replace magneto chain cover.

CARBURETTOR. SCRAMBLES MODELS.

The main jet size in technical data is for an open exhaust pipe system.

The correct exhaust pipe length is most important, namely 42 inches long measured along centre line.

GEAR RATIOS. SCRAMBLES MODELS.

Internal Ratios.

Engine sprocket size	1.1 First gear	1.35 Second gear	1.77 Third gear	2.67 Fourth gear (top)
16 teeth	18.39 to 1	12.19 to 1	9.30 to 1	6.89 to 1
(a) 17 teeth	17.30 to 1	11.47 to 1	8.74 to 1	6.48 to 1
18 teeth	16.34 to 1	10.83 to 1	8.26 to 1	6.12 to 1
(b) 19 teeth	15.48 to 1	10.26 to 1	7.83 to 1	5.80 to 1
20 teeth	14.71 to 1	9.75 to 1	7.43 to 1	5.51 to 1
21 teeth	14.01 to 1	9.29 to 1	7.08 to 1	5.25 to 1
22 teeth	13.37 to 1	8.86 to 1	6.76 to 1	5.01 to 1

(a) Standard for 350 cc. Scrambles Models.

(b) Standard for 500 cc. Scrambles Models.

GEAR RATIOS. TRIALS MODELS.

Internal Ratios.

Engine sprocket size	1.1 First gear	1.47 Second gear	2.39 Third gear	3.28 Fourth gear (top)
16 teeth	22.59 to 1	16.46 to 1	10.12 to 1	6.89 to 1
(a) 17 teeth Standard	21.25 to 1	15.48 to 1	9.52 to 1	6.48 to 1
18 teeth	20.07 to 1	14.62 to 1	8.99 to 1	6.12 to 1
(b) 19 teeth	19.02 to 1	13.86 to 1	8.52 to 1	5.80 to 1
20 teeth	18.07 to 1	13.16 to 1	8.10 to 1	5.51 to 1
21 teeth	17.22 to 1	12.54 to 1	7.71 to 1	5.25 to 1
22 teeth	16.43 to 1	11.97 to 1	7.36 to 1	5.01 to 1

(a) Standard for 350 cc. Trials Models.

(b) Standard for 500 cc. Trials Models.

GEAR RATIOS. SPORTS TWINS.

Internal Ratios.

Engine sprocket size	1.1 First gear	1.35 Second gear	1.77 Third gear	2.67 Fourth gear (top)
(a) 19 teeth	15.48	10.26	7.83	5.80
20 teeth	14.71	9.75	7.43	5.51
21 teeth	14.01	9.29	7.08	5.25
(b) 22 teeth	13.37	8.86	6.76	5.01

(a) Competition Sprocket.

(b) Standard 600 cc. Engine Sprocket.

NOTES

INSTRUCTION BOOK
A·J·S

MODEL 14-250 c.c. O.H.V.
MODEL 14/CS 250 c.c. O.H.V. SCRAMBLER
MODEL 8-350 c.c. O.H.V.

MATCHLESS

MODEL G2-250 c.c. O.H.V.
MODEL G5-350 c.c. O.H.V.

Factories:
BURRAGE GROVE and MAXEY ROAD
PLUMSTEAD, S.E.18

Telephone: WOOlwich 1223 (7 lines)
Telegrams: "ICANHOPIT, WOL-LONDON"
Cables; "ICANHOPIT, WOL-LONDON" TELEX 22617
Codes: A.B.C. 5th and 6th Edition; Bentley's; and Private Codes

Registered Offices:
PLUMSTEAD ROAD, PLUMSTEAD
LONDON, S.E.18 :: ENGLAND

--- Issued by ---

A.M.C. MOTOR CYCLES : LONDON S.E.18
Proprietors: ASSOCIATED MOTOR CYCLES LTD.

CONTENTS

	Page
Carburetter	22
Controls	7
Data	4
Driving	8
Electrical Equipment	40
Engine	15
Forks and Frame	30
Free Service	52
Guarantee	55
Information	47
Lubrication	10
Maintenance	14
Repairs and Service	49
Spare Parts	53
Tools and Special Equipment	54
Transmission	25
Wheels and Brakes	37

THE MODERN MOTOR CYCLE unquestionably provides one of the most healthy, economical and pleasant means of transport. In addition, by reason of its superb braking, high power to weight ratio and ease of control it is, if used with due care, one of the safest vehicles on the road.

It is our sincere desire that every owner should obtain from his mount the service, comfort and innumerable miles of low cost travel that we have earnestly endeavoured to build into it.

It must be borne in mind, however, that although of simple design and construction, it is nevertheless a highly specialised piece of engineering and must in consequence be intelligently and efficiently maintained in order to provide unfailing reliability.

In this book we provide non-technical instructions for carrying out all the maintenance operations likely to be called for in normal service, together with assisting illustrations.

To owners of long experience we tender apologies for the elementary nature of some of the contents of this handbook, but owners, whether novice or expert, are advised to read the contents from beginning to end. We are at all times pleased to give owners the full benefit of our wide experience in matters relating to motor cycles of our manufacture and elsewhere will be found details of the particulars required when making enquiries of our Service Department.

Safety on the Road

IN the interest of Safety on the Road, a few words of warning will not be out of place.

The outstanding manoeuvrability of a motor cycle over most other vehicles on the road makes it necessary to exercise caution at all times.

There are, unfortunately, a few motor-cyclists whose reckless driving constitutes a menace not only to themselves but also to other road users resulting in the totally false impression in some quarters that motor-cycling is a dangerous pastime.

REMEMBER IT IS NOT THE MOTOR CYCLE THAT CAUSES ACCIDENTS, IT IS THE MAN WHO IS RIDING IT.

Take a pride in your riding technique and never rely upon the other fellow doing the right thing.

Your example of careful and courteous riding will materially contribute to road safety and to the reputation of a fine sporting pastime.

NO ACCIDENTS PLEASE

Your motor cycle, as issued from the factory, is fitted with an efficient silencing system, and with careful and unobtruse driving, particularly in built-up areas, will not cause annoyance to the general public.

Owners who interfere with the silencing system by removing the baffles are purely exhibitionists and such conduct can only bring motor-cyclists in general into disrepute.

Data 350 c.c.

Identity

Engine Number	On the crankcase near engine plate cowling
Frame Number	On right side of frame head lug
Cylinder bore	72 mm.
Stroke	85.5 mm.
Cubic capacity	347 c.c. (21.17 cu. ins.)

Carburetter

Type 389/42	Amal Monobloc (12° inclination)
Main jet (without air filter)	220
Main jet (with air filter)	220
Choke size	1⅛"
Throttle slide	3½
Needle position	central (.106) pilot 25

Capacities

Petrol tank	3¼ gallons (12.5 litres)
Oil capacity	2½ pints (1.4 litres)
Gear box	3 pints (1.8 litres)
Front chain case	568 c.c.

Compression ratio
6.9 to 1

General

Seat height	29.5" (74 cms.)
Wheelbase	53" (134.5 cms.)
Weight	340 lbs. (154 kilos)
Ground clearance	6" (15 cms.)

Cylinder bore

Nominal size	2.8345 + .0005" / − .0005"

Piston size

Skirt diameter (taken at right angle to gudgeon pin top of the skirt)

High limit	2.8286"
Low limit	2.8276"

Piston rings

Compression rings	diameter 72 mm.
Compression rings	3/64" width
Compression rings	radial thickness .115"—.109"
Scraper ring	diameter 72 mm.
Scraper ring	width 5/32"
Scraper ring	radial thickness .109"—.101"
Piston ring gap	.008"—.013"

Ignition timing
¼" B.T.D.C.

Valve timing

Inlet valve opens	40° B.T.D.C. } with .01" rocker clearance
Exhaust valve closes	40° A.T.D.C.

Sparking plug
K.L.G. FE. 80

Chain sizes

Front (72 links)	.315" x .628" Duplex
Rear (123 links)	½" x .305

Gear ratios

Internal ratios	1.30 to 1, 1.85 to 1, 2.92 to 1
Actual ratios—Top	6.39 to 1
Third	8.32 to 1
Second	11.82 to 1
First	18.68 to 1

Sprockets

Engine	22 teeth
Clutch	46 teeth
Final drive	18 teeth
Rear wheel	55 teeth

Data 250 c.c.

Identity

Engine Number	On the crankcase near engine plate cowling
Frame Number	On right side of frame head lug
Cylinder bore	69·85 mm.
Stroke	64·84 mm.
Cubic capacity	248·5 c.c. (15·2 cu. ins.)

Carburetter

Type 376/250	Amal Monobloc (12° inclination)
Main jet (without air filter)	180
Main jet (with air filter)	180
Choke size	1 1/32"
Throttle slide	3½
Needle position	central (·106) pilot 25

Capacities

Petrol tank	3¼ gallons (18 litres)
Oil capacity	2½ pints (1·4 litres)
Gear box	3 pints (1·8 litres)
Front chain case	568 c.c.

Compression ratio
7·8 to 1

General

Seat height	30" (76 cms.)
Wheelbase	53" (134·5 cms.)
Weight	325 lbs. (148 kilos)
Ground clearance	5½" (14 cms.)

Cylinder bore

Nominal size	2·7500 + ·0005" − ·0005"

Piston size

Skirt diameter (taken at right angle to gudgeon pin top of the skirt)	
High limit	2·7488"
Low limit	2·7480"

Piston rings

Compression rings	diameter 2¾" (69·85 mm.)
Compression rings	width ·0625"—·0615"
Compression rings	radial thickness ·112—·106"
Scraper ring	diameter 2¾" (69·85 mm.)
Scraper ring	width ·156"—·155"
Scraper ring	radial thickness ·112—·106"
Piston ring gap	0·008—·013"

Ignition timing
¼" B.T.D.C.

Valve timing

Inlet valve opens	40° B.T.D.C. } with ·01" rocker clearance
Exhaust valve closes	40° A.T.D.C.

Sparking plug
K.L.G. FE. 80

Chain sizes

Front (73 links)	⅜" x ·225
Rear (125 links)	½" x ·305

Gear ratios

Internal ratios	1·30 to 1, 1·85 to 1, 2·92 to 1
Actual ratios—Top	6·89 to 1
Third	8·96 to 1
Second	12·75 to 1
First	20·12 to 1

Sprockets

Engine	21 teeth
Clutch	50 teeth
Final drive	19 teeth
Rear wheel	55 teeth

250 SCRAMBLES MODEL.

TECHNICAL DATA.

Engine capacity	248 c.c.
Bore and stroke	70 x 65 mm.
Compression ratio	11.5 : 1
Carburetter AMAL Monobloc	376/250
Choke Diameter	1 1/16"
Main Jet No.	180
Pilot Jet No.	25
Slide No.	3
Needle Position	Four
Needle Jet	.107
Petrol Tank Capacity	2.75 gallons
Oil Tank Capacity	2.5 pints
Brakes	6" dia.
Rear Chain	131 links 1/2" x .305"
Primary Chain	55 links 1/2" x .205"
Sparking Plug (for running-in)	FE. 80
Sparking Plug (for racing)	FE. 220
Front Fork capacity	6.5 ozs. S.A.E. 20
Ignition Timing	32° B.T.D.C.
Engine Sprocket	17 teeth
Rear Wheel Sprocket	70 "
Clutch Sprocket	37 "
Gear Box Sprocket	17 "

GEAR RATIOS. 250 c.c. SCRAMBLES MODELS.

Internal Ratios.

First Gear	Second Gear	Third Gear
2.42 to 1	1.85 to 1	1.30 to 1

Gear Ratios with 17 teeth Engine Sprocket.

First Gear	Second Gear	Third Gear	Top Gear
21.62 to 1	16.55 to 1	11.63 to 1	8.95 to 1

Controls

Throttle twist grip. On right handlebar. Twist inwards to open. When fully closed engine should just idle when hot.

Valve Lifter. Small lever on left side handlebar.

Air lever. Small lever on right handlebar. Pull inwards to increase air supply to carburetter. Once set, when engine has warmed up, requires no alteration for different road speeds. Should be fully closed when starting engine from cold.

Clutch lever. Large lever on left handlebar. Grip to release clutch so that drive to rear wheel is disconnected.

Front brake lever. Large lever on right handlebar. Grip to operate front wheel brake and, for normal braking, use in conjunction with rear brake application.

Rear brake lever. Pedal close to left side foot rest. Depress with left foot to apply rear brake. Apply gently and use increasing pressure as the road speed decreases.

Gear change lever. Pedal in horizontal position close to right foot rest. Controls selection of the four speeds, or ratios, between engine and rear wheel revolutions, with a "free" or neutral, position.

Kick-starter lever. Vertical pedal on right hand side of gear box.

Gear indicator. Moves under the control of the gear change lever and the number registering with a line on gear box indicates gear in engagement (or neutral).

Gear box filler cap. Located on side of gear case cover. Allows insertion of lubricant and access to clutch inner wire and internal clutch operating level.

Petrol tank filler cap. Located in top of fuel tank. To release, slightly depress, turn fully to the left, and then lift away. There are two locking positions. The middle position, between the fully tightened down and "lift away" positions, is in the nature of a "safety" device to prevent loss that might be occasioned by unauthorised meddling.

Oil reservoir filler cap. Located on right side crankcase. To remove, unscrew.

Lighting switch. Left hand one on top of head lamp, with three positions:

OFF ... Off.
L. ... Pilot, rear and speedometer ON.
H. ... Main, rear and speedometer ON.

Ignition switch. Right hand one on head lamp. Three positions—EMG., OFF., IGN. Turn clockwise for Ignition.

Ammeter. In top of head lamp. Indicates charge or discharge.

Dipping switch. On left handlebar. Operates when lamp switch is at "H".

Horn switch. On **left** handlebar, incorporated with Dip Switch.

Speedometer. In top of head lamp.

Before using the machine, sit on the saddle and become familiar with the position and operation of the various controls. Pay particular attention to the gear positions.

If any adjustment is made to the rear brake pedal make certain the brake does not bind and also see there Is not excessive free pedal movement before the brake comes "on".

Driving

FUEL

Although various quality fuels are again available owners are advised to use only the best. The small economy that might be considered to accrue by using the cheaper grades is more than offset by the advantages obtained by using only Premium Grades.

FUEL SUPPLY

Two fuel feed taps are situated underneath the rear end of the petrol tank. (One each side). Both must be shut off when the machine is left standing for more than a few minutes.

Normally, only use the tap on the right hand side of the machine and then the other side will act as a reserve supply. *Always re-fuel as soon as possible after being forced to call upon the reserve and then, at once, close the "reserve" tap.*

STARTING THE ENGINE FROM COLD

SPECIAL NOTE

It is NOT necessary to flood the carburetter, by depressing the plunger on the float chamber, before attempting to start the engine. Flooding the carburetter unnecessarily will result in difficult starting.

Check that there is sufficient fuel in the petrol tank.
Check that there is sufficient oil in the oil reservoir.
Check that the gear pedal is in the neutral position.
Pull outward the plunger of off-side petrol tap.
Check that the air control lever is in the fully closed position.
Depress the kickstarter two or three times to rotate and free the engine.
Open the throttle to the slightest amount possible.
Turn the ignition switch to IGN. Raise valve lifter to release compression.
Give the kickstarter a long, deliberate swinging kick when the engine should commence running.
Do not allow the kickstarter to return violently against its stop.
The kickstarter mechanism must be allowed to engage properly before putting heavy pressure on the kickstarter crank pedal pin. That means there are two definite and separate movements when operating the mechanism by depressing the crank.
The first is a slow and gentle movement which ends when it is felt the pawl has engaged with the teeth on the ratchet pinion.
After the engine has started, slowly open the air lever. Then set the throttle so that the engine is running at a moderate speed (neither racing nor ticking over) and allow to warm up. While doing this, check the oil circulation as detailed in page 11. The machine can then be taken on the road.

STOPPING THE ENGINE

To stop the engine, close the throttle, TURN OFF IGNITION. Before leaving the machine, turn off the fuel supply.

ON THE ROAD

Having started and warmed up the engine, take the machine off the stand, sit astride it, free the clutch by pulling up the large lever on the left bar and engage the lowest gear. Next, slowly release the clutch lever and the machine will commence to move forward. As it does this, the engine speed will tend to drop as it picks up the load so it will be necessary to increase the throttle opening, gradually, to keep the engine speed gently rising.

When well under way, disengage the clutch, slightly close the throttle, engage second gear and release the clutch lever, then open up the throttle to increase the speed of the machine. Repeat these operations in order to engage third and top gears.

To engage a higher gear the pedal is pressed downward with the toe and a lower gear is obtained by raising the pedal with the instep. To engage first gear from the neutral position, the pedal is therefore raised. After each pedal movement, internal springs return the pedal to its normal horizontal position.

The pedal must be moved to the full extent of its travel when selecting a gear, either up or down. It must not be "stamped down" or jabbed, but firmly and decisively moved till it stops. A half-hearted movement may not give full engagement. Keep the foot off the pedal when driving and between each gear change because, unless the lever can freely return to its normal central position, the next gear cannot be engaged.

RUNNING IN THE ENGINE

It is a natural desire to learn the capabilities of one's machine, similarly it can be irritating to be overtaken by a rider of a machine fitted with a smaller capacity engine. Nevertheless, the owner of a new machine must, in his own interest, strictly adhere to the principles of running in, which will result in a quieter engine, with a better performance than a similar machine owned by a rider who is unwilling to drive with restraint during the initial stage of running in.

The load imposed on the engine is governed by the amount of throttle that is used, and the makers of your machine, know from experience, that if the throttle or twist grip is not opened in excess of *one-third of its total movement* for the first 1,000 miles independent of road speed, the engine cannot be overloaded.

After this distance the amount of throttle can be progressively increased.
Special attention must be given, during the running in period, to such details as valve rocker adjustment, chains, brakes, contact breaker points, and steering head bearings, all of which tend to bed down in the first hundred miles or so. Particular note must be made of the adjustment of steering head bearings, which, if run in a slack condition, will be quickly ruined. After this bedding down process has taken place, adjustments to such details will only be necessary at lengthy intervals.

Do not overlook instructions for changing oil (see page 14).

Lubrication

LUBRICANTS TO USE

Efficient lubrication is of vital importance and it is false economy to use cheap oils and greases. The use of multigrade oils is not recommended.

We recommend the following lubricants to use in machines of our make.

FOR ENGINE LUBRICATION

HOT above 50° F	COLD 32° F to 50° F	EXTREME COLD below freezing point (32° F)
SAE 50	SAE 30	SAE 20
Mobiloil **D** Castrol **Grand Prix** Energol SAE 50 Essolube 50 Shell **X-100** Motor Oil **50**	Mobiloil **A** Castrol **XL** Energol SAE 30 Essolube 30 Shell **X-100** Motor Oil 30	Mobiloil **Arctic** Castrolite Energol SAE 20 Essolube 20 Shell **X-100** Motor Oil **20/20W**

NOTE—For the British Isles and much of Europe the **Cold** and **Hot** recommendations approximate to **Winter** and **Summer** conditions respectively. The **Extreme Cold** recommendations refer to wintry conditions in parts of Northern Europe, Canada, the Baltic and Scandinavian countries, and high mountainous districts where extreme cold is the average condition.

FOR GEAR BOX LUBRICATION

HOT above 50° F	COLD 32° F to 50° F	EXTREME COLD below freezing point (32° F)
SAE 50	SAE 50	SAE 30
Mobiloil **D** Castrol **Grand Prix** Energol SAE 50 Essolube 50 Shell **X-100** Motor Oil 50	Mobiloil **D** Castrol **Grand Prix** Energol SAE 50 Essolube 50 Shell **X-100** Motor Oil 50	Mobiloil **A** Castrol **XL** Energol SAE 30 Essolube 30 Shell **X-100** Motor Oil 30

NOTE—For the British Isles and much of Europe the **Cold** and **Hot** recommendations approximate to **Winter** and **Summer** conditions respectively. The **Extreme Cold** recommendations refer to wintry conditions in parts of Northern Europe, Canada, the Baltic and Scandinavian countries, and high mountainous districts where extreme cold is the average condition.

FOR HUB LUBRICATION AND ALL FRAME PARTS USING GREASE

Mobilgrease No. 4   Castrolease Heavy   Energrease C3
Esso Pressure Gun Grease.   Shell **Retinax A.** or **C D**.

250 c.c. TELEDRAULIC FRONT FORKS

Mobiloil A (SAE-30)   Castrol XL (SAE-30)   Energol (SAE-30)
Essolube 30 (SAE-30)   Shell **X-100** Motor Oil 30 (SAE-30)

350 c.c. TELEDRAULIC FRONT FORKS

Mobiloil Arctic (SAE-20)   Castrolite (SAE-20)   Energol (SAE-20)
Essolube 20 (SAE-20)   Shell **X-100** Motor Oil 20 (SAE-20)

FOR REAR CHAINS

Mobilgrease No. 2   Esso Fluid Grease   Energrease A.O
Castrolease Grease Graphited
Heated Until Just Fluid.

When buying oils and greases it is advisable to specify the **Brand** as well as the grade and, as an additional precaution, to buy only in sealed containers or from branded cabinets.

CHECKING OIL CIRCULATION

Provision is made to observe the oil circulating, which is visible after removing the oil filler cap on the right side of the crankcase.

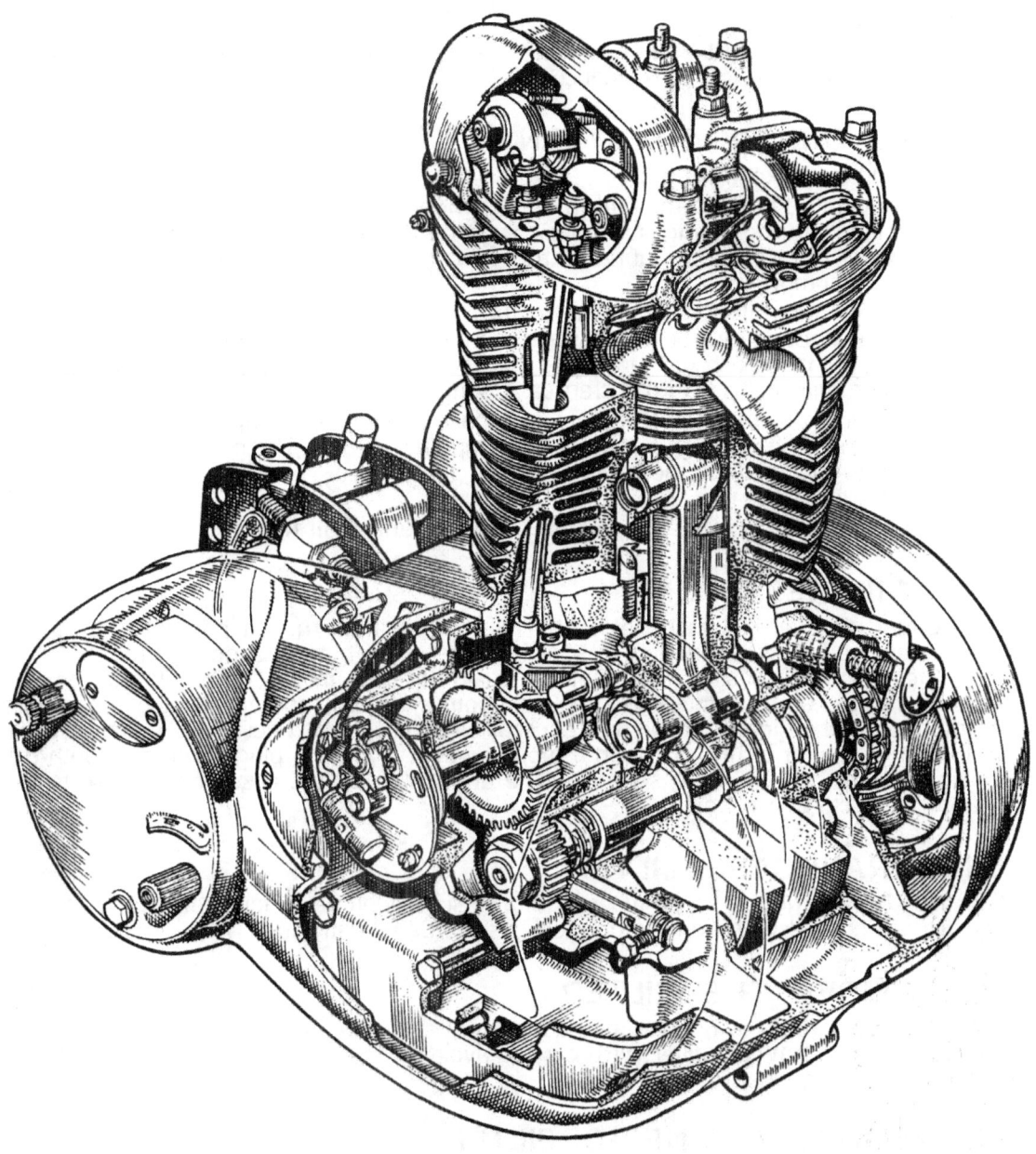

Illustration 1
Cut-away section of engine

ENGINE LUBRICATION SYSTEM

This is by true dry sump system. The oil tank, or reservoir, is integral with the crankcase. The oil pump has only one moving part, i.e., the oil pump plunger, which rotates and reciprocates. Rotation is created by the worm gear on the timing side flywheel axle. Reciprocation is caused by engagement of the oil pump guide pin with the profiled groove in the oil pump plunger. The oil pump is designed so that the sump scavenging capacity is greater than the delivery, thus keeping the crankcase sump free of oil during normal running conditions

Whilst the oil reservoir is integral with the crankcase, oil is fed to the pump by gravity, on the same principle as a machine fitted with a separate oil tank, but without the use of external oil pipes.

ENGINE OIL PUMP (see Illustration 1)

If, for any reason, the crankcase is dismantled the oil pump plunger must be removed from its housing before attempting to separate the crankcase halves. It is also necessary to remove the small timing pinion.

IMPORTANT

Under no circumstances must either the pump plunger or guide screw be disturbed in ordinary routine maintenance.

ENGINE OIL CIRCULATION

The oil pump forces oil through:—

(a) Passages drilled through the timing side flywheel axle, timing side flywheel and crank pin to lubricate the timing side bearing and the big-end bearing. The splash passes to interior of cylinder, to lubricate the cylinder and piston, and then falls into the crankcase sump.

(b) From the front oil pump housing to the rocker box via passages in the cylinder barrel, lubricating the rocker gear and valve stems. Oil from the rocker gear drains by gravity via the push rod tunnels to the timing gear case at a pre-determined level. The over-spill drains into the crankcase sump.

(c) The oil pump extracts oil from the crankcase sump, metal impurities are collected by a magnetic filter incorporated in the sump drain plug. The oil is again filtered by a felt filter located in the crankcase (see illustration 1), before returning to the oil tank reservoir.

For valve guide lubrication see paragraph "Adjustment of oil feed".

THE OIL RESERVOIR

The normal oil level is 1 inch below the filler cap orifice, the oil content is 2½ pints. Run the engine for a short period to scavenge the sump, before "topping up".
After the first 500 miles (800 kilometres) again at 1,000 miles (1,600 kilometres) and subsequently at 5,000 mile intervals (8,000 kilometres) the oil reservoir should be drained the oil filter cleaned in petrol and the reservoir replenished with new oil. It is preferable to drain the oil after a run and when the oil is warm. A drain plug is fitted to both the crankcase sump also the oil reservoir. The drain plug for the reservoir is close to the bottom front crankcase bolt.

THE CRANKCASE FILTER

The filter is cylindrical in shape made from a close-grained felt, supported by a wire cage. The filter is housed in the drive-side crankcase. (See illustration 1).

TO REMOVE THE FILTER

Use Allen Key 018667 to unscrew the domed nut and take out the spring. Remove the cap washer, withdraw the filter with care to avoid damage. Thoroughly clean filter in petrol and replace when dry.

TO REMOVE MAGNETIC FILTER

Incorporated with the crankcase sump plug is a powerful magnet, which does not require frequent attention. For cleaning place a tray under the crankcase, unscrew the sump plug, with the use of a good fitting ring spanner.
Metal particles adhering to the magnet can be removed by wiping with a grease coated rag, the grease will collect metal particles on the rag. Keep the magnet away from large pieces of steel or iron, as contact can impair the efficiency of the magnet.

ADJUSTMENT OF OIL FEED

The internal flow of oil is controlled by fixed restrictions, with the exception of the oil feed to the inlet valve guide, which is regulated by a needle pointed screw located in the cylinder head (see illustration 3) and secured by a locknut.
To adjust the oil feed loosen the lock nut and screw home lightly the regulating screw, then unscrew it the smallest amount possible and retighten the lock nut.
An excess of oil to the inlet valve guide will cause a smoky exhaust and heavy oil consumption.

EXHAUST VALVE STEM LUBRICATION

From a drilling in the exhaust rocker axle boss in the rocker box, oil is fed to a cavity in the cylinder head. A further drilling from this cavity, through the cylinder head to an oil hole in the valve guide, provides positive lubrication for this part of the engine and needs no adjustment.

CRANKCASE RELEASE VALVE

Crankcase pressure is released into the atmosphere through a timed and ported release valve. The ported portion for this valve is situated between the two driving side bearings, the valve outlet is adjacent to the gear box housing. The valve cannot become deranged and needs no attention.

GEAR BOX LUBRICATION

To top up or replenish oil for the gear box remove the inspection plate secured by two screws on the gear box end cover.
Use one of the grades of oil specified, on no account must grease be used.
The normal oil content is 3 pints (1·8 litres), the gear box must not be completely filled with oil. After draining and replenishing the oil at the first 500 miles (800 kilometres) top up every subsequent 1,000 miles (1,600 kilometres) to a level just below the bottom of the orifice for the inspection plate.

FRONT CHAIN LUBRICATION

The front chain is lubricated with engine oil filled to the front chain case, which forms an oil bath. If the lower of the two slotted screwed caps on the chain case is removed, the oil level can be observed. The correct oil level is just above the bottom run of the primary chain. To top up, remove both slotted screwed caps and fill oil through the uppermost aperture, checking the level through the lower. A drain plug is situated immediately below the clutch assembly. If the chaincase is drained, refill with 1 pint (·6 litres) of engine oil.

REAR CHAIN LUBRICATION

When a totally enclosed rear chaincase is fitted, the chain is lubricated by oil mist discharged from the crankcase release valve tube on to the chain. Additional lubrication should not be necessary. Where the rear chain is exposed it should be lubricated periodically particularly during wintry or prolonged inclement weather. For effective lubrication the chain should be removed, cleaned in paraffin (kerosene) and immersed in grease that is heated until it becomes fluid. Remove surplus grease before refitting.
CAUTION: When refitting the chain connecting link, the **closed end** of the spring clip must face the way the chain travels.

WHEEL HUB LUBRICATION

Both hubs are pre-packed with grease during assembly, which prevents the entry of water as well as lubricating the bearings. After the first 5,000 miles (8,000 kilometres) and before 10,000 miles (16,000 kilometres) dismantle and clean the hub bearings and repack with fresh grease.

SPEEDOMETER LUBRICATION

Manual lubrication is not necessary, if a grease nipple is not fitted to the speedometer gearbox.

REAR FORK HINGE (SWINGING ARM)

Apply grease gun on nipple mounted on the right side of the fork hinge, during routine maintenance (use S.A.E. 140 oil).

REAR BRAKE PEDAL

A grease nipple is fitted underneath the pivot part of the pedal.

GENERAL

Occasionally apply a little engine oil to parts such as control levers, and cables, brake rods, stands, etc. Use a little grease to lubricate the twist grip rotor.

Maintenance

PERIODICAL MAINTENANCE

Regular maintenance attention to lubrication and certain adjustments must be made to ensure unfailing reliability and satisfactory service. This necessary attention is detailed below and owners are strongly recommended to carefully follow these suggestions and to make a regular practice of doing so from the first.

DAILY

Oil Reservoir	Inspect oil level and top-up if necessary. Check oil circulation.
Petrol tank	Check level and refill if necessary.

WEEKLY

Oil reservoir	Check level and top-up if necessary.
Tyres	Check pressures and inflate if necessary. Inflator under twin seat.

EVERY 500 MILES (800 KILOMETRES)

Oil reservoir	Drain at first 500 miles and re-fill with new oil, and clean filters.
Ignition	Check contact breaker points. Regrease felt pad.
Gear box	Drain at first 500 miles and re-fill 3 pints (1·8 litres).
Chaincase	Check level of oil when machine is standing vertically on level ground. (See chain lubrication).
Battery	Inspect each cell for level of electrolyte and top up with distilled water if necessary. Level of electrolyte should just be over top of plates. Beware of overfilling.

EVERY 1,000 MILES (1,600 KILOMETRES)

Oil reservoir	Drain at first 1,000 miles and re-fill with new oil.
Rear chain	In wet weather remove and soak in molten grease. See page 13.
Gear box	Check oil level.
Small parts	Smear all moving parts with engine oil and wipe off surplus.
Chaincase	Drain, and re-fill, or monthly.

EVERY 2,000 to 5,000 MILES (3,200 to 8,000 KILOMETRES)
(according to road conditions)

Air filter	(If fitted) clean and re-oil filter element.

EVERY 3,000 MILES (4,800 KILOMETRES)

Rear chain	In dry weather remove and soak in molten grease.
Brake pedal	Inject small amount of grease.
Speedometer.	Inject grease into gear box if nipple is fitted.
Ignition	Clean contact breaker points and re-set if necessary. Regrease felt pad.
Plug	Clean sparkling plug and re-set points as necessary.
Steering head	Test steering head for up and down movement and adjust if necessary.
Bolts and Nuts	Check all nuts and bolts for tightness and tighten if necessary but beware of over-tightening.
Rockers	Check O.H.V. rocker adjustment and correct if necessary.

EVERY 5,000 MILES (8,000 KILOMETRES)

Oil reservoir	Drain and re-fill with new oil. If machine is only used for short runs renew oil every three months instead of mileage interval.
Filter	Clean filter in crankcase.
Ignition	Clean and adjust contact points. Check gap.
Front fork	Drain and re-fill with fresh oil. Insufficient oil content is indicated by abnormally lively action.
Carburetter	Remove carburetter float chamber side cover and clean interior. Also detach petrol pipe banjo and clean gauze strainer.

Engine Service

TAPPET ADJUSTMENT

The top ends of the two long push rods have screwed extensions. These are locked in position by nuts, thereby providing tappet adjustment.

The correct tappet clearances, with valves closed and engine warm (not hot) is **NIL**. This means the push rods should be free enough to revolve and, at the same time, there should be no appreciable up and down play.

Prepare to adjust tappets by:

Set piston to T.D.C. (both valves closed).
Remove the three nuts, and fibre washers under them, retaining tappet cover to rocker box.
Take away cover.

Adjust tappets by:

With spanners, hold the sleeve 5, either valve (illustration 2) and slacken lock nut 2. Then screw, in or out, the head 3 until the clearance is nil.
Tighten lock nut 2 and re-check the clearance.

Finally

Check adjustments so that, with no up and down movement, the long push rods are free to revolve when the valves are closed.

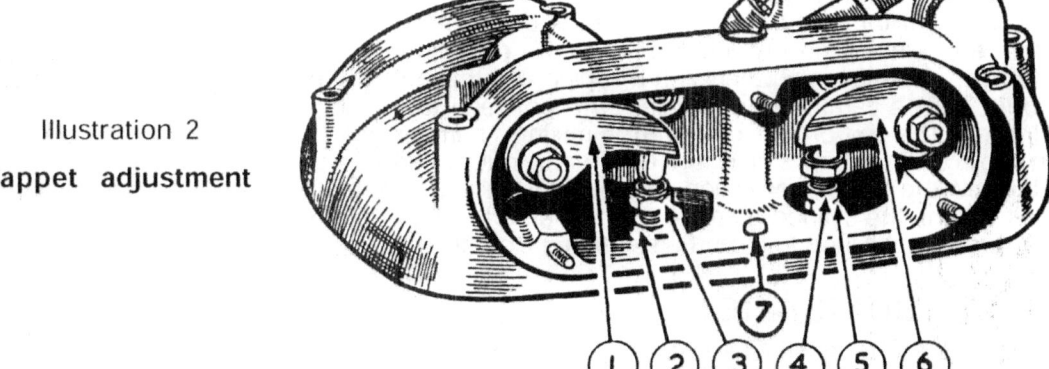

Illustration 2

Tappet adjustment

1. INLET ROCKER ARM (TAPPET END).
2. NUT, LOCKING ADJUSTING CUPPED SCREW.
3. CUPPED ADJUSTING SCREW.
4. CUPPED ADJUSTING SCREW AND LOCK NUT.
5. SLEEVE, TO ACCOMMODATE ADJUSTING SCREW, ON TOP END OF PUSH ROD.
6. EXHAUST ROCKER ARM (TAPPET END).
7. ROCKER BOX BOLT.

Complete adjustment by:

Replace rocker tappet cover taking care to replace the fibre washer that is under each retaining nut.

As mentioned elsewhere do not over-tighten the nuts because the joint is made with a rubber fillet and undue pressure is not necessary.

NOTE—In normal conditions tappet adjustment should not be necessary more frequently than about every five thousand miles or after decarbonising and grinding valves. If adjustment is found necessary more frequently the cause should be investigated at once.

> For service work on the upper part of the engine, with the exception of tappet adjustment, the twin seat and petrol tank should be removed for accessibility.

TO REMOVE TWIN SEAT

Remove two bolts under the rear end of the seat, release the nuts securing the front portion of the seat, which now can be lifted off.

TO REMOVE THE PETROL TANK

Close both petrol taps, unscrew the two cap nuts securing the petrol pipe (watch for 4 fibre washers each side of the banjo unions). Take out two bolts securing the front of the petrol tank and a further bolt securing the rear, noting the location of the tank bolt rubbers and spacers, the front ones are **thick** the rear are **thin,** the steel washers are also dissimilar.

TO REMOVE THE ROCKER BOX

Remove the three nuts and fibre washers securing the rocker box cover, also the sparking plug.
Turn the engine until both valves are closed, i.e., after the inlet valve has opened and just closed.
Remove two nuts and the bolt securing the engine steady bracket to the rocker box and frame. Disconnect valve lifter cable.
Take out the nine bolts securing the rocker box to the cylinder head (one of these bolts is inside the rocker box (see illustration 2), the location of these bolts must be noted as they are dissimilar.
Tilt upwards the right side of the rocker box, extract both push rods and identify their location for replacement in their original positions, remove the rocker box from the cylinder head.

TO REMOVE THE CYLINDER HEAD

Remove the exhaust pipe and silencer as one unit, then the accessory compartment cover and air filter tube if fitted. Do not rock the exhaust pipe sideways unduly to extract it from the exhaust port which can cause the end of the pipe to close in and result in gas leakage, also movement between the pipe and the port when the engine is hot. Instead squirt a little paraffin or petrol into the port and try again.
Unscrew the cap on the carburetter mixing chamber, take out both slides, wrap them in a piece of rag and attach it to the frame, out of harm's way.
Unscrew the petrol pipe union and take away the petrol pipe. Four sleeve nuts and one bolt retains the cylinder head to the barrel, with these removed, the cylinder head with carburetter attached to it can be separated from the cylinder.

DECARBONISATION

Instead of the usual stipulated mileage interval between periods of decarbonisation, it is recommended that this is undertaken only when the need becomes apparent because of loss in power, heavy petrol consumption or generally reduced performance.
When undertaken, unless it is thought necessary to inspect the piston and rings, the cylinder barrel is best left undisturbed.
Before starting this work have available a gasket set, and if the machine has covered considerable mileage, a new set of piston rings also.
Carbon formed on the piston crown and in the sphere of the cylinder head, can be scraped off with a cheap steel rule, with the sharp corners removed, or similar tool. **Deal** with the cylinder head before removing the valves, and do not use emery cloth or other abrasives for this work.

TO REMOVE AND REPLACE THE VALVES AND GUIDES

The valve springs are removed by inserting the index finger through the coil of the spring and pulling upwards sharply.
A light tap on the valve spring collar will expose the valve split collets (which should be put in a place of safety), then take out the valve.
Both valve guides are located by an external circlip, the cylinder head must be gently and uniformly heated before attempting to remove or replace the guides.
With the head pre-heated tap the guide upwards out of the port sufficiently to enable the circlip to be prised out of its groove. Reheat the head and drive out the guides through the cylinder head. When refitting the guides, pre-heat the head and verify that the oil holes are in alignment with holes in the cylinder head.

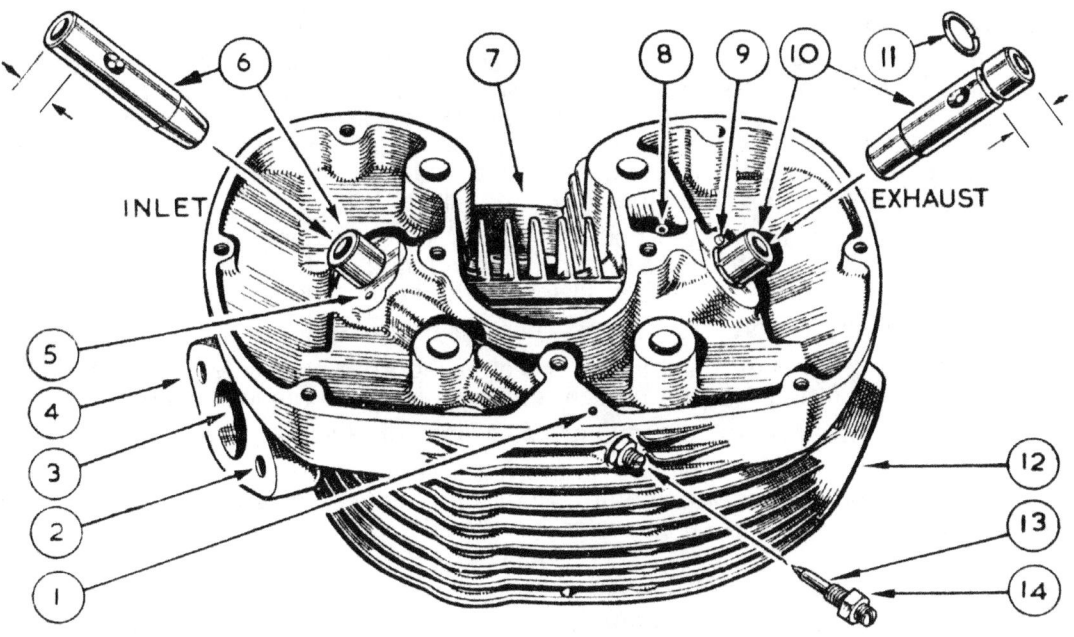

Illustration 3

The valve guides and the needle adjusting screw are also shown withdrawn

1. PLAIN HOLE, FOR OIL FEED TO INLET VALVE.
2. TAPPED HOLE, TO ACCOMMODATE CARBURETTER RETAINING STUD.
3. INLET PORT.
4. TAPPED HOLE, TO ACCOMMODATE CARBURETTER RETAINING STUD.
5. HOLE, TO ACCOMMODATE DOWEL LOCATING VALVE SPRING SEAT.
6. GUIDE, FOR INLET VALVE.
7. TAPPED HOLE, FOR SPARKING PLUG.
8. PLAIN HOLE, FOR OIL FEED TO EXHAUST VALVE.
9. HOLE, TO ACCOMMODATE DOWEL PIN LOCATING VALVE SPRING SEAT.
10. GUIDE, FOR EXHAUST VALVE.
11. CIRCLIP (BOTH GUIDES).
12. EXHAUST PORT.
13. NEEDLE SCREW, ADJUSTING OIL FEED TO INLET VALVE.
14. LOCK NUT, FOR NEEDLE ADJUSTING SCREW.

VALVE GRINDING

The grinding is accomplished by smearing a thin layer of fine grinding paste (obtainable ready for use at any garage) on the valve face and then, after inserting the valve in the head, partially revolve, forwards and backwards, while applying light finger pressure to the head, raising the valve off its seat and turning to another position after every few movements. (Never revolve the valve continuously in one direction.)

When the abrasive ceases to bite, remove the valve and examine its face.

The grinding may be considered to be satisfactorily completed when a continuous matt ring is observed on both valve face and seat.

After grinding, all traces of abrasive must be carefully washed off with petrol and a piece of rag, moistened in petrol, should be pulled through the bore of each valve guide to remove any abrasive that may have entered.

A holder for the valve, when grinding in the valve, can be supplied. The part number is 017482.

REPLACING THE VALVES

A valve spring compressor is required to compress the springs, a special tool which is inexpensive, can be obtained from dealers, or from our Spare Parts Department. The application of this tool is shown in illustration 4. Before fitting the valve springs, position correctly the valve spring seat—the raised portion on the underside is located with the depression (5) in cylinder head. (See illustration 3).

The inlet valve is the larger of the two valves and it is vitally important to locate correctly the two split collets into the grooves on each valve stem.

Clean the valve guide bores with a piece of clean rag, apply a little oil on the valve stems and also inside each guide before assembly.

REMOVING THE CYLINDER AND PISTON

With the cylinder head removed, the barrel can be raised vertically to clear the holding down studs. Before doing so, position the engine with the piston on the top of its stroke, have available a piece of clean rag. Raise the cylinder sufficiently to enable the rag to be put into the throat of the crankcase (under the piston) as a precaution against a broken ring falling into the crankcase, then lift the cylinder clear of the four studs passing through it. Make a mark inside the piston to indicate front.

The gudgeon pin is a sliding fit in both the piston and connecting rod. Use round nose pliers to compress and extract the circlip (it is immaterial which one is removed) then push out the gudgeon pin and lift the piston off the connecting rod.

Do not disturb the piston rings unless absolutely necessary.

If new piston rings are fitted and if they are obtained from our Spare Parts Department they are ready for fitting, as the ring gap is allowed for during manufacture.

The **top** compression ring is chromium plated and has a slightly tapered extension.

When new, the word TOP is etched on the ring face to indicate which way it should be fitted. Fit first the scraper or oil control ring, then the two compression rings, to avoid breakage do not expand these rings unnecessarily.

REFITTING THE PISTON

Before refitting the piston apply a little oil to the gudgeon pin, also to the bosses for the gudgeon pin in the piston. Place the piston over the connecting rod in the same way as it was removed, or in accordance with the marking made, and then introduce the gudgeon pin through the piston, connecting rod and piston bosses.

It is vitally important to correctly locate the gudgeon pin circlip, and a little extra care and time should be devoted to this most simple and important operation. Use round-nosed pliers to introduce the circlip into its groove, using a rotary motion then verify that the circlip is correctly located.

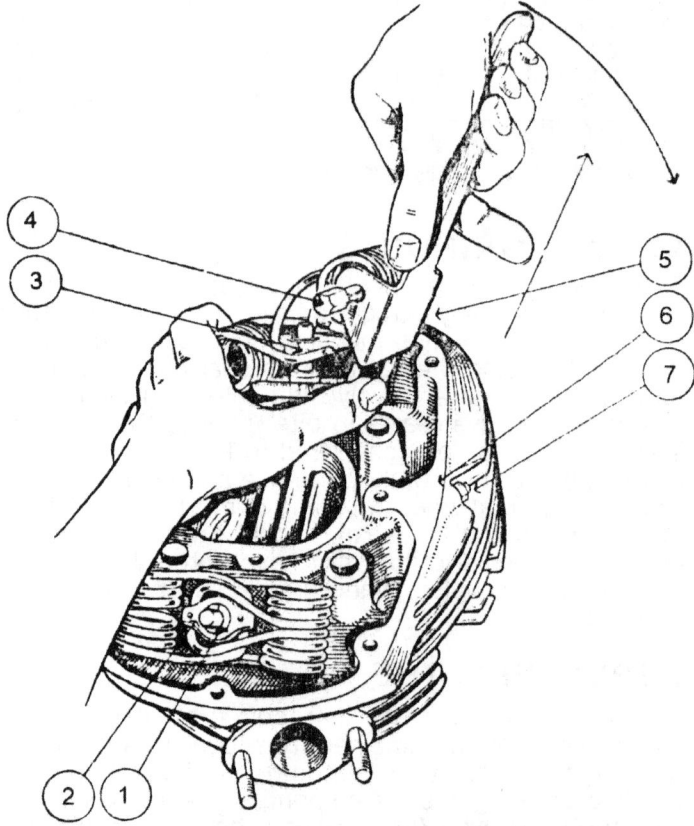

Illustration 4

Application of valve spring compressor

1. COLLET, FOR VALVE.
2. COLLAR, FOR VALVE SPRING.
3. COLLAR, FOR VALVE SPRING.
4. BOLT THROUGH TOOLS AND COILS OF VALVE SPRING.
5. VALVE SPRING COMPRESSOR TOOL.
6. OIL PASSAGE FROM ROCKER BOX TO INLET VALVE GUIDE.
7. SCREW WITH LOCK NUT ADJUSTING OIL FEED TO INLET VALVE.

REFITTING THE CYLINDER BARREL

Fit a new cylinder base gasket, after removing broken pieces of the old one. Use a little jointing compound on the base of the cylinder and stick a new gasket to it, no jointing compound should be on the crankcase face. Set the piston ring gaps at 120°, pass the cylinder over the four long studs and lower it gently at the same time compressing each piston ring in turn with the fingers, until the cylinder has passed the scraper ring when it can be lowered on to the crankcase.

NOTE—Some clean rag under the piston to fill the throat of the crankcase will safeguard against a broken piston ring falling into the crankcase.

REFITTING THE CYLINDER HEAD

The cylinder head gasket also acts as an oil seal for the push rod tunnels, consequently it must be in good order if it is to be used again. To avoid the possibility of subsequent attention a new gasket is desirable.

This gasket is neither symmetrical nor reversible and it must be placed on the cylinder in the correct way.

A study of the cylinder barrel face will show an elongated hole (where the push rods operate).

Just behind is a tapped hole for the cylinder head bolt.

Close to the cylinder bore and to the right of the cylinder head bolt hole is a smaller hole, which is the oil feed passage from the pump to the rocker gear.

Place the gasket on the cylinder so that the oil feed hole in the cylinder registers with the small hole in the gasket.

Put the cylinder head in position, refit the four cylinder head sleeve nuts and the long cylinder head bolt, do not omit the five washers.

First tighten the four sleeve nuts diagonally—not one side at a time—then tighten the long bolt, until all are firmly tightened.

If a torque spanner is available it should be set to 35 foot lbs. for the four sleeve nuts only.

REFITTING THE ROCKER BOX

Before attempting to refit, make sure the piston is on T.D.C. of the firing stroke, with both cam followers down.

Use a new rocker box gasket for this assembly. In the centre portion of this gasket is a projection with a small hole in it. There is also a similar size hole in the cylinder head which is the oil feed passage from the oil pump through the cylinder to the rocker gear. It will be readily seen that if the rocker box gasket is reversed the oil feed passage will be sealed, therefore ensure that the gasket is properly located before fitting the rocker box.

With the rocker box gasket correctly located, take up the rocker box, pass all the holding down bolts through it, put the rocker box into position.

Take up the two engine push rods, tilt the right side of the rocker box upwards, then introduce the push rods through the head and cylinder. The exhaust push rod operates with the cam follower nearest to the contact breaker. (See illustration 1).

Locate the rocker arms in the push rod adjusters and first tighten the two central rocker box bolts which have screwed extensions.

Tighten the remainder diagonally including the one inside the rocker box.

Washers are fitted under the heads of all these bolts.

It should be remembered that a soft gasket is used between the cylinder head and the rocker box, therefore the degree of tightness for these bolts is a matter of good judgment and commonsense.

Re-adjust the tappets as previously described.

IGNITION TIMING

Before setting or checking the ignition timing, make sure the contact gap, at full separation, is ·012".

(See details on Contact Breaker).

Reference to illustration 5 will indicate the principle used.

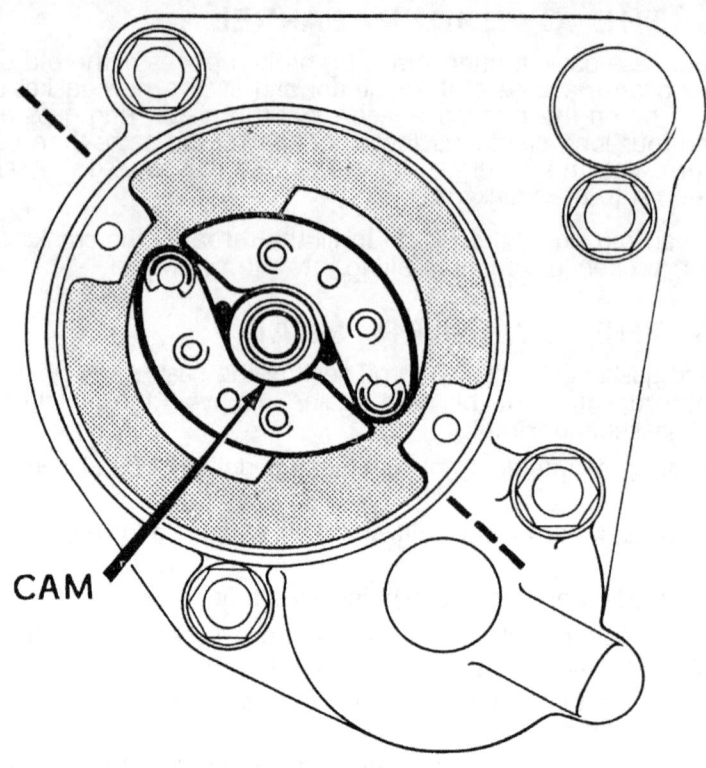

Illustration 5

Automatic Ignition Advance Mechanism
(Approximate Ignition Setting)

TO CHECK THE TIMING

Position the engine as detailed for tappet adjustment. Remove the sparking plug, the cover for the contact breaker and engage top gear.

Obtain a short length of stiff wire or wheel spoke about 5" long. Insert the wire through the sparking plug hole, until it touches the piston crown. By slowly moving the rear wheel backwards and forwards the top dead centre of the piston travel can be ascertained. Keep the wire vertical as far as the plug hole will permit—make a mark on the wire to register with the seating for the sparking plug on the cylinder head. Take out the wire and make a further mark on it ¼" ABOVE the previous mark.

Put the wire through the sparking plug hole, then turn the engine **BACKWARDS** until the top mark on the wire registers with the seating for the sparking plug, the piston is now ¼" before top dead centre.

A ⅝" hole is drilled in the contact breaker base plate to enable a small screwdriver to be inserted, and engaged between the two bob weights for the automatic ignition control. (See illustration 5).

Turning the screwdriver clockwise will separate the bob weights to the fully advanced position. If the timing is correct the contact points should be just about to separate.

The exact point of separation can best be found by inserting a thin piece of cigarette paper between the points, which when pulled lightly will be free when the contact points separate.

TO ADJUST IGNITION TIMING

By slackening the two screws in the slotted holes on the contact breaker base plate, the plate can be moved either clockwise or anti-clockwise to adjust the timing as required. Move the plate clockwise to advance and use the method described for checking to obtain the correct timing.

TO RESET IGNITION TIMING

As the ignition advance is limited to ¼" B.T.D.C, this setting is critical and must be carefully carried out. The automatic ignition control unit is a taper fit on the camshaft, retained by a central bolt. To remove this unit take out the retaining bolt, use in its place a withdrawal bolt, Part No. 042247. Screw home this bolt—do not use undue force—then tap the head of the bolt lightly which will separate the unit from the shaft.

NOTE—The contact breaker cam is detachable and if it is inadvertently removed, the timing should be rechecked after refitting the cam, before attempting to start the engine.

VALVE TIMING (including Scrambles Models)

The cam wheel, also the small timing pinion which drives it, are both marked to facilitate assembly.

If, for any reason, the cam wheel *is* removed, to re-assemble rotate the engine until the piston is on T.D.C. of the stroke, the mark on the small timing pinion tooth will then be at 11 o'clock. Take up the cam wheel, raise both cam followers, then introduce the cam into the crankcase with the mark on the tooth gap to register with the mark on the small pinion.

These markings have been selected to give the most effective valve timing and best engine performance.

To check the valve timing, as a single piece camshaft is used, it is only necessary to record the inlet valve opening also the exhaust valve closing positions to verify that the valve timing is correct. The average valve timing, taken with ·010" rocker clearance is:—

Inlet valve opens   40° B.T.D.C.
Exhaust valve closes   40° A.T.D.C.

See TAPPET ADJUSTMENT for running pushrod clearance.

250 c.c. SCRAMBLES MODEL

IGNITION TIMING

The ignition timing must be restricted to the maker's recommendation of 32° before top dead centre. Any deviation from this setting can only result in difficult starting accompanied with misfiring at high engine revolutions.

CONTACT BREAKER

The contact breaker gap is also vitally important and should be maintained at ·012" at full separation of the contact points. Check and reset the gap if necessary before checking or re-setting the ignition timing.

Carburetter Service

The information given in this section includes all that will normally be required by the average rider. For further details, particularly those connected with racing and the use of special fuels, we refer the enquirer to the manufacturers of the carburetter, **Amal Ltd., Holford Road, Witton, Birmingham, 6.**

Our Spare Parts Department does not stock every part of the carburetter but confines its stock to those parts that, from time to time, may be required. Those parts include floats and float needles, jet taper needles, pilot jets, main jets, needle jets and washers.

CARBURETTER FUNCTION

The petrol level is maintained by a float and needle valve and, in no circumstances, should any alteration be made to these parts. In the event of a leaky float, or a worn needle valve, the part should be replaced with new. (Do not attempt to grind a needle to its seat.)

The petrol supply to the engine is controlled, firstly, by the main jet and, secondly, by means of a taper needle (see illustration 6) which is attached to the throttle valve and operates in a tubular extension of the main jet.

The main jet controls the mixture from three-quarters to full throttle, the adjustable taper needle from three-quarters down to one-quarter throttle, the cut-away portion of the intake side of the throttle valve from one-quarter down to about one-eighth throttle, and a pilot jet, having an independently adjusted air supply, takes care of the idling from one-eighth throttle down to the almost closed position. These various stages of control must be kept in mind when any adjustment is contemplated. (See illustration 6, for location of the pilot jet air adjustment screw). The pilot jet unlike earlier models is now detachable for cleaning.

The size of the main jet should not be altered save for some very good reason. See "DATA" for details of standard sizes of jet, throttle valve, and jet taper needle.

Weak mixture is always indicated by popping, or spitting, at the air intake.

A rich mixture usually causes bumpy, or jerky, running and, in cases of extreme richness, is accompanied by the emission of black smoke from the exhaust.

CARBURETTER ADJUSTMENT

With the taper needle projection, main jet size, and type of throttle slide specified correct carburation except at idling speed is assured.

In the event of difficulty being experienced look for cause under heading Useful Information (pages 46 and 47).

To check for correct idling mixture, first run the engine until it is just warm but not hot when with the throttle nearly closed and air fully open it should fire evenly and slowly. If it fails to do so, first of all make certain that the sparking plug is clean and the point setting correct. Having done this and idling is still uneven try re-setting the pilot jet air screw.

Adjustment of this air screw is not unduly sensitive and it should be possible to obtain the correct setting for even firing in a few seconds.

In the event of even firing at idling speed being unobtainable by adjustment of the air screw look for obstruction in the pilot jet.

Having obtained even firing all that remains is to adjust if necessary the position of the throttle stop screw until the desired idling speed is obtained.

TWIST GRIP ADJUSTMENT

A screw is provided in one of the halves of the twist grip body to regulate the spring tension on the grip rotating sleeve. This screw must be screwed into the body to increase the tension.

The most desirable state of adjustment is that when the grip is quite free and easy to operate but, at the same time, will stay in the position in which it is placed.

The complete twist grip can be moved on the handlebar by slackening the two screws that clamp together the two halves of the body. The most desirable position is that in which the throttle cable makes the cleanest and most straight path to the under-side of the petrol tank.

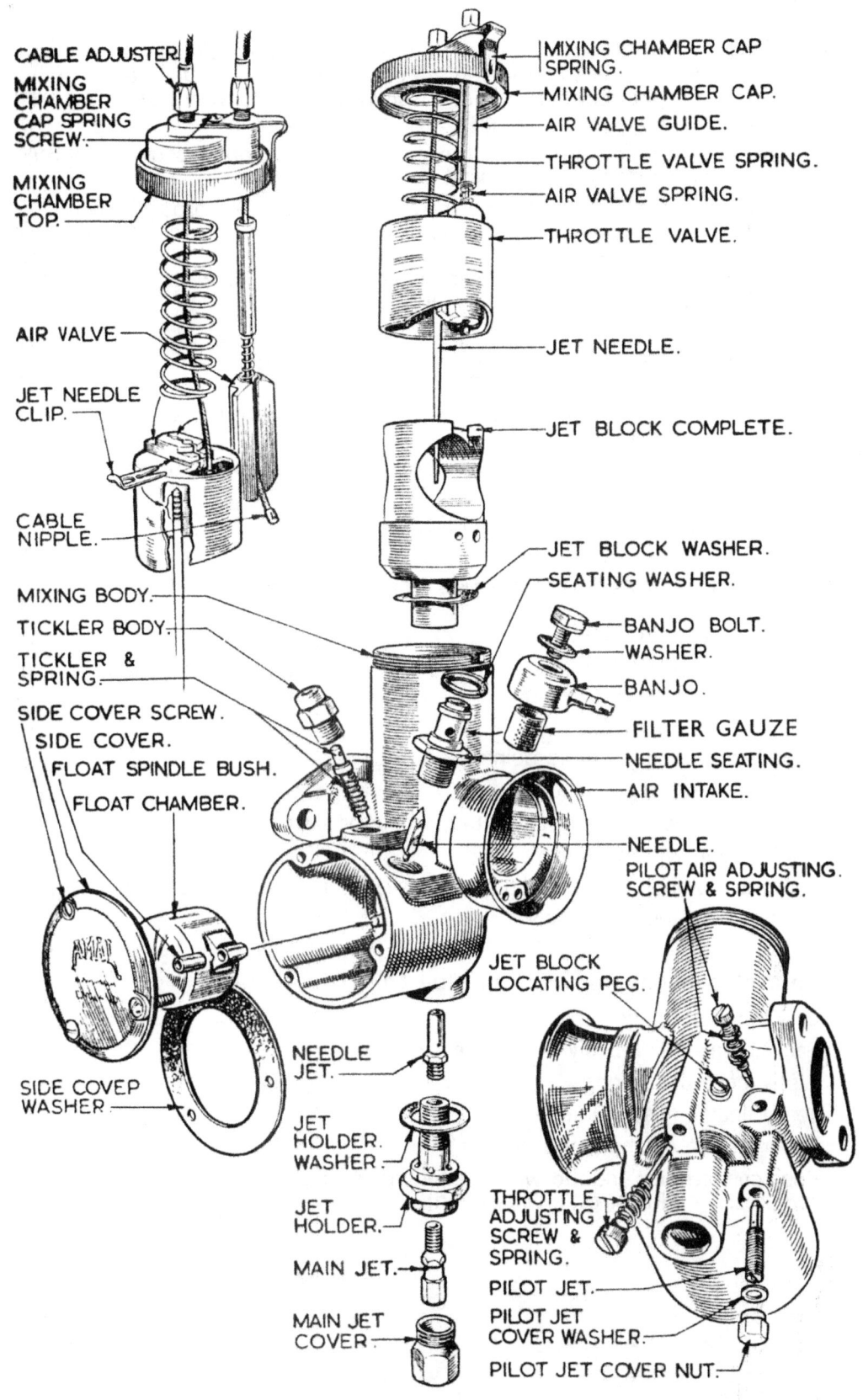

Illustration 6

Carburetter details in assembly order

AIR FILTER

In locations, such as the United Kingdom, where the roads and atmosphere are particularly free from dust, it is not considered necessary to have an air filter fitted to the carburetter, but in countries where the atmosphere contains a very heavy dust content, an air filter is essential in order to prevent abrasive wear.

The filter available (optional extra) for the conditions mentioned above is of the "Oil Wetted" type, and this requires periodical servicing.

When servicing the air filter, withdraw the filter element. Thoroughly wash this In petrol, paraffin or other suitable solvent and allow to dry. Then re-oil, using one of the light oils (SAE-20), enumerated in the final table on page 10, and allow to drain before replacing in the filter case. Clean at intervals of 2,500 to 5,000 miles according to road conditions, and renew the element every 10,000 miles.

TO REMOVE THE AIR FILTER ELEMENT

Remove the accessory compartment cover, by unscrewing the top central screw, then take out the bolts under the cover.

Slide the rubber connection along the carburetter intake, remove the nut for the filter clamp, take out the filter.

To dismantle the filter remove the central bolt.

CARBURETTER TUNING INFORMATION

Poor idling may be due to:

Air leaks. At function of carburetter and cylinder head, or by reason of badly worn inlet valve stems or guides.

Faulty engine valve seatings.

Sparking plug faulty, or its points set too closely.

Ignition advanced too much.

Contact breaker points dirty, pitted, loose, or set too closely.

High-tension wire defective.

Pilot jet not operating correctly. Partially choked or incorrect air supply.

Rockers adjusted too closely.

Heavy petrol consumption may be due to:

Late ignition setting.

Bad air leaks. Probably at carburetter joints.

Weakened valve springs.

Leaky float. (Causing flooding).

Taper needle extension insufficient.

Poor compression, due to worn piston rings or defective valve seatings. (Test compression with throttle wide open).

Transmission Service

THE GEAR BOX

The gear box, cylindrical in shape, is housed in an arc machined on the crankcase, and retained by two high tensile steel straps. As the gear box mainshaft is eccentric to the gear box shell, partial movement of the gear box in its housing provides latitude for front chain adjustment.

The gear box provides four speeds and has a positive foot change, operated by the right foot and a kickstarter.

The transmission shock absorber Is incorporated in the clutch assembly.

TO REMOVE GEAR BOX OUTER COVER

Remove the silencer fixing nut, the two nuts on the exhaust pipe bracket and take off the silencer and pipe as a unit.
Remove the right side footrest.
Remove gear indicator and bolt.
Remove footchange pedal (release the pinch bolt).
Remove kickstarter pinch bolt, then the crank.
Remove four screws securing timing cover.
The cover can now be removed.

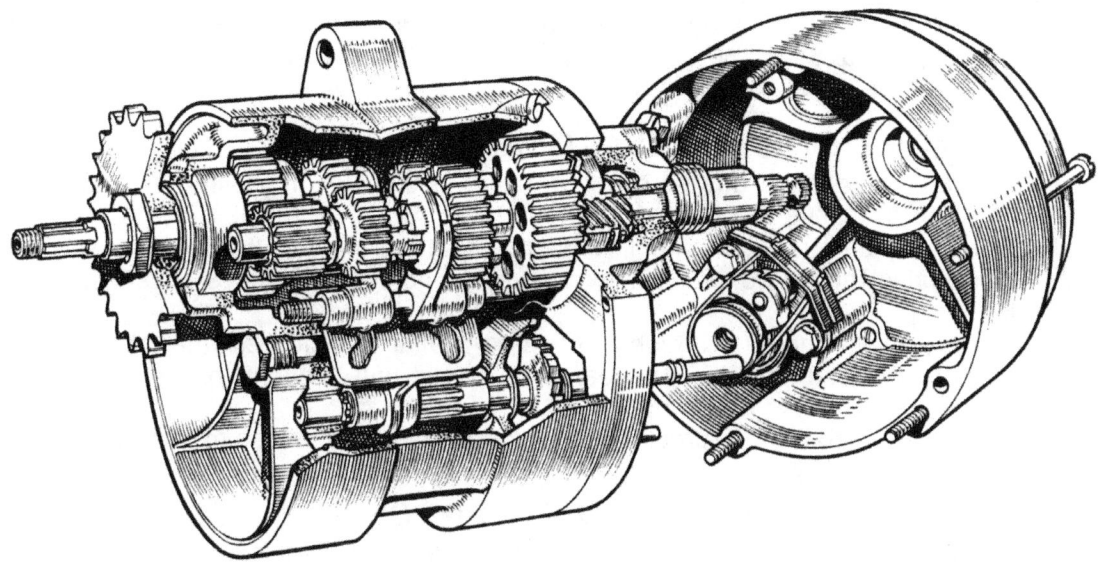

Illustration 7
Gearbox with end cover removed

TO REMOVE GEAR BOX END COVER

Remove the outer cover as described.
Use a tray under gear box to catch oil and remove drain plug.
Remove six screws securing end cover.
Temporarily refit footchange pedal to pull off the cover.
NOTE—If the gasket is renewed, the cut-away for clutch cable entry is at 11 o'clock.
Replace parts in reverse order, after again removing footchange pedal.
The gear box with end cover removed is shown in illustration 7.

TO REMOVE GEAR BOX INNER COVER

Follow instructions for removing the outer and end cover, after selecting neutral position.
Disconnect clutch cable.
Unscrew clutch body lock ring, take out the body (watch for the ⅜" ball bearing, also the locating peg, which can fall out of position).
The gear box mainshaft nut is now exposed, remove the nut, also the nut on the footchange quadrant spindle—the end cover can then be removed.

DISMANTLING THE KICKSTARTER

When the gear box cover is removed, the kick-starter mechanism will come out with the cover.

The face ratchet pinion is under tension of the ratchet spring, to remove this pinion temporarily fit the kick-starter crank and relieve the spring tension, the pinion will then be released.

Remove the circlip located in the kick-starter shaft if fitted.

To remove the kick-starter shaft prise out the end of the return spring from its anchorage, the shaft can then be extracted.

REFITTING THE GEAR BOX END COVER

With the kick-starter mechanism assembled the end plate can be refitted in the reverse order described for dismantling.

The gasket must be undamaged to avoid oil leakage. The only necessary precaution is to ensure that the foot change operating parts are in correct order by first fitting the thin washer with the largest diameter hole over the shaft for the foot change spindle before the gear box end cover is fitted. After fitting the end cover the thick washer goes over the spindle followed by the foot change ratchet, the washer for the pawl spring and finally the foot change ratchet and shaft nut. The assembly is clearly shown in the illustration, particular note should be made of the pawl spring location.

The outer pawl spring washer is shaped to hold it in position, whilst the cover is refitted. When the assembly is completed, ensure the gear box drain plug is firmly tightened and refill with 3 pints of S.A.E. 50 oil, as shown in the list of recommended lubricants. Allow time for the oil to seep through.

TO REMOVE THE SLEEVE GEAR SPROCKET

It is preferable to remove this sprocket with the end plate in position. Follow the instructions to dismantle the clutch.

Take off the rear portion of the primary drive cover, after removing the six fixing screws. The nut securing the sleeve gear sprocket is firmly tightened and has a LEFT HAND thread.

A well fitting ring spanner is required to release it after turning back the tab washer. Engaging top gear and pressing the rear brake pedal will prevent the gear sprocket turning, whilst the nut is unscrewed.

Disconnect the rear chain, the sprocket is on a splined gear and can be extracted without difficulty.

REFITTING THE SLEEVE GEAR SPROCKET

As this sprocket is part of the transmission and subjected to reversal loads, the importance of firmly tightening the fixing nut cannot be too highly stressed. Turn down the tab washer and assemble in the reverse order given for dismantling.

TO REMOVE GEAR BOX INTERNALS

If the gear box is to be completely dismantled, remove parts in the following order:— the clutch, sleeve gear sprocket and the gear box end cover.

With the gears exposed unscrew the selector fork shaft, using a spanner on the two flats machined on it, the gears, shafts and operating mechanism can then be withdrawn.

The spring loaded plunger and cam plunger bolt are situated immediately below the sleeve gear sprocket.

TO ASSEMBLE GEAR BOX INTERNALS

Fit the mainshaft with gears in the sequence shown in the illustration. Ensure the plunger and spring for the cam segment are in position, then insert the cam segment assembly.

Take up the selector fork with the projection at three o'clock and put the fork in the slot for the slider gear with the projection in the profiled slot in the cam segment.

Fit the layshaft with gears, i.e., fixed and free pinion. Take up the sliding gear, fit the remaining selector fork into the sliding gear, slip the gear on the layshaft and engage the projection in the cam segment slot. Line up the selector forks and refit the shaft and tighten. Fit the low gear pinion to complete the assembly.

TO REMOVE CHAINCASE OUTER COVER

Use a tray under chain case to catch oil.
Remove drain plug.
Remove near side footrest.
Remove engine plate cowling (two screws).
Remove three snap connectors on wire in BLACK sheath, push the sheath towards the chain case a small amount.
Remove six cover screws and inspection cap.
Carefully pull off the cover, without strain on the alternator cables.
If the cover is completely removed, turn back one of the snap connectors, to permit the black sheath to pass through the metal duct on the chain case rear portion.
When refitting the case, the gasket must be undamaged, ensure the cable colours match with those in the connector block.
Replace parts in reverse order, gently take up the cable slack by pulling the sheath at the rear of the case.

Screw locations length (under head)

Top right and bottom left 1⅞".
Top left 2¼".
Top centre 15/16".
Bottom centre 1 5/16".
Bottom right 1 1/16".

TO REMOVE ALTERNATOR ROTOR AND ENGINE SPROCKET

Remove the chain case outer cover as described previously.
Release and remove the engine shaft nut (nut measures 1" across flats).
Take off the shaft washer, rotor, shaft key and finally the engine sprocket.
(See front chain removal, 350 Model.)

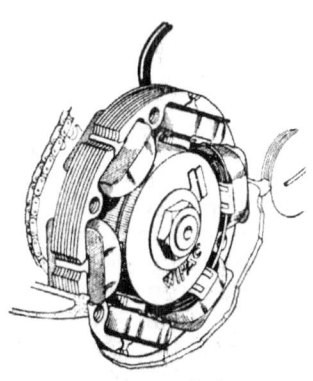

Illustration 8

Rotor

TO REMOVE CLUTCH CONTROL CABLE

Remove the oil filler cap from the kick-starter case cover.
Screw right home the clutch cable adjuster (adjacent to the handlebar lever).
Disengage, from the operating lever, the clutch cable inner wire by operating through the oil filler cap opening.
Disengage, from the handlebar operating control lever, the clutch inner wire.
Pull cable, by its lower end, till removed from the machine, easing it through the frame cable clips while doing so.

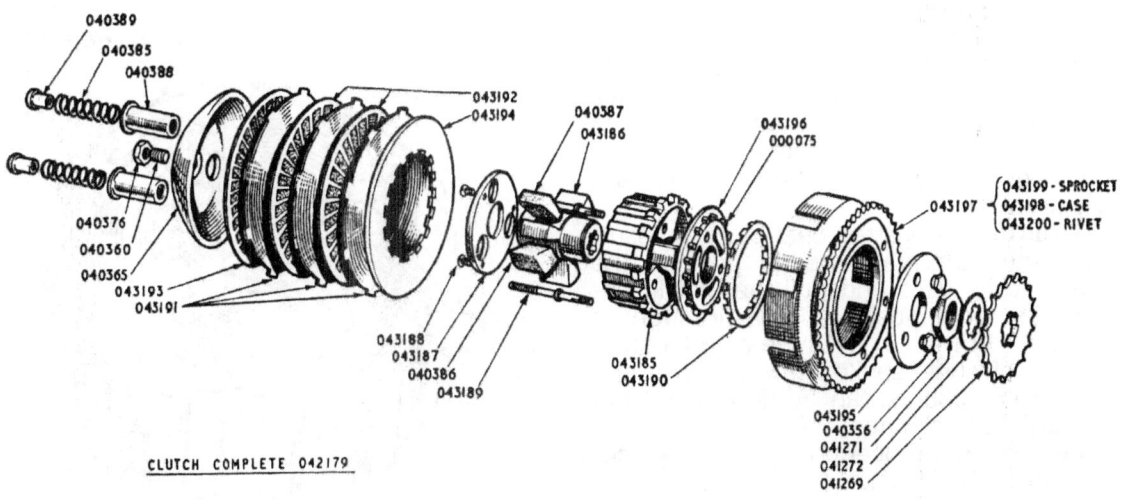

Illustration 9

Exploded view of Clutch Mechanism

TO REPLACE CLUTCH CONTROL CABLE

Reverse the above instructions and, finally, adjust as detailed earlier. Locate the cable in front of the gear box clamp bolt.

CLUTCH ADJUSTMENT

Attention to the clutch is usually confined to adjustment of the operating mechanism. To avoid clutch slip or clutch drag, it is essential to have 3/16 of an inch free movement between the clutch outer casing and the clutch cable adjuster. Without such movement the operating mechanism will be pre-loaded causing wear on the operating parts, also clutch slip. Conversely, excessive movement in the clutch cable will prevent separation of the friction plates and cause the clutch to drag, thus making the gear selection difficult. As the clutch inserts tend to settle down, this has the effect of lengthening the clutch push rod, as the width of the friction inserts are slightly reduced. To deal with clutch drag, or clutch slip, first unscrew the clutch cable adjuster lock nut which is located at the handlebar end, run down the adjuster as far as it will go.

Remove the clutch inspection cap, unscrew one or two turns the adjuster lock nut, shown in illustration of clutch assembly on page 27.

With a screwdriver, screw in the adjuster until contact with the push rod can be felt, unscrew the adjuster exactly half a turn and retighten the lock nut, taking care the adjuster does not move. Complete the adjustment by unscrewing the clutch cable adjuster until there is 3/16" movement between the outer casing and the adjuster, tighten the lock nut. Replace the inspection cap.

Clutch slip should be dealt with promptly otherwise the friction plates will be damaged and the clutch springs affected by heat. The normal free length of the clutch springs is 1¾", the clutch push rod length is 10".

DISMANTLING THE CLUTCH

NOTE—Nuts and screws in the clutch and gear box assembly have a right hand thread, with the exception of the nut retaining the gear box rear chain sprocket, which has a LEFT HAND THREAD.

Commence by removing the primary drive cover.

Unscrew in turn the three clutch spring adjusting screws, take away the clutch spring pressure plate complete with the spring cups and springs, leaving the steel and friction plates free for removal. A box key is required to unscrew the nut and sprocket. The shaft nut is 23/32" across flats.

Engage top gear, apply pressure on the rear brake pedal.

With a box key unscrew the gear box shaft nut.

Remove the chain connecting link, the clutch hub which is on a splined shaft can be pulled off after nut has been removed.

For access to the clutch bearing unscrew the three nuts securing the clutch studs and back plate. The clutch bearing arrangement is shown in illustration 9, page 27.

TO DISMANTLE CLUTCH SHOCK ABSORBER

The six rubber blocks used in the shock absorber can be replaced by:
Removing front chaincase.
Removing clutch spring pressure plate together with spring and spring cups.
Removing three screws also plate for shock absorber compartment (see illustration 10).

A "C" shaped spanner engaged with two slots in the clutch hub or a clutch steel plate with an extension handle welded to it can be used to compress the thick rubbers, whilst the thin rubbers are extracted.

To do this engage **top** gear, apply pressure on the rear brake pedal, position the tool to be used and pull the handle upwards, or opposite to the direction of clutch rotation. With the aid of a short piece of wheel spoke with a pointed end the thin rubbers can be first prised out then the thick ones.

Reverse this procedure to refit replacement rubber blocks.

NOTE—If clutch hub is removed, a tool similar to a gear box mainshaft held in a vice will be required to hold the hub, whilst rubber blocks are extracted.

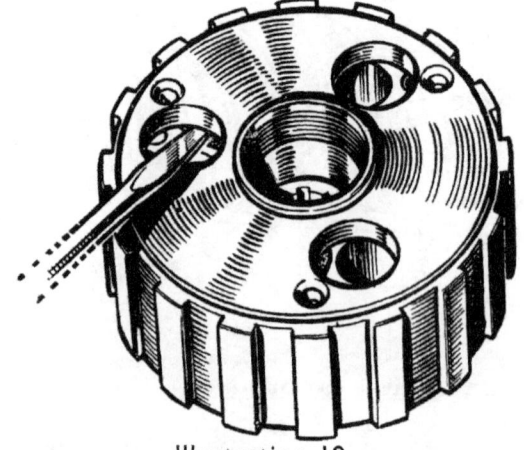

Illustration 10

CLUTCH SPRING ADJUSTMENT

In the event of clutch slip, first ascertain that the operating mechanism is correctly adjusted (see clutch adjustment).
After dismantling the clutch, when refitting the clutch spring adjusting nuts, they should be screwed on until the spring stud just protrudes through the bottom of the recess in the adjuster nut.

FRONT CHAIN ADJUSTMENT

Remove inspection cap from front chaincase, remove the two securing screws on the rear engine cowling, lift the cowling to expose the gear box adjuster bolt.
Slacken: Nut on left hand side of gear box top fixing bolt.
   Two clamping strap bolts.
Adjust chain by means of adjuster eye-bolt and two nuts.
(The correct chain whip is ⅜").
Check the adjustment in several positions and adjust at tightest part of chain.
Tighten two clamping strap bolts, top gear box fixing bolt.
Refit rear engine cowling and securing screws.
Replace chaincase inspection cap.
NOTE—After adjusting front chain, check rear chain adjustment.

REMOVING THE FRONT CHAIN (350 c.c. Model)

The front chain fitted to this model is duplex and endless, which means that the clutch sprocket, also the engine sprocket must be withdrawn simultaneously if the front chain is to be removed. To proceed, follow the instructions given for dismantling the clutch, as far as removing the gearbox main axle shaft nut. Then remove the nut and washer retaining the rotor to the driving side engine shaft, take out the key for the rotor from the shaft. The engine sprocket and clutch, together with the chain in position, can then be withdrawn.
NOTE—One or more shim washers may be fitted at the rear of the engine sprocket, which must be replaced during assembly.

REAR CHAIN ADJUSTMENT

Prior to adjusting rear chain, check front chain and adjust if required.
Loosen both nuts on the rear wheel spindle.
Loosen lock nuts on the adjusters and turn the adjusters until correct chain adjustment is obtained, taking care to move both adjusters exactly the same amount to maintain wheel alignment.
While on the stand the chain whip should be ¾" to ensure ½" whip when rider is seated.
Check the adjustment in several positions and adjust at tightest part of chain.
Remove the rubber cap on the totally enclosed chain guard to check chain tension.
Retighten wheel spindle nuts, and adjuster lock nuts.
NOTE—After chain adjustment rear brake should be checked and readjusted as necessary. See brake adjustment.

REMOVING AND REFITTING REAR CHAIN

To protect the rear chain from mud and water it is very closely shrouded by the chain guard and removing the chain without first detaching the chain guard, can present considerable difficulty. A simple procedure however, is as follows:—
First obtain a piece of thin string about ten feet long.
With cycle on the stand turn the rear wheel until the chain connecting link is at a position near the rear sprocket, and remove the connecting link.
Now pass the string through the centre hole of the end link of the top run, draw the two-ends of the string level and tie together.
Then pull the bottom run of the chain backwards with one hand while keeping the string taut at the rear end with the other hand.
As the end of the top run of the chain disengages with the gear box sprocket it will leave the string attached lying one strand each side of the sprocket teeth.
When the chain is well clear cut the string one side only at a point about one foot from where it is looped through the chain (ink.
Leave the string then *in situ* awaiting chain refitting.

To refit the chain
Pass the longer cut end of the string through the centre hole of the end chain link and then tie the two loose ends of the string together.
Then pull the string from the rear end, at the same time guiding the chain up to engage with the gear box sprocket.
Continue pulling until the chain encircles the sprocket. Remove the string, refit the connecting link with the spring clip closed end facing direction of rotation.

Fork and Frame Service
250 c.c. MODEL

STEERING HEAD ADJUSTMENT

With the machine on the stand, need for adjustment of the steering head bearings may be detected by trying to rock the forks with hands holding the fork legs. The bearings should be tested for slackness after the first 200 miles and subsequently every 1,000 miles. Two spanners should be used, one turning the adjusting nut (34) the other to slacken and retighten the lock nut when the adjustment has been carried out.

Adjustment should be such that no play be felt, yet the bearings are free to rotate and are not over tight.

Adjusting the bearings too tightly will ruin them, and induce heavy steering.

NOTE.—It is important that adjusting and locking nuts are tightly locked together.

FRONT FORKS

The construction of the forks is clearly illustrated in the exploded drawing, and it will be noted that the structure comprises of two main tubes with fixed external bearings, and welded up crown and top pressings. Long coil springs are attached to the top pressing and to damper posts fitted at the Tower ends of the slider tubes.

As the fork slider and damper tube move upwards against the resistance of the main spring, oil is forced up through the annular clearance between the damper tube and the slider leg. Because the damper tube is tapered, the clearance diminishes progressively, resulting in increased hydraulic resistance to upward movement of the fork slider.

When the maximum diameter of the damper post enters the end of the tube, the oil flow is restricted, thus providing a hydraulic lock which prevents "fork bottoming".

FRONT FORK MAINTENANCE

The forks are self lubricating and normally require no attention beyond changing the oil every 5,000 miles.

The oil should be drained by removing plugs (7).

After the fork legs have drained, the drain plugs and washers should be replaced. With the machine on the stand, remove the filler Plugs (2) and refill each leg with 70 ccs. of SAE 30 oil.

Since 30 ccs. of oil will remain trapped in the damper plugs after draining, the addition of the above mentioned 70 cc. of oil will give the correct 100 ccs. of oil in each leg.

After refilling, the machine should be rolled off the stand to locate the top spring adaptors and to replace the top filler plugs and washers.

TO REMOVE THE COMPLETE FRONT FORK ASSEMBLY

Owners are advised not to interfere with the forks unless absolutely necessary. If the fork has been damaged, it is best to remove it complete and obtain a service exchange unit.

To remove the fork assembly follow this sequence:—

Place the machine on the centre stand and remove the front wheel and mudguard.

Remove the battery, headlamp shell speedometer cable, reflector unit, ignition warning light, ammeter leads, lighting and ignition sockets. Disconnect the control cables and the two wires from the dip switch harness to the main harness. Remove the handlebar.

Remove steering column top nut (24) and withdraw column itself (26) from the bottom whilst holding the fork in position. The fork unit can be taken away after removal of distance piece and washer (watch for 34 ball bearings).

If it is desired to dismantle the slider units, the fork sliders complete with oil seals and springs may be withdrawn after removing top filler plug screws.

Care should be taken not to damage the oil seals when pulling them over the bearings.

TO REFIT THE FORKS AS A UNIT

Reassemble in reverse sequence.

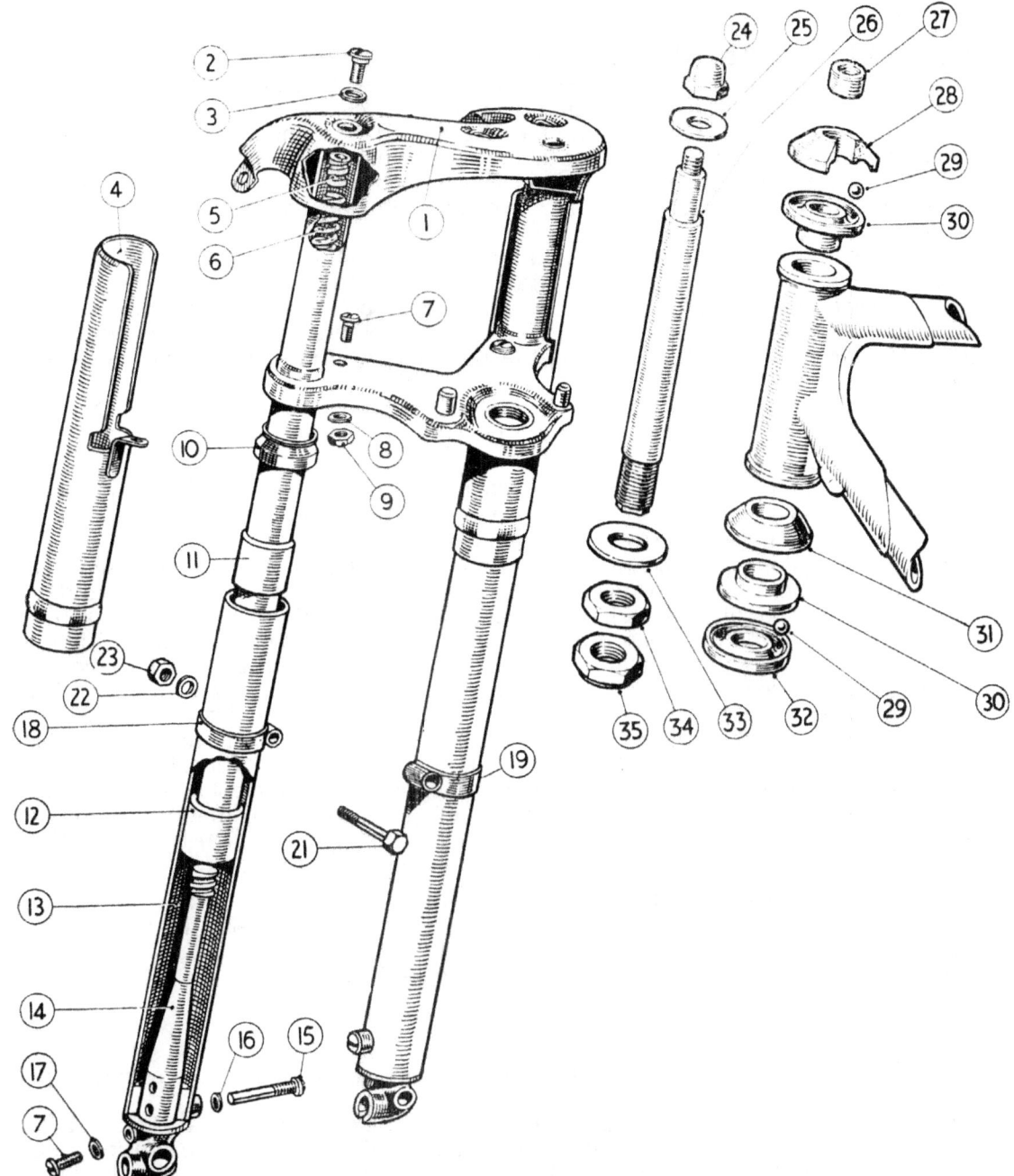

Illustration 11

250 c.c. Front Forks

1. FORK, H.
2. INNER TUBE TOP SCREW.
3. INNER TUBE TOP SCREW FIBRE WASHER.
4. TOP COVER TUBE.
5. INNER TUBE TOP ADAPTOR
6. MAIN SPRING.
7. DRAIN SCREW.
8. TOP COVER TUBE SHAKEPROOF WASHER.
9. TOP COVER TUBE FIXING SCREW NUT.
10. OIL SEAL.
11. ASSEMBLED PART.
12. ASSEMBLED PART.
13. SLIDER EXTENSION.
14. DAMPER TUBE.
15. DAMPER TUBE RETAINING SCREW.
16. DAMPER TUBE RETAINING SCREW FIBRE WASHER.
17. DRAIN SCREW FIBRE WASHER.
18. MUDGUARD CLIP LEFT.
19. MUDGUARD CLIP RIGHT.
21. MUDGUARD CLIP BOLT.
22. MUDGUARD CLIP BOLT WASHER.
23. MUDGUARD CLIP BOLT NUT.
24. NUT, DOMED TOP
25. WASHER TOP DOMED NUT
26. HEAD STEM.
27. SPACER FOR HEAD STEM.
28. ADJUSTING RACE.
29. BALLS STEERING.
30. FRAME RACE TOP AND BOTTOM.
31. DUST COVER FOR BALL RACE.
32. CROWN RACE.
33. WASHER HEAD STEM BOTTOM NUTS.
34. HEAD STEM ADJUSTING NUT. BOTTOM.
35. HEAD STEM LOCK NUT, BOTTOM.

350 c.c. MODEL

STEERING HEAD ADJUSTMENT
The steering head bearing must be kept in close adjustment otherwise if movement develops which is not promptly corrected damage can occur to the ball-races. To make this adjustment the front wheel must be raised clear of the ground by using a box under the crankcase or two boxes, one placed under each footrest.

To tighten the steering head bearing, first release the two alien screws which pass through the fork crown (No. 39, illustration 12). These screws clamp the fork tube to the fork crown.

Unscrew the dome nut at the end of the fork crown (No. 44, illustration 12) and tighten the nut underneath it half-a-turn only. Place the fingers of the left hand on the handlebar lug at the rear, and then lift up the front wheel assembly with the right hand on the mudguard. Any movement will then be felt, and retighten the dome nut as necessary until all movement is taken up, leaving the bearings free from friction and not over-tightened.

It is vitally important to very firmly tighten the two alien screws that clamp the fork tubes, otherwise "fretting" between the tube and the crown will take place.

FRONT FORKS
A breakdown of the front forks is shown in Illustration 12, and the only attention necessary is to check the oil content say every 5,000-8,000 miles. The normal oil content with the forks dry is 6½ fluid ozs. (184.6 c.c.) in each fork leg.

To top up or change the oil, first unscrew the two hexagonal bolts (No. 47, illustration 12) from each fork tube. Use a suitable receptacle to trap the oil when draining, and then remove the drain screw fitted to each fork slider (No. 56, illustration 12). The handlebars should be turned to the left when draining the left side slider, conversely turned to the right when draining the right side slider. When the oil has ceased to flow, take hold of the hexagonal bolt and lift it up sharply to create a pumping action, with the object of ejecting oil trapped in the damper tubes. After a period of 2-3 minutes a little more oil will drain, then the drain screw can be replaced and 6 ozs. of SAE-20 oil should be poured down the fork inner tube through the aperture exposed by the removal of the hexagonal bolt. The reason why 6 ozs. is refilled, is due to the fact that there must be a little oil left in the fork tube that cannot be extracted by draining. If, however, the forks are completely dismantled, then the contents should be 6½ fluid ozs. as previously stated. Six-and-a-half fluid ozs. represents 184.6 c.c, and 6 fluid ozs. is 170.4 c.c.

TO DISMANTLE THE FRONT FORKS
First unscrew both slider extensions (No. 7, illustration 12), then raise the front wheel clear of the ground as previously described.

Remove the following parts in the sequence described:
    (1) The front brake cable from the forks.
    (2) The front wheel.
    (3) The front mudguard.
    (4) The headlamp. (Before removing the headlamp, disconnect the speedometer drive cable.)

It will be seen that the damper rods are attached to the hexagonal bolt, and these bolts must be detached by releasing the locknut (No. 23). With the slider extension clear of the slider, a sharp jerk downwards should enable the fork slider, together with the damper rod and tube attached, to be withdrawn from the fork inner tube.

The fork oil seal (No. 8) is a close fit in the slider, and if difficulty exists in separating the slider from the fork tubes, an application of gentle heat to the top part of the slider where the seal is situated will cause it to expand and thus enable it to be withdrawn without difficulty.

TO REMOVE THE FORK INNER TUBE
These are retained in the fork crown and clamped by the alien screws (No. 39) and with these screws removed the fork tube can then be pulled clear of both the handlebar lug and the fork crown. To dismantle the forks further, the assembly sequence is clearly shown in illustration 12.

When replacing the oil seal, make sure that the metal face is pointing upwards as illustrated.

TO REMOVE THE FORK CROWN
Take off the dome nut and the locknut underneath it from the fork stem, then with a soft mallet tap the handlebar lug clear of the stem and watch for the steering head balls which will probably drop out during this process. Twenty-eight balls are used in the top frame race and 28 balls in the bottom race, which are retained by grease applied to the bearing cups before assembly.

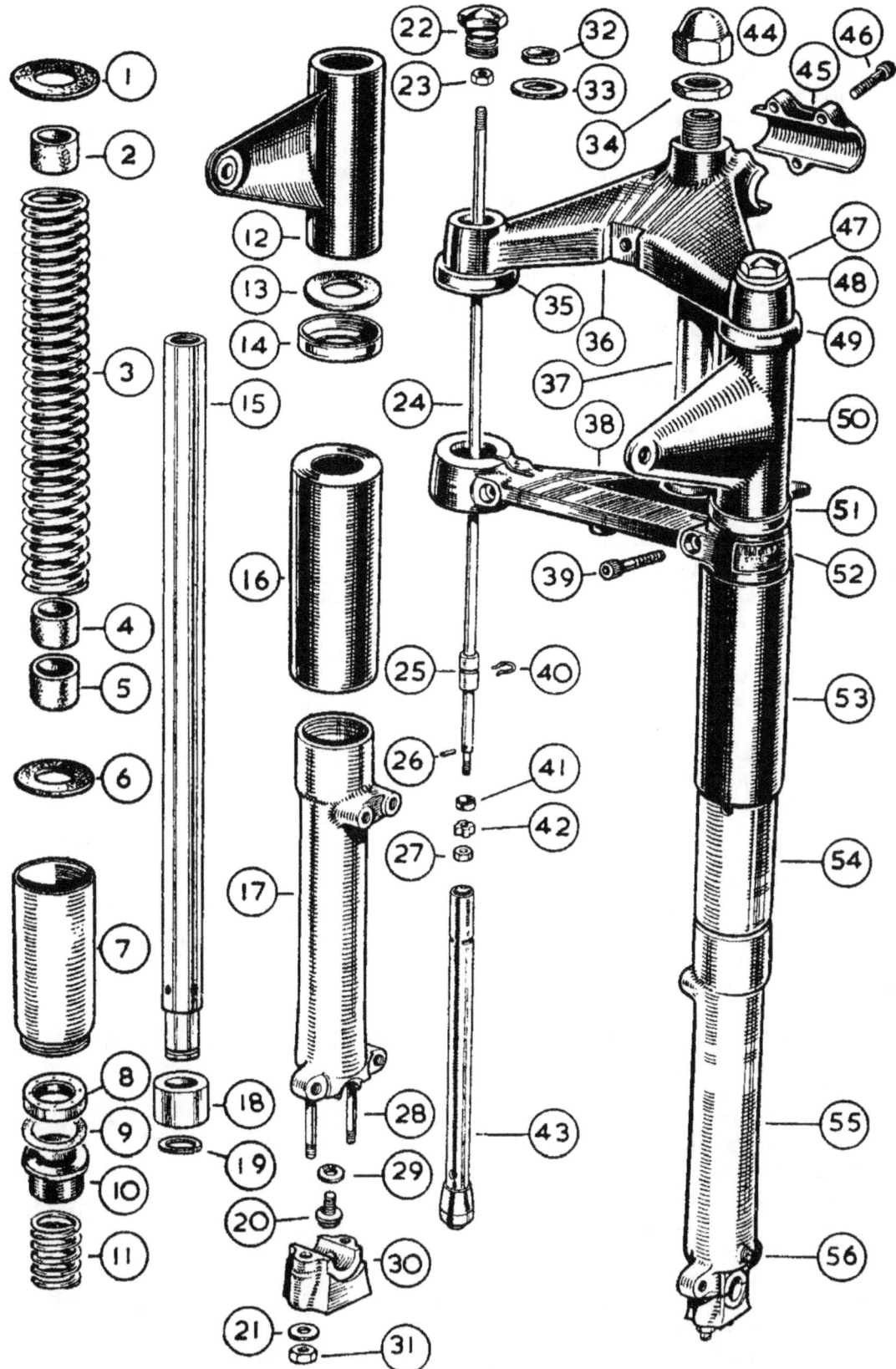

Illustration 12

350 c.c. Front Forks

For description see page 34

REF. NO.	DESCRIPTION
1.	WASHER, LEATHER, FOR FORK SPRING TOP SEATING.
2.	BUFFER, RUBBER, FOR FORK INNER TUBE (ONE OF THREE).
3.	SPRING. MAIN, FOR FRONT FORK.
4.	BUFFER, RUBBER, FOR FORK INNER TUBE (ONE OF THREE).
5.	BUFFER, RUBBER, FOR FORK INNER TUBE (ONE OF THREE).
6.	WASHER, LEATHER, FOR FORK SPRING BOTTOM SEATING.
7.	EXTENSION, FOR FORK SLIDER.
8.	OIL SEAL, RUBBER, FOR FORK INNER TUBE (AN ALTERNATIVE OIL SEAL IS MADE OF LEATHER)
9.	WASHER, PAPER, FOR USE ONLY WITH *LEATHER* OIL SEAL.
10.	BUSH, TOP, PLASTIC, FOR FORK INNER TUBE.
11.	SPRING. BUFFER, FOR FRONT FORK.
12.	TUBE, FORK COVER, TOP, RIGHT, WITH LAMP LUG.
13.	WASHER, RUBBER, FOR TOP COVER TUBE BOTTOM CAP.
14.	CAP, FOR FORK TOP COVER TUBE, BOTTOM LOCATION.
15.	TUBE, FORK, INNER.
16.	TUBE. FORK, COVER, BOTTOM.
17.	SLIDER, FOR FORK, WITH STUDS.
18.	BUSH, BOTTOM, STEEL, FOR FORK INNER TUBE.
19.	CIRCLIP. LOCATING FORK INNER TUBE BOTTOM BUSH.
20.	BOLT, FIXING DAMPER TUBE TO SLIDER.
21.	WASHER, PLAIN, FOR FORK SLIDER CAP SECURING STUD.
22.	BOLT, TOP, FOR FORK INNER TUBE.
23.	NUT. LOCK, FOR TOP END OF DAMPER ROD.
24.	ROD, FOR FORK DAMPER.
25.	SLEEVE, PLUNGER. ON FORK DAMPER ROD.
26.	PIN, STOP. FOR FORK DAMPER VALVE.
27.	NUT, LOCK, FOR DAMPER VALVE SEAT.
28.	STUD, SECURING CAP TO FORK SLIDER.
29.	WASHER, FIBRE. FOR DAMPER TUBE BOLT
30.	CAP, FOR FORK SLIDER.
31.	NUT, FOR FORK SLIDER CAP SECURING STUD.
32.	RING, RUBBER, SEALING, FOR INNER TUBE TOP BOLT.
33.	WASHER, PLAIN, FOR INNER TUBE TOP BOLT.
34.	NUT, ADJUSTING, FOR FORK STEM.
35.	CAP, FOR FORK TOP COVER TUBE, TOP LOCATION.
36.	LUG. FOR HANDLEBAR AND STEERING HEAD.
37.	STEM, FOR FORK CROWN (NOT SOLD SEPARATELY).
38.	FORK CROWN (SOLD ONLY AS AN ASSEMBLY OF CROWN, STEM AND STEM CIRCLIP).
39.	SCREW, PINCH, FOR FORK CROWN.
40.	CLIP, RETAINING DAMPER ROD SLEEVE.
41.	VALVE, FOR FORK DAMPER.
42.	SEAT, FOR FORK DAMPER VALVE.
43.	TUBE. FOR FORK DAMPER.
44.	NUT, LOCK (DOMED), FOR FORK STEM.
45.	CLIP (HALF ONLY) FOR HANDLEBAR LUG.
46.	SCREW, PINCH, FOR HANDLEBAR LUG CLIP.
47.	BOLT, TOP, FOR FORK INNER TUBE.
48.	WASHER. PLAIN, FOR INNER TUBE TOP BOLT.
49.	CAP, FOR FORK TOP COVER TUBE, TOP LOCATION.
50.	TUBE. FORK COVER, TOP, LEFT, WITH LAMP LUG.
51.	CAP, FOR FORK TOP COVER TUBE, BOTTOM LOCATION.
52.	FORK CROWN.
53.	TUBE, FORK COVER, BOTTOM.
54.	EXTENSION, FOR FORK SLIDER.
55.	SLIDER, FOR FORK, WITH CAP, STUDS AND NUTS.
56.	SCREW, PLUG, WITH FIBRE WASHER, FOR FORK SLIDER OIL DRAIN HOLE.

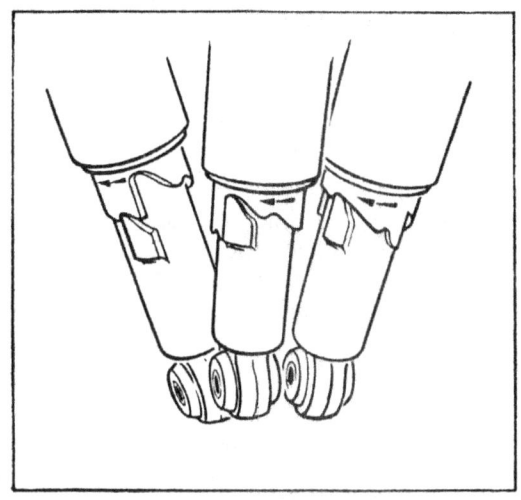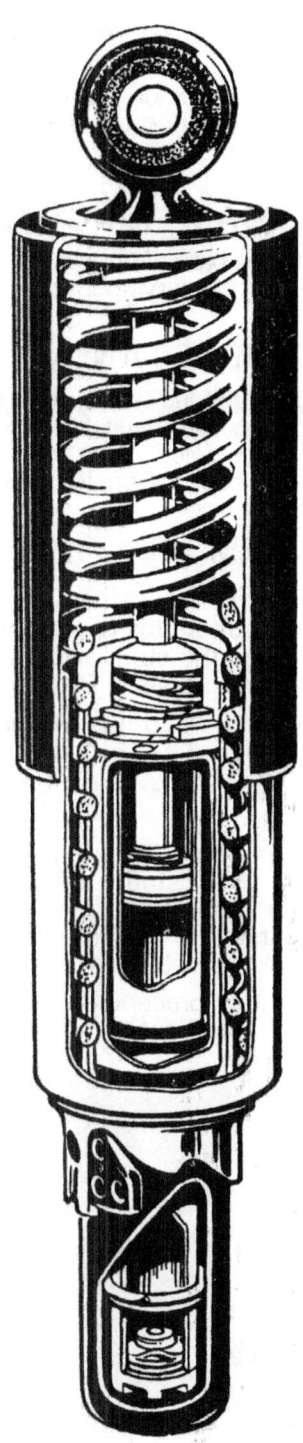

Illustration 13

"Ghost" view of Rear Suspension Unit

REAR SUSPENSION

The rear wheel is mounted in a fork which is hinged just behind the gear box.

The fork works in bronze bearings and is lubricated by an oil reservoir around the bushes and this can be replenished with heavy gear oil (SAE 140) by means of a grease nipple situated above the pivot on the right hand side. Movement of the fork is controlled by Girling suspension units. These units are of the sealed unit type, and topping up is not necessary. The springs are lubricated before assembly and the fluid in the damper unit is the exact quantity and sufficient for life of the unit.

The unit is shown in illustration 13.

Maintenance is confined to external cleaning and occasional greasing of the cam ring adjuster.

Should a squeak or rubbing noise develop as the units move, remove in turn each unit, uncover the spring by removing the top split collars, grease the external diameter of the springs and reassemble.

THE CAM RING ADJUSTER

Raising the base of the spring by turning the cam clockwise (see illustration 13), preloads the spring for varying loads.

CENTRE STAND

The centre stand is mounted on the footrest spindle and can be removed by supporting the machine on a suitable box and removing the exhaust system, both footrests and the stand stop plates. The footrest spindle can then be removed and after unhooking the operating rod, the centre stand can be removed.

TO REMOVE THE REAR CHAIN GUARD

Fully Enclosed Type

Remove bottom fixing nut on left hand rear suspension unit, and slide the lower end of the unit off the stud, slacken the left hand wheel spindle nut. Remove the two chain case securing bolts. The large spindle washer is used outside the guard.

The top and bottom halves of the chain case can then be removed.

Reverse this procedure for reassembly.

Standard type

Remove bottom fixing nut on left hand rear suspension unit and slide the lower end of the unit off the stud. Remove rear brake rod adjuster nut, rear chain and speedometer cable, slacken wheel spindle nuts. Remove the two chain guard securing bolts, lift the rear of the chain guard and slide the rear wheel out of the fork ends. The rear chain guard can now be removed.

Reverse this procedure for reassembly.

Wheels and Brakes

TO REMOVE THE FRONT WHEEL (350 c.c. Model)

With the front wheel clear of the ground, disconnect the front brake cable, then remove the nut that secures the brake torque arm to the front brake cover plate. Release the four nuts (No. 31, illustration 12), unscrew the front wheel spindle right side sleeve nut, then the wheel spindle can be withdrawn, leaving the wheel free to be taken away.

TO REMOVE THE FRONT WHEEL (250 c.c. Model)

Place the machine on the centre stand and disconnect the front brake cable.

Release the two nuts at the back of each fork slider which secure the bottom front mudguard stay, and tap the threaded end of the extension slightly to centralise the stay which clamps on to the sleeve nut and spindle. Take away the right side axle sleeve nut, then the wheel spindle can be withdrawn and the wheel will then come away from the fork.

TO REMOVE REAR WHEEL

Remove the fully enclosed chain guard if fitted. Disconnect speedo drive cable; release both wheel spindle nuts. With the rider standing on left side of the machine, lean the machine to the left and take away the wheel. When refitting ensure speedo drive is correctly located.

HUBS AND BEARINGS

Both hubs are greased when new and no further lubrication will be required for 5,000 miles, it is then advisable to renew the grease, the old grease should be removed by washing in petrol or paraffin.

When dismantling and reassembling the hubs refer to illustration for assembly order. If bearings show any signs of wear, fit replacements.

BRAKES

If the brakes are correctly adjusted and oil is not used to lubricate the bearings, the brakes will not require attention for many thousands of miles. Petrol or paraffin should not be used to wash brake shoes, these liquids have an adverse effect on the linings and braking efficiency will be lost.

Front brake adjustment is effected by a cable adjuster on the left hand fork slider.

Rear brake adjustment is effected by a knurled nut at the rear end of the brake rod.

BRAKE PEDAL ADJUSTMENT

To adjust the position of the pedal, slacken the brake pedal spindle nut, move the pedal to the desired position, hold the pedal in this position and tighten the spindle nut.

After altering the pedal position check the brake rod adjustment.

REAR BRAKE ADJUSTMENT

With the rear wheel clear of the ground screw down the adjuster on the rear brake rod until the brake is just binding. Then unscrew the adjuster four to five complete turns. On machines with a frame number before 5858, the brake adjuster should be unscrewed eight complete turns.

TYRES

To obtain maximum mileage from the tyres, maintenance should be regular and painstaking. Once a week check tyre pressures with a gauge and at the same time remove any road grit which is wedged in the treads.

A comprehensive booklet produced by Messrs. Dunlops, on "How to keep your motor cycle tyres fit", which includes instructions on tyre removal and refitting is issued with each new machine. A table of minimum inflation pressures for specified loads per tyre is also included. As a rough guide, and with a rider of average weight and normal equipment, without a pillion passenger, the pressures should be 18 lbs. for the front tyre and 22 lbs. for the rear tyre.

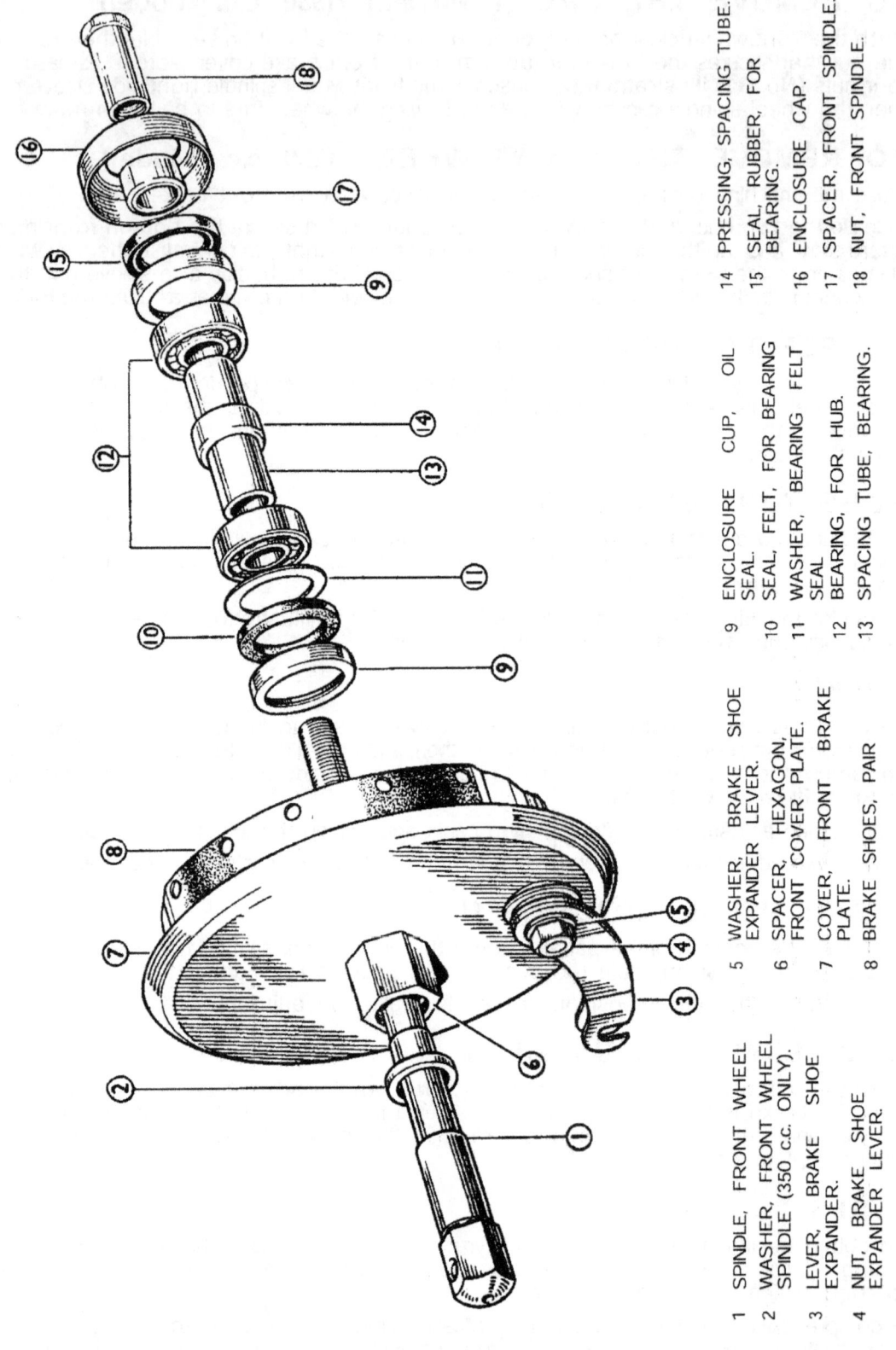

Illustration 14

Front Hub Assembly

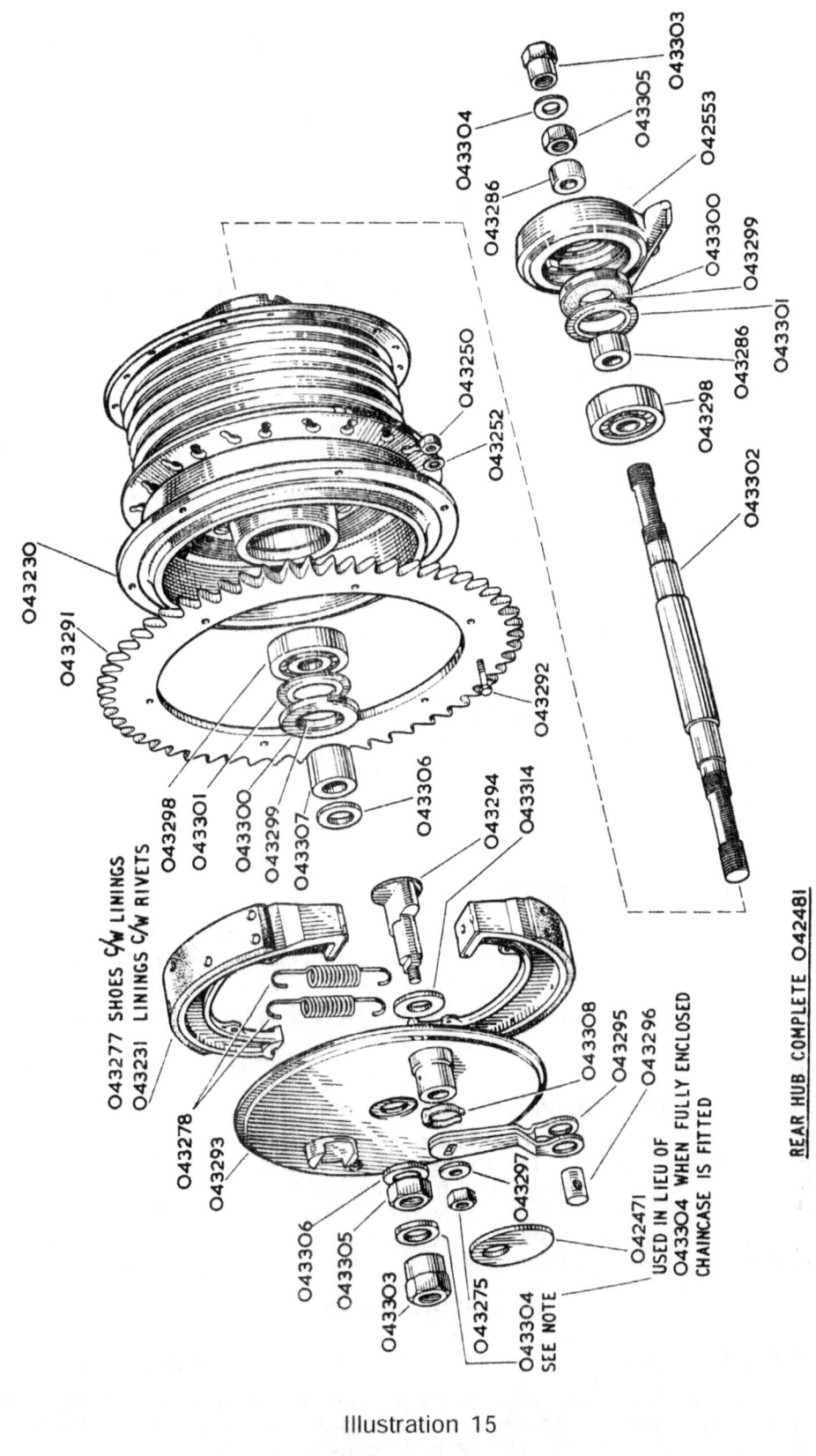

Illustration 15

Rear Hub Assembly

Electrical Service

GENERAL

The lighting and ignition systems are combined, using a six pole permanent magnet excited A.C. generator, which charges the battery via a selenium rectifier. The remaining electrical units are fed from the battery in the normal manner.

The alternator unit has inherent regulating properties which combined with circuit switching gives the correct charge rate under all conditions.

Emergency starting is provided by switching the six generator coils on to the battery, which gives immediate voltage supply for the ignition coil. The emergency switch position may also be used to provide high rate boost charge where the state of charge of the battery is low. The use of the high charge rate should be limited to fifteen minutes.

Prolonged use of the high charge rate will cause evaporation of water from the electrolyte (acid) with possible damage to the battery.

SIX POLE ALTERNATOR

The A.C. Generator used is called an "Alternator". The rotating member is a six pole permanent magnet unit, which is of special design and magnet quality, and may, therefore, be removed from the Stator Coil assembly without loss of magnetism.

The six coils of the Stator are connected in two sets of three in series. As three leads only are brought out, one is common to both sets (this is WHITE). For test purposes, the same output is obtained between green and white as between orange and white.

By switching in a resistance unit we can obtain the following changes in the circuits to provide varying outputs from the alternator.

The resistance unit is wound in the main loom of wires and is not visible as a separate unit. Its location can be seen in the wiring diagram.

The switch positions are:

OFF/IGN	Normal charge rate.
LOW/IGN	Normal charge rate.
HIGH/IGN	Normal charge rate.
OFF/EMG	Boost charge rate.
LOW/EMG	Boost charge rate.
HIGH/EMG	Normal charge.

EMERGENCY STARTING

An EMERGENCY starting position is provided in the ignition switch for use if the battery has become discharged. Under these conditions, the alternator is connected direct to the ignition coil, allowing the engine to be started independently of the battery.

Once the engine is running, turn the ignition switch back to the normal running position.

RECTIFIER

The rectifier is a full-wave bridge connected unit.

The case must be earthed to the machine, and this earth is connected POSITIVE. The three bullet type terminal connectors should be checked for tightness, and also the centre fastening bolt. This bolt forms the "earth" connection and so must meet clean faces on the machine frame and rectifier case.

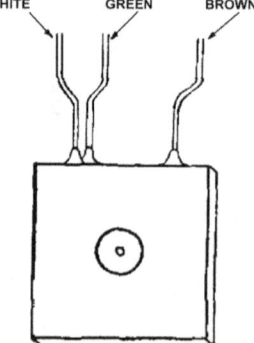

Illustration 16—**Rectifier**

COIL IGNITION

The coil, also the air filter body (when fitted) is housed in the accessory compartment on the left side of the machine. To remove the compartment cover unscrew the top cover screw, then take away the two bolts located below the cover.

The coil needs no attention beyond keeping the exterior clean, particularly between the terminals, which must be securely tightened.

CONTACT BREAKER UNIT

This unit comprises the contact set, condenser and cam lubricating pad.

The contacts are adjusted by releasing the locking screw and then setting the distance by a slight movement of the eccentric screw whilst the rocker arm heel is on the peak of the cam lobe, and finally tightening the locking screw firmly.

When dry the lubrication pad should be removed, and have H.M.P. grease kneaded into it, and then replaced. Oil is not advised, but if used sparingly and frequently is better than complete neglect. Excess oil may reach the contact surfaces and would be harmful.

When service attention is given to the breaker unit always check tightness of the live condenser connection and earth fixing screw.

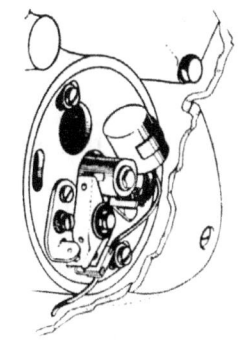

Illustration 17
Contact Breaker

AUTO-ADVANCE MECHANISM

Behind the contact breaker base plate is the advance mechanism which by means of weights and springs moves the cam in order to provide a retarded position for starting and gradually to advance the ignition setting as the engine speed increases.

HEADLAMP

The reflector is of the latest pattern aluminised thin coating deposited in high vacuum, and gives a much greater light reflection than the older plated types.

As this high efficiency coating is extremely thin, the reflecting surface should never be touched. This also means that reflectors cannot be supplied as spares without the glass front, which acts as protection during transit and stocking.

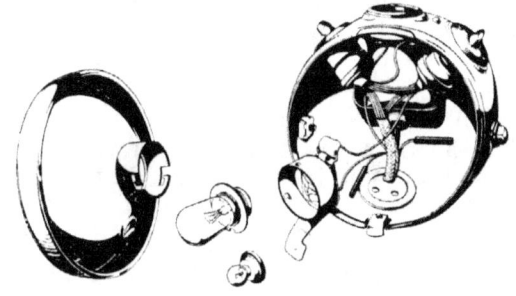

Illustration 18—**Headlamp**

HEADLAMP BULB—30 x 24 Watts

The bulb is a double filament pre-focus type, and is removed after the contact unit has been taken off. By holding the reflector and rim unit upside down and taking care to CATCH the bulb, it will DROP out, as no other fastening is employed.

HEADLAMP SWITCHES

The switches are connected inside the lamp to the wiring system by multi pin plug sockets. These are arranged with a missing pin and hole, so that incorrect mating is impossible. The operating portion with the brass contact legs is the same in both the IGN and LIGHTS switches—the only difference being the names on the escutcheon plates.

The female rubber socket portions which are connected to the wiring loom are coloured BLUE and BLACK. The BLUE one is the LIGHTING switch connector and the BLACK one is for the IGNITION switch.

SPARKING PLUG (SINGLE OR 3-POINT)

The K.L.G. Type FE80 "Corundite" Plug is fitted to all models.
It has a thread of 14 mm. and the reach is ¾". The point gap is ·020 to ·022°. Check the point gaps *every* time the engine is decarbonised and, if necessary, re-set the points. See that the plug is fitted with its external seating washer.

Coat the thread with "Oil Dag" or Graphite paste.

Firmly tighten the plug by using the standard box spanner and tommy bar (Part No. 017252). All that is required is a GAS-TIGHT joint. Therefore do not over tighten, which will **not** make a gas-tight joint more gas-tight, but can. and possibly will, distort and damage the body of the plug.

Set the gaps to ·020 to ·022". Never try to move the central electrode. To widen or narrow the gap between the electrodes only move the earth (side electrodes). Check the gaps first with a gap gauge. If they are too wide tap the earth (side electrodes) towards the central electrode using preferably a small copper drift and light hammer. Check the gaps between each tap and stop when the gauge is a nice sliding fit between the central electrode and the three earth side electrodes.

If the gaps are too small to start with gently lever the earth electrodes away from the centre electrode using a small screwdriver and then tap them back as described above. Avoid damaging the centre electrode and do not attempt to move the electrodes apart by forcing anything between them.

For maximum efficiency, plugs should be cleaned at every 3,000 miles. To take the plug to pieces for cleaning, unscrew the gland nut by holding the smaller hexagon on the gland nut upside down in a vice and then using the box spanner to unscrew the larger hexagon on the body.

Then lift away the central electrode assembly which should be washed in petrol or paraffin. Then, using fairly coarse glass paper, remove the carbon deposit and wash again.

The central firing point should be cleaned with fine emery cloth. The inside of the body should be scraped clean with a knife and finally rinsed in petrol.

There is an internal washer, between the insulator and its seating in the body. On re-assembly lightly smear this with thin oil and then screw up the gland nut sufficiently tight to give a gas-tight joint.

Finally adjust the gap to ·020 to ·022".

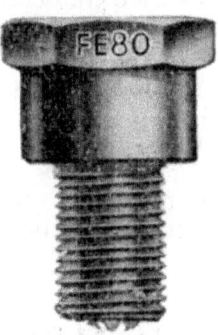

Illustration 19

BATTERY TYPE 3-ER7L POSITIVE EARTH

"Dry charged" batteries are supplied without electrolyte, but with their plates in a charged condition. No initial charging is required and to bring the battery into service it is only necessary to fill the cells with electrolyte, prepared by mixing concentrated sulphuric acid and distilled water. The cell filler holes are sealed to exclude moisture and air before the battery is brought into service and the seals should be removed immediately before electrolyte is poured in.

PREPARATION OF ELECTROLYTE. In the U.K. and countries where the temperatures are normally below 90° F. (32° C.) electrolyte of 1·270 S.G. is required, viz. 1 part acid (1·835 S.G.) to 2·8 parts distilled water. In tropical climates where temperatures frequently rise above 90° F., electrolyte of 1·210 S.G. is recommended, viz., 1 part acid (1·835 S.G.) to 4 parts distilled water.

WARNING. ALWAYS ADD ACID TO WATER—NOT WATER TO ACID.

ON DRY CHARGED BATTERIES THE FILLING OF EACH CELL MUST BE COMPLETED IN ONE OPERATION AND LEVELS RESTORED AFTER STANDING FOR AN HOUR OR MORE BY SYPHONING OFF EXCESS ELECTROLYTE.

Electrolyte should be mixed in a glass or earthenware vessel, or lead lined tank.

Temperature of filling room, battery and electrolyte should be maintained between 60° F. and 80° F.

Batteries filled in this way are 90 per cent. charged. After filling, a dry charged battery needs only the attention normally given to lead-acid type batteries.

BATTERY MAINTENANCE. Deterioration soon sets in if left standing without attention for any length of time. To keep the battery in good condition, maintenance must be carried out whether the machine is in use or not.

Every month (every fortnight in summer) remove battery, clean terminals and top up the three cells to ⅛" above the level of the plates with distilled water—NOT tap water, as this contains impurities detrimental to the battery. Pour the distilled water through a glass funnel or syringe.

Many lighting troubles can be traced to unseen corrosion between the surfaces of the battery terminals; keep the terminals clean. A little grease smeared on them will help prevent corrosion.

Do not keep distilled water in receptacles made of any kind of metal as this will quickly render it impure—make use of a clean glass bottle or jar. Rain water collected in a jar makes a satisfactory substitute for distilled water.

Never bring a naked light near a battery with vent plugs removed or when the battery is being charged; the gas given off by the electrolyte is dangerously explosive.

Battery acid is highly corrosive; therefore, throw away any cleaning rags used to clean the battery lest their use on other parts of the machine causes rust.

Never let a battery completely run down; if this does occur get it charged as soon as possible, or its length of life may be seriously shortened.

BULBS BLOWING

This can only be due to an open circuit in the battery line and the fault should be located before new bulbs are fitted. To locate the fault, check in the following order:—

(1) Bad earth connection on battery positive lead.
(2) Loose or corroded battery terminals.
(3) Loose or dirty contact in the 4-hole 2-way connector which is interposed in the battery negative lead. (Brown wire).
(5) Loose ammeter connection.
(6) Battery dry due to electrolyte evaporating.

250 c.c. SCRAMBLES MODEL

ELECTRICAL AND IGNITION EQUIPMENT

When a lighting set is fitted two separate electrical circuits are used to enable the lamps and lighting circuit to be removed for competition events. The necessary connections to be made when the lighting circuit is removed can be seen in the wiring diagram.

The main lamp bulb uses alternating current direct from the stator coils.

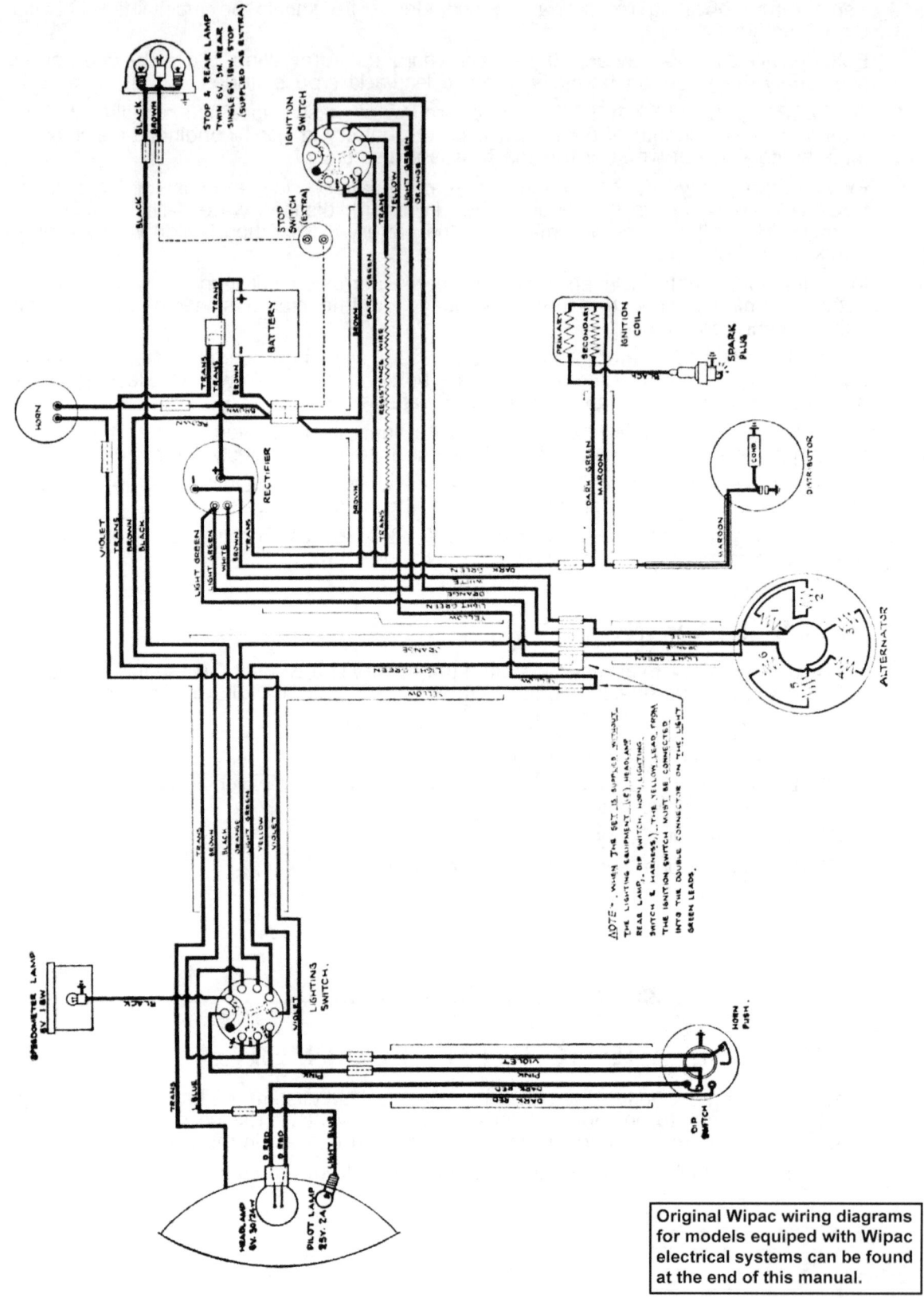

Illustration 20

Wiring Diagram: 250 c.c. Scrambler

Original Wipac wiring diagrams for models equiped with Wipac electrical systems can be found at the end of this manual.

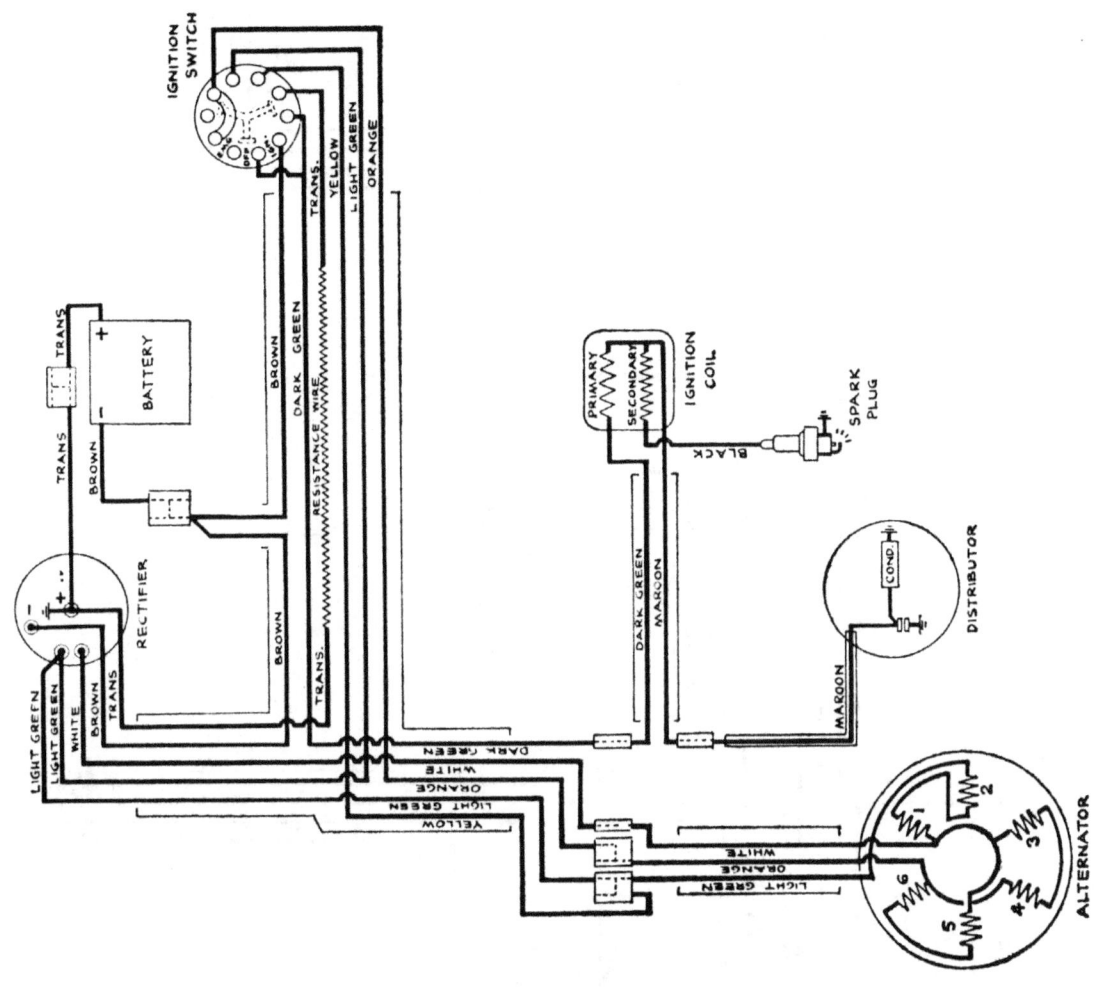

Illustration 21

Wiring diagram: 250 c.c. Scrambler (with lights removed)

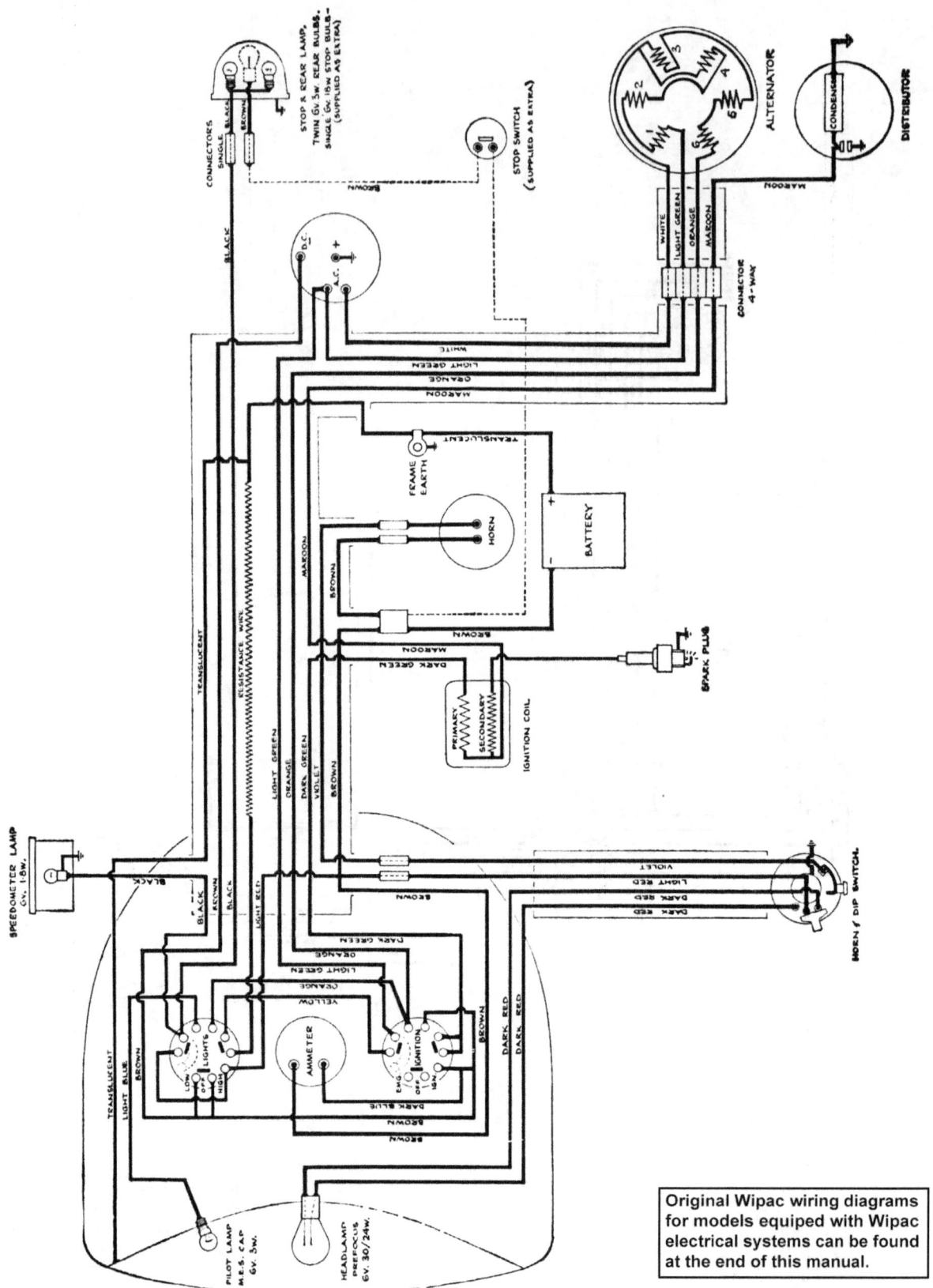

Illustration 22

Wiring Diagram 250 and 350.

Useful Information

TRACING TROUBLES

Engine fails to start, or is difficult to start, may be due to:
Carburetter flooded unnecessarily.
Water on high-tension cable.
Moisture on sparking plug.
Oiled up, or fouled, sparking plug.
Throttle opening too large.
Pilot jet choked.
Air lever in open position or bad air leak at carburetter joint.
Lack of fuel because of pipe, or tap, obstruction.
Valve not seating properly.
Contact points dirty.
Incorrect contact point gap.
Ignition not switched **on.**
Faulty coil or condenser.

Engine misses fire may be due to:
Defective, or oiled, sparking plug.
Incorrect contact point gap.
Contact breaker rocker arm sticking.
Rocker adjustment incorrect.
Oil on contact breaker points.
Weak valve springs.
Defective sparking plug wire.
Partially obstructed petrol supply.

Loss of power may be due to:
Faulty sparking plug.
Lack of oil in tank.
No rocker clearance, or too much clearance.
Weak, or broken, valve spring.
Sticky valve stem.
Valve not seating properly.
Brake adjusted too closely.
Badly fitting, or broken, piston rings.
Punctured carburetter float.
Engine carbonised.
Choked silencer.
Bad air leak between carburetter and head.

Engine overheats may be due to:
Lack of proper lubrication.   (Quality or quantity of oil).
Faulty sparking plug.
Air control to carburetter out of order.
Punctured carburetter float.
Engine carbonised.
Weak valve springs.
Pitted valve seats.
Worn piston rings.
Ignition setting incorrect.
Choked silencer.
Automatic timing control faulty.

Engine stops suddenly may be due to:
Stuck up valve.
No petrol in tank, or choked petrol supply.
Choked main jet.
Oiled up, or fouled, sparking plug.
Water on sparking plug.
Water in float chamber.
Vent hole in petrol tank filler cap choked.
Loose coil connections.

EXCESSIVE OIL CONSUMPTION

Excessive oil consumption may be due to:
Badly worn, or stuck up, piston rings. (Causing high pressure in the crankcase).
Worn valve stems.

EXCESSIVE PETROL CONSUMPTION

Excessive petrol consumption may be due to:
Leaks in the petrol feed system. (Damaged fibre washers, loose union nuts on piping, defective float needle action).
Incorrect ignition setting. (Ignition not advanced sufficiently).
Defective engine valve action.
Incorrect use of air control lever.
Moving parts of carburetter badly worn. (Only possible after very considerable mileage).
Bad air leak at carburetter junction.

STEERING UNSATISFACTORY

Incorrect steering head adjustment (too tight or excessively slack).
Pitted steering head ball races resulting from loose adjustment.
Wheels out of alignment.
Front and/or rear tyre tread not correctly manipulated to run true with wheel (causes handlebar oscillation at low road speed).
Damaged front fork main tubes resulting from impact.

ABNORMAL TYRE WEAR

Abnormal tyre wear may be due *to:*
Incorrect tyre pressure.
Wheels not in alignment.
Harsh driving methods. (Misuse of acceleration and braking).

CLEANING THE MACHINE

Do not attempt to rub, or brush, mud off the enamelled surfaces because this will soon destroy the sheen of the enamel. Mud, and other road dirt, should be soaked off with water.
The best method is to use a small hose, taking care not to direct water on to the engine, carburetter, magneto and other such parts. As a poorer substitute, a pail of water and a sponge may be used.
After washing down with water, the surplus moisture should be removed with a chamois leather, and, when the enamelled surfaces are thoroughly dry, they may be polished with a good wax polish and soft dusters.
Such parts as the engine crankcase and the gear-box can be cleaned by applying paraffin with a stiff brush, and, with a final application of petrol, will come up like new.

CHROMIUM PLATING

Under some climatic conditions, a rusty looking deposit may be observed on ferrous parts that are chromium plated. This is not ordinary rust (ferric oxide) but is a salt deposit that, in most cases and in its early stages, can be quickly and easily removed with a damp chamois leather. In stubborn cases, it may be necessary to use a special chromium cleaning compound.
The safest precaution during winter is to wipe over all chromium plated parts with a soft rag soaked in **"TEKALL",** which is a lanoline base rust preventative marketed in small tins and available at most garages. This material, so applied, leaves an almost invisible film that is impervious to moisture and its use cannot be too highly recommended to owners who value the appearance of their mounts.
In summer, when those conditions do not prevail, chromium parts should be frequently cleaned with a damp chamois leather and afterwards polished with a soft duster.
If a polish is used it must be one of the special compounds for chromium plating only. Ordinary metal polishing liquids, in particular, must not, on any account, be used because these, almost without exception, contain acids, which attack chromium,
NOTE—"Tekall" is a product of **20th Century Finishes Ltd., 175-177, Kirkgate, Wakefield,** and is retailed in ½ pint and 1 pint tins. It can be obtained from our Spare Parts Department, as follows:
½ pint tin "Tekall", Part number 011957.
1 pint tin "Tekall", Part number 011958.

Repairs and Service

REPAIRS

The instructions regarding repairs should be clear and definite, otherwise the cost may be greater than that expected. We shall be pleased to give estimates for repairs if parts are sent to us for that purpose. If the estimate is accepted, no charge is made for the preliminary examination, but, should it be decided not to have the work carried out, it **MAY** be necessary to make a charge to cover the cost of whatever dismantling and re-assembly may have been done to prepare the estimate.

Customers desiring that old parts which are replaced with new during the course of overhaul or repair be retained must make the fact known prior to the work being put in hand because, normally, such parts, having no further useful life, are scrapped upon removal.

Parts sent to us as patterns, or for repair, should have attached to them a label bearing the sender's full name and address. The instructions regarding such parts should be sent under separate cover.

If it is necessary to bring a machine, or parts, to the Works for an urgent repair, **IT IS ESSENTIAL** you **MAKE AN APPOINTMENT** beforehand to **AVOID DISAPPOINTMENT**. This can be done by letter or telephone.

CORRESPONDENCE AND ORDERS

Our routine is organised into different departments, therefore delay cannot be avoided if matters relating to more than one department are contained in one letter.

Consequently, it is desirable, when communicating with more than one department, to do so on **SEPARATE SHEETS**, each of which should bear your name and address. When writing on a technical matter, or when ordering spares, it is essential to quote the **COMPLETE ENGINE NUMBER**. Some numbers have one, or more, letters incorporated in them and these letters **MUST BE QUOTED**, otherwise model identification is not possible.

Orders should always be sent in list form and not as part of a letter.

Owners are strongly advised to purchase a Spare Parts List so that correct part numbers can be quoted. Most parts are clearly illustrated in this list which makes it very easy to recognise the part or parts required.

PROPRIETARY FITTINGS

No expense is spared to secure and fit the most suitable, and highest quality, instruments and accessories for the standard equipment of our machines.

Nevertheless, our Guarantee does not cover such parts and, in the event of trouble being experienced, the parts in question should be returned to, and claims made, direct on the actual manufacturers who will deal with them on the terms of their respective guarantees.

Those manufacturers are:

Carburetters	Messrs. Amalgamated Carburetters Ltd., Holford Road, Witton, Birmingham, 6.
Chains	The Renold and Coventry Chain Co. Ltd., Didsbury, Manchester.
Electrical Equipment	Wico-Pacy Sales Corporation, Bletchley, Bucks.
Sparking Plugs	K.L.G. Sparking Plugs Ltd., Putney Vale, London, S.W.15.
Speedometers	Messrs. S. Smith & Sons (M.A.) Ltd., Cricklewood, London.
Tyres!	Messrs. Dunlop Rubber Co. Ltd., Fort Dunlop, Birmingham.
Rear Suspension	Girling Ltd., King's Road, Tyseley, Birmingham, 11.

All the above manufacturers except S. Smith & Sons (M.A.) Ltd., issue instructive literature regarding their products which is obtainable by writing to them.

To register a new machine:

Send to the Local Registration Authority the following:
- (a) Form "RF1/2", duly completed.
- (b) The certificate of insurance.
- (c) The invoice you received from your dealer when you purchased the machine.
- (d) The appropriate registration fee.

In due course you will receive:
- (1) A Registration Book. (Commonly called the "log" book).
- (2) A Licence Disc.
- (3) Your Insurance Certificate.
- (4) Your Invoice.

The Registration Book and the Licence Disc will bear the registration numbers that have been allotted to your machine and will also show the date the Road Licence expires.

Your number plates must then be painted, in white upon a black background, with the registration numbers in characters of even thickness as follows:

The numbers on the front plate must be 1¾" high, 1¼" wide and ⁵⁄₁₆" thick with spaces of ½" between each two characters.

The numbers on the rear plate must be 2½" high, 1¾" wide and ⅜" thick with spaces ½" between each two characters.

The Licence Disc must be enclosed in a water-tight container, having a transparent front, and this must be fixed to the machine in a conspicuous position, near the front and on the left-hand side.

It is not legally necessary to carry your Driving Licence, Insurance Certificate and Registration Book while driving your machine.

Ignition Suppressors

As required by law all machines for the Home Market are issued with an approved type of radio interference suppressor already installed.

Speedometer

A speedometer MUST be fitted and it MUST BE so ILLUMINATED that it is possible to read the dial after lighting up time.

Lamps

During the official "LIGHTING UP" hours the machine must exhibit a white light facing forwards a red light facing rearwards. The rear number plate must be adequately illuminated by a white light.

Each front electric light bulb **MUST** be marked with its "Wattage". (Beware of cheap, imported, bulbs that do not have this marking).

All motor cycles made by us have electric equipment that complies with the law regarding position, size of bulbs, marking on bulbs and the correct illumination of the rear number plate.

SERVICE

The **Service and Repair Department** is situated in **Burrage Grove, Plumstead. London, S.E.18**, and is open on Mondays to Fridays from 8.30 a.m. to 12.55 p.m.— 2.0 p.m. to 5.30 p.m. It is closed on Saturdays, Sundays and National Holidays.

It exists for the purposes of:
- (a) Giving technical assistance verbally or through the post.
- (b) Supplying spare parts over the counter or through the post.
- (c) Repairing and re-conditioning machines, or parts of machines, of our make.

Burrage Grove is the first turning on the left from Burrage Road when entering Burrage Road from the Plumstead Road. (See final paragraph below).

The nearest Railway Station is WOOLWICH ARSENAL, SOUTHERN REGION RAILWAY. This Station is five minutes walk from our Service Depot in Burrage Grove. There is an excellent service of electric trains from Charing Cross, Waterloo. Cannon Street and London Bridge Stations, Southern Region Railway.

Bus routes 53, 163, 54, 99, 122 and 127 pass the end of Burrage Road (one minute from the Service Depot).

Bus routes 186, 75 and 161 serve **Beresford Square** which is three minutes walk from the **Service and Repair Department.**

Visitors from the North can pass into Woolwich via the Free Ferry between North) Woolwich and Woolwich. North Woolwich is a British Railways terminus and is also served by Bus routes. There is also a tunnel under the River Thames at this point for foot passengers. The Free Ferry accommodates all types of motor vehicles and there is a very frequent service. The Southern landing stage is less than a mile from the Service Depot.

Visitors arriving by road, if they are strangers to the locality, should enquire for **Beresford Square, Woolwich.** Upon arrival there, the road skirting the Royal Arsenal should be followed in an Easterly direction for about four hundred yards, and Burrage Road is the second turning on the right after leaving the Square. Burrage Grove is then the first turning on the left.

THE DRIVER AND THE LAW

The driver of a motor cycle **MUST** be **INSURED** against Third Party Claims and **MUST** be able to produce an **INSURANCE CERTIFICATE** showing that such an insurance is in force.

If your Insurance Certificate specifies you can only drive one particular machine you **MUST NOT DRIVE** any other machine unless its owner has a current Certificate covering **"ANY DRIVER"** and it is advisable to remember that, in the absence of such a provision the penalties for doing so are very heavy.

The driver of a motor cycle **MUST** hold a current **DRIVING LICENCE**. If you are a learner and hold a Provisional Driving Licence, your machine must show, front and back, the standard "L" plates in red and white and you must not take a **PILLION PASSENGER** unless that passenger is the holder of a current **UNRESTRICTED** driving licence.

As soon as you receive your driving licence, sign it in the appropriate place and do so each time it is renewed. It is an offence not to.

Make sure you are well acquainted with the recommendations set down in the "Highway Code".

THE MACHINE AND THE LAW

Every motor cycle used on the public roads must be registered and carry the registration numbers and licence disc allotted to it. The dealer, from whom the machine is bought, will, generally, attend to all matters legally essential before it is used on the public roads.

Free Service Scheme

FREE SERVICE SCHEME

All owners of **NEW MODELS** are entitled to one **FREE SERVICE AND INSPECTION** at 500 miles, or, at latest, three months after taking delivery.

This service is arranged by the supplying dealer to whom the **Free Service Voucher** must be handed. This voucher, together with the Instruction Manual, are supplied by us upon receipt of the signed registration form found in the tool box upon taking delivery of a new motor cycle.

The **INSPECTION AND SERVICE** consists of:

(a) Check, and, if necessary, adjust:

    (1) Rocker clearances.   (6) Wheel bearings.
    (2) Contact breaker points.   (7) Brakes.
    (3) Sparking plug.   (8) Forks and steering head.
    (4) Clutch.   (9) Alignment of wheels.
    (5) Chains.   (10) Tyre pressures.

(b) Tighten all external nuts and bolts including cylinder head nuts and fork crown pinch screws.

(c) Top-up battery and check all lighting equipment.

(d) Clean out carburetter and check for correct idling.

(e) Adjust all cables.

(f) Grease all nipples.

(g) Drain oil system. Clean filter and replenish.

(h) Check oil level in front chaincase.

(i) Top-up gear box.

(j) Test machine on the road.

NOTE—Oils, greases and materials used are chargeable to the customer.

FOR THE CONVENIENCE OF OWNERS,

SPARES STOCKISTS

ARE APPOINTED FOR MOST DISTRICTS. TO SAVE DELAY AND THE DELIVERY SURCHARGE, CUSTOMERS ARE RECOMMENDED TO ALWAYS APPLY TO THEIR NEAREST SPARES STOCKIST.

Spare Parts

GENUINE SPARE PARTS purchased from an Authorised Dealer, or from the Factory, are identical with the parts originally built into your motor cycle. By using them you are assured that they will fit accurately and give satisfactory service.

SPARES STOCKISTS

For the convenience of owners Spares Stockists are appointed for most districts. To prevent delay and save the delivery surcharge, customers are recommended always to apply to their nearest Spares Stockist.

CORRESPONDENCE AND SPARES ORDERS

Always quote the complete engine number, including all the letters in it. This will enable us to identify the machine.

Each series of frames is numbered from zero upwards, therefore, the quotation of a frame number only does not facilitate identification.

SPARES LIST

An illustrated spares list covering the models described in this Instruction Book is available on application. Price 3s. 6d. each.

PART NUMBERS

If there is any doubt about the names of parts required, or their part numbers, please send the old parts as patterns.

REMINDER

Do not forget to include your name and full postal address. We do receive orders without this very necessary information.

PAYMENT

(1) Cash with order.*
(2) Cash against pro-forma invoice.
(3) Approved ledger account.
We do not send C.O.D. (Cash on Delivery).

* Add 5 per cent of total value for carriage and packing. Minimum 1/-.

GUARANTEE

Full details of the guarantee relating to the models described in this book are given on page 54.

INSTRUCTION BOOKS

A copy of this book is issued free of charge to all purchasers of a new machine.

Tools and Special Equipment

TOOLS

The standard tool kit, issued with each new machine, contains:

1	017253	Tool Roll.
2	017007	Tyre Lever.
1	017114	Pump.
1	017249	Adjustable Spanner.
1	017257	⅛" x 3⁄16" Spanner.
2	017052	3⁄16" x ¼" Spanner.
1	017053	5⁄16" x ⅜" Spanner.
1	017252	Plug spanner and tommy bar.
1	023284	Suspension unit spanner.
1	021625	6" Screwdriver.
1	042540	Feeler gauge.
1	018667	Allen key.
1	042570	Steering head adjusting spanner.

SPECIAL TOOLS (Not supplied in tool kit)

1	043332	Timing pinion extractor.
1	042247	Automatic advance unit extractor bolt.
1	022011	Timing disc. A circular timing disc, graduated in degrees and made of ivorine. A very useful device.
1	017482	Holder for valve grinding.
1	018276	Valve spring compressor.

OPTIONAL EQUIPMENT

The following items of optional equipment are available. They are described and priced in the Spares List:

Prop Stand Assembly (Part Number 043389).

Air Cleaner.

GASKET SETS

For convenience in ordering, standard sets of engine washers and gaskets are stocked. Full details of contents and prices are included in the Spares List.

BADGES

Neat monogram badges are now available at a cost of 1/6, plus 6d. postage. They can be supplied as a brooch or for fitting in a button hole. When ordering state type required.

GUARANTEE

1. In this Guarantee the word "machine" refers to the motor cycle, scooter, motor cycle combination or sidecar as the case may be purchased by the Purchaser.

2. In order to obtain the benefit of this Guarantee, the Purchaser must correctly complete the attached registration form and return it to us within fourteen days of the purchase.

3. We will supply, free of charge, a new part in exchange for, or, if we consider repair sufficient, will repair free of charge any part proved within six months of the date of purchase of any new machine, or within three months of its renewal or repair in the case of a part already renewed or repaired, to be defective by reason of our faulty workmanship or materials. We do not undertake to bear the cost of fitting such new or repaired part or accessory.

4. Any part considered to be defective must be sent to our Works, carriage paid, accompanied by the following information:—
    (a) Name of purchaser and his address.
    (b) Date of purchase of machine.
    (c) Name of dealer from where the purchase was made.
    (d) Engine and frame numbers of machine.

5. This Guarantee shall not extend to defects or damage appearing after misuse, neglect, abnormal stress or strain, or the incorporation or affixing of unsuitable attachments or parts and in particular:
    (a) Hiring out.
    (b) Racing and Competitions.
    (c) Adaptation or alteration of any part or parts after leaving our Works.
    (d) The attaching of a sidecar in a manner not approved by us or to an unsuitable motor cycle.

    This Guarantee shall not extend to machines whose trade mark, name or manufacturing number has been altered or removed, or in which has been used any part not supplied or approved by us, or to tyres, saddles, chains, speedometers, revolution counters and electrical equipment or to parts supplied to the order of the Purchaser and different from our standard specification.

6. Our liability and that of our dealer who sells the machine, shall be limited to that set out in paragraph 3, and no other claims including claims for consequential damage or injury to person or property, shall be admissible.

    All other conditions and warranties statutory or otherwise and whether express or implied are hereby excluded and no guarantee other than that expressly herein contained applies to the machine to which this Guarantee relates or any accessory or part thereof.

REPAIRS GUARANTEE

1. Whilst the highest standard of workmanship and materials is aimed at, we cannot accept liability for any defects appearing more than three months after the machine, assembly or component has left our Works after being repaired.

2. We will repair or replace at our option free of charge any defective work, materials or parts relating to the repairs carried out by us appearing within that time but shall not be under any further or other liability for any other loss or damage whether direct or consequential and our liability shall be limited to the cost of so making good.

3. We do not accept liability in respect of parts of proprietary manufacture, e.g. tyres, saddles, chains, speedometers, revolution counters and electrical equipment which may be used by us in effecting a repair. All other conditions and warranties statutory or otherwise express or implied are hereby excluded.

WIRING WIPAC DIAGRAM

MATCHLESS G2CS and A.J.S. 14CS
SCRAMBLER MODELS
250 c.c. O.H.V. MOTOR CYCLES
A.C./D.C. TRICKLE CHARGE
MODELS PRODUCED FROM OCTOBER 1958 TO AUGUST 1960

THE WIPAC GROUP · BUCKINGHAM · BUCKS·

SPARES UNITS	PART No.
*Headlamp (less harness and speedometer)	S0910
Harness (Main)	S0911
Cut-out, Horn and Dipper Switch	S3858
Harness (Dipper Switch)	S0860
Alternator Unit	G1569
Distributor Unit	S1122
Rectifier	S0862
Coil-12v. Ignition	S0810
Rear Lamp	††S3704
Rear Lamp	†S0201
L.T. Lead Set (Ignition)	S0861

*Speedometer not supplied by Wipac
†Fitted to models prior Aug. 1964
††Fitted to models from Aug. 1964

REF. WD/26/748/2

WIRING WIPAC DIAGRAM

MATCHLESS G2 250 c.c., G5 350 c.c., G2S, G2CSR
A.J.S. Models 14, 14S, 14CSR 250 c.c., 8 350 c.c.
MODELS PRODUCED FROM MAY 1958 TO DECEMBER 1964

THE WIPAC GROUP · BUCKINGHAM · BUCKS

SPARES UNITS	PART No.
†*Headlamp (less harness and speedometer)	SEE NOTE
Harness (Main)	S2616
Horn and Dipper Switch	S3857
Harness (Dipper Switch)	S0612
Alternator	G1521
Distributor Unit	S1141
Rectifier	S2642
Coil—6v. Ignition	S0793
Stop & Rear Lamp	S3704
Stop Switch	S0754
Leads Set (Stop Switch)	S2857
Ammeter Unit	S0062

*Speedometer not supplied by Wipac
†NOTE. Headlamp Units S0777 fitted from May, 1958 to Sept. 1959
S2615 fitted from Aug. 1959 to Dec. 1964.

REPLACING RECTIFIER
The Square type Rectifier will replace the Round type without any difficulty.

Connections:
White Lead to Terminal A.C. White
Brown Lead to Terminal D.C. Brown
Light Green to Terminal A.C. Green

REAR LAMP REPLACEMENT
From August 1965 the Rear Lamp has been modified to the Ministry of Transport Grade 1 Regulations.
The Three Bulb type is replaced by the Single Bulb (Double Contact) Model.
No rewiring is required.

REF. WD/16/715/1

WIRING WIPAC DIAGRAM

MATCHLESS G2CS and A.J.S. 14CS
SCRAMBLER MODELS
250 c.c. O.H.V. MOTOR CYCLES
A.C./D.C. TRICKLE CHARGE
MODEL PRODUCED FROM SEPTEMBER 1960

THE WIPAC GROUP   BUCKINGHAM   BUCKS

SPARES UNITS	PART No.
*Headlamp (less harness and speedometer)	S0933
Harness (Main)	S2624
Horn and Dipper	S3704
Switch	S3857
Harness (Dipper Switch)	S2622
Alternator Unit	G1632
Distributor Unit	S1141
Rectifier	S2642
Coil-12v. Ignition	S0793
L.T. Lead Set (Ignition)	S2620
Rear Lamp	S2872
Harness (Ignition)	S2621
Switch (Ignition)	S0782

*Speedometer not supplied by Wipac

NOTE:—WHEN THE SET IS SUPPLIED WITHOUT THE LIGHTING EQUIPMENT (i.e. HEADLAMP, REAR LAMP, DIP SWITCH, HORN, LIGHTING SWITCH & HARNESS) THE YELLOW LEAD FROM THE IGNITION SWITCH MUST BE CONNECTED INTO THE DOUBLE CONNECTOR ON THE LIGHT GREEN LEADS.

REPLACING RECTIFIER

The Square type Rectifier will replace the Round type without any difficulty.

Connections:

White Lead to Terminal A.C. White
Brown Lead to Terminal D.C. Brown
Light Green Lead to Terminal A.C. Green

REAR LAMP REPLACEMENT

From August, 1965 the Rear Lamp has been modified to the Ministry of Transport Grade 1 Regulations.

The Three Bulb type is replaced by the Single Bulb (Double Contact) Model.

No rewiring is required when fitting a replacement Lamp.

REF. WD 79 803 1

WIRING WIPAC DIAGRAM

MATCHLESS G2 CSR 250 c.c. and A.J.S. 14 CSR 250 c.c. "SAPPHIRE NINETY"
MODELS PRODUCED FROM MARCH 1965

THE WIPAC GROUP · BUCKINGHAM · BUCKS

SPARES UNITS	PART No.
*Headlamp (less harness and speedometer)	S2615
Harness (Main)	S4084
Horn and Dipper Switch	S3857
Harness (Dipper Switch)	S0612
Alternator	G1521
Distributor Unit	S3881
Rectifier	S2642
Coil—6v. Ignition	S0793
Stop & Rear Lamp	S3704
Stop Switch	S0754
Leads Set (Stop Switch)	S2857
Ammeter Unit	S0062

*Speedometer not supplied by Wipac

REF. WD 86 811

VELOCEPRESS MANUALS – MOTORCYCLE BY MAKE

AJS 1932-1948 SINGLES & TWINS 250cc THRU 1000cc (BOOK OF)
AJS 1945-1960 SINGLES 350cc & 500cc MODELS 16 & 18 (BOOK OF)
AJS 1955-1965 SINGLES 350cc & 500cc (BOOK OF)
AJS 1957-1966 FACTORY WSM - ALL SINGLES & TWINS
ARIEL UP TO 1932 (BOOK OF)
ARIEL 1932-1939 PREWAR MODELS (BOOK OF)
ARIEL 1933-1951 (WORKSHOP MANUAL)
ARIEL 1939-1960 4 STROKE SINGLES (BOOK OF)
ARIEL 1958-1964 LEADER & ARROW (BOOK OF)
BMW R26 R27 (1956-1967) FACTORY WORKSHOP MANUAL
BMW R50 R50S R60 R69S (1955-1969) FACTORY WORKSHOP MANUAL
BRIDGESTONE 90 SERIES FACTORY WSM & PARTS CATALOGUE
BRIDGESTONE 175 SERIES FACTORY WSM & PARTS CATALOGUE
BRIDGESTONE 350 SERIES FACTORY WSM & PARTS CATALOGUES
BSA SERVICE SHEETS MASTER CATALOGUE ALL MODELS 1945-1967
BSA BANTAM D1 TO D7 1948-1966 FACTORY SERVICE SHEETS MANUAL
BSA BANTAM ALL MODELS FROM 1948 ONWARDS (BOOK OF)
BSA BANTAM D14 FACTORY WORKSHOP & INSTRUCTION MANUAL
BSA SINGLES & V-TWINS UP TO 1927 (BOOK OF)
BSA SINGLES & V-TWINS UP TO 1930 (BOOK OF)
BSA SINGLES & V-TWINS UP TO 1935 (BOOK OF)
BSA SINGLES & V-TWINS 1936-1939 (BOOK OF)
BSA C10, C11 & C12 1945-1958 FACTORY SERVICE SHEETS MANUAL
BSA OHV & SV SINGLES 250-600cc 1945-1959 (BOOK OF)
BSA C15 & B40 1958-1967 FACTORY SERVICE SHEETS MANUAL
BSA OHV & SV SINGLES 250cc (ONLY) 1954-1970 (BOOK OF)
BSA B31, B32, B33 & B34 1945-60 FACTORY SERVICE SHEETS MANUAL
BSA OHV SINGLES 350 & 500cc 1955-1967 (BOOK OF)
BSA M20, M21 & M33 1945-1963 FACTORY SERVICE SHEETS MANUAL
BSA TWINS A7 & A10 1948-1962 FACTORY SERVICE SHEETS MANUAL
BSA TWINS A7 & A10 1948-1962 (BOOK OF)
BSA TWINS A50 & A65 1962-1965 FACTORY WORKSHOP MANUAL
BSA TWINS A50 & A65 1962-1969 (SECOND BOOK OF)
DOUGLAS 1929-1939 PREWAR ALL MODELS (BOOK OF)
DOUGLAS 1948-1957 POSTWAR ALL MODELS FACTORY SHOP MANUAL
DUCATI 160cc, 250cc & 350cc OHC MODELS FACTORY SHOP MANUAL
HONDA 50 ALL MODELS UP TO 1970 INC MONKEY & TRAIL (BOOK OF)
HONDA 90 ALL MODELS UP TO 1966 (BOOK OF)
HONDA 125-150cc TWINS C/CS/CB/CA FACTORY WORKSHOP MANUAL
HONDA 250-305 TWINS C/CS/CB FACTORY WORKSHOP MANUAL
HONDA 450 CB/CL 1965-1974 K0 TO K7 WORKSHOP MANUAL
HONDA C100 SUPER CUB FACTORY WORKSHOP MANUAL
HONDA C110 SPORT CUB 1962-1969 FACTORY WORKSHOP MANUAL
HONDA TWINS & SINGLES 50cc THRU 305cc 1960-1966 (BOOK OF)
HONDA TWINS ALL MODELS 125cc THRU 450cc UP TO 1968 (BOOK OF)
INDIAN PONYBIKE, BOY RACER & PAPOOSE ILL PARTS LIST & SALES LIT
J.A.P. ENGINES 1927-1952 & MOTORCYCLES 1934-1952 (BOOK OF)
MATCHLESS 1931-1939 ALL MODELS 250cc THRU 990cc (BOOK OF)
MATCHLESS 1945-1956 350 & 500cc SINGLES (BOOK OF)
MATCHLESS 1955-1966 350 & 500cc SINGLES (BOOK OF)
MATCHLESS 1957-1966 FACTORY WSM - ALL SINGLES & TWINS
NEW IMPERIAL ALL SV & OHV FROM 1935 ONWARDS (BOOK OF)
NORTON 1932-1939 PREWAR MODELS (BOOK OF)
NORTON 1932-1947 (BOOK OF)
NORTON 1938-1956 (BOOK OF)
NORTON 1955-1963 MODELS 19, 50 & ES2 (BOOK OF)
NORTON 1955-1965 DOMINATOR TWINS (BOOK OF)
NORTON 1960-1970 TWIN CYLINDER FACTORY WORKSHOP MANUAL
NORTON 1970-1975 COMMANDO FACTORY WORKSHOP MANUAL
NORTON 1975-1978 MK 3 COMMANDO FACTORY WORKSHOP MANUAL
PANTHER 1932-1958 LIGHTWEIGHT MODELS 250 & 350cc (BOOK OF)
PANTHER 1938-1966 HEAVYWEIGHT MODELS 600 & 650cc (BOOK OF)
RALEIGH MOTORCYCLES 1919-1933 (BOOK OF)
ROYAL ENFIELD 1934-1946 SINGLES & V TWINS (BOOK OF)
ROYAL ENFIELD 1937-1953 SINGLES & V TWINS (BOOK OF)
ROYAL ENFIELD 1946-1962 SINGLES (BOOK OF)
ROYAL ENFIELD 1958-1966 250cc & 350cc SINGLES (SECOND BOOK OF)
ROYAL ENFIELD 736cc INTERCEPTOR FACTORY WORKSHOP MANUAL
RUDGE 1933-1939 (BOOK OF)
SUNBEAM 1928-1939 (BOOK OF)
SUNBEAM 1946-1957 S7 & S8 (BOOK OF)
SUZUKI 50cc & 80cc UP TO 1966 (BOOK OF)
SUZUKI T10 1963-1967 FACTORY WORKSHOP MANUAL
SUZUKI T20 & T200 1965-1969 FACTORY WORKSHOP MANUAL
SUZUKI TWINS 1962 ONWARDS 125-500cc WORKSHOP MANUAL
TRIUMPH 1935-1939 PREWAR MODELS (BOOK OF)
TRIUMPH 1935-1949 (BOOK OF)
TRIUMPH 1937-1951 (WORKSHOP MANUAL)
TRIUMPH 1945-1955 FACTORY WORKSHOP MANUAL
TRIUMPH 1945-1958 TWINS (BOOK OF)
TRIUMPH 1956-1969 TWINS (BOOK OF)
VELOCETTE 1925-1970 ALL SINGLES & TWINS (BOOK OF)
VILLIERS ENGINE UP TO 1959 INC. 3 WHEELERS (BOOK OF)
VILLIERS ENGINE UP TO 1969 (BOOK OF)
VINCENT 1935-1955 (WORKSHOP MANUAL)
YAMAHA 1961-1967 YA5 & YA6 (WORKSHOP MANUAL & ILL PARTS LIST)
YAMAHA 1971-1972 JT1& JT2 (WORKSHOP MANUAL & ILL PARTS LIST)

VELOCEPRESS TECHNICAL BOOKS – MOTORCYCLE

1930'S BRITISH MOTORCYCLE CARBS & ELEC COMPONENTS (BOOK OF)
1930'S BRITISH MOTORCYCLE ENGINES (OVERHAUL & MAINTENANCE)
1930'S BRITISH MOTORCYCLE GEARBOXES & CLUTCHES (BOOK OF)
CATALOG OF BRITISH MOTORCYCLES (1951 MODELS)
LUCAS ELECTRONICS BRITISH M/CYCLES REPAIR & PARTS (1950-1977)
MOTORCYCLE ENGINEERING (P.E. Irving)
MOTORCYCLE ROAD TESTS 1949-1953 (Motor Cycle Magazine UK)
SPEED AND HOW TO OBTAIN IT (Motor Cycle Magazine UK)
TUNING FOR SPEED (P.E. Irving)

VELOCEPRESS MANUALS – SCOOTERS BY MAKE

BSA SUNBEAM SCOOTER WORKSHOP MANUAL 1959-1965
BSA SUNBEAM SCOOTER 1959-1965 (BOOK OF)
LAMBRETTA 1947-1957 ALL 125 & 150cc MODELS (BOOK OF)
LAMBRETTA 1957-1970 LI & TV MODELS (SECOND BOOK OF)
NSU PRIMA 1956-1964 ALL MODELS (BOOK OF)
TRIUMPH TIGRESS SCOOTER WORKSHOP MANUAL 1959-1965
TRIUMPH TIGRESS SCOOTER (BOOK OF)
VESPA 1951-1961 (BOOK OF)
VESPA 1955-1963 125 & 150cc & GS MODELS (SECOND BOOK OF)
VESPA 1955-1968 GS & SS (BOOK OF)
VESPA 1963-1972 90, 125 & 150cc (THIRD BOOK OF)

VELOCEPRESS MANUALS – MOPEDS & MOTORIZED BICYCLES

CYCLEMOTOR (BOOK OF)
NSU QUICKLY 1953-1963 ALL MODELS (BOOK OF)
PUCH MAXI N & S MAINTENANCE & REPAIR (3 MANUAL COMPILATION)
RALEIGH MOPEDS 1960-1969 (BOOK OF)

VELOCEPRESS MANUALS - THREE WHEELER'S

BOND MINICAR THREE WHEELER (BOOK OF)
BMW ISETTA FACTORY WORKSHOP MANUAL
BSA THREE WHEELER (BOOK OF)
VINTAGE MORGAN THREE WHEELER (BOOK OF)

VELOCEPRESS MANUALS – AUTOMOBILE BY MAKE

ALFA ROMEO GIULIA WORKSHOP MANUAL 1300 TO 2000cc 1962-1975
ALFA ROMEO GIULIA TECH MANUAL CARBURETED CARS FROM 1962
ALFA ROMEO GIULIA TECH MANUAL FUEL INJECTED CARS FROM 1969
ALFA ROMEO GIULIETTA & GIULIA 750 & 101 SERIES 1955-1965 WSM
AUSTIN-HEALEY SPRITE & MG MIDGET WORKSHOP MANUAL 1958-1971
BMW 600 LIMOUSINE FACTORY WORKSHOP MANUAL
BMW 600 LIMOUSINE OWNERS HAND BOOK & SERVICE MANUAL
BMW 2000 & 2002 1966-1976 WORKSHOP MANUAL
CORVAIR 1960-1969 WORKSHOP MANUAL
CORVETTE V8 1955-1962 WORKSHOP MANUAL
FIAT 500 FACTORY WORKSHOP MANUAL 1957-1973
FIAT 600, 600D & MULTIPLA FACTORY WORKSHOP MANUAL 1955-1969
JAGUAR E-TYPE 3.8 & 4.2 SERIES 1 & 2 WORKSHOP MANUAL
JAGUAR MK 7, 8, 9 & XK120, 140, 150 WORKSHOP MANUAL 1948-1961
METROPOLITAN FACTORY WORKSHOP MANUAL
MGA & MGB OWNERS HANDBOOK & WORKSHOP MANUAL
MG MIDGET TC, TD, TF & TF1500 WORKSHOP MANUAL
PORSCHE 356 1948-1965 WORKSHOP MANUAL
PORSCHE 911 2.0, 2.2, 2.4 LITRE 1964-1973 WORKSHOP MANUAL
PORSCHE 911 2.7, 3.0, 3.2 LITRE 1973-1989 WORKSHOP MANUAL
PORSCHE 912 WORKSHOP MANUAL
TRIUMPH TR2, TR3, TR4 1953-1965 WORKSHOP MANUAL
VOLKSWAGEN TRANSPORTER, TRUCKS & WAGONS 1950-1979 WSM
VOLVO 1944-1968 ALL MODELS WORKSHOP MANUAL

VELOCEPRESS TECHNICAL BOOKS - AUTOMOBILE

FERRARI 250/GT SERVICE AND MAINTENANCE
FERRARI GUIDE TO PERFORMANCE
FERRARI OWNER'S HANDBOOK
FERRARI TUNING TIPS & MAINTENANCE TECHNIQUES
HOW TO BUILD A FIBERGLASS CAR
HOW TO BUILD A RACING CAR
HOW TO RESTORE THE MODEL 'A' FORD
MASERATI OWNER'S HANDBOOK
OBERT'S FIAT GUIDE
PERFORMANCE TUNING THE SUNBEAM TIGER
SOUPING THE VOLKSWAGEN
SOLEX CARBURETORS (EMPHASIS ON UK & EU AUTOMOBILES)
SU CARBURETORS (EMPHASIS ON UK AUTOMOBILES)
WEBER CARBURETORS (EMPHASIS ON ALFA & FIAT)

VELOCEPRESS BOOKS & GUIDES - AUTOMOBILE

ABARTH BUYERS GUIDE
COMPLETE CATALOG OF JAPANESE MOTOR VEHICLES
FERRARI 308 SERIES BUYER'S AND OWNER'S GUIDE
FERRARI BERLINETTA LUSSO
FERRARI BROCHURES AND SALES LITERATURE 1946-1967
FERRARI BROCHURES AND SALES LITERATURE 1968-1989
FERRARI SERIAL NUMBERS PART I - ODD NUMBERS TO 21399
FERRARI SERIAL NUMBERS PART II - EVEN NUMBERS TO 1050
FERRARI SPYDER CALIFORNIA
HENRY'S FABULOUS MODEL "A" FORD
MASERATI BROCHURES AND SALES LITERATURE

VELOCEPRESS BOOKS – RACING

CARRERA PANAMERICANA - MEXICAN ROAD RACE (BOOK OF)
DIALED IN - THE JAN OPPERMAN STORY
IF HEMINGWAY HAD WRITTEN A RACING NOVEL
VEDA ORR'S NEW REVISED HOT ROD PICTORIAL

AUTOBOOKS WORKSHOP MANUALS & BROOKLANDS ROAD TEST PORTFOLIOS

FOR A COMPLETE LISTING OF THE AUTOBOOKS & BROOKLANDS TITLES THAT WE CURRENTLY HAVE AVAILABLE, PLEASE VISIT OUR WEBSITE.

www.VelocePress.com